D0956602

THE
PALEO
HEALING BIBLE

METRO BOOKS
New York

An Imprint of Sterling Publishing
1166 Avenue of the Americas
New York, NY 10036

This book was designed, conceived, and produced by
Quantum Books Ltd
6 Blundell Street
London N7 9BH
United Kingdom

Publisher: Kerry Enzor
Design: Paul Turner and Sue Pressley,
Stonecastle Graphics
Copyeditors: Philip de Ste. Croix and Kathy Steer
Senior Editor: Philippa Davis
Publishing Assistant: Emma Harverson
Production Manager: Zarni Win
Cover Design: Tokiko Morishima

ISBN 978-1-4351-6116-0 (print format)

For information about custom editions, special sales, and premium and corporate purchases, please contact Sterling Special Sales at 800-805-5489 or specialsales@sterlingpublishing.com.

Printed in China by 1010 Printing International Ltd

2 4 6 8 10 9 7 5 3 1

www.sterlingpublishing.com

THE
PALEO
HEALING BIBLE

Christine Bailey

METRO BOOKS
New York

Contents

Introduction

Welcome to *The Paleo Healing Bible*. Whether you are new to the Paleo lifestyle or are looking for inspiration to add variety to your diet, this book is for you. In this book, we have focused on providing you with detailed information about the recommended foods in a Paleo diet together with a range of healthy recipes to get you started.

The Paleo Healing Bible is a fabulous resource and trusted guidebook explaining the beneficial reasons for following the Paleo diet. We have included practical strategies to ensure your food is healthy and high in valuable nutrients, which will enable you to optimize the health benefits of a Paleo diet. We also provide clear guidance on the best foods to include and—just as importantly—those to avoid.

About the Author

Christine Bailey is an award winning nutritional therapist, chef, author, and broadcaster with over 18 years of experience. With a passion for creating delicious nourishing recipes, Christine has a reputation for transforming people's health and inspiring love of real food. In this book Christine combines her knowledge and scientific research in the field of functional nutrition with easy-to-follow guidance that is realistic, practical, and achievable.

Living
Paleo

What is the Paleo Diet?

The Paleo diet is not simply a diet. It is a lifestyle; it involves changing the way you eat and live. It is also a personalized plan designed to find the foods that make you feel healthy and energized. The Paleo diet is more accurately described as the Paleo movement, because we know that a lot of the ill health in the Western world comes from the contemporary choices we make. We never evolved to eat refined sugar, and were never meant to spend half our lives sitting down or to live in isolation without a sense of community.

The Paleo diet was originally based on research led by the American academic Dr. Loren Cordain and others. It is a wholefood diet that includes only the most nutritionally dense, natural foods.

The thinking behind the Paleo diet focuses on our biochemical makeup and the interaction of our genes and our environment. Our genetics have changed little since we lived as hunter gatherers and optimal health depends on basing our diet around food we are genetically suited to eat. The Paleo diet is based on ideas about the way we ate in the past before processed foods, sugars, salts, high-fructose corn syrups, and modified produce became commonplace. The diet concentrates on foods that were available to our Paleolithic

ancestors around 2.5 million years ago. Our diet and the food now available to us have changed significantly, so the diet has to be adapted to our modern lives. It makes the most of high quality, nutrient-rich foods in their natural form that are readily available today.

A Paleo diet emphasizes a high intake of a wide variety of seasonal vegetables, a moderate intake of seasonal fruit, and plenty of high-quality meat, game, fish, seafood, nuts, and seeds. It removes all grains, dairy products, and legumes (beans) from the diet.

Within this framework variations in the diet can be accommodated. For example, people with autoimmune-related conditions find the Paleo approach beneficial but may exclude some foods, which can promote an immune reaction and inflammation.

What Does the Paleo Diet Include?

- Grass-fed red meats
- Wild game
- Organ meats
- Variety meats
- Grass-fed/organic poultry
- Eggs
- Fish
- Shellfish and seafood
- Fresh vegetables
- Starchy vegetables
- Sea vegetables
- Nuts
- Seeds
- Fresh fruits and berries
- Quality fats and oils (lard, duck fat plus olive, walnut, flaxseed, macadamia, avocado, and coconut oil etc.)
- Honey, stevia, coconut sugar, xylitol (okay to consume in moderation)
- Herbs and spices
- Fermented foods (kefir, sauerkraut, kombucha, etc.)
- Water, herbal teas, green and black tea (in moderation), green juices and smoothies, coconut water, nut and seed milks
- Bone broth
- Coffee (occasionally)
- Alcohol (occasionally).

What Foods Should Be Avoided?

- Grains including gluten and nongluten grains (wheat, spelt, rye, barley, oats, corn, quinoa, rice, amaranth, millet, buckwheat, teff, wild rice, sorghum)
- Beans and legumes (including peanuts and soy)
- Dairy products (see page 28)
- Processed fatty meats (hot dogs, etc.)
- Soft drinks, sodas, fruit juice
- Sugars, syrups, and artificial sweeteners
- Processed foods and ready meals
- Refined vegetable oils
- Milk and white chocolate and candies
- Refined table salt.

Adopting the Lifestyle

While this book focuses on the food and drinks that we consume, it is important to bear in mind that the Paleo approach is a non-sedentary lifestyle—getting enough rest and relaxation, and spending time socializing in a supportive environment is equally important to your health.

The Paleo Food Pyramid

The Paleo diet is based on what our ancestors ate and how they lived, so the diet focuses on unprocessed whole food, fresh vegetables, grass-fed meat, eggs, fish, fruit, and healthy fats (including saturated fat) and cuts out dairy, refined sugars, grains, beans, and processed food. The pyramid opposite shows what to include in the diet and how much of each group you should eat. For example, consume lots of fresh vegetables and grass-fed meat, poultry, eggs, and fish. Eat less fruit as it is high in natural sugars, and eat nuts and seeds in moderation as they are high in monounsaturated fats. In every meal you should try to eat some fresh vegetables and/or fruit, lean meat, nuts and seeds, and include some healthy oil.

Herbs and spices are packed with beneficial nutrients, so use them to flavor your food. In addition, spices contain zero calories, carbs, sugar, fiber, protein, or fat.

Eat nuts and seeds in moderation as they are rich in monounsaturated fats. Only eat healthy fats and oils like olive oil, avocado oil, coconut oil, or butter.

Eat fruits and berries that are low in sugar daily and save high-sugar fruit, like bananas or mangoes, for days when you need a higher carbohydrate intake.

Eat lots of grass-fed lean meat, organic poultry, and wild fresh-caught fish and seafood. Only eat moderate amounts of eggs as they are relatively high in fat.

Fresh vegetables are packed with nutrients, so eat plenty of them, especially leafy greens and nonstarchy tubers and root vegetables.

Left: Consume a wide variety of fresh, locally grown, and seasonal produce every day.

Herbs
and
spices

Nuts, seeds,
nut butters,
healthy fats,
and oils

Organic fruit

Grass-fed organic
meat, fish, shellfish,
poultry, game, and eggs

Organic locally grown
vegetables

The Importance of Hydration

As part of a healthy Paleo diet it is essential to make sure you drink plenty of water, either on its own or with a tangy squeeze of lemon or lime. Drinking water can flush out toxins and improves the skin.

Making the Transition

If you are looking to adopt a Paleo diet but you don't feel ready to dive straight in, there is no reason why you cannot take your time and transition to the diet over several weeks. This may be particularly suitable if you are suffering with significant health concerns such as diabetes. You can allow yourself to switch gradually to the Paleo diet as well as increasing other key elements of a healthy lifestyle such as exercise, stress reduction, and getting enough sleep.

There may be many aspects in your diet that you will need to change and doing this all at once can be too stressful. For example, if you are addicted to coffee and carbs, you may wish to eliminate one of these first, rather than both together.

One of the first priorities is to exclude grains from your diet—first focus on gluten grains (barley, rye, and wheat), which are often associated with digestive problems, autoimmune diseases, and inflammation. You can then start to eliminate nongluten grains like rice, millet, quinoa, and amaranth.

You can then remove dairy from your diet and switch to alternatives such as coconut and almond milk. You can create your own nut milks and nut cheeses, and can use nut milk to make ice creams and desserts (see page 197).

Clearing out your pantry is another good way to ensure that you follow the diet. Stop buying non-Paleo products and compost or donate other foods to food banks or to friends who are not Paleo.

For many people the reduction in carbohydrates is the most difficult part of the diet. People respond differently to the reduction in carbohydrates. Initially, you might feel sluggish or foggy-headed. Reduce your intake over time and make sure you include enough medium-chain triglycerides (fatty acids), like coconut oil, which the body can readily use as an energy source to avoid fatigue.

Get Support and Stay Motivated

Keep a food/exercise/stress management journal to track your progress. There are also many free apps which can help you to monitor your dietary intake and mood. In addition to noting down the foods eaten, recording how you feel can be very motivating and help keep you on track.

One of the toughest things about adopting any new diet is dealing with lack of understanding from friends or family. Ideally encourage the whole family to follow the diet or track down blogs and forums where you can find support.

The Paleo approach is a lifestyle change. It is not about temporary fixes so it is good to take your time to help yourself adopt a new way of living that will optimize your health and promote a sense of well-being.

If you are craving carbohydrates, then try some of these Paleo alternatives:

Carb-based foods	Paleo alternative
Spaghetti, tagliatelle	Spaghetti squash, kelp noodles, spiralized zucchini, or carrot
Rice	Cauliflower Rice (p.115) or parsnip rice
French fries/chips	Mashed sweet potato, cauliflower mash, or root vegetable mash
Wraps made from flour e.g. wheat/corn	Lettuce "wraps," coconut wraps, nori wraps
Tortilla chips and other grain-based snacks	Nuts and seeds, kale chips (p.112) dehydrated vegetable chips, flaxseed crackers or nut and seed crackers
Couscous or quinoa	Cauliflower Rice (p.115)
Lasagna	Use strips of zucchini instead of the pasta and make a dairy-free white sauce flavored with nutritional yeast and spices
Muffins, cakes, cookies	Make them with coconut flour or nut-based flours instead
Granola/cereals	Paleo granola made from nuts and seeds
Oatmeal	Chia desserts (p.139)
Energy bars/protein bars	Homemade or store-bought alternatives made with nuts, seeds, and dried fruits

Why Paleo?

The Paleo diet has been widely researched and it has been shown to have numerous health benefits. Various studies have indicated that the Paleo diet can be an effective way to lose weight, to make sure you are eating enough nutrients, and to reduce the risk of many chronic diseases.

Blood Glucose Balance

As the Paleo diet avoids refined sugar and carbohydrates, it can help to improve blood glucose levels, counteract metabolic syndrome, and reduce the risk of diabetes and insulin resistance.

Inflammation

Imbalances in blood sugar not only lead to weight gain and increased body fat but also promote inflammation. The Paleo diet includes plenty of anti-inflammatory nutrients, omega-3 fats, and monounsaturated fats to lower the inflammatory response. A Paleo diet can therefore help to address inflammatory conditions such as asthma, arthritis, and eczema.

Reduction in Allergies

The Paleo diet avoids key food groups known to be allergens, particularly gluten and dairy. By removing these foods you may find allergic reactions and associated inflammation are reduced.

Improved Digestion

The Paleo diet eliminates gluten and grains as well as other foods known to be gut irritants. The diet also includes foods beneficial for gut health and digestion, such as bone broth and fermented foods.

Body Composition

One of the benefits of the Paleo diet is a greater emphasis on high quality, protein-rich foods. These are essential for improving muscle mass and reducing body fat. Following a Paleo diet can lead to improved body composition and increased muscle mass and strength.

Cardiovascular Disease

The Paleo diet is rich in antioxidants, healthy fats, and nutrients essential for a healthy heart. By avoiding sugar and processed foods including trans fats, it also eliminates ingredients known to contribute to cardiovascular disease.

Improved Energy

The Paleo diet focuses on low glycemic foods—this means that sugars are released slowly into the bloodstream promoting sustained energy levels. By excluding refined carbohydrates and sugars, you avoid sudden highs and lows in energy that result in fatigue and a low mood.

Autoimmune Disease

Autoimmunity is a process whereby our body's own immune system attacks our cells, tissues, and organs. Examples of autoimmune diseases include celiac disease, multiple sclerosis, rheumatoid arthritis, lupus, and vitiligo. Autoimmune diseases all share a common link—damage to the intestinal lining. This is sometimes referred to as "leaky gut" or intestinal permeability. A leaky gut arises when the gut lining is damaged and some of the contents of the gut leaks into the bloodstream resulting in an immune response. This can lead to generalized inflammation and production of antibodies and autoantibodies, which attack the cells and tissues of the body. The gut can become leaky for many reasons. It may be linked to the consumption of certain foods (gluten, grains, dairy, etc.) and lifestyle (e.g. high stress or taking medications). The Paleo diet addresses this by removing key food triggers and focuses on healing the gut to reduce the inflammatory response.

Your Daily Vitamins and Minerals

The table below shows the recommended daily amounts of some of the important vitamins and minerals needed for optimal health in the Paleo diet.

Vitamin/Mineral	Daily Requirement	Best Paleo Sources
Vitamin A	Men: 900 mcg Women: 700 mcg	Sweet potato, carrots, eggs, cantaloupe melon, butternut squash
Vitamin B_6	Men: 1.3 mg Women: 1.3 mg	Salmon, chicken, spinach, bananas, hazelnuts
Vitamin B_{12}	Men: 2.4 mcg Women: 2.4 mcg	Salmon, sardines, clams, beef, pork, chicken, eggs
Vitamin C	Men: 90 mg Women: 75 mg	Citrus fruit, strawberries, tomatoes, red bell peppers, broccoli
Vitamin D	Men: 15 mcg Women: 15 mcg	Salmon, sardines, eggs
Vitamin E	Men: 15 mg Women: 15 mg	Avocado, olive oil, almonds, dried apricots, papaya, spinach
Calcium	Men: 1,000 mg Women: 1,000 mg	Spinach, sea vegetables, bok choy, rhubarb, canned sardines, almonds
Copper	Men: 900 mcg Women: 900 mcg	Raw mushrooms, cooked liver, prunes, sundried tomatoes
Iron	Men: 8 mg Women: 18 mg	Liver, heart, kidney, kale, spinach, mussels, clams, oysters, bone broth
Magnesium	Men: 400 mg Women: 310 mg	Cooked spinach, kale, bananas, almonds, cashews, pumpkin seeds
Potassium	Men: 2,000 mg Women: 2,000 mg	Plums, bananas, artichokes, cilantro, mushrooms, almonds, walnuts
Zinc	Men: 11 mg Women: 8 mg	Beef, turkey, oysters, crab, pork, shiitake mushrooms, cashews

Why Take Supplements?

If you have been struggling with an ongoing health condition for some time, then as well as following the Paleo diet certain supplements may be helpful to you.

For many people, regardless of the diet they follow, vitamin D levels are often low. Short daily exposure (ten to 15 minutes) to the sun without sunscreen during the warmer months is enough for most people to get sufficient vitamin D. You can also get some vitamin D from foods, such as eggs and fish. However, if you live in northern latitudes where the sun is not as strong in the colder months of the year, vitamin D supplementation may be beneficial at that time. It is sensible to get your vitamin D levels tested before supplementing.

For people who do not eat much oily fish, taking a fish oil supplement daily may be a valuable addition.

Despite the benefit of taking supplements, the focus should be on getting nutrients directly from food. If you decide to take a supplement, then do so under the supervision of a health-care practitioner. Some supplements are also not appropriate if you are taking certain medications.

If you are following the Paleo diet to support digestion and gut health, then you may benefit from including collagen and gelatin powders. There are other supplements to support gut healing and these may include glutamine, vitamin A, probiotics, colostrum, and omega-3 fats. Always seek professional advice to check if supplements are appropriate for you.

The Paleo Lifestyle

The Paleo approach is not just about diet but a whole lifestyle movement. It means modeling your life after that of your ancestors in order to promote optimal health and wellness. Our genes are not just influenced by what we eat, but by how we live our lives too.

Get Moving

Most people's lives are very sedentary yet our forebears would have been moving through much of the day. They hunted, gathered, foraged, and at times even migrated. Sometimes this would have been gentle exercise and at other times much more intense activity. Keeping active enables us to burn energy and support muscle mass. Gentle exercise is also a great way to unwind and reduce stress. It can also be a social experience enjoyed with other people, which in itself can be very beneficial to our health and well-being. Aim to move regularly during the day to get as much exercise as you can. In addition, include some high-intensity exercise such as sprinting. Intense bursts of activity for short periods helps to stimulate the release of growth hormone, this signals to the body to synthesize muscle tissue and can improve muscle mass and fat loss, and aerobic fitness by strengthening the heart.

Include Muscle Boosting Exercise

As we age we naturally lose muscle mass unless we deliberately exercise our muscles. Regular weight-bearing exercise is crucial for strengthening bones and supporting a healthy muscle mass. Resistance workouts, such as weight lifting, stimulate the release of anabolic hormones, particularly testosterone and growth hormone, which helps to keep you lean.

Get Quality Sleep

Sleep is essential for good health. Poor sleep can lead to blood sugar imbalances, a low mood, listlessness, and a lowered immune system. It is often associated with weight gain. Sleep is vital for the release of growth hormone, which works hard during the night to repair and rejuvenate tissues. Research shows that regular, good-quality sleep is vital for emotional health, with poor sleep resulting in irritability, short-temperedness, and depression. Aim for six to eight hours a night.

Socialize and Meet People

Humans are social and even spiritual beings. For optimal health and well-being it is important to spend time with friends and family who share common goals and values. If you wish to age healthily, then

focus on surrounding yourself with people who support and love you. Having a sense of community, a feeling of belonging, and living with a sense of purpose are key aspects of a healthy fulfilling life.

Get Outdoors

Our ancestors spent most of their time outdoors. Regular exposure to sun provides lots of vitamin D, an essential vitamin for health and longevity that is not readily available through food. Spending time outdoors in the natural world is also a valuable way of relieving stress.

Keep an Eye on Stress

There is no easy way of escaping the day-to-day stress of modern living, but too much stress can contribute to poor health. Take steps to reduce levels of stress in your life if needed and make more time for fun, rest, and relaxation.

Use Your Mind

As we age its important to ensure that we exercise our minds as well as our bodies. Keep your brain sharp with stimulating mental activities, crosswords, quizzes, reading, and learning throughout your life.

Paleo Vegetarians

The Paleo focus on meat, fish, and animal products means that it isn't very vegetarian-friendly. It is difficult to follow a Paleo diet if you wish to avoid all meat and fish. However, it is possible to improve a vegetarian diet following key principles of the Paleo diet.

One of the chief difficulties with a strict Paleo diet for vegetarians is that it cuts out many of the key protein sources (beans and dairy). While nuts contain protein, they can also be inflammatory if they are eaten in excess. This is because they contain higher levels of omega-6 fats compared to omega-3. Nuts and seeds should also be soaked before using to reduce phytate levels and make them easier to digest.

Eggs are one of the best Paleo vegetarian sources of protein, and they are also rich in nutrients. Vegetarians should therefore aim to consume eggs regularly. Dairy products are not included in a strict Paleo diet, but for a vegetarian who can tolerate dairy they may be a useful addition to the diet. If you are going to include dairy then focus on grass-fed dairy products and fermented dairy. Beans, including soy, are not consumed on the Paleo diet but vegetarians and vegans may need to add them in moderate quantities to ensure they are getting enough protein. Soaking and sprouting beans may make them easier to digest. In addition vegans may like to include the occasional bowl of cooked quinoa or amaranth, which are reasonable sources of protein.

In view of the difficulty of obtaining enough protein, some vegetarians may feel comfortable eating a little fish and shellfish as a protein source. Vegan protein powders are available but traditionally they are based on rice, hemp, soy, or pea proteins, which may not be well tolerated. Spirulina is a green algae available as a supplement that is rich in protein and it can also be a useful addition to the diet. For those with autoimmune conditions, however, it may not be appropriate as it can activate an immune response.

Nonmeat-eaters will also need to ensure they are getting adequate amounts of certain nutrients—in particular omega-3 fats and vitamins D and B_{12}. Another micronutrient that vegetarians and vegans might need to watch is iron. While many vegetables contain iron, it is not as readily absorbed as it is from meat sources.

It is advisable to see your doctor before adopting a Paleo vegetarian or vegan diet.

Opposite: Eggs are an excellent protein-rich, nutrient-dense Paleo food for vegetarians.

Quality Matters

The quality of the food you eat is crucial to maintain optimal health. Ideally only meat from animals raised organically on pasture and fed grass should be eaten. These animals are unlikely to have been dosed with antibiotics or hormones and the nutritional profile of their meat is generally superior. Organic is not necessarily the same as grass-fed as some farmers may include supplemental grain. From a welfare perspective grass-fed and/or organic animals are often healthier and better treated. They are less likely to be contaminated with *E. coli* as the contamination can come from the slaughterhouse where manure from an animal comes into contact with the meat. There is less manure on grass-fed cattle than on cattle reared indoors.

Grass-fed meats generally have a better omega-6 to omega-3 ratio and are often leaner with a higher protein content. Micronutrients and antioxidant levels are often higher. Meat and dairy products from grass-fed animals are rich in conjugated linoleic acid (CLA), which helps to support lean body composition, improve insulin sensitivity, and strengthen the body's immune function.

With regards to fish, both farmed fish and fish caught in the sea or river are an excellent protein source. However, commercially farmed fish may include additives and food dyes, so if you cannot access wild fish, select organic farmed fish. Wild salmon typically contains more protein and less saturated fat than farmed fish. Both are good sources of omega-3 fats. There is also concern that farmed fish may contain more pollutants than wild-caught fish. However, as many people do not eat enough fish you are better off eating quality farm-raised salmon (without added dyes) than not eating salmon at all.

With vegetables and fruits, if possible select organically grown, local, and seasonal produce. This avoids the risk of consuming pesticides. Certain produce contains more pesticide residues than others so if you cannot afford to buy all organic, then prioritize and focus on buying organic foods that are more likely to be contaminated. These include apples, celery, tomatoes, cucumber, grapes, strawberries, red bell peppers, potatoes, peaches, and nectarines. In any case, ideally choose local produce from farmers' markets where the produce is guaranteed to be fresh.

Opposite: Wild Alaskan salmon is an excellent source of protein and essential omega-3 fats.

Paleo Autoimmune Diet

Within the framework of the Paleo diet there are many variations from which to choose. One commonly adopted is the autoimmune Paleo diet. This is valuable for anyone suffering from an autoimmune condition or chronic inflammation of the gut. The autoimmune approach removes some foods from the diet while attention is given to repairing the gut lining.

One of the principles of the Paleo diet is to avoid foods known to irritate the gut and cause intestinal permeability. This includes lectins, a class of carbohydrate-binding proteins found in many foods including grains, legumes, and pseudograins (e.g. quinoa, chia, and amaranth). The consumption of lectins is associated with a number of diseases, particularly autoimmune conditions. Gluten in particular is implicated in many inflammatory and autoimmune diseases. In addition, certain food proteins, especially those found in dairy, have the ability to cross-react with gluten. This is the situation when antibodies formed against gluten by the body recognize proteins in other foods such as dairy. This means that even if gluten has been removed from the diet, the body will still mount an immune response if dairy or other cross-reactive foods are consumed. While not all people

who are sensitive to gluten will cross-react to other foods, for those with an autoimmune condition it is normally recommended that cross-reactive foods are eliminated at least initially as the gut heals.

While the majority of these problem foods are avoided in the standard Paleo diet (gluten and grains, legumes, etc.), there are some additional foods that may be aggravating for certain people. Lectins, for example, are also present in vegetables from the nightshade family—this includes tomatoes, eggplants, potatoes, chili, and bell peppers. Eggs are also a common allergenic food and contain lysozyme, an enzyme that may cause damage to the gut lining. While eggs are normally suitable for people on a Paleo diet, if there is damage to the gut lining it is sensible to avoid them while the gut heals. Nuts and seeds (except coconut) and sugar alcohols (such as xylitol) are also commonly excluded. Other foods that are known gut irritants, such as caffeine and alcohol, are also removed from the diet during the healing phase.

Opposite: Broiled chicken provides plenty of lean protein and makes a great salad with some leafy greens. Avoid dressing with mayonnaise as it is generally not autoimmune-friendly.

Is Dairy Paleo?

Dairy was not part of our ancestors' diet and so it is not included in the Paleo (or Paleolithic) diet. Milk and dairy products only became part of our diet about 10,000 years ago when people started to settle down and work the land in agriculture. Subsequently animals became domesticated and people began to drink milk. Milk and dairy products became part of the diet in this period, which was called the New Stone Age or Neolithic era. However, the main principle of a strict Paleo diet is to avoid all agricultural foods such as grains, legumes, and dairy—like milk, cheese, and yogurt.

Today dairy is prevalent in the modern Western diet and it is frequently added to many processed foods. Some people are intolerant to dairy products and research has demonstrated that milk proteins and peptides have the potential to cause allergies, inflammation, autoimmune conditions, and other health problems. Many people find the proteins difficult to digest and they may irritate the gut lining and cross into the bloodstream initiating an immune response. Dairy allergy is one of the more common food allergies, particularly in children. In addition, milk is highly insulinogenic (i.e. stimulating the production of insulin), which can promote inflammation and insulin resistance. Cow's milk proteins are also known to cross-react with gluten peptides, which means that people with gluten sensitivities may also react to dairy products.

Milk and other dairy products also contain lactose, a milk sugar that must be broken down by our bodies via the enzyme lactase so that we can digest it. It is estimated that about 65 percent of people do not have enough enzyme to digest lactose and so are lactose intolerant.

One of the concerns about eliminating dairy is how to obtain enough calcium for healthy bones. However, for optimum bone health many nutrients are required which are not provided in a good balance by eating dairy products. Key nutrients include vitamin D, calcium, magnesium, zinc, protein, collagen, boron, silicon, vitamin K, and vitamin C. In fact excess calcium has also been associated with the risk of cardiovascular disease.

Some variations of the Paleo diet do include dairy products in moderation. If you wish to consume dairy, it is worth noting that there is a big difference in nutritional profile between grass-fed dairy and conventional grain-fed dairy products. Grass-fed dairy is a good source of fat-soluble vitamins and CLA, an anti-

inflammatory fat. In addition, fermented dairy products such as yogurt and kefir provide a valuable source of probiotics. Dairy, particularly butter, contains butyric acid; this is a short-chain fatty acid that can lower inflammation in our gut. Dairy fat may also help to lower blood pressure. It is filling and so may help reduce cravings and blood sugar imbalances.

If you are tolerant to dairy and wish to include it in your diet, it is best to choose whole grass-fed dairy products. Low-fat

Above: Dairy products such as milk, yogurt, butter, cream, and cheese are generally excluded from a Paleo diet.

dairy is not a rich source of fat-soluble vitamins and does not appear to have the same satiating properties. If you are sensitive to lactose, then stick to low lactose dairy products such as butter or hard cheese. Homemade yogurt or kefir, which has been fermented for 12 to 24 hours, is also likely to be very low in lactose.

The Paleo Menu

Following the Paleo diet may feel daunting at first. Here are some suggestions to help you to get started.

Paleo Breakfast

Eggs are a classic breakfast meal that works well for a Paleo diet. Prepare them in different ways to add variety to your menu. Try and include a choice of vegetables alongside them. Many people following a Paleo diet will simply eat leftovers from the night before. This may mean eating a piece of meat or fish with cooked or raw vegetables.

For those who don't like a heavy breakfast, then simple no-cook options could include green smoothies, Raspberry Chia Dessert (see page 139), sliced avocado and fruit, nut cream or Homemade Coconut Yogurt (see page 187) and fruit, hard-boiled eggs, and vegetable sticks. You could also make up some Paleo pancakes, Paleo bread, or granola and serve it with Homemade Coconut Milk (see page 197).

If you are typically in a hurry, prepare some foods in advance that you can simply reheat. Simple meat patties made with lean ground turkey or beef can be made in advance and even frozen in batches. You can cook them and pair the dish with steamed vegetables.

Your Paleo Lunch and Dinner

Lunch and dinner options are interchangeable depending on preferences. A colorful salad with some protein is light and energizing. If you fancy a little starch add some baked sweet potato. Soups are great on cooler days, but always ensure that there is enough protein in the meal. For a less starchy substitute, try spiralized zucchini and carrots or kelp noodles instead of pasta. Coconut flour wraps are also available and can be used like traditional wheat wraps.

For something more substantial, your Paleo dinner should focus on lean meats, fish, or seafood cooked with spices featuring flavors that you really enjoy with a variety of vegetables.

Paleo Snacks

Snacking is not encouraged unless you are really hungry. If you do need a snack, it is best to keep it simple. This could include a handful of nuts and seeds, some fruits, vegetable sticks with nut butter, beef jerky, or a smoothie. Other examples are homemade Paleo breads, canned fish such as tuna, salmon, or sardines, hard-boiled eggs, cooked meats, coconut, avocado, olives, Sauerkraut (see page 186), or Coconut Kefir (see page 185).

Example Meal Planner

Below is an example of a typical meal planner for a Paleo week. You can follow it directly or tweak it to meet your own needs. Remember to drink plenty of Paleo fluids as well.

Breakfast	Lunch	Dinner	Snacks
Omelet with vegetables	Chicken with Arugula and Orange Salad with Vinaigrette Dressing (p.156)	Spiced Venison Burgers (p.56) with vegetables; Creamy Coconut Chocolate Mousse (p.180)	Sauerkraut (p.188); Matcha Green Smoothie (p.198)
Raspberry Chia Dessert (p.139)	Salmon and Seafood Salad with Gremolata (p.98)	Hoisin Spiced Ribs (p.44), sweet potato wedges, vegetables	Chocolate Chip Banana Bread (p.160); Berry Ice Cream (p.144)
Pan-Fried Indian Spiced Liver (p.62)	Tom Yum Soup with Dulse (p.130), mixed salad	Buffalo Steak (p.52), steamed vegetables; Apricot Peach Crisp (p.151)	Handful of berries with homemade yogurt, nuts, and seeds
Harissa Baked Eggs with Spinach (p.88)	Mediterranean Chili and Herb Shrimp (p.104), large mixed salad	Sticky Chicken (p.70), sweet potato and vegetables; Paleo Pumpkin Tart (p.126)	Tangy "Cheese" Kale Chips (p.112); Coconut Kefir (p.185)
Spiced Venison Burgers (p.56) with Beet, Carrot, and Pear Coleslaw (p.122)	Crispy Quail with Fig and Beet Salad and pomegranate dressing (p.82)	Almond Turkey and Green Bean Curry (p.74); Cauliflower Rice (p.115)	Berry Ice Cream (p.144), handful of nuts
Asparagus and Poached Egg with Hollandaise Sauce (p.91)	Seared Raspberry Duck with Berry Honey Dressing (p.78)	Balsamic Lamb Chops with Mint and Parsley Dressing (p.48), mixed salad	Chocolate Chip Banana Bread (p.160); Coconut Yogurt (p.187)

10 Key Principles

1 Focus on Quality
The Paleo approach is not about eating particular amounts or counting calories, but focuses on nutritional density. One of the best ways of ensuring quality is to start eating grass-fed and pasture-raised meat, wild-caught fish, and organic, locally grown, seasonal fruit and vegetables.

2 Ensure Enough Protein
Many people do not consume enough protein for their body's needs, especially if they need to recover from injury. Ensure that each meal includes some protein—a palm-size portion is enough for most people, others may need more depending if they are in training or recovering from an injury. It may seem strange to eat meat or fish at breakfast, but it doesn't take long before it becomes second nature.

3 Don't be Afraid of Fats
If you have previously followed a low-fat diet, it may seem strange to be recommending animal and saturated fats. However, these are essential for your health and are a useful energy source for your body. Switch to high quality saturated fats for cooking and eliminate all processed vegetable oils.

4 Get Variety
Look through this book to get an idea of the vast range of foods that can be included in the Paleo diet. Each week aim to include a new food—by consuming a greater variety of foods you will get a diverse range of nutrients and antioxidants in your diet that are beneficial to health.

5 Cook From Scratch
The easiest way to follow a diet is to choose a recipe and start cooking! Cooking for yourself will eliminate additives, sugars, and processed oils found in commercially prepared foods and ready meals. Use the recipes in this book to get you started. You can also double recipes and then freeze in batches to help save time later.

6 Limit Sugars
While honey and other sweeteners are included in the Paleo diet, they should only be used in moderation. Sugar is inflammatory and promotes oxidative damage, which is the precursor to chronic diseases. It also leads to weight gain and an increase in body fat rather than muscle. If you suffer with blood sugar imbalances, then you may also wish to limit your intake of fruit to one or two portions a day and avoid dried fruits.

7 Include Fermented Foods

Foods containing healthy bacteria (known as probiotic-rich foods) are essential for our digestive health and overall well-being. One of the best ways to increase the levels of healthy microbes in your gut is to eat fermented foods daily. These include homemade yogurt, kefir, sauerkraut, kimchi, kombucha, and pickled vegetables.

8 Keep Hydrated

Don't overlook the importance of fluids in your diet. Water is essential for digesting and absorbing foods, transporting nutrients around the body, keeping cells functioning properly, and removing toxins via the liver and kidneys. If you do not drink enough water, you may feel tired and toxins can build up in your body. Ideally, choose filtered water, as it's free from potential contaminants, and either drink it plain or in broths and herbal teas. Aim for eight glasses a day. Eating fresh fruits and vegetables, soups, and smoothies will also contribute to your fluid intake.

9 Construct a Balanced Plate

The easiest way to ensure that your diet is balanced is to look at what you put on your plate. Each meal should include high quality protein (at least a quarter of your plate); roughly half of your plate should be low-starch vegetables, including dark green leafy vegetables, but aim for lots of color and variety. On the remaining quarter, you can add some starchy vegetables like butternut squash, sweet potato, carrots, or beets. Always include healthy fats—these may occur naturally in meat or fish, or avocado and olives for example, or you may drizzle over a dressing or sauté the food lightly in fat.

10 Eat Mindfully

Take your time over meals. Rather than eating on the run, sit at a table and eat slowly and mindfully. Doing so will promote healthy digestion, slow down the release of glucose into the bloodstream keeping blood sugars more stable, and will make you less likely to overeat. Listen to your body and only eat if you are truly hungry. Many people following a Paleo diet enjoy intermittent fasting while others find that their high activity levels mean they require regular meals and snacks.

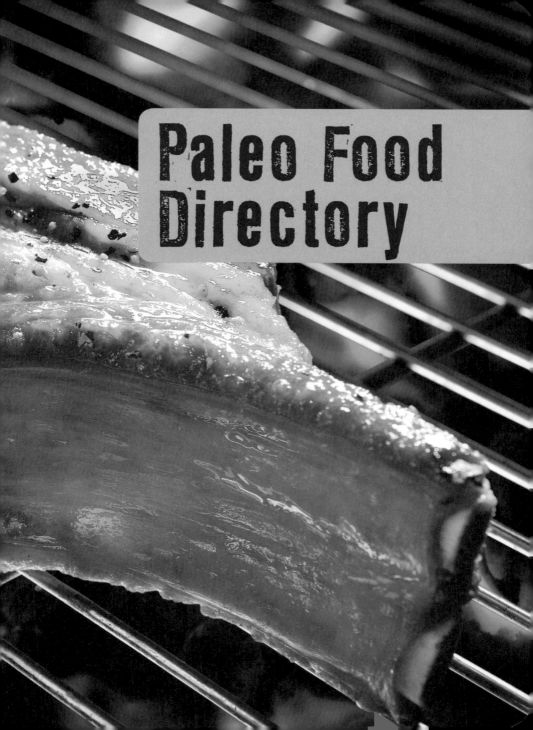

Paleo Food
Directory

Paleo Meat

Proteins are the building blocks for our bodies: from enzymes and hormones to bones, muscles, and skin. One of the best sources of protein is lean meat, which also contains a wealth of essential nutrients to boost health and energy levels.

When selecting the best meats for a Paleo diet, it is important to think lean. Lean meats are generally considered to be those that contain less than 10 g of fat per serving (3½ oz/100 g) and less than 4.5 g of saturated fat. Extra lean cuts contain less than 5 g of total fat and less than 2 g of saturated fat. When selecting cuts look for varieties with "loin" or "tenderloin" in the name. Choose organic, grass-fed meats which have a higher protein content, lower overall fat, and contain a healthier composition of essential omega-3 fats and the fatty conjugated linoleic acid (CLA). CLA has been shown to help reduce body fat and improve body composition. Grass-fed meats are also richer in certain health-promoting nutrients including antioxidants, beta-carotene, and vitamin E.

Lean meats are packed with important nutrients: B vitamins (niacin, thiamin, riboflavin, and B_6) and iron to maintain energy levels; magnesium, which is vital for building bones and supporting metabolism; and zinc, which is essential for our immune system. As it is a good source of protein, lean meat can promote muscle mass and assist in maintaining a healthy weight by helping us feel more satiated.

Left: Juicy grass-fed steaks are low in fat and are a great source of muscle-building protein.

Health Benefits of Paleo Meat

 Eye health: Grass-fed beef contains significant amounts of beta-carotene, which is converted by the body into retinol. This nutrient is particularly important for maintaining healthy eyesight as we age.

 Heart health: Paleo meats are a good source of CLA, a fatty acid with numerous health benefits including reducing inflammation in the body, cutting body fat, and lowering the risk of heart attack. Grass-fed meats also contain a higher level of omega-3 fatty acids, which are known to benefit the health of the heart.

 Immune system: Grass-fed meats are a rich source of protein (needed for the production of white blood cells) as well as minerals, selenium, zinc, antioxidants, vitamin E, and beta-carotene, which all help to promote a healthy immune system.

 Pregnancy health: Paleo meats are rich in essential nutrients that help to ensure a healthy pregnancy, including B vitamins (B_{12}, folate, B_6) for production of healthy red blood cells, protein for growth and development of the fetus, and choline and omega-3 fats for brain health.

 Growth and development: Grass-fed meats supply valuable nutrients that aid growth and development in children and teenagers, including B vitamins, iron, and zinc that are often lacking from children's diets.

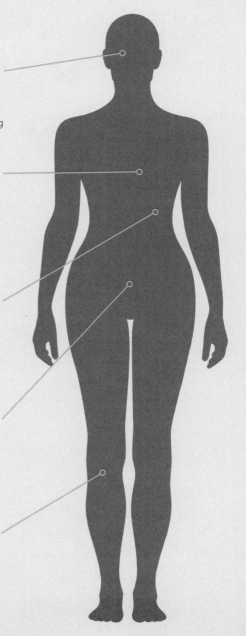

Grass-Fed Beef

Grass-fed beef comes from cows that have grazed in pasture year-round rather than being fed a processed grain-based diet for much of their lives. Grass feeding improves the quality of beef, and makes the beef richer in omega-3 fats, vitamin E, beta-carotene, and CLA. Beef is also an excellent source of high quality protein, vitamins, and minerals such as B vitamins, iron, selenium, magnesium, zinc, and choline.

Grass-fed beef may contain more than twice the amount of beta-carotene and lutein that is present in conventionally fed beef. The cholesterol content of grass-fed beef is also lower than that in conventionally fed animals. Grass-fed beef is also two to three times higher in CLA compared to the levels found in nongrass-fed beef. CLA is derived from linoleic acid, an omega-6 fatty acid which is associated

Nutrition: Grass-fed beef is a major source of omega-3 fatty acids and is naturally leaner than grain-fed beef. **Benefits:** Has lower cholesterol than grain-fed beef and may have cancer-fighting properties.

with a range of health benefits, including immune and inflammatory system support, greater bone mass, sugar regulation, and reduced body fat.

Beef is a particularly important source of a number of key nutrients that are often low in people's diets including children and teenagers—they include B12, B6, zinc, and iron. Beef also provides reasonable amounts of potassium and phosphorous to help keep the heart healthy.

Roast Beef

A joint of top round, sirloin, or rib of beef all make succulent roasting cuts.

- Roast beef is an excellent source of immune system-supporting minerals including selenium and zinc.
- This is a particularly rich source of iron (important for maintaining healthy red blood cells), potassium, niacin, and other essential nutrients.

Steak

Choose lean cuts of steak for a high-protein, low-fat meal. This includes top sirloin, top round, and eye of round steak.

■ A 3-oz (85-g) portion of top sirloin steak contains no carbohydrates but has all of the essential amino acids, which makes it a complete protein. This macronutrient is important for cell rebuilding, boosting the immune system, and muscle growth.

Ground Beef

Lean or extra lean ground beef is a good high-protein, low-fat option. Ideal for homemade burgers, meatloaf, meatballs, and taco fillings. Serve with flavorsome sauces to keep the meat moist and tender.

■ Lean ground beef is a useful source of coenzyme Q_{10}, an antioxidant that helps to prevent damage to your cell membrane proteins and DNA.

Beef Ribs

A favorite for slow cooking, beef short ribs are also a popular choice for braising, slow roasting, and barbecues. Marinate the ribs to ensure they are full of flavor.

■ Beef ribs are an excellent source of several important vitamins. For instance, a 3-oz (85-g) serving contains more than 80 percent of the daily recommended intake of vitamin B_{12}.

Meatloaf

HIGH PROTEIN

Meatloaf is delicious hot or cold—the addition of tomato sauce keeps the meat beautifully moist while cooking. Serve with a leafy green salad or steamed vegetables.

Prep: 20 mins/Cook: 50 mins

Ingredients (serves 4)

1 tablespoon balsamic vinegar
Scant ½ cup (60 g) tomato paste
Pinch of cayenne pepper
Squeeze of lemon juice
Pinch of garlic powder
18 oz (500 g) ground beef
2 tablespoons coconut flour
1 onion, finely chopped
2 oz (60 g) pancetta, finely chopped
1 garlic clove, chopped
1 egg, beaten
Salt and freshly ground black pepper

Method

1 Preheat the oven to 370°F (190°C/gas mark 5). Line a 2-lb (500-g) loaf pan with double-thickness parchment paper.

2 For the tomato sauce, mix the vinegar, tomato paste, cayenne, lemon juice, and garlic powder together. Add a splash of water if needed and continue to mix until the sauce is smooth.

3 Tip the remaining ingredients and half of the tomato sauce into a large bowl and season with salt and pepper. Mix thoroughly—your hands are the best implements for this job.

4 Press the mixture into the loaf pan and spread the remaining sauce over the top. Bake for 40 to 45 minutes until the top is golden and crunchy. If the top does not color in the oven, pop the pan under the broiler and brown for 5 minutes.

5 Cool in the pan for 5 minutes, then lift out using the parchment paper and put on a board. Slice and serve.

ENERGIZING AND BUILDS MUSCLES	
Calories (per serving)	399
Protein	30.9 g
Total fat	27.0 g
of which saturates	11.5 g
Carbohydrates	7.5 g
of which sugars	2.9 g
Vitamins/minerals	B, zinc, iron, selenium

Pastured Pork

A popular white meat packed with plenty of health-promoting nutrients. Pork is a high-protein food making it ideal for building muscle and supporting the immune system. The fat content varies depending on the cut of meat.

Pork is useful for building energy levels as it is packed with an array of vitamins and

Nutrition: Pastured pork is high in omega-3 fatty acids and contains more vitamin E than grain-fed pork.
Benefits: May help to lower cholesterol, good for cardiovascular health, and helps with energy levels.

minerals. A 3½-oz (100-g) serving of pork provides 65 percent of your RDA of thiamin, the B vitamin necessary for the efficient metabolism of carbohydrates into energy. It is also essential for the growth and repair of muscle fibers. High levels of vitamins B_2 and B_3 (riboflavin and niacin) together with minerals such as phosphorus, magnesium, iron, and zinc regulate energy release throughout the day and help your immune system to fight off illness.

Pork Tenderloin

The leanest cut of pork comes from the loin. Pork tenderloin has a similar fat content to a skinless chicken breast. Marinades can stop the meat from drying out during cooking.

- Tenderloin is considered an excellent source of vitamin B_{12} and the B vitamins thiamin and niacin, all of which help to keep your heart healthy.

Pork Chops

Look for pork loin or sirloin chops for the leanest cuts, which may be broiled, baked, sautéed, or braised. A good source of protein and, depending on the cut, most of the fat content is unsaturated.

- Pork chops are particularly high in selenium, important for thyroid function.
- This meat provides iron and B vitamins, important for maintaining energy levels.

Pork Belly

Pork belly is composed of layers of fat and meat that cook down into a flavorsome dish. 1 oz (30 g) of raw pork belly contains 15 g fat, a third of which is in the form of saturated fat.

- Pork belly has a lower protein content than other cuts of pork.
- This cut contains small amounts of iron, vitamin E, and B vitamins.

Pork Spare Ribs

Pork spare ribs are inexpensive, full of flavor, and can be broiled, roasted, or slow-cooked. But they are a fattier cut of meat.

- Rich in B vitamins, pork spare ribs can assist in the metabolism of fat, protein, and carbohydrates and promote cardiovascular health.
- Pork spare ribs provide a good source of zinc, iron, selenium, and magnesium.

Hoisin Spiced Ribs

HIGH ENERGY

Slow cooking the pork keeps the meat moist and full of flavor. Hoisin sauce typically contains gluten and peanuts so this recipe includes a healthier Paleo option. This will make more homemade hoisin sauce than the recipe needs, so store it in the refrigerator to use in other recipes, or to drizzle over the cooked ribs when served.

Prep: 15 mins/Cook: 2 hrs 10 mins

Ingredients (makes about 16 ribs)

30 oz (650 g) pork spare ribs cut into single
    ribs and halved
½ teaspoon Chinese five-spice powder
1 tablespoon coconut oil
1 teaspoon grated ginger root
1 garlic clove, crushed
1 tablespoon tamari or coconut aminos
1 tablespoon sweet chili sauce
¼ cup (60 g) honey
2 tablespoons dry sherry, optional
Salt and freshly ground black pepper

Homemade hoisin sauce

4 tablespoons tamari
2 tablespoons almond nut butter
1 tablespoon honey
2 teaspoons rice wine vinegar
1 garlic clove, finely minced
2 teaspoons sesame seed oil
1 teaspoon chili hot sauce
Pinch of black pepper

Method

1 Make up the homemade hoisin sauce by placing all the ingredients in a food processor and processing until smooth. Store in the refrigerator until required.

2 Preheat the oven to 285°F (140°C, gas mark 1). Rub the ribs with the Chinese five-spice powder and season. Place on a roasting tray and cover with foil. Cook in the oven for 1 hour.

BOOSTS THE IMMUNE SYSTEM	
Calories (per rib)	103
Protein	7.8 g
Total fat	6.3 g
of which saturated fat	2.7 g
Carbohydrates	3.3 g
of which sugars	3.3 g
Vitamins/minerals	B, niacin, zinc, selenium

3 To make the sauce for the ribs, heat the oil in a skillet and sauté the ginger and garlic for 1 minute. Add 2 tablespoons of the homemade hoisin sauce with the remaining ingredients and mix well. Remove the ribs from the oven and pour over the sauce. Mix well to coat them all over.

4 Cook for another 30 minutes. Remove the foil and continue to cook for another 30 minutes until golden.

Grass-Fed Lamb

Select organic, grass-fed lamb, which has a higher nutritional profile. Unfortunately, even the term "grass-fed" is not a guarantee of quality since grass-fed lambs may have spent a relatively small amount of time feeding on grass. The standard to look for on the label is "100% grass-fed." Lamb can only technically be called lamb for the first year of its life. In its second year it is called hogget, while in its third year, the meat is classed as mutton.

Grass-fed lamb contains an impressive amount of omega-3 and conjugated linoleic acid (CLA) which has anti-inflammatory and immune-system supportive properties. As pasture-fed lambs are more active, they also contain less fat and more protein than lambs reared indoors. Lamb contains many nutrients beneficial for heart health—the fatty acid profile with a high level of protective monounsaturated fats together with omega-3 and CLA are associated with low levels of inflammation. Grass-fed lamb is a source of the antioxidant minerals selenium and zinc, which help protect the body from oxidative stress. It is a rich source of B vitamins which help to maintain healthy levels of homocysteine. As a high-protein food it can also have a beneficial effect on blood sugar levels.

Nutrition: Grass-fed lamb is a good source of vitamin B_{12}, protein, selenium, zinc, and niacin.
Benefits: Reduces the risk of heart disease, and helps with the regulation of blood sugar.

Lamb Shank

Lamb shanks are a popular cheaper cut of meat. They are best braised and slow cooked, as there is too much muscle on them to be roasted. To tenderize the meat, marinate lamb shanks before cooking.

- One 3-oz (85-g) serving of lamb shank contains 22.7 g of protein.
- Lamb shanks provide a good source of iron, zinc, potassium, and selenium.

Leg of Lamb

A popular roasting joint, which can be cooked quickly or slow roasted for many hours so that the meat eventually falls off the bone.

- One 3-oz (85-g) serving contains around 24 g of protein and 7.8 g of fat.
- Leg of lamb is high in zinc, an important mineral for hormone production and maintaining fertility.

Ground Lamb

This is a convenient and tasty choice for homemade burgers, patties, or chilis. For a lower fat option, look for lean or extra lean ground lamb.

- Ground lamb is a good source of niacin (vitamin B_3), which helps to boost your cognitive function and also promotes healthy skin.

Shoulder of Lamb

A popular roasting joint, lamb shoulder is generally cheaper than a leg joint and fattier—which can enhance its flavor. Lamb shoulder has a strong taste which means it works well with spices, herbs, and sauces. It can also be diced or ground to use in curries, tagines, and casseroles.

- Shoulder of lamb is high in iron, good for the formation of red blood cells.

Balsamic Lamb Chops with Mint and Parsley Dressing

GOOD FAT

A simple dish that works well with lamb steaks. To maximize the flavor, marinate the lamb overnight. The dressing is equally delicious served with a roasted lamb joint.

Prep: 1 hr 15 mins/Cook: 8 mins

Ingredients (serves 4)

1 tablespoon olive oil
2 tablespoons balsamic vinegar
1 teaspoon chopped rosemary
8 small lamb chops or 4 lamb steaks

Dressing

2 tablespoons minced fresh mint
2 tablespoons minced fresh parsley
1 teaspoon capers, chopped
1 anchovy, finely chopped
1 tablespoon honey
1 tablespoon balsamic vinegar
2 tablespoons red wine vinegar
4 tablespoons olive oil

Method

1 Combine the oil, vinegar, and rosemary in a bowl. Flatten the lamb chops or steaks slightly with a rolling pin. Place in a shallow dish and cover with the oil mixture. Turn the meat over to coat them on both sides and marinate for at least 1 hour.

2 Whisk all the ingredients together for the dressing and set aside.

3 Remove the lamb from the marinade and place on a lined baking sheet. Put under the broiler for 3 to 4 minutes on each side until cooked. Cover with foil and let rest for 5 minutes. Serve with salad greens and the herb dressing.

PROMOTES A HEALTHY HEART	
Calories (per serving)	457
Protein	23.6 g
Total fat	37.9 g
of which saturated fat	12 g
Carbohydrates	4.5 g
of which sugars	4.5 g
Vitamins/minerals	B, zinc, iron, selenium

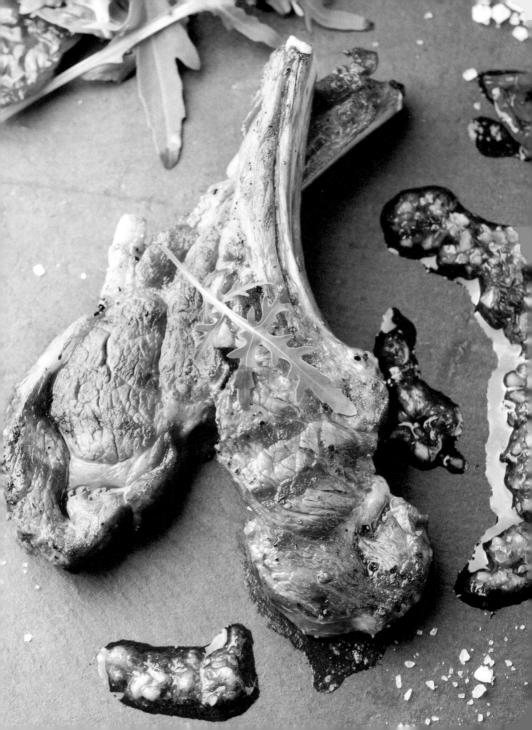

Bison and Buffalo

Bison and buffalo are different animals but the names are sometimes used interchangeably. In the United States buffalo is typically used to describe the American bison. The bison is North America's largest native animal which has been extensively farmed since the 1990s. Water buffalo originally came from Asia, and are different from North American buffalo, or bison.

Bison is a low-fat meat and varies in tenderness dependent on the cut. A 3-oz (85-g) serving of bison contains 16 g of protein, 190 calories, and 14 g of fat. Bison is also a good source of B$_{12}$ for a healthy nervous system. A similar serving of water buffalo contains 23 g of protein, 111 calories, and 2 g of fat.

Both bison and water buffalo meat contain significant amounts of omega-3 polyunsaturated fats, which are believed to protect against heart disease and other inflammatory disorders. They are a valuable source of iron, selenium, and zinc and are high in beta-carotene, an antioxidant which can reduce the risk of cancer. You can cook the meat like beef in burgers, roasts, steaks, and casseroles, but as they are naturally lower in fat than beef, it is important that they are not overcooked.

In parts of Europe, water buffalo are an important farm animal. They originally

Nutrition: Bison and buffalo are excellent sources of vitamin E, iron, and other essential fatty acids. **Benefits:** May reduce the risk of cancer, diabetes, obesity, and some immune disorders.

descended from Asian buffalo. They are called water buffalo as in the wild they inhabit swampy, wet areas. The taste of water buffalo meat and bison is very similar to beef. Water buffalo meat also contains less fat and cholesterol, and more protein, than beef and is now available in the United States.

In Europe water buffalo are also farmed to produce buffalo mozzarella and buffalo milk. Buffalo milk contains 50 percent more protein than cow's milk, 40 percent more energy in calories, nearly 40 percent more calcium, and high levels of the antioxidant tocopherol. It also has twice as much fat—spread evenly across saturated, mono-, and polyunsaturated fats. This high fat content makes it excellent for cheese making. Some people who are allergic to or intolerant of cow's milk can tolerate buffalo milk. It does contain lactose so it is unlikely to be suitable for anyone with a lactose intolerance or anyone on a strict Paleo diet.

Bison/Buffalo Steak

Bison or buffalo steaks come in a wide variety of cuts, like beef. They are an ideal choice for frying in a grill pan and stir-frying. Do not overcook as they require less cooking time than beef steaks.

- Grass-fed bison or buffalo steak is lower in calories, fat, and cholesterol than either chicken or fish and contains nearly 70 percent more iron than beef.

Ground Bison/Buffalo Meat

Ground bison or buffalo meat can be used in the same way as ground beef. It is generally leaner than ground beef and so will cook slightly more quickly. It is best to cook it over a low temperature to keep the meat moist.

- Ground bison or buffalo meat is a good source of B vitamins including niacin, which keeps the skin and hair healthy.

Roast Bison/Buffalo

Chuck and hump, which are less tender cuts of bison or buffalo, are delicious roasted but are best marinated or pot-roasted in a liquid meat stock.

- Roast bison or buffalo meat is a good source of thiamin, which is helps to maintain a healthy nervous system.
- This meat contains zinc and selenium, which can boost the immune system.

Buffalo Steak with Mushroom Stroganoff Sauce

LOW FAT

Seared buffalo steaks drizzled with a light mushroom sauce make a delicious alternative to beef steak. Cook the steaks for just a short time to keep the meat beautifully tender and moist. You can serve sweet potato fries and salad as a tasty accompaniment.

Prep: 10 mins/Cook: 26 mins

Ingredients (serves 4)

4 buffalo steaks
Salt and freshly ground black pepper
Sprigs of oregano, to garnish

Dressing

2 tablespoons coconut oil or butter
1 onion, chopped
2 garlic cloves, chopped
18 oz (500 g) cremini mushrooms, sliced
2 teaspoons arrowroot
1½ teaspoons smoked paprika
2 teaspoons tomato paste
1¾ cups (400 ml) beef stock
Dash of brandy, optional
4 tablespoons coconut cream
Handful of parsley, chopped

Method

1 To make the sauce, heat 1 tablespoon of the coconut oil in a skillet and sauté the onion over low heat for about 10 minutes until soft. Add the garlic and mushrooms, increase the heat, and fry until all the liquid has evaporated. Mix the arrowroot with 1 tablespoon of water to form a paste and set aside.

2 Add the paprika and tomato paste to the mushrooms. Pour in the beef stock and brandy (if you are using it) and simmer to reduce the sauce by half. Add the arrowroot paste, coconut cream, and parsley and stir for 1 minute to thicken the sauce. Season to taste.

3 Keep the sauce warm while you cook the buffalo steaks.

4 Heat the remaining coconut oil in a skillet over medium-high heat. Season the buffalo steaks and cook for 3 minutes on each side for medium-rare, depending on the thickness of the meat. Remove from the skillet and let rest covered with foil for 5 minutes. Serve the steaks with the sauce poured over, garnished with oregano.

AIDS GROWTH AND DEVELOPMENT	
Calories (per serving)	298
Protein	37.5 g
Total fat	13.1 g
of which saturated fat	9.8 g
Carbohydrates	6.7 g
of which sugars	3.4 g
Vitamins/minerals B, zinc, iron, magnesium	

Venison, Hare, and Rabbit

Wild or pasture-fed venison (such as deer), hare, and rabbit are high quality, nutritious meats. Venison is particularly rich in protein and is an excellent source of vitamins B_6 and B_{12}. Hare and rabbit contain high levels of iron and are low in calories. They all contain lower amounts of omega-6 fatty acids and higher amounts of omega -3.

Nutrition: Venison, hare, and rabbit are low in saturated fat and contain high levels of iron and selenium.
Benefits: May help to reduce risk of heart attacks, prevent anemia, and is good for keeping up energy levels.

Osso Buco

The osso buco part of the deer comes from the shank of the leg. It is considered to be a particularly flavorsome portion of meat. This part of the leg bone has a hole containing marrow in it and that allows for even cooking throughout the steak.

- Wild or pasture-fed deer meat is a particularly good source of omega-3 fatty acids to help protect the heart.

Venison Loin (Saddle)

Prime cuts of deer such as loin are lean cuts. To keep the meat moist during cooking you need to add a little extra fat or bacon. Try serving it with watercress salad and horseradish sauce.

- Venison contains more iron than beef, making it an ideal meat to serve growing children and teenagers, and women during pregnancy.

Roast Venison

The roast is what is taken from the rump or hindquarter of a game animal such as deer. The haunch, or back leg, is popular for roasting on or off the bone, like a leg of lamb. Leftover venison meat is delicious cold and thinly sliced in salads.

- A typical serving of roasted venison contains 140 calories, less than 1 g of fat, and 26 g of protein.

Hare

Known for its rich, gamey flavor, hare is a true wild meat. The brown hare is most commonly sold. It is hung to allow the flavor to develop. As the meat has a tendency to dry out, braising is the preferred cooking method. It is also popular in casseroles and stews.

- Good protein with high levels of vitamin B_3—a key nutrient for brain health.

Rabbit

Rabbit is more delicate in flavor than hare. It is also low in fat, particularly saturated fat. It provides a range of B vitamins including B_{12} and niacin. Niacin aids the conversion of carbohydrates to energy and supports healthy cholesterol levels.

- Rabbit provides us with several useful minerals including selenium, iron, and phosphorus to keep body cells healthy.

Spiced Venison Burgers

ENERGIZING

Ground venison is widely available and is perfect for making homemade burgers. To keep it moist, this recipe includes a little bacon. Serve the burgers with raw fermented pickles or sauerkraut and accompany them with salad.

Prep: 15 mins/Cook: 20 mins

Ingredients (serves 4)

1 teaspoon coconut oil, plus extra
   for frying
½ onion, diced
1 garlic clove, crushed
1 lb (450 g) ground venison
4 slices of lean bacon, minced
1 tablespoon chopped fresh cilantro
1 teaspoon ground cumin
1 teaspoon garam masala
1 egg
Salt and freshly ground black pepper

Method

1 Heat the coconut oil in a skillet and gently sauté the onion and garlic for about 3 to 4 minutes until soft. Set aside to cool.

2 Place all the ingredients in a large bowl and mix them together well. Season with salt and pepper.

3 Divide the mixture into four burgers. Ensure the burgers are squeezed tightly into shape so that they will hold together when cooking.

4 Heat a little coconut oil in a large nonstick skillet and fry the burgers. Turn them once only, cooking for about 5 to 6 minutes each side. Alternatively, you can cook them under a broiler for the same time, turning them halfway through.

BUILDING HEALTHY MUSCLES	
Calories (per serving)	181
Protein	29.2 g
Total fat	7.0 g
of which saturated fat	2.5 g
Carbohydrates	0.7 g
of which sugars	0.4 g
Vitamins/minerals	B, magnesium, iron

Nose-to-Tail Meat

Eating every part of an animal makes good ecological sense and is a more sustainable approach to consuming meat than discarding parts of the carcass. Variety meats refer to the edible parts other than muscle meat. It is therefore meat including organ and other cuts such as cheek, tripe (stomach), and tongue, as well as bones (including marrow bones). Organ meat is the most nutrient-dense part of the animal. For those with inflammatory or autoimmune conditions, nose-to-tail meat provides a concentrated source of key nutrients to support gut healing.

If you don't like the taste of organ meat then try grinding some in a food processor and adding it to ground beef or lamb when you prepare some of your favorite dishes. You can also cook it and then blend it into tasty gravies, sauces, and stews.

Nutrition: Nose-to-tail meat, especially liver, is rich in vitamin A, while heart is high in iron.
Benefits: Helps to keep the immune system, skin, and gut healthy, and helps prevent bleeding gums.

Try including organ meat weekly in your diet to support overall health, sustain energy levels, and to aid healing.

Liver is one of the most popular types of organ meat and one of the most concentrated sources of vitamin A—good for maintaining a healthy immune system.

Remember that meat products from pasture-raised animals are much higher in nutrients than similar cuts that come from commercially fed livestock.

What About Toxins in Liver?

Some people worry about consuming liver as they think that the liver is a storage organ for toxins in the body, and so it may itself be high in toxins. While it is true that the liver does help to eliminate toxins, it does not actually store these substances. In fact, toxins are more likely to accumulate in the body's other fatty tissues. As with all meat, it is better to source organ meats from animals that have been raised on fresh pasture and are free of any addition of hormones, antibiotics, or commercial feed additives.

Beef and Calves' Liver

Beef—and calves'—liver is stronger in flavor than some other animal livers. It is popular sautéed with onions. To tenderize liver and tone down the flavor and aroma, cut it into strips and soak in lemon juice for a few hours before draining and cooking.

- Beef liver provides a concentrated source of many key nutrients including the B vitamins (B_2, B_3, B_5, B_6, B_{12} choline, and folate), which benefit some of your most important cognitive and neurological processes. Choline is important for improving the memory and it may also help to protect against fatty liver disease. The iron in liver is especially useful for people who suffer from fatigue as well as for growing children.

- Beef liver also contains CoQ10 (Coenzyme Q10), an antioxidant that helps your body to produce energy and promotes a healthy heart.

Lambs' Liver

Lambs' liver is high in protein and iron and while it also contains cholesterol, this is essential for the production of hormones in our body.

- Lamb's liver is rich in B_{12}, iron, and copper—essential for the production of healthy red blood cells.

- This is a good source of vitamin A to keep eyes, skin, and hair healthy.

Chicken Liver

Milder in flavor than beef or lambs' liver. Chicken liver is popular in pâtés and parfaits. Remove and discard any sinew on the chicken livers before cooking, as they will make them taste bitter if left on.

- A good source of vitamins A and C for immune health and all the B vitamins. It is a high-protein, low-calorie food rich in the antioxidants zinc and selenium.

Tongue

In general, beef and veal tongues are the most commonly consumed. They tend to have a slightly grainy, firm texture. As they can be quite chewy, they are normally stewed, boiled, or poached.

- A rich source of zinc, which keeps the immune system healthy.
- Tongue provides a reasonable level of iron and B_{12} to help prevent anemia.

Kidney

Beef, lamb, and pork kidneys are generally sold trimmed, with the outer membranes removed. Beef kidneys have a milder flavor. To prepare, rinse well then soak in water with a little salt for several hours.

- A good source of B vitamins that help to maintain a healthy nervous system and metabolism.
- Kidneys contain vitamin A for vision.

Heart

Because it is a muscle meat, heart is very similar to steak or ground beef. It is often sautéed or broiled after soaking in brine for a couple of hours.

- Heart is rich in a number of nutrients including B vitamins, selenium, zinc, phosphorus, and CoQ10.
- High in protein, which makes it a valuable muscle-boosting food.

Sweetbreads

Sweetbreads principally comprise the thymus and pancreas glands of a calf or young cow, lamb, or pig. In general, sweetbreads are pinkish-white in color. They have a slightly sweet taste and can be coated in ground nuts or coconut flour and sautéed in oil until crispy.

- Sweetbreads are a good high-protein food, but high in fat and cholesterol.

Tripe

Tripe is generally defined as the stomach lining of sheep, goats, pigs, or deer. It has a somewhat rubbery texture, and is normally boiled for at least two to three hours to make it tender. It is then usually served in stews or casseroles or used in salads.

- Tripe is rich in potassium, which is important for heart health, muscle strength, and kidney function.

Pan-Fried Indian Spiced Liver

PROTEIN RICH

A delicious dish that is quick to produce and which makes an energizing breakfast or light lunch option. It is nutrient-rich and anti-inflammatory thanks to the addition of the spices. Serve with some wilted spinach or a salad, if desired.

Prep: 15 mins/Cook: 10 mins

Ingredients (serves 4)

9 oz (250 g) organic chicken livers
1 tablespoon coconut oil
1 teaspoon cumin seeds
1 tablespoon grated ginger root
1 onion, finely sliced
2 oz (60 g) white mushrooms, quartered
¼ teaspoon turmeric
½ teaspoon chili powder
½ teaspoon ground coriander
1 tomato, seeded and chopped
Pinch of sea salt
1 tablespoon lime juice
Handful of cilantro leaves, chopped

Method

1 Cut the chicken livers into cubes about 1 inch (2.5 cm) in size and set them aside. Heat the oil in a shallow pan and sauté the cumin seeds. Add the ginger and onion and cook until they are soft.

2 Add the chicken livers and sauté for 1 minute. Add the mushrooms and sauté for 2 minutes, then add the ground spices and cook for another 30 seconds. Add the tomato and season with the salt. Stir in the lime juice then remove the pan from the heat.

3 Scatter the chopped cilantro leaves over the spiced liver and serve.

HAS ANTI-INFLAMMATORY PROPERTIES	
Calories (per serving)	97
Protein	12.2 g
Total fat	4.2 g
of which saturated fat	2.4 g
Carbohydrates	3.4 g
of which sugars	2.6 g
Vitamins/minerals	A, B, iron, zinc, copper

Eating Processed Meats

Cured meats (e.g. bacon, ham, salami, prosciutto, and cooked sausage) have been a traditional way of preserving animal foods for hundreds of years. However, nowadays there is understandable concern not only about the quality of some of these meats, but also the presence of additives and preservatives that may increase the risk of certain cancers.

Cheap luncheon-type meats often contain less desirable cuts and animal scraps and they are often preserved with sugars, salts, and nitrites. They typically also contain other fillers and additives to plump up the meat.

However, you can source naturally cured or uncured deli meats from grass-fed animals. These will be made from high quality meat, spices, salt, and sugar and be smoked. They are often cured, fermented, and dried for months or even years. Although sugar is usually used in the curing process, very little remains in the finished product. Bacon, ham, sausages, and other smoked meats tend to be the fattiest meats, so it is important to select grass-fed examples. The occasional addition of good quality cured meats can be useful as a quick, convenient meal option. However, these are high in sodium which can exacerbate hypertension in salt-sensitive individuals and lead to excessive water retention. If you are concerned about nitrites, look for cured meats labeled "nitrite free."

When selecting cured meats, choose high quality, grass-fed products and check the ingredients carefully. Only eat such foods occasionally—possibly as a trail food, a snack, or as a topping on other dishes.

Bacon

Bacon is most commonly made from pork, although you can also find "bacon" made from the meat of other animals like turkey. Quality bacon is an excellent source of high-protein, low-carbohydrate energy that helps to support muscle mass. Bacon

from grass-fed meats will have a healthier fat composition, supplying some omega-3 fatty acids and monounsaturated fats.

When cooking bacon, avoid making it too crispy and burned. Burning foods can lead to the production of harmful compounds like polycyclic aromatic hydrocarbons and heterocyclic amines which are associated with cancer risk.

- A typical 3½-oz (100-g) portion of cooked bacon contains around 37 g of high quality animal protein.
- Bacon is a good source of choline, which is necessary for memory building and cognitive function.
- It also contains a range of B vitamins to boost energy levels.

Sausages

Traditionally made from pork, sausages are now available based on a wide range of animal meats. They are a convenient meat product that can be used in a range of Paleo recipes. Not all sausages are Paleo so it is important to check the ingredients. Cheaper sausages are likely to contain fillers such as soy, refined sugar, MSG, dairy, vegetable oils, or wheat starch.

Paleo-friendly sausages should consist of high quality meat, spices, possibly some vegetables, and natural animal casing. Higher quality brands will state the source of the meat used.

- A 3½-oz (100-g) pork sausage will provide around 16 g of protein.
- Pork sausages contain iron, essential for keeping muscles and tissues healthy.

Poultry and Game

Cage-free and organic poultry and game are another great source of protein and they are particularly rich in an array of essential minerals including selenium, potassium, iron, magnesium, manganese, and calcium, as well as plenty of B vitamins.

Proteins are the building blocks for key functions in our bodies including the production of enzymes and hormones and the maintenance of healthy bones, muscle, and skin. Most adults require roughly three servings of protein-rich foods daily. Poultry and game provide a complete source of protein that is easily digested and generally low in fat. Lean meats are particularly useful for boosting energy levels as they are rich in B vitamins, which assist the body's metabolism and production of red blood cells.

It is best to choose cage-free or organic poultry. Organic chicken is raised without the addition of antibiotics, synthetic hormones, or pesticides and so promotes a more sustainable environment. They can roam freely and their diet contributes to healthier, cleaner meat. This means they are typically higher in protein and lower in fat than factory-farmed birds.

Health Benefits of Poultry and Game

Brain health and stress: Poultry is high in an amino acid called tryptophan, which the body converts to the mood-boosting neurotransmitter serotonin. Serotonin can also be converted to melatonin to promote restful sleep. Poultry contains vitamin B₅ that has a calming effect on the nerves and helps to combat stress.

Heart health: Poultry is rich in B vitamins, particularly B₆ and B₁₂ that help to lower the levels of homocysteine—high levels of this amino acid are linked to an increased risk of cardiovascular disease. Poultry also provides a good source of niacin (Vitamin B₃) known to decrease the LDL (low-density lipoprotein) cholesterol and triglyceride levels.

Metabolism and energy: Poultry and game supply plenty of selenium, an essential mineral involved in metabolic function including thyroid health. They are a good source of B vitamins, which also aid metabolism and conversion of carbohydrates into energy.

Men's health: Rich in zinc and selenium, poultry has special health benefits for men by assisting in the production of testosterone. Selenium has a protective role against prostate cancer too.

Bone health: Chicken and other poultry is rich in phosphorus, an essential mineral that strengthens your teeth and bones. Its high protein content is equally important as a key nutrient for bone health and helping to prevent osteoporosis.

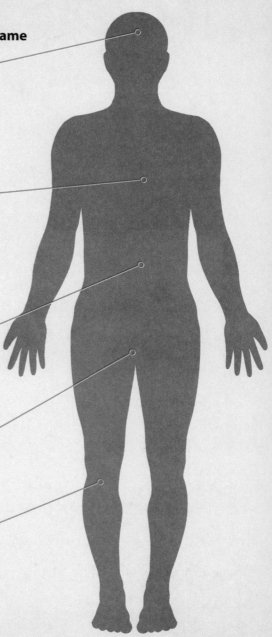

Chicken

A popular meat and excellent source of protein, chicken is also crammed with many essential vitamins and minerals to promote good health. For optimal benefits choose pasture-fed and/or organic chicken as this increases the omega-3 content of the meat and typically results in a leaner bird meaning more protein and less fat.

Nutrition: Chicken is very rich in B vitamins, vitamin E, and the minerals selenium, zinc, and niacin.
Benefits: Boosts the immune system, regulates digestion, strengthens the bones, and may help with weight loss.

Chicken Breast

This is probably the most popular part of the chicken. It can be sold as a whole breast, with or without the skin, or sliced up into smaller pieces. It can be pan-fried, stuffed with herbs and spices, baked, roasted, or barbecued. Use diced breast meat in stir-fries, curries, or in casseroles.

- Chicken breast is a low-fat, high-protein option if you remove the skin.

Whole Chicken

While organic chicken may be more expensive, using the whole chicken can be a more economical option than buying individual cuts.

- Use the chicken bones to make a broth, which is rich in protein, minerals, like calcium for healthy strong bones, and lots of amino acids including glycine and proline to fight inflammation.

Chicken Drumsticks

These are the chicken's shins. They are cheap and easy to cook. Remove the skin to reduce the fat content of the meat.

- Being rich in darker meat, chicken drumsticks contain more myoglobin than white meat. Myoglobin is the primary oxygen-carrying protein in muscle tissue and so essential for endurance activities.

Chicken Thighs

Thighs are often considered the tastiest part of the chicken. The meat is firmer and needs longer cooking time than breast meat so are delicious roasted or in slow-cooked casseroles.

- The dark meat on chicken thighs has more fat than breast meat.
- Chicken thighs are rich in minerals such as iron and zinc and B vitamins.

Chicken Wings

These are the cheapest part of the chicken but are still fantastic to eat. They come on the bone and are typically roasted or broiled for a quick and convenient meal. Cook a batch of chicken wings and use them as a healthy protein-packed snack through the day.

- Chicken wings are rich in niacin, beneficial for healthy skin, hair, and eyes.

Sticky Chicken

HIGH PROTEIN

This is a wonderful recipe for the whole family and a delicious way to use the cheaper cuts, such as thighs, drumsticks, and wings. It is equally delicious with chicken breasts. Make up a big batch and use them for packed lunches or salads. You could accompany these with roasted sweet potato wedges.

Prep: 50 mins/Cook: 30 mins

Ingredients (serves 4)

1 lb (450 g) chicken drumsticks and thighs

Sticky sauce

5 tablespoons homemade low-sugar tomato ketchup

3 tablespoons balsamic vinegar

3 tablespoons tamari

2 tablespoons Chinese five spice powder

1 tablespoon honey

2 teaspoons olive oil

Salt and freshly ground black pepper

Method

1 Preheat the oven to 400°F (200°C, gas mark 6). Place the chicken pieces in a large roasting pan. Whisk all the sauce ingredients together and season with salt and pepper.

2 Pour the sauce over the chicken. Toss together and make sure that the chicken is well coated and not heaped in more than one layer in the pan. Ideally marinate for 30 minutes.

3 Place the roasting pan in the oven and bake for around 30 minutes—check to see if it is done by piercing the flesh in its thickest part with a knife—it should be hot in the middle with no pinkness.

4 Serve the sticky chicken pieces hot or cold with salad and some homemade tomato ketchup, if desired.

A GREAT IMMUNE SYSTEM BOOSTER	
Calories (per serving)	270
Protein	20.8 g
Total fat	17.0 g
of which saturated fat	4.5 g
Carbohydrates	8.3 g
of which sugars	8.3 g
Vitamins/minerals	niacin, riboflavin, zinc

Turkey

Turkey is a high-protein lean meat that is also packed with energizing B vitamins and iron. It is an excellent source of the amino acid tryptophan, which produces serotonin and plays an important role in strengthening the immune system and lifting mood. Turkey meat is sold in various forms, including whole, prepackaged slices, breast, thighs, ground, and tenderloins. If you can, buy organic. Turkeys raised organically on pasture will have been treated humanely and are less likely to contain hormones, antibiotics, and traces of pesticide. Organic, pasture-raised turkey usually has higher nutrient quality. Allowed ample time to forage, the birds' meat is higher in healthy omega-3 fatty acids. Avoid buying prepackaged slices which may be processed and full of additives and sugars. Refrigerated raw turkey can keep for one or two days, while cooked turkey will keep for about three to four days. Be careful when handling raw turkey and ensure that it does not come in contact with other food, particularly any that will be served uncooked.

The most popular way to serve turkey is as a roast. The bird comprises white breast meat and dark leg meat. Any leftovers can be used for other dishes and the bones can be boiled to make a nourishing broth.

Nutrition: Turkey is packed with B vitamins, potassium, iron, zinc, niacin, and phosphorus.
Benefits: Boosts the immune system, helps with proper functioning of the thyroid, and helps to lower cholesterol.

Turkey Breast

A high-protein lean option. Just 4 oz (110 g) of skinned breast will provide 30–35 g of protein, with less than 1 g of total fat.

- Turkey breast is high in protein so can help keep postmeal insulin levels in a healthy range, encourage muscle mass, and aid weight loss.
- This meat is rich in niacin to help the release of energy from foods.

Turkey Thigh

Thigh joints are delicious stuffed and roasted and ideal for feeding two to three people.

- Turkey thigh contains more iron than breast meat, which helps anemia.
- Turkey contains the amino acid tryptophan, which produces serotinin that helps to keep the immune system healthy and promotes sleep.

Turkey Leg

A typical serving of turkey leg contains slightly less protein than breast does.

- Turkey leg is high in health-promoting minerals, such as zinc and iron.
- This meat is also a good source of selenium, a mineral needed to protect cells in the body from damage and to support the immune system.

Ground Turkey

Ground breast and thigh is readily available. Use in exactly the same way as other kinds of ground meat—slow-cooked chili, burgers, and meatballs are all easy and flavorsome options.

- Ground thigh meat tends to have a higher fat content than ground turkey breast, but it also has a deeper flavor.

Almond Turkey and Green Bean Curry

BRAIN BOOSTING

A rich-tasting creamy curry packed with anti-inflammatory ingredients useful for stimulating immune system health. This warming dish is an ideal way to use up leftover cooked turkey as well. Simply add the cooked turkey meat at the end of cooking. This dish can be prepared ahead of time and reheated when needed. Serve with Cauliflower Rice (see page 115) and a leafy green salad.

Prep: 2 hrs 20 mins/Cook: 30 mins

Ingredients (serves 4)

1 lb (450 g) turkey meat, cut into cubes
2 teaspoons olive oil
¼ teaspoon sea salt
2 teaspoons turmeric
1 tablespoon coconut oil
1 red onion, diced
10 oz (300 g) green beans, halved
4 tomatoes, chopped
1 x 14 oz (400 g) can whole coconut milk
6 kaffir lime leaves, finely shredded

Juice and grated zest of 1 lime
1 tablespoon coconut sugar or xylitol
⅓ cup (30 g) slivered almonds, toasted
Few cilantro leaves, chopped
Strips of ginger root

Spice paste

1 onion, chopped
2 teaspoons fresh ginger root, grated
4 garlic cloves, peeled
2 teaspoons ground cumin
1 teaspoon turmeric
1 teaspoon ground coriander
1 red chili, seeded and chopped
½ cup (60 g) blanched almonds
1 tablespoon tomato paste

Method

1 Place the turkey meat in a dish and rub over the olive oil, salt, and turmeric. Marinate the turkey for a couple of hours, or overnight if possible.

ANTI-INFLAMMATORY	
Calories (per serving)	420
Protein	42.5 g
Total fat	21.4 g
of which saturated fat	5.5 g
Carbohydrates	16 g
of which sugars	10.5 g
Vitamins/minerals	C, phosphorous, iron

2 Put all the ingredients for the spice paste in a blender and process to form a thick paste. Add a splash of water if needed to create a smooth mixture.

3 Heat a large skillet over high heat, add the coconut oil, and fry the turkey meat for 4 to 6 minutes, or until golden brown on all sides. Remove the turkey from the skillet.

4 Add the onion and the spice paste to the pan and stir-fry for 2 to 3 minutes, or until fragrant. Add the green beans, tomatoes, and turkey and cook for 5 to 6 minutes. Add the coconut milk, lime leaves, lime juice, zest, and sugar. Simmer, uncovered, for another 10 minutes, or until the turkey is tender and cooked through.

5 Scatter over the toasted slivered almonds, chopped cilantro, and strips of ginger root to serve.

Duck

Often dismissed as a fatty meat, duck is a good source of high quality protein and with the skin removed it is actually low in fat and calories. Rich and full of flavor, duck meat is extremely nutritious, with high levels of B vitamins, vitamins C and A, and minerals such as zinc, potassium, selenium, magnesium, and iron.

Nutrition: Duck is a good source of protein and contains riboflavin, folate, thiamin, and niacin.
Benefits: Improves the immune system, helps keep the skin healthy, and encourages hair growth.

Duck Breast

A popular choice which, without the skin, is a lean, high protein meat. Marinate duck breasts to add extra flavor and moisture. Slash the skin a couple of times to help the marinade penetrate further. Often pan-fried, broiled, or roasted.
- Duck breast is a useful source of selenium—an essential immune-supporting mineral.

Duck Thighs/Legs

Duck thigh and leg meat is slightly fattier than breast meat. Duck is a good source of iron, which plays a crucial role in the production of healthy red blood cells. This makes duck a good choice for growing children and teenagers. Use in stews.
- Duck thighs contain iron, which regulates numerous metabolic activities and plays an important role in growth.

Why Eat Ostrich?

Ostrich meat is becoming a popular healthy option and for good reason. Lower in calories and fat than chicken, it is an excellent source of protein and creatine, both important for building muscle. Ostrich is sold in the form of steaks, fillets, burgers, sausages, roasts, and ground meat, and it provides plenty of energizing iron and B vitamins. Ostrich meat is similar to beef in taste and texture making it an ideal lean alternative to red meat.

As it is a lean meat, ostrich steak cooks faster than some other white meats and is usually grilled, broiled, pan-fried, roasted, or braised. Marinate or drizzle the ostrich meat with a little olive oil to keep the flesh moist when cooking. As it is high in protein and low in fat, it is a useful choice if you want to lose weight.

Below: Ostrich steak is delicious pan-fried with pepper and spices.

Seared Raspberry Duck with Berry Honey Dressing

ENERGIZING

An easy-to-make dish, which is sweet and tangy thanks to the addition of raspberry vinegar and honey. If time allows, marinate the duck breasts for a couple of hours before cooking. The dressing is equally delicious drizzled over steamed vegetables or salad.

Prep: 2 hrs 20 mins/Cook: 25 mins

Ingredients (serves 4)
4 duck breasts
1 red onion, diced
Salt and freshly ground black pepper

Marinade
4 tablespoons tamari
1½ tablespoons honey
4 tablespoons raspberry vinegar
2 tablespoons olive oil

Dressing
4 tablespoons raspberry vinegar
2 tablespoons balsamic vinegar
2 tablespoons olive oil
3 tablespoons walnut oil
½ teaspoon Dijon mustard

Method

1 Whisk all the ingredients for the dressing together, season, and set aside.

2 Score the skin on the duck breasts with a sharp knife and season with salt and pepper. Combine all the ingredients for the marinade and season. Place the duck in a shallow ceramic dish and pour over the marinade. Toss to coat, cover, and let marinate for 1 to 2 hours.

3 Heat a nonstick sauté pan until hot. Drain the duck breasts, discarding the marinade, and sear the breasts with the skin side down. Reduce the heat to medium and cook for 10 minutes until the fat has rendered.

4 Preheat the oven to 400°F (200°C, gas mark 6). Transfer the duck breasts to a roasting pan and cook in the hot oven for 10 minutes.

5 Remove from the oven and let rest for 10 minutes. Slice thinly and arrange on a plate.

6 Sauté the onion in the sauté pan with the duck fat for 1 to 2 minutes until softened. Sprinkle the onion over the duck breasts and drizzle over the dressing.

7 Serve with steamed vegetables or mixed salad.

BOOSTS THE IMMUNE SYSTEM	
Calories (per serving)	449
Protein	25.5 g
Total fat	34.4 g
of which saturated fat	5.7 g
Carbohydrates	7.8 g
of which sugars	7.5 g
Vitamins/minerals	B, copper, selenium

Wild Game

Game birds are wild and free range in their natural habitats so if you are looking for something low in fat and high in protein, game is a delicious and healthy alternative to other red meats. They have a lower content of pro-inflammatory omega-6 fats and a higher content of anti-inflammatory omega-3 fats than other red meats.

Nutrition: Wild game is rich in iron, B vitamins, zinc, selenium, and essential fatty acids.
Benefits: Boosts energy levels, helps support the immune system, and reduces the risk of heart attacks.

Pheasant

For maximum flavor pheasant should be hung for three days before plucking.
- Pheasant contains high levels of magnesium that is essential for stress management.
- Pheasant is rich in vitamin B_6 which plays a crucial role in the synthesis of neurotransmitters such as dopamine and serotonin, helping to boost mood.

Grouse

Grouse is the darkest of game bird meats with a rich red, almost maroon flesh, and has an intensely deep flavor to match. Red grouse is the most commonly eaten variety. As these are wild birds, they are low in fat and high in protein.
- Grouse is an excellent source of iron, important for the production of red blood cells and can help with fatigue.

Quail

Quail is a sweet and delicate white game meat that is low in fat and high in protein. Quail is generally farmed so check its provenance to make sure that it has not been intensively reared.

- Quail meat is a great source of copper, vitamin C, iron, and various B vitamins, which are all important for generating and sustaining energy.

Partridge

Partridge is more mild in flavor than other game birds and is incredibly tender.

- Partridge is packed with iron, which helps your body's uptake of oxygen and energy production.
- This meat provides the trace element selenium, which has been linked to reducing feelings of depression and also boosts the immune system.

Pigeon

Wood pigeon is a small game bird and a good source of sustainable meat. High in satisfying protein, it helps your body to repair and renew cells. Gamey pigeon works well with roasted root vegetables and is delicious in pies and casseroles.

- Pigeon is a particularly good source of iron, zinc, and selenium to encourage a healthy immune system.

Crispy Quail with Fig and Beet Salad

MEN'S HEALTH

A delicious dish inspired by the cuisine of the Middle East, and sweet and tangy thanks to the addition of pomegranate molasses. The dressing can be prepared in advance and is a fabulous addition to any salad. This recipe would also work well with other game birds.

Prep: 2 hrs 20 mins/Cook: 35 mins

Ingredients (serves 4)

4 tablespoons pomegranate molasses
1 tablespoon ground cinnamon
2 garlic cloves, crushed
8 small boneless quail
Large handful of green salad leaves
2 cooked beet, sliced
2 figs, quartered
1 tablespoon pine nuts
Seeds of 1 pomegranate
Salt and freshly ground black pepper

Pomegranate Dressing

5 tablespoons pomegranate molasses
Juice of ½ lemon
1 garlic clove, crushed
Pinch of ground cumin
1 teaspoon honey
4 tablespoons olive oil

Method

1 Combine the pomegranate molasses, cinnamon, and garlic and rub the mixture over the quail. Ideally marinate for 1 to 2 hours, or overnight.

2 Make the dressing by mixing all the ingredients together, then season, and set aside.

3 Preheat the oven to 400°F (200°C, gas mark 6). Place the quail in a roasting pan and cover with aluminum foil. Roast in the oven for 25 minutes.

HELPS TO BOOST MALE FERTILITY	
Calories (per serving)	410
Protein	41.8 g
Total fat	19.8 g
of which saturated fat	3.5 g
Carbohydrates	33 g
of which sugars	26.1 g
Vitamins/minerals	C, D, zinc, selenium

4 Remove the foil and cook for 10 more minutes, or until the quail are completely cooked through. Remove from the oven and let rest for 5 minutes.

5 Place the salad greens in a dish with the beet, figs, and pine nuts. Sit the quail on top and sprinkle over the pomegranate seeds. Drizzle over the dressing just before serving.

Eggs

Eggs are one of the healthiest foods you can eat. In fact, whole eggs are among the most nutritious foods in the world, as they contain a little bit of virtually every nutrient we need. Choose omega-3 enriched or pastured eggs as they are even healthier.

Eggs contain high quality proteins, fats, vitamins, and minerals and are particularly rich in two amino acids—tryptophan and tyrosine—that are known to help boost our mood. While egg yolks are relatively high in cholesterol, numerous studies have confirmed that for most people eating eggs will have a minimal effect on raising cholesterol levels.

Egg yolks are also a rich source of the antioxidants lutein and zeaxanthin, which are types of carotenoids. These have powerful preventive effects for age-related macular degeneration of the eyes.

Cage-free or organic eggs are far superior to cage-bird grain-fed eggs when it comes to nutrient content. They have a higher omega-3 content and are good sources of antioxidants, vitamins A and E, and beta-carotene. Eggs are also rich in brain fats like phosphatidylcholine, which the body converts to acetylcholine, a neurotransmitter that acts on our nervous system.

Egg allergy is quite common, affecting on average two percent of the population, particularly children—although they often outgrow it. There are also concerns that eggs may cause damage to the gut lining and stimulate the immune system. For this reason people with an autoimmune condition may find it beneficial to avoid eggs initially while they heal the gut lining and lower levels of inflammation.

Health Benefits of Eggs

Brain health: Cage-free and organic eggs supply brain-boosting omega-3 fats. Two eggs provide nearly half your daily requirements for choline. Choline is a key component of acetylcholine, a neurotransmitter that carries messages between nerves and muscles and enhances memory capacity.

Eye health: Eggs are rich in vitamin A and the carotenoids lutein and zeaxanthin that are known to be important for protecting your eyes from age-related damage. Vitamin A is also important in night vision. If you're deficient in vitamin A, your body may be producing less rhodopsin, the visual pigment enabling us to see in low-light levels.

Muscle health: Eggs are a useful muscle-boosting food. Easy to digest, the amino acids in eggs are converted into muscle, skin, collagen, and other body tissue very efficiently. One egg contains 6 g of complete protein. This is a useful food postworkout to aid muscle recovery and repair.

Weight loss: Eggs are a high-protein satisfying food that help you feel fuller for longer and prevent cravings between meals. Eating eggs regularly can aid weight loss and boost energy levels.

Bone health: Eggs are one of the few food sources of vitamin D. Vitamin D is an essential substance required for the absorption of calcium and maintenance of healthy bones. Eggs also supply sulfur, which aids the production of collagen, important for the formation of bone and connective tissue.

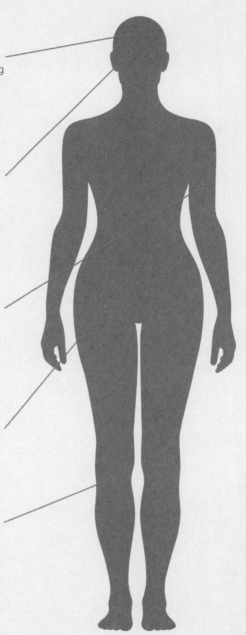

Hens' Eggs

Choose organic or pastured, cage-free eggs, which provide a useful source of healthy omega-3 fats.

- Eggs deliver B vitamins for energy production and plenty of B_{12} and folate to help maintain healthy levels of homocysteine. Too much homocysteine is linked to higher risk of cardiovascular disease and cognitive decline.

Quail Eggs

Quail eggs are little eggs with a slightly richer taste than hens' eggs. You can use them in baking—usually five to six quail eggs will replace one chicken egg.

- Quail eggs are very nutrient-dense and particularly rich in B_1 thiamin, which is important for a healthy nervous system.
- Quail eggs provide more iron and potassium than hens' eggs.

Duck Eggs

Duck eggs taste almost identical to chicken eggs and are roughly the same size, so you can substitute them in your recipes very easily. However, they are very high in cholesterol so they should be only eaten in moderation.

- Duck eggs are higher in protein, calcium, iron, potassium, and pretty much every other major mineral than hens' eggs.

Eggs and the Autoimmune Paleo Diet

Eggs are an important part of the Paleo diet, but be aware that they may aggravate the symptoms of people with autoimmune conditions. One of the main functions of the egg white is to protect the yolk from microbial damage through the presence of enzymes, particularly lysozyme. Lysozyme can form complexes with other proteins, which can be resistant to digestion. These can cross through the gut barrier initiating an immune response that causes inflammation and damage to the gut lining. These proteins therefore damage the integrity of the gut lining leading to increased intestinal permeability. Lysozyme appears to be the most significant enzyme that causes cell membrane damage. As intestinal permeability is one of the factors linked to the initiation of autoimmune diseases, anyone with an autoimmune disease may find they benefit from avoiding eggs while they allow the gut lining to heal.

Eggs are unlikely to be an issue for people with a healthy gut lining (as long as they are not one of the relatively small number of people who suffer from an egg allergy). They make a nutritious addition to a Paleo diet.

Harissa Baked Eggs with Spinach

BRAIN BOOSTING

A delicious breakfast or lunch dish. You can cook the vegetables in advance to save time—then just crack in the eggs and bake when ready to eat. This recipe allows for one egg per person, but for additional protein it is fine to add an extra egg.

Prep: 15 mins/Cook: 20 mins

Ingredients (serves 4)

1 tablespoon coconut oil
1 red onion, finely chopped
2 red bell peppers, cut into chunks
2 yellow bell peppers, cut into chunks
2 garlic cloves, crushed
1 teaspoon harissa paste, or to taste
Pinch of smoked paprika
1 x 14 oz (400 g) can chopped tomatoes
3½ oz (100 g) baby spinach leaves
1 tablespoon chopped fresh parsley
4 eggs
Freshly ground black pepper

Method

1 Preheat the oven to 320°F (160°C, gas mark 3). Warm the coconut oil in a skillet and add the onion, bell peppers, garlic, and spices. Cook slowly for 10 minutes until the peppers are soft.

2 Add the canned tomatoes and simmer the mixture for 1 to 2 minutes, or until the sauce has thickened. Stir in the spinach leaves and parsley.

3 Spoon the mixture into a baking dish or individual ramekins. Make four dips into the vegetable mixture and break in the eggs. Season with pepper.

4 Bake in the oven for 6 to 8 minutes until the whites are fully set but the yolks are still creamy.

PROMOTES HEALTHY EYES AND BONES	
Calories (per serving)	156
Protein	9.4 g
Total fat	8.5 g
of which saturated fat	3.6 g
Carbohydrates	10.4 g
of which sugars	9.1 g
Vitamins/minerals	D, B, C, K, A, calcium

Cooking Eggs

Eggs are a convenient, inexpensive, nutrient-dense, protein-packed food and are incredibly versatile. Here are some of the healthier ways to cook them.

Poached

The antioxidant properties in eggs are greatly reduced during cooking, particularly when eggs are fried or microwaved. Poaching eggs is one of the

healthiest options as it retains more of the valuable nutrients. As well as poaching eggs in water, you can crack eggs into a baking dish with vegetables and bake them briefly in the oven. Avoid cooking at excessively high temperatures which may damage the eggs.

Soft Boiled

When you soft boil an egg, the yolk isn't exposed to a high heat. This protects the cholesterol in the eggs from being oxidized, which could be harmful to health.

Scrambled

If you do wish to scramble eggs then use a heat-stable saturated fat such as coconut oil and cook over low heat for as short a time as possible. Scrambling eggs can promote oxidation of the cholesterol in the egg yolk and reduce significantly the antioxidant content of the eggs.

Can I Eat Raw Eggs?

Eggs are a common allergen food and cooking eggs may change the protein structure increasing its allergenic property. For this reason some people prefer to consume raw eggs. However, eating raw eggs raises the risk of salmonella. This is more of a concern with caged birds which are intensively reared in unhygienic conditions. Cage-free birds raised in clean,

spacious environments are less likely to be contaminated. Raw egg whites contain a glycoprotein called avidin that is very effective at binding biotin, one of the B vitamins. Thus consumption of egg whites on their own could lead to a biotin deficiency. As egg yolks are very rich in biotin, it is unlikely that consuming raw whole eggs will cause a problem but if this concerns you, just eat the raw yolk.

Asparagus and Poached Egg with Hollandaise Sauce

LOW CARB

Prep: 15 mins/Cook: 15 mins

Ingredients (serves 4)

16 asparagus spears, woody ends trimmed
1 tablespoon olive oil
1 tablespoon white wine vinegar
4 cage-free organic eggs
Salt and freshly ground black pepper

Hollandaise Sauce

2 teaspoons freshly squeezed lemon juice
2 teaspoons white wine vinegar
2 cage-free organic egg yolks
½ cup (125 g) coconut oil, melted
Pinch of cayenne pepper
Sea salt and freshly ground black pepper

Method

1 For the hollandaise, heat the lemon juice and vinegar in a small pan until just boiling. Cool slightly. Place the egg yolks and a pinch of salt into a food processor. With the motor running, gradually add the vinegar mixture to the egg yolks in a thin stream, until incorporated. Gradually pour in the melted coconut oil until combined and thick. If too thick, add a splash of hot water. Season with salt, pepper and cayenne.

2 Bring a pan of salted water to a boil, add the asparagus spears, and cook for 1 to 2 minutes. Drain, place in a bowl, and toss with the olive oil. Season to taste.

3 Heat a pan of water to a gentle simmer then add the vinegar. Carefully crack 2 eggs into the water. Poach for 2 to 3 minutes, or until the eggs are cooked to your liking, then set aside to drain on paper towels. Repeat with the remaining 2 eggs.

4 Divide the asparagus spears equally among four serving plates. Place one poached egg on top of each serving of asparagus. Drizzle over the hollandaise sauce and serve.

GREAT SOURCE OF CALCIUM	
Calories (per serving)	406
Protein	7.7 g
Total fat	41 g
of which saturated fat	29.7 g
Carbohydrates	0.1 g
of which sugars	0.1 g
Vitamins/minerals	D, E, C, B, iron, zinc

Fish and Seafood

Fish, particularly oily fish, and seafood are very nutrient dense and are your best dietary source of essential omega-3 fatty acids known as EPA and DHA. They provide proteins which are also highly digestible making them an important part of your diet.

For a healthy Paleo diet, it is extremely important to include seafood in your food choices. The amino acids found in fish are easy to digest and readily bioavailable which is important for anyone with digestive issues. As they are the richest sources of long-chain omega-3 fatty acids, they can be helpful if you suffer with inflammation or autoimmune conditions.

Fish is also generally cheaper than grass-fed meat making it a cost-effective choice. Fish contains a wide range of minerals and vitamins including calcium, phosphorous, zinc, magnesium, iron, and fat-soluble vitamins A, D, E, K, and B_{12}. It also provides two essential minerals which are often lacking in people's diets—selenium and iodine.

The fresh fish that is available will vary according to your location and the season, but aim to include a wide variety in order to provide an array of essential nutrients. Canned fish can also be a useful pantry ingredient—try and select fish in BPA-free cans where possible. BPA (bisphenol A) is an industrial chemical that is used to make resins which often line the insides of metal cans. Research in recent years has revealed the possible adverse health effects of BPA on the brains, behavior, and prostate glands of fetuses, infants, and children.

Left: A selection of delicious fish and seafood.

Health Benefits of Fish and Seafood

 Thyroid function and metabolism: Seafood provides iodine and selenium which are often lacking in people's diet. Iodine is critical to healthy thyroid function. Inadequate levels of iodine causes weight gain, low energy, depression, cognitive decline, and has been linked to certain cancers.

 Heart health: Oily fish provides the omega-3 fats EPA and DHA known for their heart-protective and anti-inflammatory benefits. Regular consumption of omega-3 fats has been shown to reduce the risk of heart attacks and strokes. Seafood also provides vitamins B_6 and B_{12} which can lower levels of homocysteine—a key marker for heart disease.

 Immune health: Seafood is a useful source of antioxidants including vitamin E, selenium, and zinc that are important for maintaining a healthy immune system. Adequate dietary selenium has been shown to help prevent certain cancers including prostate and colorectal cancer.

Men's health: Seafood is a rich source of zinc which supports reproductive and sexual function—especially in men. They are high-protein foods and the zinc in seafood is also important for building muscle by stimulating the production of testosterone and growth hormone.

 Bone health: Seafood, particularly oily fish, is one of the best dietary sources of fat-soluble vitamin D, as well as calcium and magnesium, all essential nutrients for strong healthy bones.

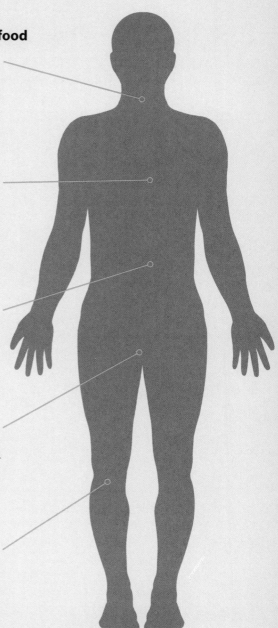

Fish

Eating fish is generally beneficial for health. Fish contains omega-3 fatty acids, which can improve blood circulation, protect the heart from disease, lower cholesterol in the blood, and make the skin glow. Fish also contains retinol, a form of vitamin A, which boosts night vision, and iodine, necessary for the proper functioning of the thyroid.

Nutrition: Fish is high in protein, vitamins, minerals, omega-3 fatty acids, and low in calories.
Benefits: Helps with memory and keeps the brain healthy, skin firm and flexible, and lowers blood pressure.

Wild Salmon

There are a number of species of North American salmon which are all healthy choices. These include king or chinook, sockeye, coho, pink, and chum.

- This fish is especially rich in brain- and heart-healthy omega-3 fats.
- Salmon provides plenty of vitamin D needed for healthy bones and a robust immune system.

Mackerel

This protein-rich oily fish provides plenty of omega-3 fats and fat-soluble vitamins A, D, E, and K to keep bones and eyes healthy.

- Mackerel contains calcium, iron, magnesium, potassium, and selenium, important for keeping the heart healthy.
- Mackerel contains the antioxidant Coenzyme Q10 which helps to protect cells from damage.

Sardines

Available fresh and canned, sardines are an oily fish rich in omega-3 fatty acids.
- Sardines are a good source of vitamin D and calcium to maintain healthy bones.
- Canned sardines with their bones, which can be eaten, are high in calcium.
- Sardines contain energizing minerals like iron, copper, and magnesium plus immune-supporting selenium and zinc.

Albacore

Albacore is a smallish species of tuna and is commonly available canned, labeled as white meat tuna.
- Albacore is rich in protein, selenium, and vitamin B_{12} and is a good source of heart-healthy omega-3 fatty acids.
- This fish is higher in mercury, so pregnant women and children should limit the amount they eat.

Tuna

Canned tuna is inexpensive and is packed with protein.
- Canned tuna is rich in niacin, a B-vitamin that supports healthy skin and the nervous system.
- Tuna provides B_{12} which aids the formation of red blood cells.
- Fresh tuna supplies more omega-3 fatty acids than canned.

Sea Bass

Both sea and freshwater bass are a low-calorie, high-protein food rich in selenium and essential omega-3 fatty acids. Buy line-caught sea bass if possible.

- Sea bass is a good source of vitamin A, important for the immune system and a healthy skin.
- Sea bass contains B vitamins including B6, B12, niacin, riboflavin, and thiamin.

Halibut

Halibut is a member of the flatfish family that is typically sold as steaks or fillets. Low in fat and calories, it is an excellent source of good quality protein. It has a fairly mild taste making it amenable to a wide variety of flavorings. Delicious baked, broiled, pan-fried, or steamed.

- Halibut provides some omega-3 fats plus the antioxidants zinc and selenium.

Trout

Closely related to salmon, trout are mainly freshwater fish—rainbow trout are most widely available. Sea trout are brown trout that migrate. Like salmon, trout is often farmed but it is generally considered low in toxins and a sustainable choice.

- Trout is a good source of omega-3 fats.
- Rich in B vitamins for a healthy nervous system and boosting energy.

Worried About Toxins and Fish?

We are often warned about consuming too much fish or shellfish due to potential harmful levels of mercury and other pollutants, including dioxins and PCBs (polychlorinated biphenyls). Fish can contain high levels of mercury as they absorb mercury from the water in which they live and from the organisms they consume.

Toxins are generally concentrated in the muscle and fat. The older the fish grows, the more toxins will accumulate in its tissues. Small fish at the lower end of the food chain tend to contain lower levels compared to larger fish higher up the food chain.

High levels of mercury in our bodies are known to cause damage to the nervous system. Mercury can cross the blood-brain barrier and placenta. However, seafood also contains high levels of selenium—this is an important antioxidant that can bind to methyl mercury preventing it from being absorbed readily by our bodies. For this reason most seafood, which is rich in selenium, is unlikely to be of real concern to our health. The fish with the lowest levels of methyl mercury include salmon, trout, haddock, sole, mackerel, sardines, herring (right),

and pollock. The main fish that are of concern are the larger carnivores such as shark, marlin, swordfish, and (to a lesser extent) tuna. For this reason authorities recommend that pregnant women, women who intend to become pregnant, infants, and children under 16 years of age should avoid eating shark, swordfish, and marlin. For everyone else, it is recommended as a precaution that these fish are eaten occasionally (e.g. one portion of them a week).

Other pollutants such as dioxins and PCBs are an additional concern because of their carcinogenic properties. Typically wild fish are lower in these toxins than farmed stock, but even with farmed fish the health benefits of eating fish far outweigh the risks, particularly oily fish which contain lots of omega-3 fatty acids.

Salmon and Seafood Salad with Gremolata

LOW CARB

This is a delicious Mediterranean-style dish flavored with a gremolata dressing—a mixture of crushed garlic, lemon, parsley, and olive oil. You can vary the seafood in this salad—scallops, mussels, shrimp, and baby squid are all wonderful additions.

Prep: 10 mins/Cook: 15 mins

Ingredients (serves 4)

8 scallops, cleaned

9 oz (250 g) large raw shrimp

2 tablespoons olive oil

Juice of ½ lemon

4 wild salmon fillets, boneless, skin on

Sea salt and freshly ground black pepper

Gremolata Dressing

Handful of fresh flat-leaf parsley, chopped

1 garlic clove, crushed

Juice and grated zest of 1 lemon

4 tablespoons olive oil

2 teaspoons manuka honey or xylitol

Method

1 Heat a sauté pan until hot. Drizzle the scallops and shrimp with a little oil and season with salt and pepper. Cook the scallops for 1 to 2 minutes on each side and remove from the pan. Drain them on paper towels. Add the shrimp to the pan and cook for 2 to 3 minutes each side until they turn pink and are cooked through. Remove the shrimp from the pan and place them on the paper towels.

2 Sprinkle a little oil and lemon juice over the salmon fillets and pan-fry for 3 to 4 minutes, turning them once. Remove from the heat and let cool.

3 Combine all the dressing ingredients and season. Arrange lamb's lettuce, watercress, spinach, and tomatoes on a plate. Add the seafood and top with the salmon. Drizzle over the dressing and serve.

RICH IN OMEGA-3 FOR A HEALTHY HEART	
Calories (per serving)	460
Protein	46 g
Total fat	28.2 g
of which saturated fat	4.5 g
Carbohydrates	5.6 g
of which sugars	4.3 g
Vitamins/minerals	A, C, B, potassium, zinc

Can I Eat Canned Fish?

While it is preferable to choose fresh, unprocessed foods, canned fish can be a useful and healthy pantry ingredient. Popular canned fish include tuna, mackerel, sardines, herring, salmon, and pilchards. These are all oily fish valuable for their omega-3 content. Canned fish can be a convenient, cheap alternative to fresh fish, which is not always available.

Canned tuna (unlike other canned fish) is lower in omega-3 fats than fresh fish. This is because tuna loses a lot of its essential fatty acids when it goes through the food processing system to be canned, so a fresh tuna steak would be a better choice. Canned "light" tuna, normally made from skipjack tuna, poses a lower risk in terms of exposure to mercury toxins than fresh yellowfin or albacore tuna. So if you wish to eat canned tuna, ideally choose skipjack.

When selecting canned fish, choose products canned in water, brine, or olive oil rather than in sunflower oil. Sunflower oil is a polyunsaturated fat which is more prone to triggering free-radical damage in the body and promoting inflammation.

Canned salmon is often packed in its own oil, meaning you may be getting the benefit of some extra omega-3 fatty acids. Canned salmon also includes the fish bones which are softened during the canning process making them safe to eat. These bones provide calcium. For example, a 3-oz (85-g) serving of salmon has over half the calcium found in a 1-cup (227-ml) glass of cow's milk. Canned sardines including their bones are another excellent source of calcium. If the canned fish is packed in tomato sauce, you'll also be getting plenty of lycopene—a phytochemical known for its antioxidant and anticancer benefits —but choose one which is low in sugar and other additives.

Top Omega-3 Sources

If you are looking to optimize your intake of omega-3 fats, then it is best to consume fish rich in EPA (eicosapentaenoic acid) and DHA (docosahexaenoic acid) two to three times a week. For some inflammatory and autoimmune conditions you may benefit from a higher level. This table will help you to select the best sources:

High omega-3 fish with > 500 mg of omega-3 per serving (3½ oz/100 g)

- Mackerel
- Sardines
- Coho and sockeye salmon
- Trout
- Canned albacore tuna
- Canned wild Alaskan salmon
- Canned sardines
- Canned skinless pink salmon.

Medium omega-3 fish with 150–500 mg of omega-3 per serving (3½ oz/100 g)

- Haddock
- Cod
- Hake
- Halibut
- Shrimp
- Sole
- Flounder
- Perch
- Bass
- Swordfish
- Oysters
- Alaskan king crab
- Farmed salmon.

Lower omega-3 fish with < 150 mg of omega-3 per serving (3½ oz/100 g)

- Mahi-mahi
- Skate
- Bluefin tuna
- Monkfish
- Red snapper
- Grouper.

Left: A portion of broiled wild sockeye salmon is a tasty way of ensuring you get plenty of healthy omega-3 fats in your diet.

Shellfish

Shellfish is important to include in your diet since it is extremely rich in nutrients. It also provides fat-soluble vitamins A, D, E, and K, as well as B vitamins to boost energy production. There are a vast range of options including squid, octopus, clams, crab, lobster, shrimp, scallops, and oysters. Allergy to shellfish is relatively common.

Nutrition: Shellfish contains zinc, copper, selenium, magnesium, potassium, phosphorus, and omega-3.
Benefits: Reduces the risk of heart attacks and strokes, and keeps the immune system healthy.

Shrimp

Shrimp are high in muscle-building protein, omega-3 fats, and are an excellent source of betaine, a nutrient necessary for improving liver function and maintaining healthy levels of homocysteine, a common amino acid found in the blood.

- Shrimp contain B_{12} to promote healthy nerves and boost energy levels.
- Shrimp are rich in selenium and copper.

Mussels

Mussels are particularly high in iodine, which helps to regulate thyroid function and may reduce the risk of breast cancer.

- A useful energy-boosting food, mussels are rich in folate and B_{12}, and important for maintaining healthy red blood cells. A bowlful of mussels easily provides all your daily B_{12} needs and over half of your iodine requirements.

Lobster

There are numerous varieties of lobster, such as the American (including the famous Maine) and the smaller European.

- Lobsters provide plenty of protein with less cholesterol, calories, and saturated fat than beef and pork. They also contain calcium for healthy nerve function and bone health. The vitamin E in lobster helps to protect cells from damage.

Crab

This popular crustacean is high in protein and low in calories—only 128 calories in 3½ oz (100 g)—and in saturated fat.

- Crab contains trace elements of selenium and chromium as well as calcium, copper, and zinc.
- Crab contains lots of omega-3, which has anti-inflammatory properties so may be good for those with arthritis.

Oysters

Fresh oysters are high in protein, zinc, and omega-3 fatty acids. Oysters also contain beneficial amounts of the amino acid tyrosine, which helps to support thyroid function and adrenal health. It may also help to improve mood.

- The high zinc levels in oysters are good for reproductive health and sexual function, particularly in men.

Mediterranean Chili and Herb Shrimp

HIGH PROTEIN

Succulent king shrimp marinated in a herb dressing and pan-fried with chili make this a protein-packed meal that is quick and easy to prepare. For plenty of flavor marinate the shrimp in the dressing for one to two hours, or overnight. Serve with a simple salad for a quick lunch or Cauliflower Rice (see page 115) for a more substantial meal.

Prep: 2 hrs 25 mins/Cook: 5 mins

Ingredients (serves 4)

24 large raw shrimp, peeled
1 red chili, seeded and sliced
2 garlic cloves, sliced
4 scallions, sliced
1 teaspoon coconut oil

Dressing

2 tablespoons capers
1 anchovy
Handful of mint leaves
Handful of cilantro leaves
Handful of parsley leaves
3 tablespoons balsamic or sherry vinegar
6 tablespoons extra virgin olive oil
Salt and freshly ground black pepper

Method

1 To make the dressing, place all the ingredients in a mini blender or food processor and pulse until smooth.

2 Place the shrimp in a shallow dish with the chili, garlic, and scallions and pour over half of the dressing. Cover the dish and let the shrimp marinate in the refrigerator for 1 to 2 hours, or overnight.

3 Heat the coconut oil in a skillet. Add the shrimp with their dressing and cook for 2 to 3 minutes until they are cooked through and look pink.

4 Serve with a salad and the rest of the dressing, stir-fry vegetables, or cauliflower rice.

ENERGIZING AND BOOSTS MUSCLES	
Calories (per serving)	158
Protein	5.8 g
Total fat	14.6 g
of which saturated fat	2.6 g
Carbohydrates	0.5 g
of which sugars	0.4 g
Vitamins/minerals	E, B, selenium, iron, zinc

Vegetables

Vegetables are an essential source of antioxidants, vitamins, and minerals. The fiber content is important for your digestive health and regulating blood sugar. They are a vital component of any diet and consuming a wide variety of colorful vegetables daily helps to keep you fit and healthy. The only vegetables excluded from the Paleo diet are legumes. For anyone following an autoimmune Paleo diet, the nightshade family of vegetables are also avoided.

If you suffer from digestive symptoms, it is a good idea to consume cooked rather than raw vegetables. Admittedly, cooking does destroy certain vitamins such as vitamin C, polyphenols, and enzymes. However, cooking helps to break down the cellular structure making nutrients more bioavailable. For example, carotenoids are more readily absorbed in cooked vegetables than in raw. Ideally eat a combination of both cooked and raw vegetables every day. As green leafy vegetables are particularly rich in nutrients and low in carbohydrates it is a good idea to include plenty of them in your daily diet.

Below: Aim to include a colorful selection of vegetables in your daily diet.

Health Benefits of Vegetables

Eye health: Many vegetables are valuable sources of vitamin C and the carotenoids lutein and zeaxanthin. Lutein and zeaxanthin are primary antioxidants that function in several regions of the eye, including the retina and the macula. A diet rich in vegetables can help to prevent age-related macular degeneration and reduce the risk of cataracts.

Skin health: Loaded with antioxidants to protect the skin from damage, vegetables also provide plenty of vitamin C to help the body make collagen, an essential protein for glowing skin. Vegetables also provide the pigment beta-carotene. Beta-carotene can protect your skin against sun damage. Beta-carotene is converted to vitamin A in the body, an essential vitamin for mucosal health.

Colon health: Leafy greens like kale and mustard greens and other brassicas, including broccoli and cabbage, have been shown to help protect against colon cancer.

Weight loss: Vegetables are rich in fiber, an important substance for weight loss because it keeps you feeling full and helps to control your feelings of hunger. Fiber can also help to balance blood sugar by slowing the absorption of carbohydrates into the bloodstream.

Bone health: Vegetables, particularly leafy greens, provide essential minerals for strong and healthy bones including calcium, magnesium, phosphorous, and vitamin K.

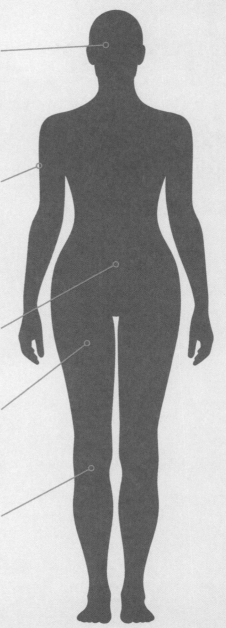

Leafy Greens and Brassicas

Leafy greens are one of the most nutritious groups of vegetables. They are packed with an array of vitamins including vitamin C, E, and K, as well as folate. They are particularly rich in minerals and provide a good source of bioavailable calcium. They also provide some omega-3 fatty acids in the form of alpha linolenic acid (ALA).

Nutrition: Dark leafy greens are very high in fiber and are an excellent source of carotenoids.
Benefits: Helps blood to clot, boosts the immune system, and reduces the risk of heart disease and strokes.

Kale

Kale can be boiled, sautéed, or steamed. Kale is rich in iron which is essential for energy. It is a good source of vitamin K that is important for heart and bone health.

- Per calorie, kale has more calcium than milk. Calcium prevents bone loss.
- Kale is a good source of vitamin C, which helps the production of collagen that is vital for cartilage and joint health.

Spinach

Spinach can be steamed or stir-fried. Rich in vitamins and minerals, spinach is a concentrated source of antioxidant carotenoids and flavonoids that are valued for their anti-inflammatory properties.

- Spinach is rich in vitamin K that is important for maintaining bone health. Vitamin K_1 helps to prevent the excessive activation of cells that break down bone.

Watercress

Watercress is an excellent source of the antioxidant vitamins A and C, as well as vitamin K. Eat watercress raw.

- Watercress is a rich source of isothiocyanates, compounds that have been shown to fight a wide range of cancers. One cup of raw watercress contains over 1,900 mcg of lutein and zeaxanthin, which sustains eye health.

Broccoli

Broccoli is rich in the sulfur compound sulforaphane that has been shown to have cancer-preventative properties. It blocks a key destructive enzyme that damages cartilage so may prevent the development of osteoarthritis. Steam or stir-fry broccoli.

- Broccoli may help to balance blood sugar levels, as it contains both soluble fiber and chromium.

Cabbage

Cabbage juice is traditionally used as a remedy to relieve stomach ulcers due to its high phytonutrient content. It is rich in indole-3-carbinol, which may help to reduce the risk of stomach cancer. Cabbage can be stir-fried, steamed, or used raw.

- Cabbage is a very good source of vitamin K, known to help prevent Alzheimer's disease.

Cauliflower

Cauliflower is a useful source of sulforophane, which maintains cell health. The glucosinolates in cauliflower reinforce detoxification pathways while its high antioxidant content helps to protect the body from free radical damage.

- Cauliflower provides choline, a nutrient known for its role in brain development, cognitive function, and memory.

Collards

Collard greens are a highly nutritious member of the brassica family closely related to kale and cabbage.

- Collards are a very good source of folate, which is important in DNA synthesis and protection of the baby during pregnancy.
- Rich in vitamins C and A, collards help sustain a healthy immune system.

Turnip Greens

A member of the brassica family, turnip greens are rich in vitamin C, important for production of collagen, which provides structure to skin and hair.

- Turnip greens are very rich in iron for energy production.
- Turnip greens provide nitrate that has been shown to improve muscle oxygenation during exercise.

Swiss Chard

Like beets, chard is a valuable source of phytonutrients called betalains, which provide antioxidant, anti-inflammatory, and detoxification benefits.

- Swiss chard has calcium, magnesium, and vitamin K for healthy bones.
- A good source of manganese and zinc that help to prevent damage from chronic disease.

Why Eat Lettuce?

Don't overlook the nutritional benefits of lettuce. Romaine, bibb, Boston, and iceberg are just some of the most popular varieties. While iceberg is not particularly nutritious, other varieties —particularly romaine—are packed with vitamins and minerals, fiber, and phytonutrients that benefit health.

- Romaine lettuce is particularly rich in vitamin C, beta-carotene, folate, and potassium—all nutrients that have a positive effect on heart health.
- Lettuce is low in calories and high in fiber so can help you maintain a healthy weight and support the digestive system.

Tangy "Cheese" Kale Chips

LOW CALORIE

Crunchy kale chips make a healthy snack and are an ideal alternative to conventional high-fat processed potato chips. You can bake these in an oven or, if you have a dehydrator, dehydrate them until crispy.

Prep: 20 mins/Cook: 25 mins

Ingredients (serves 8)

¼ cup (35 g) sunflower seeds, soaked for 2 hours then drained
¼ cup (40 g) cashews, soaked for 2 hours then drained
4 sundried tomatoes in oil, drained
½ red bell pepper, seeded and chopped
½ teaspoon garlic salt
1 shallot, chopped
2 tablespoons nutritional yeast flakes
2 soft large dates, chopped
2 tablespoons lemon juice
2 tablespoons water
2 tablespoons apple cider vinegar
9 oz (250 g) bag of chopped kale

Method

1 Blend all the ingredients except the kale to form a thick paste.

2 Place the kale in a bowl and pour over the sauce. Work thoroughly with your hands to ensure the kale is entirely coated in the sauce.

3 To dehydrate, place the kale on a nonstick mesh sheet and dehydrate for 4 to 6 hours. Then flip the kale over, place on the mesh sheet, and dehydrate for another 6 to 8 hours until crisp.

4 For an oven-baked version: preheat the oven to 300°F (150°C, gas mark 2). Place the kale on a lined baking sheet and bake for 15 to 20 minutes. Carefully turn the kale over and cook for another 5 minutes until it is crisp.

5 Store the chips in an airtight container for two to three days.

GREAT FOR STRONG HEALTHY BONES	
Calories (per serving)	96
Protein	4.9 g
Total fat	6.4 g
of which saturated fat	1.0 g
Carbohydrates	4.4 g
of which sugars	1.6 g
Vitamins/minerals	K, C, A, calcium, copper

Cruciferous Vegetables and Goitrogens

Cruciferous vegetables are those in the Brassicaceae family. They are also known as Cruciferae (meaning "cross-bearing") because of the shape of their flowers, whose four petals resemble a cross. They include cauliflower, cabbage, garden cress, bok choy, broccoli, brussels sprouts, and other green leaf vegetables.

Goitrogens are compounds found in cruciferous vegetables and some other vegetables and fruits. They have been shown to suppress the function of the thyroid by interfering with iodine uptake. Iodine is an essential mineral needed for the production of thyroid hormones T4 (thyroxine) and T3 (triiodothyronine). People with Hashimoto's or Grave's disease (autoimmune thyroid conditions) or hypothyroidism are sometimes advised to avoid consumption of cruciferous vegetables for this reason. However, there is little scientific research to suggest that eating cruciferous vegetables will cause a decrease in thyroid function in the absence of iodine deficiency.

As cruciferous vegetables are highly nutritious and have been linked to many health benefits, they should form a significant part of your diet. If you do have a thyroid condition or disorder, it is a good idea to ensure your diet is rich in the necessary minerals for thyroid hormone production, especially iron, selenium, and zinc, and also consume iodine-rich foods, such as fish and sea vegetables (see page 128), regularly.

Most forms of cooking reduce goitrogen levels so if you are concerned about your thyroid function or you do have a disorder then you may be advised to lightly steam cruciferous vegetables rather than eating them raw.

Cauliflower Rice

HEALTHY HEART

Using cauliflower to create a rice is a delicious low-carb alternative to using grains. Cauliflower rice can be used in both raw and cooked dishes and works beautifully with Asian flavors.

Prep: 15 mins/Cook: 5 mins

Ingredients (serves 4)

1 medium head cauliflower, 18 oz (500 g)
1 tablespoon coconut oil
1 small onion, finely chopped
1 piece of fresh ginger root, grated
1–2 tablespoons coconut aminos or tamari
Drizzle of fish sauce
Drizzle of rice vinegar
Handful of chopped cilantro leaves
Handful of chopped basil
Handful of chopped mint
Salt and freshly ground black pepper

Method

1 Place the cauliflower in a food processor and pulse until finely chopped so it looks like little rice size pieces.

2 Add the coconut oil to a large skillet and sauté the onion and ginger. Add the cauliflower and season. Place the lid on and steam-fry for 5 minutes. Once softened, add the aminos, fish sauce, vinegar, and herbs, and your rice is ready to serve.

SUPPORTS THE DIGESTIVE SYSTEM	
Calories (per serving)	82
Protein	3.9 g
Total fat	3.7 g
of which saturated fat	3 g
Carbohydrates	10.8 g
of which sugars	2.3 g
Vitamins/minerals	A, B, C, D, calcium

Nonstarchy Vegetables

There are a variety of other nonstarchy vegetables that are equally nutritious. They typically come from the stem, flower, or flower bud rather than actual leaves. Here are just a few examples. Aim to include a wide variety of these tasty vegetables in your diet to optimize the range of nutrients you receive.

Nutrition: Nonstarchy vegetables are high in fiber, vitamins, and phytochemicals, and low in calories.
Benefits: Aids digestion, may improve memory, helps to keep the heart healthy, and lowers blood pressure.

Asparagus

The fleshy green succulent spears of asparagus are readily available in spring. Asparagus can be good for digestive health as it is rich in inulin, a type of prebiotic fiber that encourages the growth of beneficial gut bacteria.

- Known for its anti-inflammatory, antioxidant properties, asparagus contains vitamin C, beta-carotene, vitamin E, and the minerals zinc, manganese, and selenium.
- Asparagus contains a significant amount of the antioxidant glutathione which helps the body to rid itself of toxins.
- Asparagus is a good source of B vitamins including folate to help improve cognitive function.

Fennel

The crisp fennel bulb can be sautéed, stewed, braised, grilled, or eaten raw.

- Fennel is rich in a range of phytonutrients including anethole which can help reduce inflammation and the risk of certain cancers. It is a very good source of folate, an important B vitamin during pregnancy, and potassium that helps to lower high blood pressure.

Globe Artichokes

Globe artichokes can be boiled or steamed and are a good source of fiber that is beneficial for digestive health.

- Globe artichokes are packed with phytonutrients such as quercetin, rutin, gallic acid, and cynarin, which help protect against conditions like heart disease, liver dysfunction, high cholesterol, and diabetes.

Celery

Celery contains a range of antioxidant nutrients, including vitamin C, beta-carotene, and manganese, and is particularly high in phenolic antioxidants known for their anti-inflammatory benefits.

- The pectin-based polysaccharides in celery are good for stomach health.
- A useful source of vitamin K for a healthy heart and bones.

Allium Family

Alliums (also known as the onion family) are known for their powerful aroma. This is due to the concentration of sulfur compounds, which have been shown to have numerous health benefits including helping the body to rid itself of toxins. Alliums are rich in important minerals such as selenium, iron, and manganese.

Nutrition: Alliums are rich in antioxidants, vitamins C, A, B, and K, and many minerals.
Benefits: Can protect the heart, lower cholesterol, increase bone density, and are powerful anti-inflammatories.

Leeks

Leeks contain a range of B vitamins which can be good for heart health. They also strengthen the neural system of babies developing in the womb. Leeks contain the flavonoid kaempferol that helps to protect blood vessel linings from damage.

- Leeks contain vitamins A and K, and healthy amounts of folic acid, niacin, riboflavin, magnesium, and thiamin.

Garlic

Garlic contains the sulfur compound known as allicin that is responsible for its distinctive smell.

- Garlic is low in calories.
- A rich source of vitamin C, vitamin B_6, and manganese and other trace nutrients.
- Garlic supplementation has been shown to strengthen the immune system and it is valued for its antimicrobial properties.

Red Onions

Red onions are a rich source of quercetin, a bioflavonoid known for its antioxidant and antihistamine properties.

- Onions are a rich source of chromium, a trace mineral that can help control glucose levels making it beneficial for people with diabetes.
- Red onions provide significant amounts of vitamin C and vitamin B_6.

White Onions

A good source of flavonoids and sulfur-containing nutrients. The high sulfur content of onions may help to strengthen connective tissue and bone as well as benefiting cardiovascular health.

- Onions provide B vitamins including biotin, important for skin and hair.
- Onions contain copper to maintain healthy red blood cells.

Chives

Chives are a nutrient-dense herb packed with a range of vitamins and minerals including folate, choline, calcium, magnesium, phosphorus, and potassium.

- Chives are believed to have cancer-protective properties.
- The choline in chives is an important nutrient that helps memory and the structure of cellular membranes.

Roots and Tubers

Roots and tubers are generally higher in starch than other vegetables. The glycemic index (GI) varies—carrots, for example, are relatively low GI while sweet potatoes and beets are higher. These foods contribute the main part of your carbohydrate intake on a Paleo diet. Roots and tubers can be roasted, boiled, steamed, fried, and baked.

Nutrition: Roots and tubers are high in fiber and are excellent sources of vitamins, minerals, and antioxidants. **Benefits:** Helps to keep the heart healthy, reduces the risk of heart disease, and lowers blood pressure.

Sweet Potato

Orange-fleshed sweet potatoes are rich in beta-carotene which boosts our levels of vitamin A. The purple-fleshed variety is full of anthocyanins which have antioxidant and anti-inflammatory properties.

- Sweet potatoes provide plenty of vitamin C and B vitamins, and may increase levels of adiponectin that helps to improve insulin metabolism.

Carrot

A popular root vegetable, carrots are particularly rich in carotenoids and other antioxidants that are known to be good for cardiovascular health.

- Carotenoids are also important to maintain healthy vision and reduce the risk of cataracts and glaucoma.
- Carrots contain soluble fiber and may offer protection against colon cancer.

Beets

A popular root for boosting heart health and athletic performance. Beets are rich in nitrates, which are converted into nitric oxide in your body. Nitric oxide helps to relax blood vessels, improving blood flow, and lowering blood pressure.

- Beets are a unique source of betaine, a nutrient with anti-inflammatory and detoxifying properties.

Parsnips

This sweet root vegetable contains more calories and starch than carrots, but is rich in essential nutrients and fiber.

- Parsnips are packed with vitamin C that aids the immune system and keeps teeth and gums healthy.
- Parsnips are rich in B vitamins and vitamins K and E to help maintain a healthy heart.

Celeriac

A member of the celery family, celeriac, or celery root, can be used raw or cooked and is popular mashed to replace potatoes.

- Celeriac is a very good source of vitamin K, which is particularly important for promoting bone and heart health. To aid absorption of this fat-soluble vitamin, add a little fat to the dish when preparing and eating celeriac.

Beet, Carrot, and Pear Coleslaw with Lime Dressing

HIGH FIBER

A vibrant colorful salad, sweet and tangy with the addition of the Asian-style dressing. It is delicious served with meat or fish. Use a spiralizer if you want to create long noodle strips. Alternatively, you can use a mandoline or food processor to create long strips rapidly. The salad can be dressed ahead of time to intensify the flavors.

Prep: 15 mins

Ingredients (serves 4)

2 carrots, spiralized or cut into julienne
1 large beet, spiralized or cut into julienne
¼ fennel bulb, cored and cut into
   long strips
1 shallot, finely chopped
1 pear, grated or cut into long strips
1 teaspoon nigella seeds/cumin seeds

Dressing

½ teaspoon grated ginger root
2 tablespoons tamari
1 tablespoon lime juice
2 tablespoons rice wine vinegar
1 teaspoon honey
¼ red chili, seeded and diced

Method

1 Place all the spiralized or cut vegetables into a large bowl.

2 Whisk all the dressing ingredients together until smooth. Drizzle over the salad and toss completely. Store in the refrigerator until ready to serve.

GOOD FOR A HEALTHY HEART	
Calories (per serving)	64
Protein	1.5 g
Total fat	0.3 g
of which saturated fat	0.1 g
Carbohydrates	13.2 g
of which sugars	12.9 g
Vitamins/minerals	C, B, A, K, manganese

Squash

Summer and winter squashes are members of the Cucurbitaceae family and relatives of both the melon and the cucumber. They are sometimes also called the gourd family. Squashes come in numerous varieties, both winter and summer, with many that are good to eat. Some varieties, such as zucchini, also produce edible flowers.

Nutrition: Squashes are very nutritious and are high in vitamins A, C, B, and omega-3 fatty acids.
Benefits: Keeps the heart healthy, regulates blood sugar levels, and are powerful anti-inflammatories.

Zucchini

A low-calorie, low-carb vegetable that is delicious eaten raw or cooked. Very popular for making low-carb noodles too.

- Zucchini are a good source of magnesium and potassium, which can help to balance fluid levels.
- Zucchini are rich in vitamin C and the carotenoid lutein, both beneficial for their antioxidant properties.

Pumpkin

Pumpkins are very rich in vitamin A and carotenoids that are important for skin and eye health. They are valued for their cancer-protective benefits.

- Pumpkin is a good source of fiber and low in calories. This helps you feel full for longer—ideal for weight management.
- This squash is high in potassium, so replenishes electrolytes after exercise.

Butternut Squash

Butternut squash, a common winter variety, is extremely rich in vitamin A.

- Butternut squash is incredibly rich in vitamins A, C, and E. These antioxidants protect against cell damage and are good for skin, hair, and eyes.
- A good source of potassium, butternut squash is useful for maintaining healthy blood pressure.

Spaghetti Squash

Spaghetti squash gets its name from the fact that when it is cooked, the inside flesh pulls out of the shell in long strands, resembling spaghetti pasta.

- Spaghetti squash is rich in a range of vitamins including vitamins C, A, and B vitamins.
- This squash is a good source of manganese to keep bones healthy.

Acorn Squash

Acorn squash is an excellent source of vitamin C that helps to maintain a healthy immune system.

- Acorn squash is very high in dietary fiber. One cup cooked contains 6 g of fiber and 83 calories. It aids digestive health, lowers high cholesterol, and regulates the levels of blood sugar in the body.

Paleo Pumpkin Tart

HIGH FIBER

This is a healthy alternative to the traditional pumpkin pie. You can use canned pumpkin puree if you wish, or simply steam pumpkin or butternut squash and then process it in a food processor. This recipe has a spoonful of cacao powder added to the base for additional flavor. Serve with coconut cream or yogurt.

Prep: 20 mins/Cook: 1 hr

Ingredients (serves 8)

Base

1⅔ cups (250 g) pecans

1 tablespoon raw cacao powder

2 oz (60 g) pitted soft dates

1 tablespoon vanilla extract

1 tablespoon coconut oil

1 tablespoon honey

Filling

14 oz (400 g) pumpkin or butternut
   squash puree

2 eggs

½ cup (125 ml) coconut cream

1 teaspoon ground cinnamon

1 teaspoon allspice

1 teaspoon ground ginger

1 tablespoon vanilla extract

1 tablespoon lucuma powder, optional

¼ cup (60 g) coconut sugar

Dusting of raw cacao powder, to decorate

2 tablespoons pecans, optional

Method

1 Preheat the oven to 350°F (180°C, gas mark 4).

2 Place the pecans in a food processor and process until very fine. Add the cacao, dates, vanilla, oil, and honey and process until the mixture comes together.

3 Press the mixture into a greased springform loose-bottom 8-inch (20-cm) cake pan.

PACKED WITH ANTIOXIDANTS	
Calories (per serving)	374
Protein	6.1 g
Total fat	30.2 g
of which saturated fat	8.0 g
Carbohydrates	19.9 g
of which sugars	15.1 g
Vitamins/minerals	A, C, B, potassium, iron

4 Place all the filling ingredients in a blender and process until smooth. Pour the mixture into the cake pan on top of the pecan base and bake for 1 hour until the filling has puffed up in the center and turned light golden.

5 Serve the pumpkin tart warm or cold. Decorate with a dusting of cacao powder and/or the pecans, if desired.

Sea Vegetables

The numerous health benefits deriving from sea vegetables may be due to their fucoidan content. Fucoidans are starchlike sulfur-containing molecules or polysaccharides. Known for their anti-inflammatory and anticancer benefits, they also appear to support the immune system and promote cardiovascular health.

Nutrition: Sea vegetables are an excellent source of iodine and are packed with minerals and vitamins. **Benefits:** Purifies the blood and lowers blood pressure, may improve memory, and keeps the skin healthy.

Nori

Best known as the outer wrap for sushi, nori is an edible red seaweed that is popular in east Asia, especially Japan. Use to make Paleo sushi rolls, add to soups, or simply delicious as a snack toasted with a little oil.

- Nori provides protein, omega-3 fats, and is a useful source of iron and calcium. It has a low iodine content.

Wakame

Wakame is an edible brown seaweed common in Asian cuisines. To prepare, soak for 15 minutes until soft, drain, and rinse. Heat gently or simply add to salads raw.

- Wakame contains magnesium and calcium for bone health.
- This seaweed contains iron and vitamins to help keep the skin healthy and boost the immune system.

Arame

An edible brown seaweed that is rich in iodine. This thin wiry sea vegetable is sweeter and milder in taste than many others—delicious in salads and soups.

- Arame contains lots of fiber that helps the digestive system and detoxification, and may lower cholesterol.
- Arame provides a good source of vitamin A, calcium, iron, and magnesium.

Dulse

Red or purple in color, dulse is a valuable source of iodine and minerals, particularly phosphorous, iron, and potassium. It is also rich in antioxidants, which serve a protective role in the body.

- Dulse is a good source of protein and fiber to maintain blood sugar balance.
- The polysaccharides content in dulse helps the body to eliminate toxins.

Hijiki

Similar to arame, hijiki is bolder in flavor, with aniselike undertones. Some studies have shown that it can contain high levels of arsenic—for this reason, only eat hijiki if it comes from a certified organic source.

- Rich in iron to boost energy levels.
- Hijiki contains calcium and magnesium to keep the nervous system healthy and to strengthen bones.

Tom Yum Soup with Dulse

HIGH PROTEIN

Tom yum paste is readily available in grocery stores. It contains a delicious combination of galangal, lemongrass, chili, garlic, and lime. This is a simple creamy soup, packed with protein because of the shrimp and with plenty of minerals thanks to the addition of dulse.

Prep: 15 mins/Cook: 12 mins

Ingredients (serves 4)

1½ oz (40 g) dulse fronds
2 x 14 oz (400 g) cans whole coconut milk
1 tablespoon tom yum paste
Juice of ½ lime
Small pinch of saffron threads
Handful of spinach leaves
2 scallions, shredded
7 oz (200 g) cooked king shrimp
Cilantro, chopped, to garnish

Method

1 Place the dulse in water and soak for 10 minutes. Drain.

2 Pour the coconut milk into a medium pan and heat gently. Add the dulse, tom yum paste, lime juice, and saffron.

3 Stir well and bring to a gentle boil. Reduce the heat and simmer for 1 minute. Just before serving add the spinach leaves, scallions, and shrimp and cook for 1 minute to heat through.

4 Spoon the soup into bowls and sprinkle over the chopped cilantro leaves before serving.

EXCELLENT FOR BOOSTING ENERGY LEVELS	
Calories (per serving)	120
Protein	11.48 g
Total fat	4.34 g
of which saturated fat	1.20 g
Carbohydrates	8.56 g
of which sugars	5.15 g
Vitamins/minerals	B, iron, selenium, zinc

Nuts and Seeds

Nuts and seeds are included in a Paleo diet but they are typically avoided by anyone following an autoimmune program. This is because they may promote inflammation if eaten in excess.

Nuts can be high in phytic acid, which binds to minerals in food (especially iron and zinc) and prevents us from absorbing them. Phytic acid interferes with enzymes that we need to digest our food. Levels of phytate may be reduced by soaking and dehydrating nuts before eating them. Nut flours do not contain much phytic acid. This is because the flour

is made from blanched nuts and the phytic acid is found mostly in the skin of the nuts. Avoid nuts packaged or roasted in oil or containing added sugars; instead, eat them raw or lightly roasted.

While seeds (pumpkin, sunflower, sesame, chia, flaxseed, etc.) feature in a Paleo diet, processed seed oils do not. These seed oils are high in omega-6 polyunsaturated fats, and a significant disproportion between omega-3 and omega-6 fatty acid intake can cause inflammation. Cold pressed nut and seed oils can be used in dressings but they should not be heated as their nutritional content may be damaged.

Nuts and seeds, however, are packed with nutrients and provide plenty of protein, vitamins, and minerals. They also provide some healthy monounsaturated and omega-3 fatty acids, which can be good for heart health. Their high fiber and protein content makes them very satisfying. Some nuts and seeds also contain plant sterols, which can help to lower high LDL cholesterol.

Health Benefits of Nuts and Seeds

 Brain health: Nuts and seeds are a good source of zinc and magnesium that are important for the production of brain neurotransmitters and omega-3 fats to assist cognitive function.

 Sleep: Many nuts and seeds are rich in calcium and magnesium that help relax the muscles and nervous system. Some provide tryptophan, an amino acid that your body converts into serotonin, which in turn is converted into melatonin, the "sleep hormone."

 Heart health: Nuts are rich in a range of heart protective nutrients including vitamin E, B vitamins, magnesium, potassium, omega-3, and monounsaturated fats. A good source of fiber and plant sterols, which can help to lower high LDL cholesterol.

 Men's health: These foods are rich in zinc, which is important for prostate health, male fertility, and the production of testosterone. Nuts and seeds also provide magnesium, which is very important for maintaining healthy levels of testosterone and also helping to keep the heart healthy.

 Skin health: All nuts and seeds are rich in vitamin E, an antioxidant that keeps your skin glowing. The omega-3 fats, selenium, and zinc in some nuts and seeds are also good for the skin. Zinc, in particular, helps to maintain collagen, which keeps your skin smooth and soft.

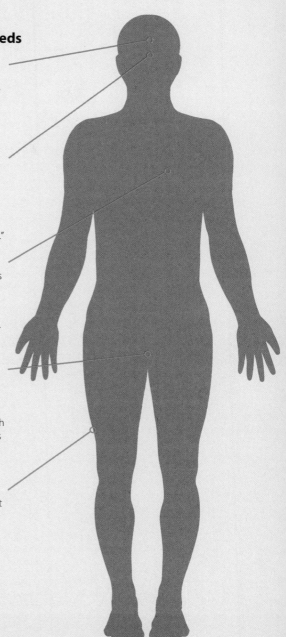

Nuts

Nuts are an excellent source of energy, antioxidants, vitamins, minerals, and essential omega-3 fatty acids. Nuts contain fiber, which can help to lower cholesterol and make you feel fuller for longer. Nuts also contain L-arginine, a substance that can help to make artery walls more flexible and less prone to blockages.

Nutrition: Nuts are packed with protein, vitamins, minerals, essential fats, and fiber.

Benefits: Helps to lower cholesterol levels, protects against heart disease, and may reduce the risk of strokes.

Almonds

Almonds are popular in Paleo baking recipes when ground up to form a flour.

- Almonds are high in monounsaturated fats, vitamin E, magnesium, potassium, and fiber, all good for a healthy heart.
- They have been shown to help lower LDL cholesterol.
- The flavonoids found in almond skins help to stabilize blood sugar.

Hazelnuts

Also known as filberts or "cobnuts," hazelnuts contain lots of minerals.

- Hazelnuts are high in folate that can help to maintain healthy levels of homocysteine and reduce the risk of neural tube defects in the fetus.
- These nuts are a good source of vitamin E that is important for the integrity of cell membranes and skin health.

Cashews

Cashews are lower in fat than many other nuts and are a good source of heart-healthy monounsaturated fats.

- Cashews are particularly rich in copper, a mineral important for iron utilization, the health of bone and connective tissue, and the production of the skin and hair pigment called melanin.

Brazil Nuts

Brazil nuts are rich in monounsaturated fats and vitamin E making them particularly good for the heart.

- Brazil nuts are one of the best food sources of selenium—just three will supply your daily recommended intake. Selenium is vital for immune function, hormone production, detoxification, and antioxidant protection.

Pecans

Popular in desserts and pies, pecans are particularly rich in phenolic antioxidants and monounsaturated fatty acids making them good for the heart.

- The antioxidant ellagic acid has been shown to possess anticancer properties.
- Pecans are a good source of B vitamins and protein, they can boost energy levels and balance blood sugar levels.

Macadamias

Macadamia nuts taste sweet and are a good source of energy.

- Macadamias have a beneficial fat profile, as they are very low in omega-6 fats and high in anti-inflammatory monounsaturated fats.
- These nuts provide palmitoleic acid, which has positive effects on blood lipids and is an effective skin moisturizer.

Walnuts

Walnuts are higher in omega-3 fats than other nuts. They also contain a number of neuroprotective compounds, including vitamin E, folate, and antioxidants.

- If you suffer from herpes, you may want to avoid or limit walnuts, as their arginine content can deplete levels of the amino acid lysine, which can trigger recurrences of herpes.

Pistachios

Pistachios are packed with antioxidants, as well as containing healthy fats and the minerals selenium and iron.

- Pistachios have been shown to improve lipid levels and lower high LDL cholesterol.
- These nuts are a good source of lutein, beta-carotene, and vitamin E. Lutein is important for vision and skin health.

Seeds

Small, but packed with an array of nutrients, seeds are a healthy addition to a Paleo diet. You can also soak and blend many seeds to create seed milks.

A valuable source of protein, seeds have a healthier ratio of omega-3 to 6 fatty acids compared to most nuts. Useful as a snack or an addition to dishes.

Nutrition: Seeds are packed with fiber, vitamins, and minerals including zinc, iron, calcium, and phosphorus.
Benefits: Strengthens bones, helps keep the immune system healthy, and promotes healthy skin and hair.

Pumpkin Seeds

Pumpkin seeds are particularly valuable for their high levels of zinc and magnesium.
- Pumpkin seed oil is rich in natural phytoestrogens that may help alleviate menopausal symptoms.
- Good for men's prostate health, pumpkin seed extracts may play a role in treating benign enlargement of the prostate gland.

Sunflower Seeds

Sunflower seeds are an excellent source of vitamin E, the body's primary fat-soluble antioxidant. Vitamin E is known for its anti-inflammatory effects and plays a role in the prevention of cardiovascular disease.
- Sunflower seeds are a good source of magnesium that can help maintain healthy nerves and muscles and reduce the severity of asthma and migraines.

Flaxseed

Flaxseeds are available whole or ground. Whole flaxseeds can be used in baking while ground can be added to oatmeal, smoothies, sprinkled onto salads, and mixed into pancake batters.

- Flaxseed is known for its high protein and fiber content, so is good for your digestive health, alleviating constipation, and regulating blood sugar levels.

Sesame Seeds

Also available as tahini which is a sesame seed paste. Sesame seeds are an excellent source of copper, which may help to relieve the pain of arthritis.

- Sesame seeds contain magnesium and calcium for healthy bones.
- These seeds contain zinc, which is important for sex hormone production and fertility.

Pine Nuts

Pine nuts are not actually nuts, but are the seeds of pine trees. Delicious eaten raw or roasted, with a sweet nutty flavor.

- These seeds are rich in nutrients that help to boost energy.
- They may help with weight loss as they contain pinolenic acid, which triggers the release of an appetite-suppressing hormone known as cholecystokinin.

Chia Seeds

Chia seeds are tiny black seeds from the plant *Salvia hispanica*, a member of the mint family. It was prized as an energy fuel by the Aztecs. They are loaded with fiber, protein, omega-3 fatty acids, and antioxidants. Because chia seeds are rich in soluble fiber, they can absorb ten to 12 times their weight in water. They should be soaked in water before they are eaten—if taken dry, you may have problems swallowing them. They are effective for balancing blood sugar and promoting weight loss, and are a good source of calcium, magnesium, phosphorus, and protein to aid bone health. There are concerns that they may damage the gut lining so it is best to avoid them on an autoimmune Paleo diet, or observe a limit of 1 heaping tablespoon daily.

Raspberry Chia Dessert

HIGH FIBER

A simple, protein-packed, omega-3-rich breakfast dessert. Soak the chia seeds overnight to make this a speedy healthy start to the day.

Prep: 15 mins/Soak: 15 mins

Ingredients (serves 1)
3 tablespoons chia seeds
1 cup (250 ml) almond milk
¼ cup (30 g) raspberries
Pinch of ground cinnamon

Method

1 Put all the ingredients into a bowl. Stir constantly for 1 minute so that the seeds don't clump together.

2 You can either soak this overnight in the refrigerator or let soak for 15 minutes in the morning. When ready to serve, place in a blender or process in a food processor to mash up the berries. Spoon into a glass and top with a few extra raspberries to serve.

KEEPS BONES HEALTHY AND STRONG	
Calories (per serving)	156
Protein	5.9 g
Total fat	9.5 g
of which saturated fat	0 g
Carbohydrates	17.9 g
of which sugars	0 g
Vitamins/minerals A, C, D, B, E, calcium, iron	

Fruits and Berries

Fruits are packed with an array of phytochemicals, antioxidants, vitamins, and minerals as well as fiber to support health. Focus on low-sugar fruits to limit your intake of fructose, and avoid fruit juices.

Fruits are an important food group in the Paleo diet. While fresh fruit does contain more sugar than vegetables, most fruits are relatively low in glycemic index (GI). Dried fruits tend to be high in sugars and glycemic load (GL) so should only be eaten in small amounts. People with blood sugar imbalances or inflammatory conditions should avoid fruit juices, smoothies, and dried fruit and limit fruit to around two portions a day. This will keep their fructose intake low.

Berries typically have the highest vitamin, mineral, and antioxidant content, as well as being lower in sugar than other fruits. They are particularly rich in compounds called anthocyanins, which are a type of flavonoid shown to be beneficial for healthy aging and reducing oxidative damage to the body caused by free radicals. To maximize your antioxidant benefits from fruits, choose organic, seasonal produce. Frozen fruit is a very healthy alternative when out of season.

Health Benefits of Fruits and Berries

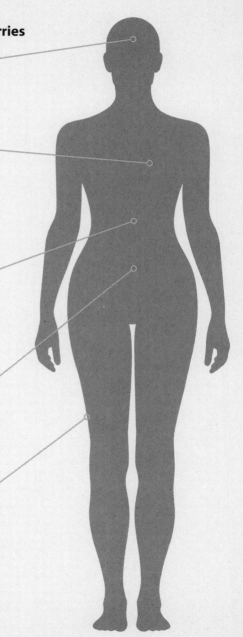

Brain health: Fruits such as berries are rich in flavonoids, especially anthocyanins, which have been shown to counteract cognitive decline and may help to reduce the risk of developing Parkinson's disease.

Heart health: Fruits contain a wealth of phytochemicals, antioxidants, vitamins, and minerals that help to protect the heart, lower blood pressure, and reduce inflammation. Some fruits like apples contain pectin, a soluble fiber that can help to maintain healthy cholesterol levels.

Cancer protective: Fruits are rich in a number of compounds such as ellagic acid and limonene that have been shown to possess anti-cancer properties. They are a good source of fiber and may help to reduce the risk of colon cancer too.

Digestive health: Many fruits are excellent sources of soluble fiber, which helps regulate bowel movements and benefits digestive health. Green bananas are particularly rich in prebiotic fiber that encourages the growth of beneficial bacteria in the gut.

Skin health: A good source of vitamin C, which helps your body to produce collagen, a protein that helps to keep your skin firm and elastic. Many fruits are also rich in carotenoids, which can help to protect the skin from damage including UV damage caused by exposure to the sun.

Berries

While all fruits and vegetables contain antioxidants, nutrient-rich berries are some of the best sources. They contain numerous powerful antioxidants, including anthocyanins, which gives them their vibrant color. Known for their anti-inflammatory, antiaging benefits, berries are one of the best fruits to eat raw.

Nutrition: Berries are packed with powerful antioxidants, vitamin C, fiber, and folate.

Benefits: Keeps skin and hair healthy, reduces the risk of arthritis, reduces inflammation, and lowers cholesterol.

Blueberries

Known for their exceptional phytonutrient and antioxidant content, blueberries seem to be very good for the nervous system and brain health and may reduce the risk of cognitive decline and Alzheimer's.

- Blueberries are beneficial for the heart.
- They have been shown to improve lipid profiles and raise the level of beneficial HDL cholesterol.

Raspberries

An excellent source of vitamin C and phytonutrients, raspberries provide anti-inflammatory and antioxidant benefits.

- The ellagic acid found in raspberries has been shown to have anticancer properties.
- Other compounds in raspberries increase metabolism in our fat cells and balance blood sugar levels.

Strawberries

Strawberries are one of the best fruits from which to obtain vitamin C. They contain a wealth of phytonutrients including antiaging anthocyanins.

- Strawberries have potent anti-inflammatory properties and seem to help balance blood sugar too.
- A good source of manganese to keep the skin healthy.

Cranberries

Rich in vitamin C, cranberries provide anti-inflammatory benefits particularly for the cardiovascular and digestive systems.

- Cranberries help to prevent urinary tract infections. The phytochemicals in cranberries contain proanthocyanidins (PACs) that stop potential pathogenic bacteria from adhering to the lining of the urinary tract.

Blackberries

Rich in vitamin C and anthocyanins, blackberries are good for cognitive function. The high tannin content of blackberries may reduce intestinal inflammation and alleviate diarrhea.

- Blackberries are a good source of vitamin K that helps blood clotting.
- They are a low-calorie high-fiber fruit and help with weight management.

Berry Ice Cream

ENERGIZING

A delicious dairy-free ice cream packed with vitamin C and antioxidants. The addition of macadamias creates a wonderful creamy texture as well as providing plenty of protein and healthy fats. You can use frozen berries if you want to. To boost the antioxidant content even more, add a spoonful of superfood berry powder.

Prep: 20 mins/Freeze: 2 to 3 hrs

Ingredients (serves 6)

Scant 2 cups (200 g) macadamia nuts
½ cup (25 ml) pure pomegranate juice
2 teaspoons vanilla extract
1 tablespoon mixed superfood berry
    powder, optional
4 oz (120 g) mixed berries, fresh or frozen
1 tablespoon lemon juice
Scant ¼ cup (60 g) xylitol or honey

Method

1 Place the nuts and juice in a high-speed blender and process to combine them. Add the remaining ingredients and process until thick and smooth.

2 Pour the mixture into an ice-cream maker and churn according to the manufacturer's directions. Or, pour into a freezerproof container and freeze for 30 minutes, then remove and mix well. Continue until firm, about 2 to 3 hours.

3 Soften the ice cream 15 minutes before serving. Serve with fresh berries and mint.

RICH IN ANTIOXIDANTS	
Calories (per serving)	288
Protein	3.0 g
Total fat	25.9 g
of which saturated fat	3.8 g
Carbohydrates	14.6 g
of which sugars	4.5 g
Vitamins/minerals	C, K, E, B, manganese

Super Berries

Berries are renowned for their health-promoting properties. As well as popular favorites like blueberries and raspberries, there are many others that are rich in an array of healthy phytonutrients, as well as other vitamins and minerals. These "super berries" are available all year round in the form of powders, dried berries, or juice.

Nutrition: Super berries contain vitamins A, C, and B and are packed with antioxidants.
Benefits: Boosts energy levels, have antiaging properties, and helps to keep the skin and eyes healthy.

Goji Berries

Also called wolfberries, goji berries are a popular superfood. They are a vibrant red and have a deliciously intense flavor.
- Rich in carotenoids, antioxidants that are particularly beneficial for skin and eyes.
- They are an extremely nutrient-dense food and surprisingly high in amino acids. This makes them a wonderfully energizing food choice.

Mulberries

The mulberry is predominantly found in subtropical areas of Africa, Asia, and North America. As they have a short shelf life, they are commonly sundried.
- Mulberries are a popular antiaging fruit due to their high antioxidant levels.
- A good source of vitamin C, mulberries are also packed with other nutrients.
- Mulberries provide protein for energy.

Acai Berries

The acai berry is the fruit of a palm tree that grows in the rainforests of the Amazon and is known as "the tree of life."

- Acai berries are one of the most concentrated sources of antioxidants, known as anthocyanins, which have potent antiaging benefits.
- These berries are a good source of fiber, vitamins C and A, calcium, and fats.

Camu Camu Berries

These berries grow on a small bush native to the swampy lowlands of Peru. They are similar in size to a cranberry and have a slightly sour, tangy flavor. Available as freeze-dried powder, camu camu berry is used in small amounts only.

- Camu camu berries are packed with vitamin C, which is helpful in preventing diseases including colds and flu.

Goldenberries

Also known as Cape gooseberries. The fresh berry looks like a small yellow-orange cherry surrounded with papery husks resembling a Chinese lantern. The harvested berries are sundried and have a citruslike, slightly sweet-sour flavor.

- The berries contain a variety of vitamins, including vitamins A and C, and many B vitamins to boost energy levels.

Rosaceae Family

Fruits from the Rosaceae family include both apples, pears, and some pit fruit including cherries, peaches, and plums. While apples are typically available all year round, others like cherries and plums have a much shorter season. However, most of these fruits freeze well, making them available throughout the year.

Nutrition: These fruits are high in fiber and packed with carotenoids and other antioxidants and minerals.
Benefits: Lowers cholesterol, helps prevent high blood pressure and strokes, and prevents constipation.

Apples

Apples contain an array of polyphenols, which are antioxidants and seem to help protect the heart as well as lowering the incidence of asthma.

- Apples are rich in soluble fiber pectin, so may help lower total and LDL cholesterol. Pectin can also help stabilize blood sugar levels and reduce cravings.
- They also stimulate healthy gut flora.

Pears

Pears contain lots of phytonutrient antioxidants, particularly in the skins. These protect against cell damage and have anti-inflammatory benefits.

- Pears are a very good source of fiber, they can help the blood sugar balance and digestion. As pear fibers bind bile acids, they can be helpful in improving cholesterol levels too.

Why Eat Cherries?

Cherries—and more specifically tart cherries—are often overlooked for their health benefits. Sweet cherries contain fiber, vitamin C, carotenoids, and anthocyanins, each of which may help to play a role in cancer prevention. Tart cherries are anti-inflammatory and may help to lower your risk of gout attacks and reduce the pain and inflammation associated with osteoarthritis. They are also beneficial in improving recovery after exercise. Cherries provide a natural source of melatonin to aid sleep. Tart cherries may help your body to metabolize fat and glucose so assisting you to lose weight. Tart cherries are available either dried or as a concentrated juice throughout the year.

Plums

The high fiber in prunes (dried plums) helps alleviate constipation, lowers cholesterol, and improves digestive health. Prunes' insoluble fiber provides food for the "friendly" bacteria in the large intestine.

- Fresh plums are a good source of vitamin C, improving the absorption of iron.
- Plums are rich in phenols which have antioxidant protective properties.

Peaches

Peaches are a good source of beta-carotene that the body converts to vitamin A, which benefits skin and eye health and the immune system.

- Peaches are rich in vitamin C and a number of phenols, vitamins, and minerals essential for heart health including potassium, magnesium, folate, choline, and vitamin E.

Nectarines

Related to peaches nutritionally, nectarines contain a slightly higher concentration of certain minerals like iron, phosphorus, and potassium. They are also a useful source of vitamins A and C and the B vitamins.

- One medium nectarine contains around 285 mg of potassium. Potassium helps the body to maintain a healthy blood pressure and balances fluid levels.

Apricots

Apricots are rich in beta-carotene, vitamin C, and fiber. The presence of carotenoids and xanthophylls may help to protect eyesight from age-related damage.

- Apricots also contain catechins, which have strong anti-inflammatory and anticancer properties.
- Dried apricots are rich in fiber making them ideal for alleviating constipation.

Apricot and Peach Crisp

HIGH FIBER

This delicious Paleo fruit dessert is similar to cobbler but much healthier. You can use this nutritious topping for all types of fruit including bags of frozen fruits when fresh are not available.

Prep: 20 mins/Cook: 50 mins

Ingredients (serves 6)

10 apricots, pitted and sliced
4 ripe nectarines or peaches, pitted
    and sliced
1 cup (150 g) almonds or almond flour
2 tablespoons ground flaxseed
Pinch of sea salt
1 tablespoon ground cinnamon
1 tablespoon ground ginger
4 tablespoons coconut oil melted
2 tablespoons honey
⅔ cup (100 g) chopped pecans

Method

1 Preheat the oven to 350°F (180°C, gas mark 4). Place the apricots and peaches in a baking dish.

2 Grind the whole almonds, if using, until very fine in a food processor. Transfer to a large bowl and combine with the flaxseeds, salt, and ground spices. Mix the oil and honey together, then using your hands, work this into the almond mixture to form a crumbly dough. Gently mix in the pecans. Sprinkle the topping over the fruit.

3 Bake in the oven for 40 to 50 minutes until golden and crisp.

HELPS TO PROTECT YOUR EYESIGHT	
Calories (per serving)	390
Protein	8.2 g
Total fat	32.5 g
of which saturated fat	7.3 g
Carbohydrates	16.4 g
of which sugars	15.5 g
Vitamins/minerals	C, A, E, folate, riboflavin

Melons

Melons include a wide variety and are valued for being relatively low in sugar. Melons are actually members of the cucurbit family of plants (Cucurbitaceae) that also includes cucumbers, pumpkins, squashes, and gourds. The seeds of melons can be dried and used as a healthy snack. Melons provide a wealth

Nutrition: Melons are excellent sources of vitamins A, C, B, K, and also fiber, magnesium, and antioxidants. **Benefits:** Aids digestion, reduces inflammation, boosts the immune system, and helps keep eyes healthy.

of antioxidants including carotenoids, vitamin C, and plenty of minerals such as calcium, potassium, manganese, selenium, magnesium, zinc, and copper. Because the nutritional benefits increase as the fruits ripen, it is best to select fully ripened melons to eat.

Melons contain almost no fat and are low in calories, making them an excellent choice for desserts, particularly if you are watching your weight.

Watermelon

Watermelons are rich in lycopene, beta-carotene, and vitamin C—all protective, anti-inflammatory nutrients and especially beneficial for skin and eyesight.

- Watermelon contains citrulline, an amino acid that is converted by our kidneys into arginine, which helps to maintain healthy blood pressure and improves blood flow.

Cantaloupe Melon

Cantaloupes are also commonly known as muskmelons, mush melons, rock melons, or Persian melons.

- Cantaloupe are a good source of carotenoids, vitamin C, potassium, a number of B vitamins, vitamin K, and fiber, which help to promote a healthy heart, lower inflammation, and maintain healthy blood pressure.

Honeydew Melon

Honeydew melons are a popular summer fruit, low in calories, and hydrating due to their plentiful water content.

- Honeydew melons are a good source of vitamin C.
- Honeydew provides vitamin B_6 that stimulates the production of serotonin, a neurotransmitter that helps regulate mood and sleep.

Galia Melon

Galia melons are a hybrid cultivar of cantaloupe and honeydew melons.

- Galia melons are high in vitamin C, carotenoids and fiber, which helps digestive health and balances blood sugar levels. Carotenoids are known for their cancer-protective properties.
- A good source of potassium to maintain healthy blood pressure.

Citrus Fruits

Citrus fruits are famous for being high in vitamin C. They also contain lots of antioxidant phytonutrients, which are thought to have anticancer properties. Low in sugar (depending on the variety) compared to other fruits and packed with water and fiber, they can satisfy your appetite and help with weight loss.

Nutrition: Citrus fruits contain a range of minerals including potassium, copper, magnesium, and selenium.
Benefits: Helps to keep the heart healthy, supports the immune system, and helps to lower cholesterol.

Oranges

A rich source of vitamin C and polyphenols, oranges are a popular fruit throughout the year. One flavanone called hesperidin has been shown to help lower blood pressure. The flavones in the peel are particularly beneficial for lowering cholesterol.

- Oranges contain lots of antioxidants to maintain cardiovascular health, reducing the risk of strokes and certain cancers.

Lemons

Rich in vitamin C, adding lemon juice to meals can help improve the absorption of iron. Lemon juice is often added to hot water and drunk to stimulate digestion and to help detoxify the body.

- The nutrients in lemons are good for immune health, fighting bacterial and viral infections, as well as helping the body's digestive system.

Limes

Limes are an excellent source of vitamin C and, like lemons, contain limonoid compounds, which have been shown to prevent certain cancers.

- Rich in citric acid, limes may help prevent the formation of kidney stones.
- Limes contain hesperidin, making them beneficial for maintaining healthy cholesterol levels.

Why Eat Grapefruit?

Grapefruits are available in red, pink, and white varieties. Grapefruit is an excellent source of vitamin C, a vitamin that helps to strengthen the immune system. Red and pink varieties are rich in lycopene, a nutrient that may help men reduce the risk of developing prostate cancer. Lycopene is also important for a healthy skin.

Grapefruit contains pectin, a form of soluble fiber that helps to lower cholesterol and assists digestive health. Grapefruits are also rich in the phytonutrients known as limonoids that are valued for inhibiting tumors and are thought to be helpful in reducing the risk of certain cancers.

Arugula and Orange Salad with Vinaigrette Dressing

LOW CALORIE

Citrus fruits are a delicious addition to salads and this recipe would work equally well with pink grapefruit segments instead of the oranges. The dressing can be prepared in advance and stored in the refrigerator until needed. Add some protein such as cooked chicken or fish to make this a speedy lunch option.

Prep: 10 mins

Ingredients (serves 4)

3½ oz (100 g) arugula, watercress, and spinach leaves
2 oranges
1 cooked beet, sliced
½ red onion, diced
Small handful of flat-leaf parsley, chopped
⅓ cup (30 g) walnut halves

Vinaigrette Dressing

2 tablespoons sherry vinegar
2 tablespoons walnut oil
2 tablespoons olive oil
Sea salt and freshly ground black pepper

Method

1 Place the arugula, watercress, and spinach leaves in a large bowl or serving platter.

2 Using a sharp knife, peel the skin and pith away from the oranges and cut them into segments. Set aside any orange juice that comes out from the fruit.

3 Scatter the beet, orange segments, onion, parsley, and walnuts over the arugula.

4 Whisk the vinegar and oils with the reserved orange juice and season to taste. Drizzle the vinaigrette dressing over the salad to serve.

KEEPS YOUR HEART HEALTHY	
Calories (per serving)	169
Protein	2.9 g
Total fat	14.5 g
of which saturated fat	1.7 g
Carbohydrates	6.6 g
of which sugars	6.4 g
Vitamins/minerals	C, B, K, A, omega-3 fats

Tropical Fruits

Typically tropical fruits are higher in sugar than other fruits, although this varies depending on the type. Often available frozen, tropical fruits are delicious in a range of both sweet and savory dishes. Many fruits can also be found in dried form, but choose those without added sugars or additives.

Nutrition: Tropical fruits are full of beneficial vitamins and minerals, as well as antioxidants.
Benefits: Boosts the immune system, aids digestion, helps to keep the skin healthy, and boosts your mood.

Papaya

The flesh of papayas is rich orange-pink in color. The seeds are edible, although their peppery flavor is slightly bitter.

- Papaya contains several unique protein-digesting enzymes that help digestion and reduce inflammation.
- This fruit is a good source of carotenes, vitamin C, and flavonoids with immune-supporting benefits.

Pineapple

Pineapple contains bromelain, a digestive enzyme known for its anti-inflammatory and digestive benefits. Eating pineapple may improve digestion of protein foods.

- Pineapple is a good source of the trace mineral manganese and B vitamin thiamin that help boost energy levels.
- This fruit is very rich in vitamin C for immune support and a healthy skin.

Pomegranate

Pomegranate is variously available as fresh fruit, freeze-dried powder, or juice.

- Pomegranates are exceptionally rich in vitamin C and high in polyphenols, including ellagic acid, which has been shown to help inhibit cancer cell growth.
- The array of antioxidants present in pomegranates has also been shown to be beneficial to cardiovascular health.

Banana

Popular as a workout fuel, bananas provide easily digestible carbohydrates and potassium to replenish electrolytes lost during exercise. Potassium can also help relieve muscle cramps during workouts.

- Bananas may help lift your mood as they are rich in tryptophan, an amino acid that the body converts to the feel-good neurotransmitter serotonin.

Kiwi

Packed with more vitamin C than an equivalent quantity of orange, kiwis are a great immune-supporting food.

- Kiwis are rich in vitamin C, which has been shown to help reduce the severity of conditions like osteoarthritis, rheumatoid arthritis, and asthma.
- These are high in fiber which can help to remove toxins from the colon.

Chocolate Chip Banana Bread

HEALTHY HEART

A great recipe for a breakfast treat or succulent snack. You can slice and freeze the bread making it a useful standby recipe. It is delicious served on its own or toasted and spread with coconut butter. You could use any nut or seed butter in this recipe.

Prep: 15 mins/Bake: 45 mins

Ingredients (makes 1 loaf)

4 ripe small bananas

4 eggs

½ cup (100 g) coconut oil

½ cup (125 g) cashew nut butter

⅔ cup (60 g) coconut flour

1 teaspoon baking soda

2 teaspoons baking powder

1 tablespoon vanilla extract

1 teaspoon ground cinnamon

⅓ cup (60 g) dairy-free, sugar-free chocolate chips

Method

1 Preheat the oven to 350°F (180°C, gas mark 4). Grease a loaf pan and line it with wax paper.

2 Combine the bananas, eggs, oil, and nut butter in a food processor. Add the coconut flour, baking soda, baking powder, vanilla, and cinnamon to the mix, and blend them together.

3 Stir in the chocolate chips. Spoon the batter into the lined loaf pan and bake for 45 minutes until it is golden and cooked through.

4 Cool in the pan for 15 minutes before turning out. Slice the loaf and serve.

PROTEIN PACKED AND HIGH IN FIBER	
Calories (per slice)	371
Protein	9.1 g
Total fat	28.0 g
of which saturated fat	16.2 g
Carbohydrates	20.2 g
of which sugars	11.0 g
Vitamins/minerals	B, K, potassium, copper

Healthy Fats and Oils

Fats in a Paleo diet are either derived from whole foods such as salmon, meat, nuts, and eggs, or from fats used for cooking like coconut oil. Unlike popular low-fat diets, the focus for a Paleo diet is to ensure the consumption of enough quality fats centered around saturated, monounsaturated, and omega-3 fats.

Long-chain saturated fatty acids (LCSFA) such as myristic, palmitic, and stearic acid are primarily derived from animal fats like lard, duck fat, and ghee if dairy is included. These fats form essential components in our cells and are useful for producing energy. They are also heat stable making them suitable for cooking at high temperatures. Saturated fats are in fact very healthy to consume presuming your insulin levels are in a normal range, and there is little evidence that they contribute to heart disease. Some plant-based oils are also great for cooking, such as avocado, palm, and coconut oil. Coconut fat is rich in medium-chain triglycerides (MCT). MCTs are metabolized differently from long-chain saturated fats; they don't require bile acids for digestion and they pass directly to the liver for energy conversion. This makes MCTs a great energizing fat.

Monounsaturated fat (MFA), or oleic acid, is found in certain meats, olive oil, avocados, lard, and some nuts like macadamias. They are also important structural fats in the body, are heat stable and possess anti-inflammatory properties.

Polyunsaturated fats (PUFA) can be divided into omega-6 and omega-3 types. PUFA are fragile and vulnerable to oxidative damage. Typically the Western diet is very high in omega-6 fats which are pro-inflammatory. Therefore these should only be eaten in small quantities. Cereal grains, some meats, and industrial processed and refined oils are also high in omega-6 fats.

Omega-3 fats include alpha-linolenic acid (ALA) and long-chain EPA and DHA fatty acids. They have anti-inflammatory properties. Conversion of ALA is poor so it is important to ensure that we have optimal levels of EPA and DHA which are found in oily fish. Vegetarian sources of omega-3 fats are poorly converted by the body into these active fats.

Health Benefits of Fats and Oils

Brain health: Your brain is mainly made of cholesterol and fat, most of which are essential fatty acids, in particular DHA. Eating the right fats can therefore improve cognitive function and mood. Medium-chain triglycerides can be used as a fuel by the brain and may help to alleviate cognitive decline.

Heart health: Healthy fats, including monounsaturated fats, can decrease inflammation, lower circulating triglycerides, and reduce insulin due to the natural antioxidants they contain. Saturated fats don't damage easily in high heat, making them the safest fats to cook with because oxidized (damaged) fats cause inflammation in the arteries. Saturated fats can help raise HDL, the "good" cholesterol that helps to lower your risk of heart disease.

Immune support: Some fats provide vitamins D and A that are important for immune health, plus the compounds lauric and capryllic acid known to have antimicrobial benefits.

Reproductive health: Fat is critical for reproductive health in both men and women because it is used to manufacture hormones and helps to regulate hormone balance. Healthy fats can also lower inflammation and improve symptoms linked to PMS and the menopause. For men, healthy fats stimulate the production of testosterone.

Body composition: Including more fat and less carbohydrate in the diet can improve insulin sensitivity, reduce inflammation, and support your metabolism.

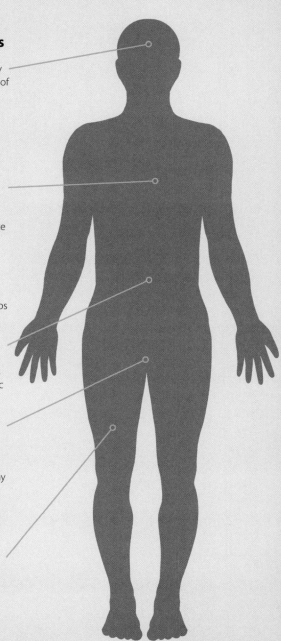

Duck Fat

Duck fat is primarily composed of long-chain saturated and monounsaturated fats. It has a high smoke point, making it ideal for cooking at very hot temperatures. Duck fat is used in classic dishes and produces delicious crisp roasted vegetables.

- Duck fat is high in monounsaturated fat that can help to lower levels of cholesterol in the blood.

Ghee

Ghee, or clarified butter, is a dietary source of fat traditionally used in Indian cooking. Although not included in all Paleo diets as it is derived from dairy, ghee has a higher smoke point than normal butter, olive oil, or coconut oil, making it a great choice for sautéing or frying foods. Because the milk solids have been removed, it's very low in lactose making it acceptable to people with lactose intolerance. Ghee provides butyrate, a short-chain fatty acid that can decrease inflammation and help support colon health.

- Ghee is rich in fat-soluble vitamins A, D, E, and K, which are important for bones and brain health, and to boost the immune system.
- Choose ghee from grass-fed cows as it is high in conjugated linoleic acid (CLA) that can improve insulin resistance and encourage healthy body composition.

Lard

Lard is an animal fat normally obtained from pigs. It is high in saturated fat making it very stable for cooking. Choose lard from grass-fed animals for a better fat profile.

- A traditional, sustainable fat, lard provides cholesterol, an important fat needed for hormone production.
- Lard provides vitamin D, an essential vitamin for immunity and bone health.

Avocado Oil

A versatile oil ideal for salad dressings, marinades, and high-temperature cooking, avocados are rich in the heart-healthy monounsaturated fat, oleic acid. Oleic acid has been linked to reduced inflammation and may have anticancer properties.

- Avocados contain the antioxidants lutein and zeaxanthin, which are important for eye health and lower the risk of macular degeneration and cataracts.

- They are packed with a number of nutrients notably vitamin K, potassium, folate, vitamin E, and vitamin C.
- Rich in fiber, avocados can help to balance blood sugar levels and may actually promote weight loss.
- Consuming avocado oil with plant foods can help the body to absorb the fat-soluble vitamins A, E, and K and also carotenoids in foods.

Olive Oil

The less refined the oil, the lower the smoking point but higher the antioxidant levels. For lower temperature cooking choose virgin olive oil and for dressings opt for extra virgin olive oil.

- The high monounsaturated fat content of olives has been linked to a reduced risk of cardiovascular disease.
- Olives are rich in phytonutrients.

Walnut Oil

Unrefined walnut oil is made from nuts that are dried and cold pressed. Use in dressings and baking.

- Walnut oil is rich in antioxidants, specifically ellagic acid that has anticancer properties.
- This oil contains high levels of monounsaturated oils which are anti-inflammatory and good for the heart.

Macadamia Oil

Macadamia oil is high in monounsaturated fats and is an excellent source of oleic acid. It imparts a mild, buttery flavor to foods making it delicious to use to make mayonnaise. Having a long shelf life, it can be used for low-temperature cooking as well as in dressings.

- Macadamia oil contains vitamin E, a potent fat-protective antioxidant.

Red Palm Oil

Naturally reddish, palm oil is extracted from the flesh of the plum-sized palm fruit. Red palm oil is the virgin unrefined oil. Refined palm oil is a good choice for high-temperature cooking. However, refining the oil reduces its antioxidant content.

- Red palm oil is packed with antioxidants including vitamin E and CoQ10 that is important for energy production.

Why Eat Coconut?

A variety of coconut-derived ingredients—from coconut oil and coconut water to coconut flour and coconut milk—are popular in Paleo diets. Coconut milk is made from a combination of coconut meat and water and is delicious used in sweet and savory dishes. Coconut water is a great hydrating liquid, rich in electrolytes sodium, potassium, and magnesium, making it a popular sports drink. The coconut flesh makes a great snack, low in carbohydrates and very satisfying due to its high fat content.

Coconut oil provides medium-chain triglycerides (MCTs) which are easier to burn as a fuel for the body and the brain. Supplementing with MCT oil has been shown to be beneficial for neurodegenerative conditions such as Alzheimer's. Coconut oil is also rich in lauric acid that boosts immune function and caprylic acid that has antimicrobial properties and may help people with a bacterial or yeast infection. MCTs have also been shown to lower inflammation and support gut barrier healing making them helpful for autoimmune conditions.

Paleo Pantry

If you're looking to adopt a Paleo style of eating, then it is worth spending time clearing out your pantry and stocking it instead with some healthy Paleo staples.

By restocking your pantry with healthy foods, you will have the essentials to create a range of dishes quickly while strengthening your resolve to follow a nutrient-dense diet.

Key products include those for cooking (oils, fats) and baking (coconut flour, almond flour), canned items (such as canned fish and coconut milk), drinks (green tea, yerba mate, herbal teas), snacks (nuts, seeds, jerky, seaweed snacks, kale chips), spices, herbs, flavorings (tamari, coconut aminos, vinegar), sweeteners (honey), and dried goods like sea vegetables and dried mushrooms, etc. These foods are not only convenient but also have numerous health benefits and nutrients to get you in the best of health.

Health Benefits of Pantry Staples

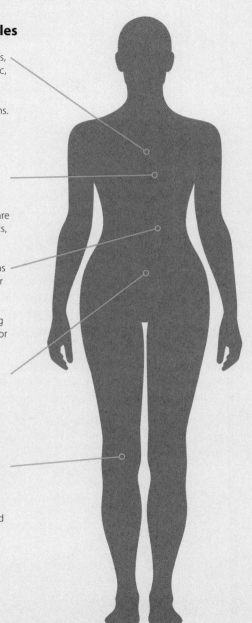

Anti-inflammatory: Many spices, such as turmeric, ginger, and garlic, are known for their powerful anti-inflammatory properties making them good for autoimmune conditions. They also benefit cardiovascular health and relieve inflammatory conditions like asthma and arthritis.

Heart health: Certain pantry ingredients like canned fish, canned tomatoes, and chocolate contain a range of nutrients that are good for the heart. These include omega-3 fats, antioxidants, and magnesium.

Blood sugar: Condiments such as vinegar can lower the blood sugar response after eating, improving insulin function, and even your feeling of fullness when taken before or during the meal. Cinnamon is also a beneficial spice for improving blood sugar regulation.

Digestive health: Some pantry ingredients like coconut flour are rich in digestible fibers that encourage bowel regularity and provide prebiotic fibers to boost levels of beneficial bacteria in our gut.

Joint health: Bone broth and gelatin contain a number of nutrients that are beneficial for connective tissues and bone health, including collagen, hyaluronic acid, and chondroitin sulfate.

Spices and Flavors

Spices not only add flavor to dishes but they are rich in antioxidants that are known to be good for our health. For those following an autoimmune Paleo diet, certain spices may not be appropriate as they are derived from the nightshade family of plants. These include chilies, paprika, and cayenne pepper.

Nutrition: Spices are packed with vitamins, minerals, and antioxidants, as well as enhancing the flavor of dishes. **Benefits:** Fights infection and boosts the immune system, alleviates nausea, aids digestion, and keeps skin healthy.

Ginger

Ginger is the underground rhizome of the ginger plant and is popular in Asian dishes as well as in baking. Known as a carminative spice, it is traditionally used to alleviate digestive disorders, wind, and nausea.

- Ginger contains anti-inflammatory compounds called gingerols which may help with inflammatory conditions including arthritis.

Turmeric

Turmeric is the spice that gives curry its yellow color. Curcumin is the main active ingredient in turmeric. It has powerful anti-inflammatory effects and is a very strong antioxidant.

- Curcumin has been shown to be effective at delaying or even reversing age-related decline in brain function including Alzheimer's disease.

Himalayan Sea Salt

Unlike refined table salt which is chemically cleaned, Himalayan sea salt is unrefined and free of additives.

- Himalayan salt provides a number of trace minerals including potassium, calcium, and magnesium that help maintain healthy fluid levels and replenish important electrolytes lost through sweating.

Cinnamon

Cinnamon is the bark of the cinnamon tree. It is available in its dried tubular form, known as a quill, or as ground powder.

- Cinnamon contains a number of volatile oils including cinnamaldehyde. These have antimicrobial benefits, anticlotting properties, and help the body to respond better to insulin so assisting with control of blood sugar levels.

Vanilla

A useful flavoring, vanilla contains chemicals called vanilloids that have anti-inflammatory properties. These are vulnerable to heat so use in cold dishes or in low-temperature baked goods. Most vanilla products are processed, so look for organic vanilla beans or pure extract.

- Traditionally vanilla was used to relieve gastrointestinal symptoms.

Garlic Flakes

Garlic flakes, sometimes called instant garlic, are small dehydrated pieces of garlic that are used as a flavoring. Use them in soups, stews, and sauces. Store in an airtight container.

- Garlic can help to lower cholesterol and reduce the risk of heart disease.
- These flakes aid detoxification due to their antimicrobial properties.

Nutritional Yeast Flakes

Nutritional yeast is a rich source of B vitamins and adds a delicious nutty, slightly cheesy flavor to dishes. It is derived from a yeast called *Saccharomyces cerevisiae* and is grown on sugar cane and beet molasses. Once harvested, it undergoes heat treatment and is then crumbled or flaked.

- Nutritional yeast flakes are a source of all essential amino acids and fiber.

Coconut Aminos

Coconut aminos is a soy-free flavoring made from the sap of the coconut tree. Available in health food stores.

- Coconut aminos is especially rich in amino acids that are important for the repair and growth of muscle tissue, keeping the nervous system and brain healthy, as well as aiding digestion and contributing to a healthy heart.

Cashew Nut Cheese

HIGH FIBER

This is a delicious alternative to dairy cheeses. Using nutritional yeast flakes provides plenty of flavor and also a health-boosting array of B vitamins. Ideally ferment the nut cheese overnight to increase the levels of probiotic bacteria in it. For a quicker option, simply blend all the ingredients together and serve. You can stir in herbs or sundried tomato for additional flavor.

**Soak: 8 hrs/Prep: 10 mins/
Stand: 24 hrs**

Ingredients (serves 8)

1⅔ cups (250 g) cashews, soaked overnight
   and drained
1 cup (250 ml) water
1 teaspoon probiotic powder
½ teaspoon Himalayan sea salt
1 tablespoon nutritional yeast flakes

Method

1 Blend the nuts, water, and probiotic powder in a high-speed blender until the mixture is smooth.

2 Place the mixture in a strainer that has been lined with cheesecloth. Fold the cheesecloth over the top and place a light weight on top. This causes any excess liquid to drain out.

3 Let stand for 24 hours. Then stir in the salt and yeast flakes. Store in the refrigerator until ready to use.

CHOLESTEROL FREE AND HEART-HEALTHY	
Calories (per serving)	185
Protein	6.4 g
Total fat	15.1 g
of which saturated fat	3.0 g
Carbohydrates	5.9 g
of which sugars	1.4 g
Vitamins/minerals	B, K, magnesium, zinc

Vinegars and Sauces

Ready-made sauces are not generally used in the Paleo diet as they are made from refined sugars, grains, and gluten, but you can use fish sauce, natural oyster sauce, and tamari, as well as making your own. Many vinegars are acceptable, including apple cider and balsamic, but malt vinegar contains gluten so should be avoided.

Nutrition: Vinegar contains vitamins, minerals and acetic acid, while fish sauce is rich in iodine.
Benefits: Lowers blood sugar levels after meals, good for keeping the heart healthy, and aiding digestion.

Apple Cider Vinegar

Organic, unfiltered apple cider vinegar is rich in acetic acid and contains "mother" strands of proteins, enzymes, and friendly bacteria that cause the cloudy appearance.

- Acetic acid has antimicrobial properties and promotes digestion.
- Apple cider vinegar improves insulin sensitivity and helps to lower blood sugar responses after meals.

Balsamic Vinegar

Choose good quality balsamic vinegar as cheaper brands often contain sugar and unwelcome additives.

- Balsamic vinegar has been shown to help inhibit LDL oxidation and lipid peroxidation making it beneficial for heart health.
- This vinegar can be helpful in maintaining healthy blood sugar levels.

Red Wine Vinegar

This vinegar is made from red wine that has been fermented for up to two years.

■ Red wine vinegar contains acetic acid, which can help curb hunger pangs and aid weight loss as it slows down the digestion process.

■ This vinegar contains the antioxidant resveratrol, which can lower blood pressure and keep the heart healthy.

Fish Sauce

Made from small fermented fish, fish sauce is an Asian condiment that adds a distinct flavor as well as salty taste to dishes. Use in small amounts due to its strong flavor.

■ Fish sauce contains the vital nutrients and minerals found in fish, but enhanced by fermentation. This includes iodine and other substances that nourish the thyroid, as well as vitamins A and D.

Tamari

Tamari is a Japanese wheat-free fermented soy sauce. It is thicker than ordinary soy sauce and can be used in a variety of savory dishes to enhance their flavor.

■ A good source of manganese to keep bones strong.

■ Tamari contains the amino acid tryptophan, which helps reduce sleeping difficulties and boosts your mood.

Flours and Setting Agents

Coconut and other nut flours are very good substitutes for non-Paleo grain and wheat flours. They are also nutritious as they are packed with protein, fiber, and healthy fats. You can buy them from health food stores. Gelatin, agar, and arrowroot are all useful setting agents that can be used in both desserts and savory dishes.

Nutrition: Full of fiber and protein, as well as vitamins and minerals, they are all highly nutritious.
Benefits: Improves digestion, keeps skin and hair healthy, helps with weight loss, and keeps bones strong.

Coconut Flour

This flour is made from coconut meat that has been dried and defatted. It is valuable for baking Paleo breads, cakes, cookies, and muffins.

- Coconut flour is relatively low in carbohydrates but high in fiber which contributes to digestive health.
- This flour helps to create a feeling of fullness and balances blood sugar levels.

Almond Flour

Almond flour or almond meal is highly nutritious, easy to use, and readily available. High in protein, low in carbohydrates, and low in sugars, it is beneficial for weight loss and improving muscle mass.

- Almond flour is particularly rich in magnesium, phosphorous, potassium, and calcium as well as heart-protective vitamin E.

Arrowroot

A useful starch in Paleo cooking obtained from the rootstock of the arrowroot plant; it is dried and then powdered into a flour. Arrowroot can be used to lighten Paleo baking recipes. It is also useful for thickening sauces, both sweet and savory. Arrowroot is gluten free.

- Arrowroot contains good levels of vitamins, including niacin and thiamin.

Gelatin

Gelatin from grass-fed animals is a nutritious addition to the Paleo diet and can be added to recipes and drinks.

- A great source of collagen, gelatin is also rich in the amino acids glycine and proline and is particularly beneficial for gut healing, the condition of skin, hair, and nails, and joint and bone health.

Agar Flakes

Derived from seaweed, agar flakes are often used to set liquids and they also act as a binder in recipes. Dissolve agar in boiling liquid for use in a range of dishes.

- Agar contains calcium and iron, and is a good source of fiber.
- This contains no sugar, no fat, and no carbohydrates and may help the body to detoxify and aid digestive health.

Why Eat Cacao?

Nutrient-rich cacao has been prized by many cultures for over 2,000 years. But it is important to remember that raw, unsweetened cacao powder and chocolate, which is high in antioxidant flavonols, is very different from the common commercial cocoa drinks and chocolates, which are loaded with sugar and low in antioxidant content.

Cacao is extracted from cacao beans, which are found in the pods (or fruit) of the cacao plant—a tropical tree that is native to Central and South America. Loaded with antioxidants, cacao is also an excellent source of minerals including magnesium, iron, chromium, manganese, zinc, and copper. It is one of the richest food sources of magnesium, which helps to relax the muscles and heart and cardiovascular system and relieve stress. Many of the health benefits appear to be due to the antioxidant content, so choose raw cacao powder for optimal benefits.

Cacao also contains the amino acid tryptophan and phenylethylamine (PEA), which has a positive effect on mood. Raw cacao powder is milder in flavor than commercial roasted cocoa powder. Processed chocolate powders generally lack many of the health benefits of the raw ingredient.

In addition to cacao powder, you can also find cacao nibs, cacao butter, and paste. Cacao nibs are slightly bitter and have a strong chocolate flavor. Cacao butter and paste are popular in raw desserts and for making homemade chocolates.

Although chocolate can be a healthy food option it is still energy dense and so will make you gain weight if you eat too much of it. Dark chocolate has been shown to offer a number of health benefits including improving blood pressure and blood flow, which may be one of the reasons it can support cognitive function. Choose dark chocolate containing 85 percent cocoa solids for a higher intake of beneficial antioxidants and lower sugar content.

Berry Gelatin Desserts with Coconut Yogurt

STRONG BONES

A simple light dessert made using grass-fed gelatin. You can use any berries, and bags of frozen berries are a great standby option if fresh are not available. By pureeing the berries, you create a more intense, thicker set dessert than by simply using juice. Instead of coconut yogurt, you could top the desserts with coconut cream.

Prep: 15 mins/Chill: 3 to 4 hrs

Ingredients (serves 2)

1 cup (150 g) strawberries
1 cup (130 g) raspberries
2 tablespoons grass-fed gelatin powder
1 cup (250 ml) water or pomegranate juice

Method

1 Puree the fruit in a blender. Place the gelatin in a pan and mix in the fruit puree and water or juice. Stir well.

2 Bring the liquid to a boil stirring constantly to dissolve the gelatin. Let the mixture cool.

3 Pour into glasses or bowls. Place in the refrigerator to set for 3 to 4 hours. Top with coconut yogurt or cream and a few berries to serve.

BOOSTS YOUR SKIN, HAIR, AND NAILS	
Calories (per serving)	144
Protein	8.8 g
Total fat	9.3 g
of which saturated fat	6.6 g
Carbohydrates	7.5 g
of which sugars	7.1 g
Vitamins/minerals	C, K, manganese

Creamy Coconut Chocolate Mousse

ENERGIZING

A rich, creamy mousse that makes an unashamedly indulgent treat. You can also turn this into a frozen dessert by spooning it into freezer-proof molds. The addition of cacao butter or coconut oil helps to set the mousse and gives it a rich flavor.

Prep: 10 mins/Chill: 3 to 4 hrs

Ingredients (serves 2)

1 x 14 oz (400 g) can coconut milk
2 tablespoons cashew or almond
   nut butter
2 tablespoons coconut oil or cacao
   butter, melted
Pinch of ground cinnamon
⅓ cup (100 g) honey
⅓ cup (30 g) raw cacao powder

Method

1 Simply place all the ingredients in a blender or food processor and process until smooth.

2 Pour into glasses or ramekins and place in the refrigerator for 3 to 4 hours to harden. Alternatively, place in the freezer for 1 hour to set. Top with berries and a sprig of mint to serve.

BURSTING WITH ANTIOXIDANTS	
Calories (per serving)	239
Protein	3.2 g
Total fat	12.3 g
of which saturated fat	7.8 g
Carbohydrates	28.5 g
of which sugars	23.3 g
Vitamins/minerals	E, iron, calcium, copper

Fermented Foods

The traditional diet of every ancient culture contained foods that were fermented. Originally this was done primarily to preserve food for longer, but we now know that it also creates very healthy, easily digested foods that are rich in probiotics.

Fermented foods are foods that have been through a process called lactofermentation where natural bacteria and yeasts from the surrounding environment—and on the vegetables and fruit themselves—feed on the sugar and starch contained in the foods to create lactic acid. This anaerobic process (fermentation) does more than just preserve the food, however, it also makes the nutrients inside the food easier to digest and more bioavailable. For example, the amount of bioavailable vitamin C in sauerkraut is 20 times higher than in the same helping of fresh cabbage. This is because in the fresh cabbage vitamin C is bound in the cellulose structure, which can be more difficult to digest and so absorb. As communities of specific health-promoting bacteria grow, they consume sugars and produce valuable enzymes. Fermented foods provide you with a beneficial bacteria to strengthen your immune and digestive systems.

Cultures all over the world have been eating fermented foods for a long time, from Sauerkraut (see page 188) in Germany to kimchi (see page 184) in Korea.

Left: Kimchi is a traditional Korean fermented dish believed to slow down aging. It is made from vegetables, including cabbage and spices.

Health Benefits of Fermented Foods

 Lower inflammation: Fermented foods can have anti-inflammatory properties making them useful for conditions such as asthma and respiratory infections.

 Immune health: Probiotic bacteria are known to strengthen immune function making them beneficial for autoimmune conditions. Some, such as kefir, also provide a wealth of amino acids that are important for immune function.

 Digestive health: Fermented foods are rich in probiotic bacteria that help digestion. This enables you to digest fats, proteins, and carbohydrates more easily, as well as giving support to the gut barrier lining. They are particularly beneficial to take after antibiotics to reinoculate the gut flora.

Child health: Probiotic bacteria are particularly important for supporting a child's digestive system, which is not fully mature. As fermented foods are predigested, it is easier for children to assimilate the valuable nutrients from them.

Urinary health: The beneficial yeasts and bacteria in fermented foods can help to fight infections in the urinary tract, which are typically caused by an overgrowth of pathogenic bacteria.

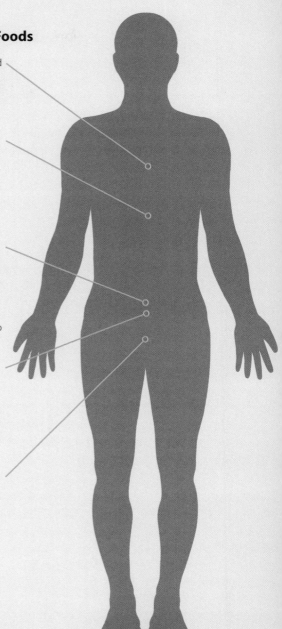

Kimchi

This is a popular Korean fermented food. While recipes vary, it normally contains fermented cabbage, radish, and other vegetables as well as spices including garlic and chili. It is popular served with spicy beef dishes.

- Kimchi is a good source of vitamins A, C, and B vitamins and its probiotic "healthy bacteria" aids digestion.

Why Eat Kefir?

An ancient cultured food, kefir is a fermented milk drink. It is rich in amino acids, enzymes, calcium, magnesium, phosphorus, and B vitamins. Kefir contains several strains of friendly bacteria as well as beneficial yeasts, which can support digestive function and immune health. It is made with kefir "grains," which are not actually a grain but are a mother culture of bacteria and yeasts. Although cow's milk is typically used, it can also be made with sheep's milk, coconut, or nut milk. You can also make water kefir using water grains.

You can purchase kefir in health food stores or make it at home using kefir grains and either organic dairy milk or coconut milk. It takes between 24 and 30 hours to ferment the cultures in milk at room temperature. Once fermented, store the kefir in the refrigerator and consume it within four days. Since the kefir grains react with metals, do not use any metal utensils when preparing. If making coconut milk kefir, you will need to refresh the kefir grains in cow's milk after four to five batches to enable it to ferment.

Homemade Coconut Kefir

PROTEIN RICH

One of the most healthy fermented foods, you can make your own effervescent kefir as a tangy, fresh, and tasty alternative to yogurt.

Prep: 20 mins/Ferment: 24 hrs

Ingredients (serves 4)

1 sachet of milk kefir grains
4 cups (1 liter) organic whole coconut milk

You need a clean, sterilized jar big enough to hold 35 oz (1 liter).

Method

1 Place the kefir in a small sterilized glass jar and pour over the coconut milk. Stir well with a wooden spoon. Cover with a lid or cloth and let ferment in a warm place, away from direct sunlight, for at least 24 hours. Do not seal the lid, as gas can build up as the mixture ferments.

2 The milk will separate to form the kefir liquid at the bottom. Carefully pour the mixture through a fine strainer and collect the kefir liquid in a clean container.

3 Store the prepared kefir in the refrigerator until required.

4 After straining, the grains should be placed straight back into a clean jar without washing them first. Fresh coconut milk is added to the grains to make the next batch of kefir.

AIDS DIGESTION	
Calories (per serving)	70
Protein	1 g
Total fat	6 g
of which saturated fat	5 g
Carbohydrates	6 g
of which sugars	3 g
Vitamins/minerals	A, C, calcium, iron

Sauerkraut

Sauerkraut is based on shredded cabbage but may also include other vegetables, such as carrot. If purchasing sauerkraut, choose an organic raw brand as many commercial brands will be heat-treated and lack any beneficial bacteria.

- Based on cabbage it provides plenty of vitamin C, vitamin K, and fiber.

Kombucha

Kombucha was called the "immortal health elixir" by the ancient Chinese and it has been consumed for more than 2,000 years. It is made from sweetened tea that has been fermented by a symbiotic colony of bacteria and yeast (known as SCOBY).

- Kombucha is rich in enzymes that your body requires for digestion and encourages blood cleansing.

Sour Cream

Sour cream is simply fermented cream. For a nondairy version, simply chill a can of coconut milk for an hour, then open the can without shaking it, scoop out the hard cream on top, put in a bowl, stir well until creamy, and add 2 tablespoons white vinegar, then chill before serving.

- Sour cream contains calcium and phosphorous to keep bones healthy.

Yogurt

A popular traditional food, yogurt is typically made from dairy ingredients. Many people on a Paleo diet avoid all dairy products including sheep and goat milk, but yogurt can be made easily from coconut or nut milks.

■ Coconut yogurt contains beneficial bacteria, fiber, vitamins, and minerals, to aid digestion and prevent constipation.

Homemade Coconut Yogurt

It's easy to make your own coconut yogurt at home. Serve with a mixture of fresh seasonal berries for a healthy and satisfying breakfast.

Prep: 30 mins/Ferment: 8 to 12 hrs

Ingredients (serves 4)

2 x 14 oz (400 g) cans organic whole
 coconut milk
1 tablespoon agar flakes or 2 teaspoons
 gelatin
1 tablespoon yogurt or 1 pack of yogurt
 starter or 1 teaspoon probiotic powder

Method

1 Place the coconut milk and agar flakes in a saucepan and simmer, stirring until the agar has dissolved. Remove from the heat and let cool to room temperature.

2 Add the yogurt starter and stir thoroughly. Pour the mixture into a yogurt maker and ferment for 8 to 12 hours. Or pour into a clean jar, cover and ferment at 110°F (43°C). Stir well and put the yogurt in the refrigerator to thicken.

SUPPORTS THE IMMUNE SYSTEM	
Calories (per serving)	199
Protein	1.7 g
Total fat	18.7 g
of which saturated fat	16 g
Carbohydrates	7.2 g
of which sugars	1.6 g
Vitamins/minerals	A, B, C, D, calcium, iron

Sauerkraut

LOW CALORIE

Unlike many store-bought versions, homemade sauerkraut is raw and therefore richer in beneficial enzymes and probiotic bacteria. Use organic, fresh vegetables and wash and dry them thoroughly. You can vary the vegetables according to taste. This version includes carrots and onions for additional flavor and beneficial nutrients.

**Prep: 8 hrs 30 mins/
Ferment: 3 to 4 days**

Ingredients (serves around 10)

1 cabbage e.g. savoy or napa, thinly sliced

3 carrots, grated or finely chopped

2 shallots, finely chopped

2 tablespoons sea salt

½ cup (125 ml) warm water

2 garlic cloves, peeled and chopped

1 teaspoon caraway seeds

2 teaspoons fennel seeds

Handful of washed, soaked sea vegetables
chopped, optional

BOOSTS YOUR IMMUNE SYSTEM	
Calories (per serving)	25
Protein	2.0 g
Total fat	0 g
of which saturated fat	0 g
Carbohydrates	4.0 g
of which sugars	1.0 g
Vitamins/minerals	C, K, B₆, sodium, folate

Method

1 Place the vegetables in a large mixing bowl. Put the salt and water in a separate small bowl and stir to dissolve. Pour over the vegetables and massage the mixture with your hands. Set aside at room temperature to soften overnight.

2 The following day, drain and set aside the salt water. Stir the garlic, caraway, and fennel seeds into the cabbage mixture and add the sea vegetables, if you are using them. Mix well. Tightly pack the mixture into a large glass jar with a lid. Pour over the saved salt water and press it firmly so there is no trapped air inside and the cabbage is covered in its own juice. Close the lid tightly.

3 Leave the jar in a warm, dark place for 3 to 4 days. It will take at least a week to ferment if left in a cool place. When ready, store in the refrigerator until required.

Beverages

The most important beverage that your body needs is water. Water makes up about 60 percent of the human body and plays a key role in all our physiological processes.

For many people who switch to a Paleo style of eating, making a change from their favorite drinks can be difficult. Whether you've been used to consuming energy drinks, beers, or soda, there are healthier alternatives that will not only hydrate the body but also provide refreshment and, in some cases, bring you additional health benefits. If you already eat a large variety of vegetables, then some water will be delivered from the food that you consume.

Remember that many of the fermented products previously discussed are also drinks—kombucha, water kefir, and milk kefir are recommended.

Water is the primary drink in the Paleo lifestyle. If you find plain water boring, try sparkling water or add a squeeze of lime or lemon for an extra kick. Just by adding various flavorings to plain water you may find that you drink more. Cucumber slices, mint, and lemon wedges in water are also refreshing. Some people like to add a splash of apple cider vinegar to warm water to drink before meals to stimulate digestion.

If you are taking strenuous exercise, consider adding lemon juice to water plus a pinch of salt. Lemons are high in potassium and the salt will help replace sodium lost when you sweat.

It is not a good idea to drink fruit juice because of its high sugar content. Green juices and smoothies, however, are beneficial, especially if you are looking for an opportunity to include a wider variety and quantity of vegetables in your diet and find eating larger amounts of vegetables difficult to achieve.

Health Benefits of Beverages

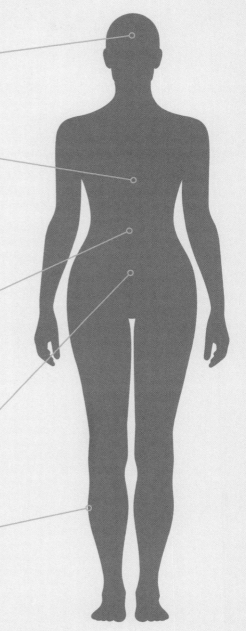

Brain health: Dehydration can affect our cognitive function. It may impair your attention span, memory, and motor skills. Drinking enough water will keep you feeling alert, allowing you to function optimally, and it can also help to relieve migraines.

Energy: Water is needed by our cells to function efficiently. Even minor dehydration can lead to low energy levels and fatigue. Drinks rich in electrolytes can replenish flagging energy while others that contain caffeine provide a more instant lift. Certain herbal teas like ginseng or licorice are adrenal adaptogens, which can also be effective energy boosters.

Weight loss: Drinking water before and between meals helps you to feel full, meaning you are likely to eat less. Many people mistake hunger for thirst so if you feel hungry, first drink a glass of water. Other drinks like green tea have also been shown to stimulate fat burning and aid weight loss.

Digestive health: Drinking enough water prevents constipation and supports kidney and liver function by helping to flush away waste products. In the large intestine, water binds with fiber to increase the bulk of the stools, reduce transit time, and make defecation easier.

Skin health: For glowing skin it is important to drink enough water. It assists cell health, lubricates the body, and by helping excretion of toxins may keep your skin looking clear.

Tea

Tea contains far less caffeine than coffee, but black tea tends to have more caffeine than green or white tea. If you want to avoid caffeine altogether, drink herbal teas.

- Green and black tea both provide a variety of health benefits including having antioxidant, anticarcinogenic, and anti-inflammatory properties.

Herbal Teas

Herbal teas are delicious served either hot or cold. Made from herbs or fruit extracts, some have specific health benefits.

- For a calming tea before bedtime try valerian, camomile, or lemon balm. Other teas can help to maintain a healthy gut, such as mint, ginger, turmeric, or marshmallow root.

Green Tea

Available as loose leaf, tea bags, or green tea matcha powder, which is the whole leaf ground up. The health benefits of matcha tea exceed those of green tea infusions.

- Green tea is rich in catechins, particularly EGCG which is a powerful antioxidant with anticancer benefits. Green tea has been shown to boost the metabolic rate and increase fat burning.

Rooibos Tea

Rooibos tea or red bush comes from a South African bush. It is caffeine free.

- Rooibos is rich in antioxidants including polyphenols, which have anti-inflammatory and anticancer properties. It contains quercetin known for its anti-inflammatory benefits, particularly for conditions such as asthma and for settling digestive upsets.

Coffee

Coffee occupies a bit of a gray area in the Paleo diet. While it was not an ancestral food, scientific research suggests that it can be beneficial to health when it is well tolerated. Some people do not metabolize it well and it can cause adverse effects.

There is concern that high coffee consumption may increase intestinal permeability, which is why it is often limited or avoided on an autoimmune protocol. Its caffeine content can adversely affect the adrenal glands by stimulating them to release the stress hormones cortisol and adrenaline, which is the same as the fight or flight response and over time this can lead to adrenal fatigue. High cortisol levels may also interfere with sleep, impair digestion, and overstimulate the immune system.

- Coffee is rich in antioxidants and polyphenols, and a number of studies have shown a range of health benefits including prevention of cancer, diabetes, cardiovascular disease, Alzheimer's, and Parkinson's disease.

- Coffee can aid weight loss due to antioxidants present including chlorogenic and caffeic acids which appear to curb overeating and reduce body fat. Unroasted coffee is richer in antioxidants and has been studied for its contribution to weight loss.

Maple Water

Maple water is liquid extracted from maple trees. It is a sweet, naturally filtered water, which contains a number of minerals such as calcium, potassium, magnesium, and manganese, which can be good for the heart and kidneys.

■ Slightly lower in sugar than coconut water, maple water contains enzymes, which help digestion and excretion.

Birch Water

Similar to maple water, this drink comes from tapping a birch tree. Birch water is often flavored. It also contains electrolytes and aids detoxification and cleansing due to its diuretic properties.

■ Birch water contains saponin, which helps to promote healthy cholesterol levels.

■ Birch water contains xylitol, a sugar alcohol that helps prevent tooth decay.

Coconut Water

Coconut water is a natural isotonic drink that provides the same energy-boosting benefits as formulated sports drinks.

■ Coconut water is rich in the electrolytes calcium, magnesium, phosphorus, sodium, and potassium, which are rapidly absorbed and assimilated by the body. It can help maintain healthy blood pressure.

Juices Versus Smoothies

Fruit juices are not recommended due to their high sugar content. Green juices and smoothies can be a valuable addition to a Paleo diet as a way of increasing vegetable intake. Green juices lack fiber, which makes vitamins, minerals, and antioxidants more easily absorbed, but can unbalance blood sugar levels as fiber helps to slow down the absorption of sugars. To avoid this, consume a green juice with a meal or limit the portion size.

Incorporating green juices can help people who have digestive problems and find it difficult to digest cooked or raw vegetables. To keep the sugar content low, make your juices using vegetables rather than fruit and try lifting the taste with a little lemon or ginger. You can add one green apple if you find that vegetable green juices taste too bitter.

Green smoothies—where the ingredients are simply blended together with water or another liquid —do contain fiber and are often more satisfying. This is an effective way to increase your intake of vegetables easily without putting a strain on your digestion. They are a useful way to sneak in various supplements and foods such as collagen powder, green superfoods, oils, nuts, seeds, or protein powders. Often green smoothies contain fruit, so it is important to keep an eye on the sugar content. Green smoothies can be an easy way to start the day if you find breakfast too difficult to manage. To make it more sustaining consider adding some soaked nuts, kefir, and dairy-free yogurt. This will help to balance your blood sugar levels.

Why Drink Bone Broth?

Bone broth is an important nutrient-rich food to include in a Paleo diet. Making your own is extremely cost effective, as you can make use of leftover carcass bones that would otherwise be thrown away.

Bone broth is simply made by slowly simmering the bones in water for several hours. To extract as many nutrients as possible, it is a good idea to cut or break up the bones before cooking. When the bone broth is ready, the bones and vegetables or flavorings should be strained and discarded. The broth can be stored in the refrigerator for two to three days for use as a drink or added to soups, stews, and casseroles. It can also be frozen. When making bone broth, it is important to select bones from organic grass-fed animals for optimal nourishment.

- Homemade bone broth is excellent for speeding healing and recuperation from illness. Chicken broth, for example, contains a natural amino acid called cysteine, which can thin mucus, making it useful for respiratory infections.
- Bone broth is rich in a number of nutrients that are important for healthy bones, including calcium, magnesium, and phosphorous.
- Bone broth contains plenty of amino acids such as glycine, proline, and arginine which all have anti-inflammatory effects.
- Popular for its role in contributing to a healthy gut, bone broth can assist the healing of the gut lining.
- The gelatin content in bone broth promotes healthy hair, nails, and joints and also helps to maintain healthy connective tissues.

Nut and Seed Milks

Nut and seed milks are a valuable addition to a Paleo diet to replace dairy. Many can be purchased ready made but it is also simple to make your own. Commercial brands often contain added sugars and thickeners like guar gum, which some people may find difficult to digest. Almond milk and coconut milk are popular for recipes or used as a dairy alternative in drinks.

- Coconut milk is a staple fat option for those following a Paleo diet.
- Almond milk is a good source of heart-protective vitamin E as well as calcium, to strengthen bones.

Homemade Coconut Milk

HIGH FIBER

Coconut milk is very easy to make at home. If storing in the refrigerator it may separate, so just give it a quick stir until mixed and then it's ready to use.

Prep: 20 mins

Ingredients (serves 2)

2 cups (500 ml) water

1 cup (90 g) unsweetened coconut flakes

ANTIFUNGAL AND ANTIBACTERIAL	
Calories (per serving)	231
Protein	1.6 g
Total fat	16.3 g
of which saturated fat	14.6 g
Carbohydrates	21.1 g
of which sugars	0 g
Vitamins/minerals	D, B$_{12}$, calcium, iron

Method

1 Heat the water until hot but not boiling. Put the coconut and water in a high-speed blender. Blend on high until thick and creamy.

2 Line a colander or strainer with cheesecloth or use a nut bag and strain the liquid. The coconut pulp can be dried and used in other recipes.

3 You can drink the coconut milk immediately or store it in the refrigerator for two to three days.

Matcha Green Smoothie

WEIGHT LOSS

This amazing creamy smoothie is sweet and nourishing. Studies have shown that exercising after drinking matcha tea can encourage fat burning even more, making this an excellent preworkout drink. Add a scoop of protein powder if you want to boost the protein content.

Prep: 5 mins

Ingredients (serves 1)

3 Brazil nuts

1 cup (250 ml) almond milk or coconut milk

5 oz (150 g) pineapple, fresh or frozen

2 handfuls of kale or spinach

¼ teaspoon matcha green tea powder

1 scoop of protein powder, optional

Method

1 Simply place all the ingredients in a high-speed blender and process until the mixture is smooth and creamy. Pour into a glass and serve.

BOOSTS YOUR BRAIN AND BURNS OFF FAT	
Calories (per serving)	208
Protein	5.4 g
Total fat	9.9 g
of which saturated fat	1.8 g
Carbohydrates	24.8 g
of which sugars	15.1 g
Vitamins/minerals	E, C, B, selenium

Alcohol in the Paleo Diet

Many people following a strict Paleo diet consider that moderate alcohol consumption is consistent with the health goals that the diet promotes.

While some people may benefit from drinking regular, small amounts, alcohol can also be bad for your health in various ways. It is a known irritant to the gut and can cause an increase in intestinal permeability. For this reason,

it is not recommended for people with autoimmune conditions where gut healing is required.

Alcohol is detoxified by the body in the liver, via an enzyme called alcohol dehydrogenase. In some people the activity of this enzyme is reduced which can mean that alcohol is not well tolerated and this can result in more extreme hangovers.

Drinking too much alcohol can also lead to weight gain, high blood sugar, and insulin problems, a fatty liver, elevated levels of fats in the blood, and homocysteine (an amino acid found in the blood and, if levels become too high, there is an increased risk of heart disease). It can also lead to increased oxidative stress. Alcohol also burdens the digestive and detoxification systems. It can lead to disturbed sleep and is addictive.

Red wine has been associated with some cardiovascular health benefits probably because of the antioxidants it contains. Alcohol in small amounts may help people to unwind and socialize—all of which can be beneficial to health.

If you want to drink alcohol, do so in moderation. Aim for no more than one small glass a day and have regular days which are alcohol free.

Paleo Dos and Don'ts

What to Include

- Grass-fed red meats
- Wild game
- Organ meats
- Variety meats
- Grass-fed/organic poultry
- Eggs
- Fish
- Shellfish and seafood
- Leafy green vegetables
- Salad vegetables
- Nonstarchy vegetables: avocado, olives, etc.
- Allium vegetables: onion, leek, chive, garlic, etc.
- Starchy vegetables: sweet potato, squashes, carrot, beet, parsnip, etc.
- Sea vegetables
- Nuts
- Seeds
- Fresh fruits: berries, pit fruits, melons, citrus, apples, pears, tropical fruits, etc.
- Quality fats and oils: lard, duck fat, tallow, red palm oil, olive, walnut, flaxseed, macadamia, avocado, coconut, etc.
- Pantry items: gelatin, agar flakes, coconut flour, almond flour, tamari, coconut aminos, nutritional yeast flakes, green banana flour, coconut milk and cream, canned fish, fish sauce, tapioca starch,

arrowroot, vinegar, cacao powder, carob powder, capers, gherkins, baking soda, baking powder, Himalayan sea salt, etc.
- Herbs and spices
- Honey and other sweeteners: stevia, coconut sugar, xylitol occasionally if tolerated
- Fermented foods: kefir, sauerkraut, kombucha, etc.
- Beverages: water, herbal teas, green and black tea, coffee (in moderation), green juices and smoothies, coconut water, nut and seed milks, kombucha, kefir, bone broth and broths, lemon or lime water
- Alcohol (occasionally).

What to Avoid

- Grains: including gluten and nongluten grains (wheat, spelt, rye, barley, kamut, couscous, semolina, oats, corn, quinoa, rice, amaranth, millet, buckwheat, teff, wild rice, sorghum, and products containing these grains)
- Beans and legumes (including peanuts and soy)
- Soy products: soy flour, soy milk and yogurt, tempeh, tofu, textured vegetable protein, okara, MSG, soy protein, edamame beans
- Dairy products: hard and soft cheeses, ghee, cottage cheese, curds, milk, yogurt, butter, ice cream, sour cream, buttermilk, foods containing dairy and lactose, whey protein powder
- Processed fatty meats (hot dogs, etc.)
- Soft drinks, sodas, and fruit juice
- Sugars, syrups, and artificial sweeteners such as aspartame and saccharin
- Processed foods and ready meals
- Refined vegetable oils
- Milk chocolate, white chocolate, and candies
- Refined table salt.

Glossary

Amino acids—these are the building blocks of muscle-building protein. They carry out important functions, have a key role in the storage of nutrients, and help in wound healing.

Antioxidants—these protect our bodies against the damaging effects of free radicals. Vitamins C, E, beta-carotene, and selenium are antioxidants.

Beta-carotene—a pigment found in large quantities in orange-fleshed and dark green fruit and vegetables and is turned into vitamin A by the body.

Fats—compounds of carbon, hydrogen, and oxygen atoms that exist in chains of varying lengths, shapes, and orders. They are one of the vital nutrients required by the body for both energy and the construction and maintenance of "structural" elements, such as cell membranes.

Free radical—a highly chemically reactive molecule often containing oxygen that can cause damage to cells in the body.

Gluten—a group of proteins found in wheat and other cereal grains. Celiac

disease is a disorder in which the body becomes intolerant to gluten.

Glycemic index (GI)—rates ingredients and dishes according to the rate at which a carbohydrate food breaks down into sugars and enters the bloodstream.

Glycemic load (GL)—this estimates how much the food will raise the person's blood sugar level after eating it.

Intestinal barrier—the lining of the intestines, often referred to as the gut barrier or mucosal barrier. It provides a physical barrier between the insides of the gut and the inside of the body.

Intestinal permeability—or leaky gut, this refers to a measure of how permeable the gut lining is. If the gut is compromised, substances that should not cross the barrier are able to do so.

Lectins—a group of carbohydrate-binding proteins found in many foods that can bind to specific carbohydrates including membranes in the gut.

Monounsaturated fat—these fatty acids contain just one double bond in their fatty acid chain. The more double bonds a fatty acid boasts, the more "fluid" it is. They are generally liquid at room temperature.

Polyunsaturated fats—these fats have more than one double bond in their fatty acid chain. They tend to be liquid even when refrigerated. They include omega-3 and 6 fatty acids.

Prebiotics—nondigestible food ingredients (for example, inulin and certain fibers) that promote the growth of beneficial microorganisms in the intestines.

Probiotics—beneficial microorganisms that live in the body, primarily in the gastrointestinal tract.

Saturated fats—these fats have all available carbon bonds paired with hydrogen atoms. They are solid at room temperature.

Index

Credits

Picture credits
(t)= top, (c)= center, (b)= bottom

Shutterstock.com: 7 sarsmis; 8-9 TDway; 10 Anna Hoychuk; 11 baranq; 12 MaraZe; 16 michaeljung; 17 BlueSkyImage; 19 Stephen VanHorn; 21 Valery Bareta; 23 YuliaKotina; 24 zoryanchik; 27 ElenaGaak; 29 nevodka; 33 Rido; 34-35 amenic181; 36 Subbotina Anna; 38 Anna Hoychuk; 39(t) Anna Hoychuk; 39(c) stockcreations; 39(b) msheldrake; 41 MSPhotographic; 42(c) Sergiy Zavgorodny; 42(b) MSPhotographic; 43(t) Milarka; 43(c) Viktor1; 43(b) svry; 45 Fanfo; 46 Michael Vesia; 47(t) margouillat photo; 47(c) Gayvoronskaya_Yana; 47(b) HLPhoto; 48 NinaM; 49 Anna_Pustynnikova; 51(t) Josef Hanus; 51(c) Wollertz; 51(b) Arsti; 53 Digivic; 54(c) Valerio Pardi; 54(b) HLPhoto; 55(t) Shaiith; 55(c) Jacques Palut; 55(b) Agnes Kantaruk; 57 stockcreations; 59(c) Dani Vincek; 59(b) Paul Cowan; 60(t) sarsmis; 60(c) svry; 60(b) Lesya Dolyuk; 61(t) Bildagentur Zoonar GmbH; 61(c) Otokimus; 61(b) Elena Fabbrili; 63 Africa Studio; 64 Ingrid Balabanova; 65(t) Kalavati; 65(b) zoryanchik; 66 amenic181; 68(c) Jacek Chabraszewski; 68(b) MaraZe; 69(t) Anna Hoychuk; 69(c) Elena Shashkina; 69(b) B. and E. Dudzinscy; 71 Peteer; 72 Dar1930; 73(t) Filipe B. Varela; 73(c) Visionsi; 73(b) Marina Onokhina; 75 Cristi Lucaci; 76(c) svry; 76(b) margouillat photo; 77 Jill Chen; 79 karelnoppe; 80(c) PHB.cz (Richard Semik); 80(b) Lilyana Vynogradova; 81(t) Gayvoronskaya_Yana; 81(c) Pawel Strykowski; 81(b) Robin Stewart; 83 sarsmis; 84 Gayvoronskaya_Yana; 86(t) Kentaro Foto; 86(c) Dream79; 86(b) pixfly; 87 Karpenkov Denis; 89 Bloor; 90 Natalia Van Doninck; 92 Lukas Gojda; 94(c) Dani Vinceks; 94(b) Alexander Raths; 95(t) Zaira Zarotti; 95(c) DJ Srki; 95(b) Troyker; 96(t) Dani Vincek; 96(c) Anna Hoychuk; 96(b) Viktory Panchenko; 97 Aneta_Gu; 99 Kondor83; 100 Photosiber; 101(t) Angorius; 101(b) Anna Hoychuk; 102(c) Dream79; 102(b) ilolab; 103(t) Olga Lyubkina; 103(c) artemisphoto; 103(b) gori910; 105 Shaiith; 106 yonibunga; 108(c) Brent Hofacker; 108(b) B. and E. Dudzinscy; 109(t) Charlotte Lake; 109(c) Elena Shashkina; 109(b) Yevgeniya Shal; 110(t) Andrii Opanasenko; 110(c) Brent Hofacker; 110(b) peuceta; 111(t) Brent Hofacker; 111(b) Tim UR; 113 Brent Hofacker; 114 stockcreations; 115 Tim UR; 116 Kati Molin; 117(t) pilipphoto; 117(c) Dani Vincek; 117(b) zhekoss; 118(c) Viktor1; 118(b) Gayvoronskaya_Yana; 119(t) Quanthem; 119(c) Chamille White; 119(b) Space Monkey Pics; 120(c) bitt24; 120(b) sarsmis; 121(t) Dream79; 121(c) Olha Afanasieva; 121(b) Handmade-Pictures; 123 pearl7; 124(c) Orlio; 124(b) Magdalena Kucova; 125(t) sarsmis; 125(c) DarZel; 125(b) Svetlana Foote; 127 PG Studija; 128(c) jreika; 128(b) yasuhiro amano; 129(t) Madlen; 129(c) Only Fabrizio; 129(b) Miyuki Satake; 131 Mr. Suttipon Yakham; 132 Brent Hofacker; 134(c) Gayvoronskaya_Yana; 134(b) Sea Wave; 135(t) Gayvoronskaya_Yana; 135(c) Diana Taliun; 135(b) marekuliasz; 136(t) Diana Taliun; 136(c) Gayvoronskaya_Yana; 136(b) Christian Jung; 137(c) Gayvoronskaya_Yana; 137(b) tharamust; 138(t) Elena Elisseeva; 138(c) Sea Wave; 138(b) HandmadePictures; 140 Yulia Davidovich; 142(c) HandmadePictures; 142(b) Dionisvera; 143(t) Volosina; 143(c) matka_Wariatka; 143(b) Wiktory; 144 Dionisvera; 145 Liv friis-larsen; 146(c) HandmadePictures; 146(b) nookieme; 147(t) id-art; 147(c) guentermanaus; 147(b) gresei; 148(c) sarsmis; 148(b) Wiktory; 149(c) Orlio;

More About the Author

Christine Bailey
www.christinebailey.co.uk

Christine is a member of the British Association for Applied Nutrition and Nutritional Therapy (BANT), Complementary and Natural Healthcare Council (CNHC) and the NHS Directory of Complementary Therapists. Christine adheres to the strict BANT Code of Ethics and Practice.

THE TRAVEL DOCTOR

YOUR GUIDE TO STAYING
HEALTHY WHILE YOU TRAVEL

Mark Wise

M.D., D.T.M.& H. (London)

FIREFLY BOOKS

A FIREFLY BOOK

Published by Firefly Books Ltd., 2002

The medical information in this book is meant as a guideline and should be used in conjunction with a visit to your doctor or travel clinic.

First Printing

National Library of Canada Cataloguing in Publication Data

Wise, Mark (Mark R.)
        The travel doctor : your guide to staying healthy while you travel / Mark Wise.
Includes index.
ISBN 1-55297-668-8
        1. Travel—Health aspects. I. Title.
RA783.5.W584 2002   613.6'8   C2002-901828-5

Publisher Cataloging-in-Publication Data (U.S.)

Wise, Mark.
  The travel doctor : your guide to staying healthy while you travel / Mark Wise.—1st ed.
[304] p. : ill., maps ; cm.
Includes index.
Summary: Guide to avoiding health risks when traveling. Includes tips on jet lag, altitude sickness, culture shock, parasites and traveling with a medical condition.
ISBN 1-55297-668-8 (pbk.)
1. Travel—Health aspects. 2. Travel. 3. Preventive Medicine—Methods. I. Title.
613.6/ 8   21   CIP   RA783.5.W57 2002

Published in Canada in 2002 by
Firefly Books Ltd.
3680 Victoria Park Avenue
Toronto, Ontario M2H 3K1

Published in the United States in 2002 by
Firefly Books (U.S.) Inc.
P.O. Box 1338, Ellicott Station
Buffalo, New York 14205

Cover and design: George Walker
Maps and diagrams: George Walker
Cartoons: Max Licht (www.maxlicht.com)

Printed and bound in Canada by
Friesens,
Altona, Manitoba

The Publisher acknowledges the financial support of the Government of Canada through the Book Publishing Industry Development Program for its publishing activities.

THE TRAVEL DOCTOR

YOUR GUIDE TO STAYING HEALTHY WHILE YOU TRAVEL

CONTENTS

Introduction

"Travel expands the mind ... but loosens the bowels" are the words you will hear most often from the mouths of travel medicine professionals. And while the latter will often be true in spite of reading this book, it's the former that is by far the most important. The reasons we travel are as infinite as the number of travelers. We travel abroad to study, to work and to volunteer, to relax, to pray, to adopt children, to visit friends and family and to explore. No corner of the world is too remote. And when we do explore, it's not just places we discover, but people, cultures, smells, colors, tastes and ideas and so much more about ourselves.

My interest in travel and travel medicine began in the mid 1970s, when I spent three months backpacking through South America in search of Butch Cassidy's resting place. My friend and colleague Dr. Howard Hamer and I never found that spot (we did find Simón Bolívar's resting place), but my memories of Cartagena, Riobamba, Otovalo, Ayacucho, Machu Picchu, Rio de Janeiro, the Pampas, Iguassu Falls and Cochabamba are all still clear in my mind. So is that near fatal flight from Rio to Santa Cruz.

Since that time, I have been most fortunate to be involved in the fields of tropical and travel medicine. I have had the pleasure of doing predeparture medical briefings for scores of remarkable young, and not so young, people from all walks of life. In addition, I have provided pretravel advice in my office to many thousands of travelers. And while my work and family have taken me to most corners of the earth, I am probably also one of the world's most experienced vicarious travelers.

Travel medicine concerns itself mainly with the health risks when we "go over there," and that's what most of this book addresses. But often travelers "come here"—and their diseases (e.g., tuberculosis) travel along. Sometimes everyone stays put and the organisms do the traveling, which is what happened in 1981 when cholera traveled by boat from Asia to Peru and reintroduced this dreaded infection to the Western Hemisphere. Guatemalan raspberries contaminated with Cyclospora have turned up in our desserts in North America. West Nile fever probably hitched a ride on a bird or mosquito from the Middle East.

This book began several years ago as a series of newsletters called *The Travel Clinic News*. The newsletters evolved into *Malaria, Montezuma and Me,* a guide written with Voluntary Service Overseas (VSO) Canada volunteers in mind. (This nongovernmental organization is one of many excellent organizations sending people abroad to share their skills with those in less fortunate countries.) *The Travel Doctor* is more comprehensive, aimed at providing just about every traveler with the health information they will require.

There is a saying, *"You've got nothing unless you have your health."* Perhaps that's not entirely true, but it sure helps, especially when you travel abroad. When we get sick at home, we have quick access to our family doctor and specialists, the local walk-in or emergency clinic, the latest technology, the Internet and our mother. We speak the local language and understand the treatment we receive. In the middle of Borneo, everything is different, including the diseases you may have. When it comes to malaria, there are more conflicting opinions than there are species of mosquitoes. Therefore, I strongly believe that all travelers should be equipped with knowledge of the health risks to which they may be exposed. A well-informed traveler is more likely to be a healthy traveler.

The purpose of this book is to provide you with the necessary information so that you will be in the best position to stay healthy while abroad. It's not a substitute for going to your doctor or a travel clinic. But I am certain it will make your visit that much more worthwhile. In fact, I am confident that the doctor or nurse in the clinic will use this book as well. Being realistic, I have also tried to give you some tips about what to do should you fall ill. And yes, I must admit that in spite of my best intentions, some of my most vivid memories over the years have been of dysentery in Ecuador, sunburns in Guatemala, scorpions in Burkina Faso, bedbugs in London and jet lag in Toronto.

I have divided the book into five main parts, which tend to overlap. Part One looks at what you need to consider during the planning stages. Where do I find out about the health risks, what medicines and supplies should I take along, what will I do if I get sick abroad? Next, people tend to worry the most about infectious diseases, especially when they go to tropical destinations. As you'll read in Part Two, some of these can be prevented with vaccines, some with condoms and others with pills; but most important is your personal behavior. Not all that might ail you is infectious. Part Three covers all these concerns—too many time zones, too much sun, too much altitude, not enough heat, too much heat, snakes and spiders, and a totally different culture. Each traveler is unique. Your age, purpose for travel and underlying medical problems are all important when it comes to maintaining your health while away. In Part Four you'll probably find a chapter on yourself or your travel companion. Finally, what do you do when you get home and your temperature hits 101.5°F, your bowels let loose, you can't stop scratching … and more? You'll find the answers— and the answers to all sorts of other questions—in Part Five.

There are no absolute responses to all the issues: Who needs what inoculation? Which antimalarial is best? What do I take for diarrhea? How can I beat jet lag? Am I fit to travel? Even travel medicine professionals have trouble agreeing on everything. But let's hope the information provided in this book will help you make informed decisions.

This book contains quite a bit of medical information. Doctors have a bad habit of speaking a language that no one else understands. That's why we studied Latin. Wherever possible I add an intelligible explanation for any *medicalisms* used. Specific medications are written in both their generic and brand names. Units of measurement have taken on an American form in most cases, despite my roots in Canada.

It's quite easy to read a book such as this, which dwells on watery diarrhea, 30-inch worms, treacherous roads, deadly viruses, sharp needles and bugs galore, and decide not to go anywhere. That's not the idea. As I tell all my travelers before they leave:

• There are lots of interesting infections and conditions out there.

- With a little bit of knowledge, common sense and luck, I'm sure you won't encounter most of them.
- I think that you should know about them anyway.
- You just might feel better than ever while you are away.

So, regardless of where you are going and what you will be doing, I hope that you enjoy this book and find it helpful. Have a great trip, and stay well.

* * *

This book is dedicated to all those who travel, especially the ones who are forced to do so out of fear of persecution.

PART ONE

Before You Go

ELEPHANTS - THEKADY - Kerala - India

Dear Dr. Wise

Hey. It's your lawyer clients,
Rob + Alysse, hopping around India
with enough pills to knock out the
elephants in the photo.
We have spent most of our
time in the South.
Thanks for your help in trip
preparation. It was invaluable.
Hope you're enjoying the snow!
Will see you again in July.
Regards,
Rob + Alysse

SWAGAT

DR. MARK WISE
2300 John Street
Thornhill, ON
L3T 6G7
CANADA

Getting Ready

CHAPTER 1

"Uncertainty and anticipation are the joys of travel."
KEN HUNDERT

Once you have decided to go away, whether for a week or for two years, the fun begins. That is, unless you just found out that you are leaving tomorrow. In any case, you will undoubtedly have many things on your mind, such as planning your itinerary, preparing a budget, deciding what to pack, getting to the airport on time ... and much more. Hopefully, one of the items on your list will be your health while you are abroad. With this in mind, you should probably ask yourself some questions, such as:

• Do I need any inoculations or shots before I go?
• Where can I get them and how soon should I begin?
• Will I be traveling in malarious areas?
• What medications should I be taking along?
• What other medical supplies will I need?
• Are there any safety precautions I should be aware of?
• Am I healthy enough to travel? Would it be best to see my doctor before I go?
• Does the fact that I plan to climb Mount Kilimanjaro three weeks after my heart attack make a difference?
• I may be pregnant. Is that OK?
• Where will I get clean water?
• Is there anything else over there that I don't know about, but should?

- What do I do and whom do I see if I become sick while I'm away?
- If something's the matter with me when I get home, who's going to figure that out?

Now that you've asked all these questions, you should probably arrange to see your doctor. If he or she isn't able to provide the accurate, up-to-date advice you need, then you should probably head off to see someone at a travel clinic. Whether it's a doctor or a nurse, this someone should know a great deal about travel medicine.

What Is a Travel Doctor ... or Nurse?

Most doctors cannot truly empathize with their patients. If that were so, the cardiologist would need to undergo a coronary artery bypass, the gastroenterologist a colonoscopy, the gynecologist, childbirth (especially the male ones) and the urologist ... well, figure it out. But for the travel doc (or nurse), things are much easier. You pick your destination, book a flight, get some shots and pack some Imodium®, and you're off. It's certainly how I have picked up a lot of practical information.

Your travel medicine professional must have a broad knowledge of many fields of medicine in order to advise the young and the elderly, the pregnant, the infected, and people with chronic illnesses or disabilities. The professional will also require a good understanding of tropical medicine—malaria, typhoid fever, hepatitis A through E, schistosomiasis, trypanosomiasis, filariasis, onchocerciasis, and many more exotic and unpronounceable infections ending in "iasis." Not all that ails us is infectious. Jet lag, culture shock and altitude sickness are only a few of the other discomforts that may need to be considered prior to travel. It is very helpful if your doctor knows the destinations to which you are going. Most doctors, and most other people for that matter, wouldn't know which way to head if they were off to Bhutan, Burkina Faso or Bolivia. Finally, your adviser should be well versed in world climate, local geography, religious customs, global politics, festivals and human behavior. Being a travel doctor, I can tell you that this is the most interesting part of the job. A few masks or photographs on the wall may suggest that the doctor has been there, or at least knows someone who has.

The travel doctor can only advise the traveler on vaccines, antimalarials and precautions. *"The doctor advises ... the patient decides."* Travelers may base their decisions upon several factors, such as their perception of the risks, their love of needles and their budget.

Pretravel advice should be about much more than just needles and pills. You should also learn how your own personal behavior can greatly lessen the likelihood of most infections and other catastrophes.

As well, you should find out how to deal with certain medical problems, should they arise.

When you go for your medical advice, there is the very real chance that you will be left with the message, *"Don't eat, don't drink, don't drive, don't go outdoors at night, don't leave your hotel, don't meet anyone ... don't have any fun."* This should not be the message. However, if I may be a bit facetious, the minimum message should be, *"Have a great time, but at least don't have sex without a condom and mosquito repellent while sipping local water in the back of a moving bus at night in rural Nigeria or Brazil or Thailand."*

I hope that the following chapters provide you with much of the information you will need to know. So on your mark, get ready ... get set!

The Common Sense Guide

CHAPTER 2

"I dislike feeling at home when I am abroad."
GEORGE BERNARD SHAW

While I do hope you read this book from cover to cover, it may be worthwhile to touch on the high points before you get going:

1. *Use your common sense.* It's the most important thing you can take along.
2. Be proactive about your health. Stay physically fit, mentally fit, well rested and well fed.
3. Get the recommended and/or required pretravel inoculations. Visit a travel clinic.
4. The most common problems will be related to your stomach and bowels. *"Boil it, bottle it, filter it, purify it, peel it, cook it ... or forget it."* And be sure to wash your hands.
5. Take along something to treat your diarrhea, such as Imodium® and Cipro®, and remember to replace your fluids if you become ill.
6. Carry the appropriate medications and medical supplies, and carry them appropriately.
7. Avoid mosquitoes and other insects. Use an insect repellent (containing DEET)—day and night. In malarious areas, sleep under a mosquito net.

8. Do not believe everything you hear or read about malaria and antimalarials. (But please believe what you read in this book.) Take your antimalarial medication as directed.
9. HIV/AIDS is transmitted through unprotected sex, through needles and through blood products. Abstain, or use a latex condom ... every time.
10. Death is transmitted through car accidents. Avoid driving in rural areas after dark.
11. Be aware of your personal safety at all times.
12. Avoid dogs and other moving animals. Know what to do if you get bitten.
13. Don't abuse alcohol.
14. Carry adequate medical and travel insurance.
15. If you can manage only one of these tips, choose number 1. And one more thing.
16. Have a great trip.

First Aid

CHAPTER 3

*"The alternative to a vacation is to stay home
and tip every third person you see."*

AUTHOR UNKNOWN

This chapter is not intended to turn you into a paramedic, an emergency nurse or a doctor. Ideally you are already traveling with one. The next best thing is to take a course in first aid and cardio-pulmonary resuscitation (CPR). Watching reruns of *ER* may help remind you of the basic measures to take in the event of a minor, or not so minor, mishap.

Keep in mind that most accidents and injuries are preventable. Some would argue that all are preventable. I wouldn't go quite that far. But appropriate clothing, plenty of fluids, strict attention to cleanliness, good footwear, staying out of fights, sensible use of alcohol, keeping away from animals, knowing when to rest, listening to good advice and, I suppose, some luck will help you avoid most unwanted catastrophes. A little bit of knowledge, and more common sense, will help you deal with problems should they arise.

Cuts and Scrapes

Cuts and scrapes are perhaps the most common minor emergencies you will encounter. Swiss Army® knives are great, but be careful when you check out those 42 different blades. Keep in mind that in a hot, humid, less-than-sanitary environment (e.g., rural Africa), simple wounds may be more prone to infection. The mouths of most animals, especially humans, are teeming with bacteria, so

bites need to be cleaned extremely well and may warrant oral
antibiotics. To look after most minor injuries:

- Thoroughly cleanse the wound with soap and water, or with any
  other antiseptic. Any foreign material should be removed if possible. If you are traveling in a far-off country, it will all be foreign. Dead, ragged skin can be carefully trimmed away.
- Apply direct pressure to the site of bleeding. Elevate the affected
  area. These two measures, especially the first, will help stop most
  types of bleeding.
- Protect the wound by covering it first with a dry, sterile dressing
  or bandage. Then add padding and protection with a covering of
  additional bandages.
- If the cut is deep or if the skin edges are apart, consider the need
  for sutures (stitches), or try to bring the edges together with a
  butterfly bandage.
- Watch for signs of infection—redness, swelling, soreness,
  increased warmth, or pus coming from the wound. Topical
  and/or oral antibiotics may be necessary.
- If you are not up to date with your tetanus shots (you should be),
  now may be the time to get a shot.
- If a dog, monkey or other furry animal has caused your cut or
  abrasion, quickly read Chapter 6, Pretravel Inoculation, and consider the need for a series of rabies shots. Call home if necessary.
- If you have a penetrating injury, such as from a knife or a branch,
  do not attempt to remove the object. Cover the wound with a
  sterile dressing and stabilize it with bulky bandages ... and go for
  help!

Burns

The day before Benjamin and I arrived in Ghorepani in the
Annapurna range of Nepal, a teahouse burned to the ground,
killing two Nepalese children. The cause was a candle burning in
one of the rooms. I would suggest that you avoid smoking in bed
(or anywhere for that matter) or reading by candlelight. The following is the first aid treatment for "minor" burns:

- Remove the "burnee" from the source of the burn.
- Immerse the affected area in cold water.
- Cleanse gently with soap and water or another antiseptic.
- Butter goes on your bagel ... not on your burn!
- For first-degree burns (redness only)—these may be left open to the air; topical remedies such as aloe vera or vitamin E cream are said to speed up healing.
- For second-degree burns, which form blisters—do not pop the blisters. (The intact skin helps to prevent infection.) Cover with a nonadherent dressing, such as Telfa® or Sofratulle®, and wrap regular gauze around this to keep the dressing in place; change the dressing daily at first, then every two or three days until it has dried up.
- Use analgesics such as aspirin, acetaminophen or ibuprofen for pain relief.

Third-degree or full-thickness burns do not blister. They appear charred black or waxy white and may lack sensation. Extensive burns may result in significant fluid losses and shock. There may also be damage to the airway and lungs. Transportation to adequate medical care is necessary.

Blisters

Not all blisters come from burns. More commonly they arise as a result of repetitive friction, which acts like a burn. In the case of your feet, your hands or anywhere else, a blister will usually be preceded by a "hot spot." This is the stage at which treatment should be started, for if it progresses on to a blister, the pain and disability may be extreme.

If you are hiking or doing something else repetitive (like playing lots of squash while on vacation), do a foot check from time to time. Should there be an area that is red or sore, fiddle with or change your socks, adjust your laces and apply a lubricant such as Vaseline® and/or some moleskin. If you do develop a blister, do the following:

- Try to leave the "bubble" intact, as it acts as a sterile barrier.

- Cover it with a sterile, nonadherent dressing.
- If the blister pops on its own, wash it with soap and water, apply a topical antibiotic and cover it with a sterile dressing. Do not remove the collapsed skin.
- If the blister is in an awkward spot, such as your heel, it may be punctured with a sterile needle or pin (sterilize with a flame or alcohol), leaving the collapsed skin in place to act as a sterile dressing. Apply an antibiotic cream and a sterile dressing.

Nosebleeds

Most nosebleeds result from blunt trauma to the nose (where else?). This is often delivered in the form of a fist, though it may occur spontaneously. The bleeding usually originates from the front of the nose along the septum, the wall dividing the two nostrils. To treat a nosebleed:

- Calm the person.
- Have the person sit forward so that the blood does not drip down the back of the throat.
- Apply firm pressure—pinch the soft parts of the nose between your thumb and index finger—for 15 minutes or so. (Do not release the pressure every other minute to check on your progress.)
- Apply ice to the nose if possible.
- Seek further medical care if the bleeding does not stop or if you suspect an underlying fracture. (These things are sometimes obvious.)

Dental Problems

No one likes to visit the dentist at home. Imagine having to see one during your vacation, where the magazines in the waiting room may be in a foreign language and, more importantly, the equipment may not be sterile (think hepatitis B and HIV). If you are going away for more than a few months, visit your dentist before you leave to make sure there are no imminent problems.

Teeth sometimes get knocked out or broken. This does not usually happen spontaneously. If you lose a tooth, retrieve it, rinse it in clean water and keep it moist in a wet washcloth or milk, or tucked away in your mouth. Handle it by the crown, that is, the chewing surface. If possible, place it back in its socket, and try to see a dentist within 30 minutes. For a fractured tooth, try to save the broken piece; again, head off to the dentist. Painkillers, ice packs or topical agents such as clove oil may give some welcome relief. Let's face it. You will not always be that close to a dentist.

A toothache is not a good sign. It may arise for several reasons, including dental cavities, a dental abscess, gum disease or irritation of the nerve root. When an infection is present, there is often associated swelling of the gum and cheek. Antibiotics and/or a dentist are the usual treatment. If you have pre-existing dental problems, you may be subject to a wicked toothache, or barodontalgia, at altitudes between 5,000 and 15,000 feet. This is due to the expansion of trapped gas in accordance with Boyle's law. The pain will resolve as you descend.

Strains and Sprains

Thankfully, most strains and sprains are minor and get better on their own within a few days. They usually result from overuse of some part of your body (e.g., your legs, when you are trekking in Nepal) or an accident (e.g., spraining your ankle, when you are trekking in Nepal). The phrase *"Take two aspirin and call me in the morning"* was designed for such injuries. These may have to be differentiated from more serious injuries such as fractures or dislocations. Often the victim can help you tell the difference, by using phrases such as *"I felt something pop out of place,"* or *"I heard it snap,"* or *"There's no way I can stand on it!"* Looking at the injury and noticing that the area appears deformed and immediately swollen should also help. In such cases, you will have to seek good medical care. In the meantime, the principles of treatment are the same as for strains and sprains.

This can be summarized with the acronym RICE:

- **Rest**—Stop the activity that caused the injury until the pain and swelling have subsided.
- **Ice**—This will help to reduce or limit the swelling, and hence the pain, by reducing blood flow to the injured area. An ice pack, a bag of frozen veggies or anything else that's cold can be applied for up to 20 minutes at a time, every few hours, for the first few days. A piece of fabric or a bandage between the ice and the skin is a good idea.
- **Compression**—Wrapping an elastic bandage around the site of the injury will also help to minimize the swelling, and will keep the affected area a bit more at rest. Bandages should be wrapped firmly, but not too tightly. If the fingers or toes are turning blue and feeling cold, this is a bit too tight!
- **Elevation**—This also helps to prevent swelling, and may make it easier for you to rest.

Heat will attract more blood flow to the injured area, and should be avoided in the acute stage. However, during the recovery stage it would be beneficial, and might feel good. Tiger Balm®, at greatly inflated prices, is one of the hottest-selling items in the streets of Kathmandu. Overpaid professional athletes may require an immediate MRI (magnetic resonance imaging) of their injury. You probably won't.

If you do suspect a more serious injury, such as a fracture or dislocation, it's best to immobilize the arm, leg, wrist, finger or whatever before going for further medical care. An appropriate splint may consist of a rigid board or plastic, a pillow, a magazine or anything else that will limit movement. Fingers can be splinted to an adjacent finger, legs to an adjacent leg. Splint the injured area above and below the injury site. If things look a bit deformed or misshapen, do not try to make corrections. *"Splint it as it lies"* is the rule of thumb. Unnecessary manipulation may damage nearby blood vessels and nerves. If possible, make a regular check of the circulation beyond the injury site. A sling will help immobilize shoulders, arms and wrists.

Cold Injury

There are many popular destinations where the risk of cold injury exists. Many of them are literally right in our own backyards. Temperature decreases with altitude, not only leading to cold injury, but aggravating altitude sickness as well. Alcohol, cigarette smoking and tight or wet clothing will also add to the risk of such injuries.

Frostbite is what occurs when our body tissues freeze. This is most likely to happen on an exposed surface, such as the ears, the nose or an extremity—the fingers and toes. When freezing occurs, ice crystals form within the cells. Remember that water expands when it freezes to ice, causing the cells to rupture and die. That, along with impairment of the local circulation, leads to death of the tissues.

Frostnip usually precedes frostbite. At this stage, only the superficial layers of the skin have frozen. This is comparable to a first-degree burn. The affected area will appear white or gray (pink or red in dark-skinned people) and will feel numb. Movement remains intact. If further exposure takes place, it may become blistered and turn black in color. Frostbite occurs when all of the tissues—skin, nerves, muscles, blood vessels—have frozen. It will appear white or bluish, and feel woody to the touch. Movement is lost and sensation is absent.

Frostnip should be treated promptly if possible, as it may continue on to frostbite if left untreated. Immersing the affected part in warm water (105°F/40.5°C) and protecting it from further cold should suffice. If you can't find your thermometer, the water should feel hot, but not too uncomfortable to touch. Warm up your body as well with some hot soup and warm clothing. An analgesic such as aspirin or ibuprofen can be taken, as the rewarming process may be quite uncomfortable.

Frostbite requires similar rewarming. The tissues should be handled carefully to avoid causing more damage. Bandages and a splint should be applied. The main pitfall in the treatment of frostbite is the danger of refreezing and, hence, more tissue damage. For that reason, rewarming should not be started until you are sure there will be no further exposure to the cold. It's better to hobble on a frostbitten foot until proper medical care is available than to thaw the extremity, only to have it freeze again. It may take several months before the extent of damage from frostbite is evident, but certainly loss of fingers, toes and ears can occur.

Chilblains and trench foot are milder injuries than frostbite, and occur when an extremity is exposed to both wet and cold. The treatment is similar, and there are usually no long-term problems.

Hypothermia

When we are exposed to cold environments, the body has two methods of coping. Number one, the blood vessels to the skin constrict or narrow, so that our blood flow is redirected to the center of the body and we lose less heat to the environment. If this doesn't work, we shiver, which produces heat through muscle action. When these mechanisms are overwhelmed, our core temperature falls below 96°F/35°C. This may occur quickly, such as when we are dropped in frigid water, or more gradually over hours or days. The very old or very young, the intoxicated or those on certain medications may be predisposed to hypothermia.

In addition to being cold and shivering, the hypothermic person may become confused, irritable and, eventually, comatose. This is not unlike high altitude cerebral edema (HACE), which may be aggravated by hypothermia.

To treat hypothermia:

- Get the person out of the cold, away from the wind and moisture, and off the cold ground.
- Remove any wet or cold clothing.
- Cover the person up with warm blankets, a sleeping bag or dry clothing. Apply heat sources such as a hot water bottle or heating pad (but not directly on the skin).
- Warm up the environment with a fire, some sunshine or warm bodies.
- Do not aim for rapid rewarming, such as immersing the person in warm water.
- Offer warm fluids and something sweet to eat.

More severe hypothermia is a medical emergency and requires transport to a medical facility.

Seizures

Seizures or convulsions occur when there is an uncoordinated burst of electrical activity in the brain. In a classical grand mal seizure, this leads to loss of consciousness (though the eyes may stay open), uncontrolled shaking (tonic-clonic) movements of the extremities, and often incontinence of urine and feces. Lacerations of the tongue are common. The seizure may be followed by a period of drowsiness and confusion. Most seizures last less than a few minutes, and there is usually a complete recovery. They may be alarming, but are rarely life-threatening.

There are many causes for a convulsion, the most common of which would be the failure to take one's regular medications (in the case of someone with pre-existing epilepsy). Children under the age of four may develop a "febrile" convulsion when they have a high fever. A convulsion in someone with a fever, particularly in the tropics, should raise the possibility of malaria or meningitis. Travelers with a history of seizures should not be taking the anti-malarial mefloquine (Lariam®).

The basic treatment of a seizure is as follows:

- Protect the person from further injury (move away from furniture, fire or water).
- Place them on their side if there is an excess of saliva, blood or vomit in the mouth.
- Do not restrain the person.
- Do not place anything in the person's mouth, especially your fingers.
- Seek medical care if there is not a full recovery or there is an associated medical problem such as a fever.
- If someone has a "first" seizure with no obvious cause, they should be assessed as soon as possible by a medical professional.

Heat Exposure

When your car's cooling mechanism breaks down, things go terribly wrong. Smoke starts coming out from under the hood and four-letter words start coming out of your mouth. Our body is no different. We have two main mechanisms to keep our core temperature at about 98.6°F/37°C in the face of extreme heat. First, our blood is redirected to the skin and our blood vessels dilate. This allows us to radiate some of the excess heat into the environment. Then we sweat, hopefully a lot. As the sweat evaporates, it acts to cool us down. When the humidity is high, the sweat may not evaporate as quickly or at all. In very dry or windy conditions, it may evaporate so quickly that you don't even notice yourself dripping. Your ability to adapt may also depend upon your age and certain medications that you may be taking.

Heat exhaustion is the first sign of trouble. It is characterized by a normal or slightly elevated temperature, headache, thirst, nausea and vomiting, dizziness and weakness, and, as the name implies, exhaustion. The skin may be pale, cool or moist. Treatment consists of:

- Moving the person into a cooler spot, such as the shade (most sensible local people are already there). Remove excess clothing.
- Replacing fluids. Oral rehydration will usually suffice (the cooler the better). Drink small amounts of fluid frequently, rather than gulping down large amounts, which may result in further vomiting. Keep track of urine output to assess the state of hydration. (Clear urine is better than dark, concentrated urine.)

True heatstroke is a medical emergency. The body's cooling mechanisms have failed. The temperature rises dramatically, often as high as 106°F/41°C. The skin is red, hot and dry. Confusion may progress to loss of consciousness. Your initial treatment may involve cooling the person with cool, wet towels or sheets, ice packs and fanning. Seeking out more sophisticated medical care is necessary.

Prickly heat or heat rash is not quite a life-threatening condition, but it can be a nuisance and it is common in hot, humid climates. It is caused when the narrow ducts through which sweat travels to the surface become clogged. This results in itching, irritation and small blisters or red bumps, mainly on the trunk and the thighs. Treatment consists of somehow keeping your skin cool and dry, and perhaps applying a cortisone cream.

As one of my dermatology professors once said, *"There's a fungus among us!"* This is especially true in Costa Rican rain forests and other such locales. "Athlete's foot" between the toes and "jock itch" in the groin are both caused by funguses. You can try to prevent these by keeping these areas dry and cool. Loose-fitting cotton clothing and some talcum powder may help. If you do develop a rash, antifungal creams such as Canesten®, Nizoral® or Lamisil® should clear it up.

Fever

An elevated core temperature, or fever, is something that we have all experienced. It is usually a sign that something is wrong—and that something is usually an infection. Heatstroke is one noninfectious cause that must be considered in the tropics. Fevers are often accompanied by other symptoms such as headache, chills and shakes, muscle aches and hot and cold spells. Other signs and symptoms such as a cough, vomiting, diarrhea, a rash or a stiff neck may be present, depending upon the underlying cause of the fever.

Our normal body temperature is about 98.6°F or 37°C. A temperature of 102°F or 39°C would be considered a high fever. Temperatures should be measured with thermometers, since not everyone who feels warm, hot or on fire actually has an elevated temperature. Very high fevers may result in confusion, delirium or —in children under the age of four—febrile convulsions or seizures. While these conditions may be frightening, they usually stop on their own and cause no permanent damage.

Fever can be treated through the following measures:

• Taking medications such as acetaminophen (Tylenol®, Tempra®) or ibuprofen (Advil®). Aspirin must be avoided in children and young adults.
• Removing excess clothing.
• Sitting in a tepid bath (not too hot, not too cold).
• Drinking plenty of fluids.

Remember, it's not the fever that is of concern; it is the cause of that fever. In the tropics, and even after you are home, remember that a fever is a sign of malaria until proven otherwise. Dengue, typhoid, intestinal infections, tick typhus, hepatitis and meningitis are other possible causes. "Nontropical" illnesses also occur. Wherever you are, seek medical care if your fever persists for longer than 24 hours. If you are in a malarious area and far from medical care, hopefully you are equipped with standby emergency treatment, as described in Chapter 8, Malaria.

Head Injuries

Head injuries happen in a variety of ways, including falls from a height, diving injuries, a blow to the head and motor vehicle/motorcycle accidents. Alcohol is often partly responsible. Helmets, seatbelts, safe vehicles, traveling during daylight hours and more common sense are all worth considering. Remember too that doorways in many foreign countries were built with shorter people in mind. Don't forget to duck. I did ... forget, that is!

Thankfully, most head injuries are mild. You see some stars, feel some pain, and that's about all. Cleansing any wounds and applying some ice may be all that is necessary. A concussion is a more serious injury, when the person loses consciousness for up to a few minutes and may wake up confused or with some amnesia. This person should be seen by a doctor if possible.

The brain is like other body tissues—it swells when it is injured. Unfortunately, it is enclosed in the skull, or cranium, a rigid box that does not allow for very much swelling (it does, however, protect your head in most instances). In a severe head injury, where there is internal bleeding or edema (swelling from fluid), increased intracranial pressure may develop, leading to other symptoms and signs. These include severe headache, nausea and vomiting, blood in the ears or the nose and change in level of consciousness (the most important finding to watch for).

We are used to seeing medical personnel shining flashlights in the eyes of head-injured patients. If you do this and if the pupils appear to be unequal, it is unlikely that your patient will do very well. Anyone suspected of having a severe head injury must be evacuated to a place with good medical care. Remember, when there is a head injury, there is often an injury to the neck and cervical spine as well. To avoid making matters worse, immobilize the neck properly before moving the person. If you do not know how to do this properly, find somebody who does.

Allergic Reactions

These are extremely common, and may be caused by drugs (e.g., penicillin, sulfa), foods (e.g., peanuts) or insect stings (e.g., bees and wasps). Anaphylaxis is the most frightening and severe, but infrequent, allergic reaction. It begins minutes after exposure to an allergic agent and progresses rapidly. The most serious consequence is a constriction or narrowing of the airways and a dilation of blood vessels, resulting in difficult breathing, a rapid pulse, a fall in blood pressure, shock and death.

The treatment of this life-threatening emergency is an immediate subcutaneous injection of adrenaline or epinephrine. Other useful medications (which you may not have) include oxygen, steroids and antihistamines (e.g., Benadryl®). If you have a serious allergy you should be wearing a MedicAlert® bracelet and carrying an EpiPen®. If you are responsible for others, you should be aware of any medical problems in the group, including allergies, and know how to deal with them.

A milder form of an allergic reaction would be hives or urticaria—those red, itchy welts that come and go all over your body. This can be treated with antihistamines alone. Somewhere in between anaphylaxis and urticaria is what is called angioedema. This consists of acute facial swelling, usually around the eyes and/or the lips. This should be treated with an antihistamine, as well as adrenaline if there is any difficulty with breathing.

Eye Problems

Most eye problems are minor and can be treated with simple measures. If you think that an injury is more serious, seek medical attention. Perhaps the commonest ailment is conjunctivitis, or "pink eye." Aside from redness, soreness and increased tearing, there is usually some pus or goop, or a lot of pus and goop, which makes your eye sticky and difficult to open in the morning. Treatment consists of bathing the eye with warm water and using antibiotic eye drops, such as 10 percent sodium sulamyd or gentamicin (Garamycin®). Keep your fingers out of your eyes, use your own towels and keep your hands off your friends, loved ones and anyone else.

A foreign body such as dust or sand may get into your eye. This may make your eye red, sore and teary. Hopefully, just flushing or washing your eye with water can remove most irritants. A Q-tip® may be helpful in removing small particles. Sometimes these specks lodge under the eyelid, so do your best to turn the lid "inside out" and take a look. Embedded foreign bodies will require a topical anesthetic, a sterile needle and a steady hand, hopefully at the end of a doctor's arm. If any sort of chemical gets into your eye, immediately flush it with lots of water.

Sometimes a scratch or a foreign body will result in a corneal abrasion. Again the eye will be red and sore, and extremely sensitive to light. A topical antibiotic, and a patch if the person is very uncomfortable, should suffice. These abrasions usually heal on their own within 24 to 48 hours.

If you wear contact lenses, make sure you take along plenty of the correct cleansing solutions, and perhaps a spare pair of glasses just in case.

Exposure to ultraviolet light at high altitudes may be particularly harmful due to the thinness of the atmosphere and the reflection from the snow. This results in keratitis. Pain is severe, there is excessive tearing and redness, and light is bothersome. Treatment consists of analgesics and perhaps an eye patch for comfort, and you can expect to be better within 24 hours. Sunglasses of the wraparound variety should be worn at high altitudes.

Well, I sincerely hope that this covers all of your travel emergencies. If not, it never hurts to ask *"Is there is a doctor in the hostel?"* At our first stop on the Annapurna circuit, an unfortunate Frenchman was carried into town late one afternoon, having slipped and injured his ankle. It was evident to me that there was a fracture, but with rest, ice (cold beer), mild compression and elevation, he was able to remain with us for the night rather than risk being carried down for a few more slippery hours in the dark. The helicopter arrived the next morning.

Don't forget that travel insurance.

First Aid Kits and Other Sundry Items

"What medicines and supplies should I take along?" is a common question we get asked when people are traveling abroad. *"That depends,"* is my usual answer. It depends upon all those risk factors, like where are you going? For how long? What are you

doing? etc. So if you plan to climb Mount Everest as the expedition doctor or sail around the world for a year, you may need slightly more than the businessman off to Bangkok for a week. If you will be residing abroad for some time, you may need to do a little more advance planning. And if you have pre-existing medical conditions or disabilities, you really had better do your homework before you leave.

My first suggestion to most people is to visit your medicine cabinet and see what you normally keep handy around the house. This includes both medications and medical supplies. Then consider how far you'll be from decent medical care. You may need to take along what you would normally get at the drugstore or emergency department. Are you responsible for others, like your children, your students, fellow climbers or a tour group? Then you had better anticipate their needs as well.

If you're taking medications abroad, keep these suggestions in mind:

- Leave your medications in their original labeled containers. Some people suggest that you carry written prescriptions for all your medications.
- Take more than you anticipate you will actually need.
- If you can't afford to lose a medication, then carry it with you at all times.
- If you're traveling with narcotic medications or syringes, carry an official-looking letter with lots of stamps from your doctor explaining why.

There are many excellent commercially available first aid kits. They can usually be personalized for your specific needs. If you're contemplating minor surgery, consider something like the Steri Aid Kit®, which contains sterile supplies such as syringes, needles and suture material. This would be appropriate for someone traveling off the beaten path, someone who is responsible for a group of travelers, or anyone who distrusts needles around the world. While this sort of kit may be of help if you need an injection or a few stitches, it will not bail you out of a serious car accident or a ruptured appendix.

The following is a brief list of some of the more common and useful things to take along. The brand names are not the only ones available. Remember, what you take along will depend upon your particular situation. If you plan to be looking after broken bones, gunshot wounds, cerebral edema and cardiac arrests, you may want to sit down with your doctor over lunch to plan a more extensive list.

Checklist of Suggested Medications

❑ altitude sickness (Diamox®, Adalat®, dexamethasone)
❑ analgesics (acetaminophen, ASA, ibuprofen, codeine, Tylenol #3® or other narcotics)
❑ antacid/ulcers (Maalox®, Zantac®, Losec®)
❑ antibiotics (amoxicillin, cephalexin, erythromycin, ciprofloxacin)
❑ antidiarrheal (Imodium®, Lomotil®, Pepto-Bismol®); antibiotic (Cipro®, Noroxin®, Zithromax®)
❑ antifungal cream (Canesten®, Monistat®, Lamisil®)
❑ antihistamine (Benadryl®)
❑ antimalarials (discuss with medical professional)
❑ antinauseant/motion sickness (Gravol®, Bonamine®, Phenergan®, Transderm V®/Transderm Scop® patches)
❑ bee sting kit (EpiPen®—for those with a history of severe allergic reactions)
❑ cream/pills for vaginal infections (Monistat®, Diflucan®)
❑ eye drops (10% sodium sulamyd, Garamycin®)
❑ an extra pair of glasses or contact lenses, and/or a copy of your prescription
❑ laxatives (Senokot®, Dulcolax®)—not everyone gets just diarrhea
❑ rehydration salts (Gastrolyte®, Pedialyte®)
❑ sunscreen
❑ topical antibiotic (Polysporin®, Fucidin®, Bactroban®)
❑ topical cortisone cream (Celestoderm®, 1% HC)
❑ other prescription and nonprescription medications used regularly

Checklist of Suggested Supplies

❏ adhesive tape
❏ antiseptic (Betadine®)
❏ Band-Aids®
❏ condoms
❏ diary
❏ first aid guide
❏ flashlight and batteries
❏ gauze rolls
❏ insect repellent (containing DEET—Muskol®, Deep Woods Off®, Ultrathon®)
❏ medical records and/or Medic Alert® bracelet
❏ moleskin
❏ mosquito net (preferably impregnated with permethrin)
❏ safety pins
❏ scissors
❏ sewing supplies
❏ small alarm clock
❏ soap, toothpaste, deodorant and other toiletries
❏ sterile dressings
❏ sterile needles, suture supplies (Steri Aid Kit®)
❏ Steri-strips®
❏ Swiss Army® knife
❏ tensor bandage
❏ thermometer
❏ toilet paper
❏ triangular bandage (sling)
❏ tweezers
❏ waterproof matches
❏ water purifier, iodine tablets, Pristine®

Not every box in the lists needs a check mark. Sharp objects such as scissors, knives and tweezers will have to be packed in your checked luggage. Now you can move on to those more mundane necessities of travel—underwear, socks and T-shirts.

Medical Care Abroad

CHAPTER 4

"I never travel without my diary. One should always have something sensational to read in the train."

OSCAR WILDE

When we are planning our trip abroad, we imagine endless beaches, historic sights, romantic dinners, exotic foods, perhaps a bit of diarrhea and probably a few other things that I won't mention. Appendicitis, kidney stones, coronary bypasses, lost baggage, hospital fees, theft and emergency evacuations tend not to enter our mind. By emergency evacuations, I am referring to hurricanes, earthquakes, *coups d'état,* volcanic eruptions and the like, not wicked cases of diarrhea. But bad things sometimes happen to good people like you and me, so it's best to travel prepared ... and insured.

Let's begin by getting prepared. Should you have any pre-existing medical problems, it's wise to carry a letter from your doctor summarizing your condition or conditions. Recent consultation letters and pertinent laboratory reports should be included. A copy of your latest electrocardiogram would be invaluable to the doctor trying to treat your chest pain in Mongolia. While you're at it, record the names and phone numbers of your doctors in case you or someone else needs to contact them.

Personally, I feel that all of your pertinent medical information should be carried with you in writing, though there are many companies that will be happy to store your medical information in their computer back home. Should you become ill abroad, either you or the doctor can access that information by calling their 24-hour toll-free line. It's also possible to have your medical information available through the Internet, as long as you are well enough to punch in your password. Finally, another elegant method is to record everything on a small CD that fits into your wallet. These methods sound great, but they may have some limitations, such as concerns about confidentiality, and the availability of Internet access and CD-ROM drives in far-off lands. Electricity is sometimes a bonus where I travel.

A MedicAlert® bracelet may be low tech, but it's an effective way of informing the local doctor that you have diabetes, dangerous allergies, epilepsy, a pacemaker, artificial valves, artificial hips or other bionic parts. Further information is available through their website (see end of chapter).

Your Medications

Learn the names of your medications and carry a written list. Many people refer to their pills affectionately as "the little round yellow one," or the "white one shaped like a football." This description will probably be inadequate if you lose your medications in Burundi, or most other countries for that matter (their football doesn't look like ours). Most drugs go by two names. The *generic* name is the actual name of the compound, like mefloquine or ciprofloxacin. The brand name is what the manufacturer likes you to call it, like Lariam® or Cipro®. While it's best to know both names, it's imperative that you know at least the generic name, as this will probably be the easiest way to find the equivalent of what you are looking for.

The availability of medications abroad will vary, depending upon your destination and also the particular medication. The more "remote" your destination, and the less "common" your medication, the more difficulty you may have. It's best to carry more medication than you will actually need for your trip and to consider storing it in more than one place. Pills should be carried in their original labeled containers, not all mixed together. Some people suggest that you also carry the written prescriptions as well. If you are carrying narcotic medications, such as codeine, you should carry a letter from your doctor explaining the reason why. This is doubly important if you are carrying syringes for diabetes, life-threatening allergies or other medical conditions. The more official-looking stamps on such a note, the better. For long-term volunteers abroad, I have had very little difficulty sending medications via courier to replenish their supplies.

In many countries, especially the less-developed ones, most medications are available over the counter, or without a prescription. Often these will be sold in their original packaging, so it's possible—hopefully—to know exactly what you are getting. On the other hand, many doctors and clinics will dispense your pills in tiny plastic bags with labeling that's both illegible and in a foreign language. There's a tendency in some countries to manufacture "combination" drugs; that is, something that will deal with your intestinal infection, stomach pain, diarrhea, gas and hair loss all with one tiny pill. This shotgun approach may work, but it does expose you to many more drugs and possible side effects.

Certain medications that we no longer use in North America, or even outdated ones, may show up on the shelves in some distant countries. The antibiotic chloramphenicol, for example, remains in widespread use in many parts of the world. It may suppress your bone marrow, a side effect we consider unacceptable back home.

Halfan® (halofantrine), an antimalarial medication, is available all over the tropics, but again, due to its rare cardiac side effects, North American experts do not recommend it.

"What is the quality of medications abroad?" you might ask. That's a good question! Widespread counterfeiting of medicines, inadequate quality assurance during the manufacturing process and poor storage may all contribute to substandard drugs. Some countries will be worse than others. Whenever possible, therefore, it's best to anticipate your medicinal needs before you leave home.

Medical Insurance

Go ahead. Skimp on your backpack or your hiking boots. But please, when it comes to your medical insurance, buy the best that you can afford. The insurance you may have at home, whether it's government sponsored or totally private, will likely not be adequate should an emergency arise while you are away. Carry proof of your insurance with you at all times. In addition, the cliché *"Read the small print"* could never be truer.

Your travel medical insurance should cover you for several things, including:
- the costs incurred for all doctors', dentists' and hospital fees
- the costs of any prescribed medications
- medical evacuation to the nearest adequate medical facility, and back home as soon as this option becomes possible and practical
- emergency replacement of lost medications or supplies
- emergency cash advances
- assistance in finding medical care abroad

If you have pre-existing medical conditions, you can be certain that your insurer will want to know about them. Unfortunately, this may increase the cost of your premium. For those who plan to engage in some higher-risk pursuit, such as climbing Everest, white water rafting, scuba diving or bungee jumping, make sure that injuries resulting from such hazardous activities are covered.

In addition to supplemental medical insurance, you should strongly consider the need for travel insurance. Important features of this plan would be:

- trip cancellation, interruption or delay protection (due to illness involving yourself, your traveling companion or your family, or other factors such as airline strikes, weather, terrorism)
- protection against the default or bankruptcy of suppliers
- replacement of travel documents such as your driver's license or credit cards
- repatriation in the case of death abroad
- reimbursement for lost luggage or personal possessions
- a 24-hour hotline to provide emergency travel advice and assistance
- legal assistance

Contained in the small print may be situations that are not covered, such as acts of God (floods, earthquakes, hurricanes, etc.), acts of terrorism or hijacking, and wars (declared and undeclared). Some policies may cover only "emergency" medical problems. The definition of "emergency" may be a bit ambiguous.

There are many good companies that provide emergency services to travelers. (See Related Websites at end of chapter.)

Many doctors and medical facilities abroad may be reluctant to bill your insurance provider directly. Make sure that you have access to the necessary funds should an emergency arise. Retain the copies of all receipts for medical services and medications. And don't forget ... read the small print.

How Do I Locate Medical Care Abroad?

There are countless ways of accessing medical care while you are away, but sometimes it pays to do your research before you leave. If you have significant pre-existing medical problems, your regular doctor or specialist may be able to provide you with the name of a long-lost colleague or classmate abroad in case of an emergency. Another option is to join IAMAT (International Association for Medical Assistance to Travellers). For a small donation, this nonprofit organization will provide you with a listing of English-speaking doctors and clinics around the world (I happen to be one of them).

In addition, they will also send you extensive information regarding inoculations, malaria risk and much more. (See Related Websites at end of chapter.)

I realize that it's not always convenient to become ill around the corner from the recommended doctor. In this case, there are a few other options. Your local embassy or consulate should be able to direct you to the best medical care available locally. (See Related Websites at end of chapter.)

The hotel where you are staying may have a "hotel doctor" who would be only too happy to make a housecall. If you are living and working abroad, the company or organization that sent you will probably be able to furnish you with a list of recommended doctors and hospitals. It's always best to know if possible where you should go for your medical care well before you need it. And it sure can't hurt to know a few handy phrases in the local language.

The quality of medical care around the world obviously varies greatly. In rural Burkina Faso, the local hospital was not somewhere you'd want to stay. The ocean view from the rooms of the hospital in Lamu (an island off the coast of Kenya) was superb. The hospital was not. The Aga Khan Hospital in Dar es Salaam, on the other hand, was. Regardless, I think that it's worth your while to know something about the diagnosis and treatment of common conditions that you may encounter. This applies particularly to malaria and diarrhea.

What If I Think I Need a Blood Transfusion?

This is one of the most frequently asked questions. Here are the answers. First, emergency blood transfusion is, thankfully, very rarely required. Fluids can usually be replaced by the use of what is known as colloid or crystalloid plasma expanders.

Blood, when it is required, cannot be guaranteed to be infection-free in many countries. HIV, hepatitis B and C, and trypanosomiasis (Chagas' disease) are all transmissible via blood transfusions. While it would be nice to carry around a pint or two of your own blood, this is just not practical. Your best available options for dealing with this issue are:

• Accept a blood transfusion only if it is absolutely necessary (assuming you have some say in the matter). Do your utmost to ensure that it is screened for HIV.

- Know your blood type, in the hope that if you do require a transfusion, you can find a "low-risk" donor among your friends or other expatriates.
- Carry adequate medical insurance so that you can quickly be evacuated to somewhere that has "safe" medical care.
- Avoid activities that may make you more "transfusion-prone," such as driving at night without a seatbelt.

Webster's definition of *insurance* is *"a means of guaranteeing protection or safety."* Well, there really isn't anything that will guarantee your protection or safety, but traveling prepared, and carrying adequate medical and travel insurance, will soften the blow and make life easier should anything go wrong.

Related Websites

MedicAlert: www.medicalert.org

Emergency services: http://www.internationalsos.com
http://travel.state.gov/medical.html

International Association for Medical Assistance to Travellers: www.sentex.net/~iamat

Government offices, Canada:
http://www.voyage.gc.ca/Consular-e/For_Dest/canadian_offices-e.htm

Government offices, U.S.:
http://www.foia.state.gov/mms/KOH/keyofficers.asp

Key Points

- Don't leave home without medical and travel insurance.
- Carry a record of your medical problems and medications.
- Try to take all the medications you may need with you.

Region-by-Region Guide

CHAPTER 5

"There are no foreign lands. It is the traveller only who is foreign."

ROBERT LOUIS STEVENSON

This chapter is meant to give you an idea of what diseases you might be exposed to while you are away. Please remember that it's only a guideline. What you may actually encounter depends upon those ubiquitous risk factors: For how long are you traveling? Are you going to be in rural areas? What will you be doing there? What time of year will you be gone? Do you have any underlying medical problems? How old are you?

Also remember that while there are a lot of interesting diseases "over there," most of you probably won't get any of them (aside from traveler's diarrhea), and you may feel even better while you are away. Certain activities, such as unsafe sex and riding in the back of a pickup truck late at night (especially having unsafe sex while riding in the back of a pickup truck late at night), are risks everywhere, and have not been mentioned in this section. Situations change, and out-breaks break out. Therefore, your information needs to be kept up to date. For more detailed information, check some of the references provided at the end of the book and visit your local travel clinic. Much of this information has been adapted from the World Health Organization (WHO) publication *International Travel and Health*.

This is not an exhaustive list of every disease present around the world. For that I would refer you to a textbook of tropical medicine. But it does include just about everything you need to know. I have divided the world up into regions:

- North America (excluding Mexico and Central America)
- Mexico, the Caribbean, Central and South America
- Africa
- Asia
- Oceania
- Europe and the Middle East

North America

Canada; United States, including Hawaii
In lesser-developed regions such as Africa, almost 70 percent of illness is from infectious diseases such as malaria, TB, diarrhea, HIV/AIDS and measles. Here in North America, that figure is closer to 10 percent. We owe this relative lack of morbidity and mortality (illness and death) from infectious disease to several factors, including a climate that is less conducive to disease-transmitting vectors; a higher standard of living, which affords us better living conditions, adequate education and medical care; and our public health system, which does its best to protect us from infectious diseases through immunization, surveillance and early intervention.

We are much more likely to die from diseases of excess—too much food, too much alcohol, too many cigarettes, too many pills, too much sitting on the couch. Therefore, most travelers are not at great risk when they travel around this continent, as long as they don't pick up our bad habits. Having said that, all is not perfect, and there are some things to watch out for.

FOOD- AND WATER-BORNE DISEASES. We pride ourselves on our clean water and well-prepared foods. In spite of this, almost every diarrhea-causing organism that we encounter in the tropics may be present in our own backyard. *Salmonella, Campylobacter, Shigella, Giardia lamblia* and *Cryptosporidium* all turn up on my lab reports on a regular basis. There have been several outbreaks of *E. coli* 0157, a potentially lethal form of food poisoning. So the rules *"Boil it, bottle it, peel it, cook it ... or forget it"* should apply to all those who go off the beaten path in search of turquoise lakes, shimmering streams, mountain peaks—and even by some who don't.

INSECT-BORNE DISEASES. Malaria was no stranger to the United States and Canada in the 19th century. The occasional case still occurs in people who have not left the country, but most doctors count on imported cases, of which there is no shortage, to gain their experience in this field. Dengue fever has occurred in recent years, particularly along the border between Texas and Mexico, with Mexico reporting the majority of cases. Hawaii and Rio de Janeiro have also experienced significant outbreaks. West Nile fever has been responsible for several deaths in the New York City area, and birds and mosquitoes carrying the virus have been found on the Canadian side of the border as well.

Ticks are responsible for a handful of infections, the most famous of which is Lyme disease. Hikers, regardless of where they plan to roam, should cover up with proper clothing and use repellents containing DEET and/or permethrin. Lyme disease has been reported from almost every U.S. state. The highest-risk areas are in the northeast, the midwest and Oregon and northern California. Most cases in Canada have been reported from southern Ontario. LYMErix®, a vaccine against this infection, may be advisable if your exposure is to be significant. Rocky Mountain spotted fever has been reported from most U.S. states, as well as western Canada. Erlichiosis is most common in the southeastern and south central United States. Babesiosis, which resembles malaria under the microscope, is found in the United States in the same areas as Lyme disease. Other tick-borne infections include Colorado tick fever and tick-borne relapsing fever.

OTHER CONCERNS. Assuming you practice safe sex, drive carefully, dress appropriately for the weather and use lots of common sense, North America is a safe place to travel from the health point of view. A word about meningococcal meningitis—the risk of this disease has been found to be increased in freshmen living in U.S. college dormitories. For this reason, vaccination of such students is recommended using the quadrivalent vaccine (A,C,Y,W-135). In Canada, it's sufficient to immunize only against the serogroup C.

Oh, yes, those snakes. Most venomous snakebites in North

America are courtesy of pit vipers, especially rattlesnakes, which come in 16 varieties. I am told that the sound of their rattle is something not easily forgotten. Coral snakes may be responsible for a small minority of bites. Rabies is transmitted by raccoons, foxes and bats. Hantavirus, which is contracted through close contact with rodents and their excretions, has been reported mainly from western Canada and the southwestern United States. No vaccines are required to enter North America.

Mexico / Central and South America / Caribbean

Mexico; **Central America:** *Belize, Costa Rica, El Salvador, Guatemala, Honduras, Nicaragua, Panama;* **South America:** *Bolivia, Brazil, Colombia, Ecuador, French Guiana, Guyana, Paraguay, Peru, Suriname, Venezuela;* **Caribbean:** *Anguilla, Antigua, Aruba, Bahamas, Barbuda, British Virgin Islands, Cayman Islands, Cuba, Dominica, Dominican Republic, Grenada, Guadeloupe, Haiti, Jamaica, Martinique, Montserrat, Netherlands Antilles, Puerto Rico, Saint Kitts and Nevis, Saint Lucia, Saint Vincent and the Grenadines, Trinidad and Tobago, Turks and Caicos, Virgin Islands (USA)*

This hemisphere certainly has its attractions for North Americans, one of them being the lack of jet lag for those who travel there. You may visit tropical rain forests, stroll around ancient Inca and Aztec ruins, lie on countless beaches, explore beautiful cities like Rio de Janeiro and Buenos Aires and trek high in the Andes. The traveler will encounter a great diversity of conditions, depending upon exact destination and "style" of travel. Working as a volunteer in rural Guyana or Haiti will entail greater risk than attending a business meeting in São Paulo.

FOOD- AND WATER-BORNE DISEASES. Diarrheal disease is prevalent throughout this region. Hepatitis A may occur everywhere, and hepatitis E is reported in Mexico. Typhoid fever is a risk to those who travel off the proverbial beaten path. Intestinal worms or helminths such as *Ascaris* and *Trichuris* would be common among poor populations without access to clean food and water. Hepatitis A vaccine is recommended for all travelers. Typhoid vaccine would be for those at higher risk.

Cholera was reintroduced to this hemisphere in 1991. The disease continues to be present in several countries of Central and South America. Vaccination is recommended only for travelers at very high risk. Outbreaks of ciguatera poisoning are common in the Caribbean. Eat coral reef fish at your own risk.

INSECT-BORNE DISEASES. In the Caribbean, malaria is present on the island of Hispaniola (Haiti/Dominican Republic), with most of the risk on the Haitian side. This is mainly with *P. falciparum*. In Mexico and the countries of Central America, malaria is a risk in rural, lowland areas. Conversely, there is little or no risk in urban areas and most coastal resort areas. The risk in Costa Rica is quite low, where it exists mainly along the northeastern border with Nicaragua and in the state of Limón on the Caribbean coast. All of Belize, excluding Belize City, may be a threat. In Guatemala, many tourists spend most of their time in the highlands, with only a brief overnight excursion to the ruins at Tikal.

Personal precautions may suffice for such brief exposure, though cases of malaria have been reported in such situations. Rural areas of Honduras, including the Bay Islands, a favorite diving destination, are a risk. *P. vivax* is the predominant strain of malaria in Central America, and chloroquine is the drug of choice for malaria prophylaxis in this area. The exception to this guideline is in Panama, east of the Panama Canal, where mefloquine, doxycycline or Malarone® would be preferred. The Canal Zone itself is malaria free, though back in the early 20th century, when the canal was being built, malaria and yellow fever claimed hundreds of lives.

In South America, there is no risk of malaria in major urban areas or at altitudes above about 5,000 feet. It's not present in Chile, Uruguay and most of Argentina. In the rest of South America, the predominant strain of malaria is *P. vivax*. Brazil reports the most cases, the majority of which come from the Amazon region. Manaus, Brasilia, Iguasu Falls and the cities along the east coast are malaria free. The interior of Guyana and Suriname are high-risk areas. Lowland areas of Peru, Ecuador and Bolivia have malaria outside of urban areas. Those who follow the common route from Quito, the Galapagos, Lima, Cuzco, Machu Picchu and Lake Titicaca are not at risk. If you are visiting the coast of Ecuador, or northern Peru where it borders Ecuador, you are. While there are areas of chloroquine-sensitive malaria in Peru, the drug of choice for all other malarious areas would be mefloquine, doxycycline or Malarone®. Many tours to Peru visit the Amazon for only a few days, at Porto Maldonaldo. The risk of malaria here is low, but present.

Dengue fever is present in almost all countries, particularly the Caribbean, Mexico, Central American countries and Brazil. It may be seasonal, being most prevalent during and after the rainy season. Use an insect repellent during the day. Louse-borne typhus is found in the Andean regions of Peru and Colombia.

The yellow fever endemic zone begins in Panama (on the east side of the Darien Gap) and includes all South American countries with the exception of Chile, Uruguay, Argentina and Paraguay. (See map at end of chapter.) In Brazil, there is increasing concern that this infection will re-emerge in urban areas. Yellow fever vaccine is recommended or required for all travelers who will be visiting rural areas of countries in the endemic zones. Many popular cruises require evidence of yellow fever inoculation, partly for the protection of their passengers, but also because they will be visiting other ports of call (e.g., Barbados) that require such documentation.

Visceral and cutaneous leishmaniasis and American trypanosomiasis (Chagas' disease) are present in Central and South American countries. Bancroftian filariasis is endemic in Guyana, Brazil and Suriname. Myiasis, caused by the larva of the botfly *(Dermatobia hominis)*, is found in most tropical rain forests, with Belize being the most common source among tourists.

OTHER CONCERNS. Rabies, mainly in dogs and bats, is present throughout the region. Vaccination would be recommended for higher-risk, longer-term travelers, especially young children.

Cutaneous larva migrans (creeping eruption) can occur on any tropical beach that's frequented by dogs. This seems to be particularly prevalent in Jamaica. Schistosomiasis may be found in the fresh waters of Brazil, Suriname and north-central Venezuela, and on a few Caribbean islands, including St. Lucia, Puerto Rico, the Dominican Republic and Martinique. The hepatitis B carrier rate is high in the Amazon basin. Higher-risk travelers should be vaccinated.

Many tropical Caribbean beaches will be home to jellyfish, sea urchins and other stinging sea creatures. Several poisonous snakes are found in this region, with pit vipers and coral snakes being the most common. The fer-de-lance is perhaps the most feared species. The anaconda, while not poisonous, may reach a length of 37½ feet (that's the record) and kills its victims by constriction. Should you find one of these sleeping quietly in your hammock, leave it alone.

Outbreaks of meningococcal meningitis have occurred in Brazil and Chile. Most cases have been due to serogroup B. As there is no vaccine against serogroup B, vaccination is not currently recommended for travel to these areas.

Altitude sickness is a concern above 7,000 feet. If you are flying into Bogotá, Quito, Cuzco or La Paz, take time to acclimatize. Trekkers in the Andes and those who climb Mount Aconcagua (22,831 feet) in Argentina must be particularly knowledgeable about the risks and treatment of altitude sickness. Carry Diamox® for prevention or treatment.

Finally, keep your personal safety in mind at all times. Peru and Guatemala are two of the most dangerous countries when it comes to motor vehicle accidents. Having ridden buses through the mountains of both countries, I am not surprised. Colombia leads the world in kidnappings.

Asia

Afghanistan, Armenia, Azerbaijan, Bangladesh, Bhutan, Brunei, Burma, Cambodia, China, East Timor, Georgia, India, Indonesia, Iran, Japan, Kazakhstan, Korea (South and North), Kyrgyzstan, Lao People's Democratic Republic (Laos), Malaysia, Maldives,

Mongolia, Nepal, Pakistan, the Philippines, Singapore, Sri Lanka, Taiwan, Tajikistan, Thailand, Turkmenistan, Uzbekistan, Vietnam

This vast region stretches from Russia and its former states in the west, across India, Pakistan and Nepal, and on to China and the countries of Southeast Asia. Jet lag is indeed a problem. North America is home to thousands of immigrants who have left countries in this region to settle here, and who frequently return home to visit friends and family.

FOOD- AND WATER-BORNE DISEASES. Diarrheal disease may be encountered throughout this region. Certainly some countries present a greater risk than others. Bacterial infections are, as always, the commonest cause of diarrhea. *Campylobacter,* one of the responsible organisms, is becoming increasingly resistant to ciprofloxacin in Thailand. Alternative antibiotics would include erythromycin. Parasitic infections such as giardiasis are reasonably common in Russia, India and Nepal. *Cyclospora* is prevalent in Nepal in the late spring and early summer.

Hepatitis A is a risk throughout Asia. Hepatitis E may also occur in this region. Typhoid is a concern for any traveler veering off the beaten path, and even for those who are on it in countries such as India and Pakistan. Southeast Asia plays home to some interesting food-borne helminthic (worm) infections, such as clonorchiasis, paragonimiasis and fasciolopsiasis. Don't worry too much about pronouncing these things. Just cook your food.

Cholera is reported in many of the countries of Asia, but once again is of little risk to the average traveler.

INSECT-BORNE DISEASES. The prevalence of malaria changes as we travel from west to east through Asia. While it is reported from some of the former Russian states such as Tajikistan, the risk is relatively low. Afghanistan, however, does have chloroquine-resistant *falciparum* malaria. India and Pakistan are the source of many of our imported malaria infections. The disease is present throughout both countries at altitudes below about 6,000 feet. In the winter months, the likelihood of contracting malaria in New Delhi and northern India is low or perhaps nonexistent. The risk in urban areas of Pakistan such as Karachi, Islamabad and Lahore is low, but present. Colombo and Dhaka, the capitals of Sri Lanka and Bangladesh, respectively, are malaria free. The Maldives, located in the Indian Ocean southwest of India, are malaria free. In Nepal, malaria is present in the Terai district in the southwestern part of the country, including Chitwan National Park. The risk is quite low, and personal protective measures may suffice for most short-term visitors. Where malaria is a risk, the predominant strain is *P. vivax*. But because of the risk of chloroquine-resistant *P. falciparum*, the preferred prophylaxis is mefloquine, doxycycline or Malarone®.

In Southeast Asia (Thailand, Myanmar [Burma], Vietnam, Indonesia, Laos, Malaysia, the Philippines), the predominant strain of malaria is chloroquine-resistant *P. falciparum*. Along the borders between Thailand and Myanmar and Thailand and Cambodia, *P. falciparum* is resistant to mefloquine as well. What differentiates this area from most of India and Africa is that there is no risk of malaria in urban areas, nor in many touristy areas such as beaches. If you are exposed to malaria, the antimalarial of choice would be mefloquine, doxycycline or Malarone®, with the exception being those border areas just mentioned, where Malarone® or doxycycline would be the drug of choice.

This means that many travelers off to this area probably do not need to be taking antimalarials. Thailand is perhaps the favorite destination in this region, and to quote the Centers for Disease Control and Prevention (CDC): *"Limited risk. No risk in cities and major tourist resorts (e.g., Bangkok, Chiang Mai, Phuket). Transmission largely confined to forested rural areas, principally along the borders with Cambodia and Myanmar (Burma), not visited by most travelers: most travel to rural areas in Thailand is during daytime hours when the risk of exposure is minimal."* The same goes for the rest of Southeast Asia. You need to be reasonably far off the beaten path before you're at risk.

Nevertheless, there is still no shortage of malaria. Borneo, Sumatra, Sulawesi, Java and many other rural areas will pose a threat. In China, risk does occur in rural areas, though not in the northern and western provinces. The greatest risk, where there is chloroquine-resistant *falciparum* malaria, is on Hainan Island and in southern China bordering Myanmar, Laos and Vietnam. Cruising on the Yangtze River is not a risk. Most "tourists" to China will not require malaria prophylaxis. Discuss your plans with your travel health professional.

Dengue fever is a risk throughout Asia, particularly Southeast Asia. It is most prevalent during and after the rainy season, and tends to occur in areas that tourists like to visit. Japanese encephalitis is present in rural agricultural areas, also during the wetter months between May and October. In more tropical regions, it may be a threat year round. Immunization would be recommended for the higher-risk traveler. Other insect-borne diseases that are uncommon in travelers include mite-borne typhus, leishmaniasis, filariasis and plague.

Yellow fever is not a risk in Asia, but proof of vaccination is required by most countries if you are arriving from a yellow fever–infected country and, sometimes, from any country in the endemic zones.

OTHER CONCERNS. Hepatitis B is a serious problem in most of Asia, with more than 10 percent of people being carriers of the virus. Vaccination is recommended for all "high-risk" travelers, and is not unreasonable for anyone traveling to this part of the world. Stray dogs, some infected with rabies, are a huge problem in India, Thailand and other countries in this region. Pre-exposure inoculation should be considered for longer-term travelers, children and anyone else at higher risk. Schistosomiasis may be transmitted through exposure to fresh water in the Philippines, central Sulawesi and parts of Vietnam. Swim in the oceans. Outbreaks of meningococcal meningitis occurred in Nepal and northern India in the late 1980s. Vaccination is no longer recommended for most vacationers, though it may be reasonable for those with prolonged exposure to local people.

Several species of snakes are found in this region, including cobras, kraits and vipers. Russell's viper, which is widespread across this region, is responsible for more human fatalities than any other venomous snake and possesses one of the most potent venoms. The saw-scaled viper is only two feet long, but its bite is frequently fatal.

Africa

Northern Africa: Algeria, Egypt, Libya, Morocco, Tunisia; Sub-Saharan Africa: Angola, Benin, Burkina Faso, Burundi, Cameroon, Cape Verde, Central African Republic, Chad, Comoros, Congo, Djibouti, Equatorial Guinea, Eritrea, Ethiopia, Gabon, Gambia, Ghana, Guinea-Bissau, Ivory Coast, Kenya, Liberia, Madagascar, Malawi, Mali, Mauritania, Mauritius, Mozambique, Niger, Nigeria, Réunion, Rwanda, São Tomé and Principe, Senegal, Seychelles, Sierra Leone, Somalia, Sudan, Tanzania, Togo, Uganda, Zambia, Zimbabwe; Southern Africa: Botswana, Lesotho, Namibia, Saint Helena, South Africa, Swaziland

I have had the good fortune to go to Africa twice, once to West Africa with Foster Parents Plan, and more recently to East Africa with Voluntary Service Overseas (VSO). Regarding infectious diseases, especially malaria, the health risks are higher than in most other parts of the world. Fortunately, most diseases can be avoided with a little bit of knowledge, some common sense and perhaps a shot or two.

The continent can be conveniently divided into three regions—northern, sub-Saharan and southern. From the health point of view, the greatest risks lie in sub-Saharan Africa.

FOOD- AND WATER-BORNE DISEASES. Gastrointestinal infections are widespread. Bacteria are responsible for most cases of diarrhea in travelers, but parasitic infections such as giardiasis and amebiasis are also common. Intestinal worms such as ascariasis, trichuriasis and hookworm are common among local populations. All travelers should be vaccinated against hepatitis A. Hepatitis E is a lesser risk. Typhoid fever is a risk to the higher-risk traveler, and cholera for those at the highest risk (e.g., going to work in a refugee camp). Other interesting infections, which are of little threat to most of you, include dracunculiasis (Guinea worm) and echinococcosis. It goes without saying, *Take great care with your food and water.*

INSECT-BORNE DISEASES. Most of the cases of malaria we see in North Americans are contracted in Africa, especially sub-Saharan Africa, where it occurs in both urban and rural areas. The islands of Réunion and the Seychelles are malaria free. Areas situated above about 6,000 feet, including the cities of Nairobi and Addis Ababa, are also free of malaria.

The majority of cases of malaria in Africa are caused by chloroquine-resistant *P. falciparum.* If you are traveling to this region, personal precautions such as insect repellents and mosquito nets are exceedingly important. Mefloquine, doxycycline or Malarone® would be the antimalarial of choice. Beware of people who tell you otherwise. Cases of mefloquine-resistant malaria have been reported. Remember, no antimalarial is likely to be 100 percent protective. Some travelers who will not have access to reasonable medical care may also wish to carry "standby emergency treatment," as described in Chapter 8, Malaria.

In northern Africa, chloroquine-sensitive malaria is present in parts of Egypt, Morocco and Algeria. The risk is low. Specifically, those off to Cairo and a cruise down the Nile do not need malaria prophylaxis. They do need something for diarrhea. In southern Africa, there is a risk in most areas, though not all. Harare and Bulawayo in Zimbabwe are risk free. In Namibia, most of the reported cases of malaria occur in the north part of the country. In South Africa, it is mainly visitors to Kruger National Park in the northeastern part of the country who are at risk.

Sub-Saharan Africa lies in the yellow fever endemic zone, and large outbreaks occur periodically in the unvaccinated local population. Vaccination may be required, and is usually recommended for visitors to this area. Although countries such as Egypt and South Africa lie outside of the endemic zones, proof of yellow fever vaccination will be required if you are arriving from a "yellow fever country" (see map at end of chapter).

Africa has a tremendous array of other insect-borne infections. Fortunately, most of them are rarely seen in travelers. These include onchocerciasis (river blindness), filariasis, leishmaniasis, West Nile fever, Rift Valley fever, plague and African trypanosomiasis (sleeping sickness). Dengue fever occurs, but is much less common than in Asia and Latin America. I have seen several travelers with tick-bite fever, or South African tick typhus. Remember to wear your long pants and socks when traipsing around in the bush.

OTHER CONCERNS. Hepatitis B vaccination is recommended for higher-risk travelers and anyone else who may be concerned about the risks of unsafe sex or medical care. The meningococcal meningitis belt extends from the Gambia in the west to Ethiopia in the east (see map at end of chapter). Those who plan extended (three weeks or more) travel to this area or who will be in close contact with the local population during the dry season from December to May should be vaccinated with Menomune® (A, C, Y, W-135). Rabies vaccine should be considered for high-risk travelers, particularly young children. Schistosomiasis is prevalent in most of Africa, including along the Nile River. You may be told locally that certain lakes and rivers (e.g., parts of Lake Malawi) are risk free. Swim in fresh water at your own risk. While fast-moving water may be safer than still water, whitewater rafters have become infected.

Several viral hemorrhagic fevers, such as Lassa, Ebola and Marburg hemorrhagic fever, occur sporadically in sub-Saharan Africa. Although they generate great interest in our press, the risk to travelers is extremely low.

Many travelers to East Africa attempt to climb Mount Kilimanjaro (19,340 feet). This typically involves a vertical ascent of between 2,000 and 3,000 feet per day over four to six days. Because this rate of ascent exceeds safe guidelines, I would recommend that you carry Diamox®, either for prevention (that's my suggestion) or for treatment.

If you are a poisonous snake, Africa is the place to be. Vipers, cobras (spitting and nonspitting), boomslangs, birdsnakes, puff adders and one of the most dreaded of them all, the black mamba, can all be found here. Cleopatra chose the bite of an Egyptian cobra or asp to end her life in 30 BC. Hopefully you do not encounter a python, a nonpoisonous snake that would rather hug you to death.

Some 70 percent of the world's 40 million people infected with HIV live in sub-Saharan Africa. More than 30 percent of pregnant women in Botswana and other southern African countries are HIV positive. The rate in commercial sex workers is much higher. HIV and other personal safety issues are of great importance to the traveler to this part of the world.

Oceania

Australia, New Zealand, the Antarctic, American Samoa, Cook Islands, Easter Island, Fiji, French Polynesia, Guam, Kiribati, Marshall Islands, Micronesia, Nauru, New Caledonia, Niue, Palau, Papua New Guinea, West Papua (Irian Jaya), Samoa, Solomon Islands, Tokelau, Tuvalu, Vanuatu, Wallis and Futuna Islands

With a few exceptions, Australia and New Zealand can be considered much the same as North America when it comes to health concerns. It's very cold in the Antarctic, and there are no mosquitoes there. Penguins do not transmit any diseases to humans.

FOOD- AND WATER-BORNE DISEASES. Diarrheal infections, hepatitis A and typhoid fever are all a risk on the islands of Oceania (excluding Australia and New Zealand). Intestinal helminths or worms such as ascariasis and trichuriasis are also found.

INSECT-BORNE DISEASES. Chloroquine-resistant *P. falciparum* is the predominant strain of malaria. It occurs in Papua New Guinea, West Papua (Irian Jaya), the Solomon Islands and Vanuatu. Other islands, including Australia and New Zealand, are malaria free. Mefloquine, doxycycline and Malarone® are the antimalarials of choice. Strains of *P. vivax* found in Papua New Guinea and West Papua may be resistant to both chloroquine and the usual doses of primaquine.

Dengue fever is a risk in most islands of this region, particularly during the rainy season from December to June. It has also been reported in Northern Queensland, a province of Australia. Ross River virus (endemic polyarthritis), a mosquito-borne infection causing a fever, flu-like symptoms and joint pains, is reported from several parts of Australia. Murray Valley encephalitis is yet another mosquito-borne infection found in Australia. Mite-borne typhus and filariasis occur on some islands, but again are usually of little threat to travelers.

Yellow fever is not present in this area, but proof of vaccination may be required if you are traveling from an infected country.

OTHER CONCERNS. The hepatitis B carrier rate in Oceania (again, excluding Australia and New Zealand) is about 15 percent. Vaccination is recommended for higher-risk travelers. Australia's rate is comparable to our own. Most of the islands of Oceania are rabies free. The poisonous snakes of Australia belong to the elapid family, with most bites coming from the brown snake, the tiger snake, the death adder and the taipan. This last species is considered to be the most venomous land snake in the world. Fortunately it is not particularly aggressive, preferring to hide or escape rather than attack. A very small amount of its venom is enough to kill a quarter of a million mice or 100 people. (How's that for useful trivia?) Coelentrates such as the box jellyfish and coral are hazards to those visiting the reefs off Australia. And don't forget those crocodiles.

Europe and the Middle East

Europe: Albania, Andorra, Austria, Belarus, Belgium, Bosnia and Herzegovina, Croatia, Czech Republic, Bulgaria, Denmark, Estonia, Finland, France, Germany, Gibraltar, Greece, Hungary, Iceland, Ireland, Italy, Latvia, Liechtenstein, Lithuania, Luxembourg, Malta, Moldova, Monaco, Netherlands, Norway, Poland, Portugal, Romania, Russian Federation, San Marino, Serbia and Montenegro, Slovakia, Slovenia, Spain, Sweden, Switzerland, Ukraine, United Kingdom, the former Yugoslav Republic of Macedonia. **Middle East:** *Bahrain, Cyprus, Iraq,*

Israel, Jordan, Kuwait, Lebanon, Oman, Qatar, Saudi Arabia, Syria, Turkey, United Arab Emirates, Yemen.

Most of Western Europe resembles North America when it comes to its relative dearth of exotic infectious diseases. But once again, all is not perfect, though the risk to most travelers is quite low. The same cannot be said for the Middle East and other parts of Europe.

FOOD- AND WATER-BORNE DISEASES. Diarrheal disease frequently affects visitors to the Middle East, and it's probably best to stick to bottled water wherever you go. Hepatitis A is a risk in Eastern European countries and the Middle East, and vaccination is recommended. Hepatitis E is present in parts of the Middle East. Typhoid is much less common, and vaccination would be recommended only for those at the highest risk. Other infections, which include trichinosis and beef, pork and fish tapeworms, occur as a result of inadequately cooked meat.

INSECT-BORNE DISEASES. Europe is free of malaria, although that was not always the case. In the Middle Eastern countries of Oman, Saudi Arabia, Iran and Iraq, both *P. vivax* and *P. falciparum* malaria occur, though they are restricted to rural areas, where most travelers do not go. Most of these countries have reported chloroquine-resistant *P. falciparum,* so Malarone®, doxycycline or mefloquine would be the antimalarial to use. Tick-borne encephalitis occurs between the spring and fall in forested areas of Central and Eastern Europe (Austria, the Czech Republic, Germany, Hungary, Poland, Switzerland), Ukraine, Russia and the Baltic states (Estonia, Latvia and Lithuania). Vaccination against this infection with FSME-Immun® is recommended for those who will spend time in rural areas during these months. Lyme disease is also present. Lymerix®, which is used to prevent this infection in North America, is ineffective against the strains found in Europe.

West Nile fever occurs in some countries surrounding the Mediterranean. Cutaneous and visceral leishmaniasis (kala-azar), which are transmitted by sandflies, may be found in southern

Europe, around the Mediterranean and in the Middle East. Onchocerciasis is found in Yemen.

There is no yellow fever in this region, but proof of vaccination may be required by some of the Middle Eastern countries if you are arriving from a yellow fever–infected country.

OTHER CONCERNS. Rabies is present in several countries in Europe and the Middle East. The majority of cases are found in wild animals, especially foxes. Human cases are rare. The carrier rate for hepatitis B is moderate (between 2 and 10 percent) in the Middle East and Eastern Europe. Vaccination is recommended for longer-term travelers and others at high risk, such as health care workers. Outbreaks of meningococcal disease have occurred in Saudi Arabia among religious pilgrims. Proof of vaccination against at least strains A and C, and preferably Y and W-135, is a requirement of entry for religious pilgrims at all times of the year. Schistosomiasis is found in certain areas of the Middle East. Snakes are not a big concern, but those that are found belong to the *Viperidae* family.

I apologize if I have neglected to mention a particular country or exotic disease. As doctors always say, *"Common things are common,"* and I think that by reading this chapter you will be aware of the most common significant health risks. Remember, personal safety and sexually transmitted diseases are a concern everywhere. By checking out the CDC's or Health Canada's website, and by visiting a travel clinic, you can find out more about the health concerns that are pertinent to you.

Related Websites

Centers for Disease Control and Prevention:
www.cdc.gov/travel

Health Canada:
www.hc-sc.gc.ca/pphb-dgspsp/tmp-pmv/index.html

Countries Reporting Cases of Malaria

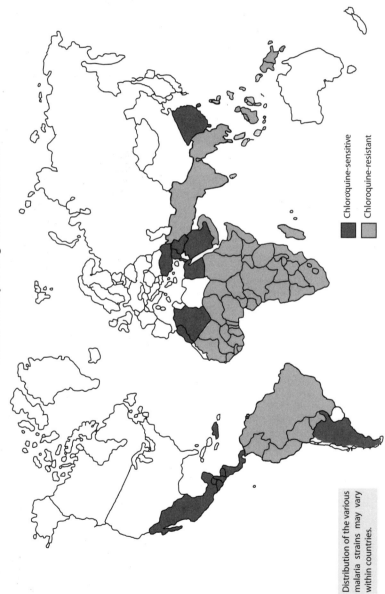

Chloroquine-sensitive

Chloroquine-resistant

Distribution of the various malaria strains may vary within countries.

Meningoccal Meningitis in Africa

Meningitis Belt:
Areas with
frequent
epidemics

Japanese Encephalitis

Yellow Fever in South America

Yellow fever endemic zone

Yellow Fever in Africa

Yellow fever endemic zone

PART TWO
Infectious Concerns

Nigeria 2000
Guy Hersant

Greetings from Nigeria
where computers are hard
to find.
Have been here 14 months
without being sick once-
something of a record! Have
been to Lagos - not nearly as
dangerous as its reputation
but not like this picture
either. All the best
Jennifer

Dr. Mark Wise
2300 John St.
Thornhill,
ON
Canada L3T 6B7

Air Mail Par avion

Pretravel Inoculation

CHAPTER 6

"Travel is fatal to prejudice, bigotry,
and narrow-mindedness."

MARK TWAIN

While it's certainly not the only topic of concern to the potential traveler, the matter of pretravel inoculation—or *"What shots do I need?"*—seems to create the most anxiety and confusion in the minds of travelers and medical personnel. Some people believe that with a few needles, they are immune to everything to which they may be exposed. Not true! In fact, infectious diseases account for only a small proportion of the morbidity (sickness) and mortality (death) in travelers. Having said that, immunization is an important and effective means of preventing specific infections that you may encounter.

How Do Vaccines Work?

As far as I am concerned, the words vaccinate, immunize and inoculate may all be used interchangeably. The word "vaccine" comes from the Latin *"of or from cows,"* referring to the substance derived from a mild virus affecting cows, which was used to prevent smallpox in humans. Vaccines work by priming the body's own immune system to prevent a variety of infectious diseases. By exposing the body to tiny amounts of the virus or bacteria (antigen), the body produces antibodies, which will, in the future, prevent the development of the disease in question should exposure occur. To avoid transmitting the actual disease through vaccination, most vaccines are modified. They may be "killed" or "inactivated," which eliminates any risk; or they may be "live" but "attenuated," which means they have been sufficiently altered that they will trick the body into producing antibodies, but will not make the person ill. You are not receiving a "small dose" of the disease.

Vaccines are not perfect. They may not be 100 percent effective, and adverse effects may occur. But they are the most efficient method of preventing infectious diseases. Look at how well we have (or haven't) done with HIV, malaria and TB, three diseases lacking an effective vaccine. But you can't please all the people all the time, and there is out there a vocal minority extolling the dangers of vaccines. Links have been made connecting the MMR (measles, mumps and rubella) vaccine with autism, and hepatitis B with multiple sclerosis. No scientific evidence exists to support these theories.

What's the Risk?

There are a lot of vaccines, and there are a lot of countries, but not everyone visiting every country needs every vaccine. How do we decide? Well, practicing travel medicine is a bit like being an insurance agent. Most of you pay big bucks to insure your home, your car, your life, your income and even your vacations. Mercifully, most of us are not rear-ended, robbed, hit by a hurricane or unexpectedly killed or disabled.

We do our best to assess the risks to which the traveler will be exposed, and recommend the most appropriate forms of insurance or protection—whether it be needles, pills, condoms or common sense. To do so requires knowledge of geography, tropical and many other fields of medicine, epidemiology and human behavior. It also requires some insight into each individual traveler and the risks that they may encounter.

The most important principle we go by is: *"Immunize according to risk ... not just the country visited."* In assessing these risks, we consider the following:

- *Duration of travel.* Someone going away for four days is at less risk than a person relocating for two years.
- *Purpose of travel.* Certain activities, such as medical work, inter

national peacekeeping or volunteering in a small rural community, present a greater risk than sitting behind a desk or sightseeing.

- *Style of travel.* The budget-minded backpacker, long-term volunteer or person returning home to visit the family will have greater exposure to disease than the businessperson who doesn't leave the five-star hotel.
- *Age.* Certain age groups may be more susceptible to certain infections, or have riskier behavior.
- *Time of year.* Some infections may be seasonal, such as malaria, meningococcal meningitis, Japanese encephalitis or tick-borne encephalitis.
- *Urban vs. rural travel.* Many infections are found only in rural areas, while others, such as hepatitis A and B, are readily available in both urban and rural settings.
- *Other medical conditions or medications.* HIV/AIDS, diabetes, heart disease and pregnancy are only a few of the conditions that will affect your risk of travel.
- *Destination.* Certainly it does make a difference where you are going. The Bahamas are not a great problem; nearby Haiti is.

Having considered these factors, we can then divide all our travelers into "high risk," "low risk," and "somewhere in between." A good example of a high-risk traveler would be Indiana Jones. He travels frequently, often to remote parts of the world where clean food and water are not always available, and where exposure to blood and blood products, high altitude, sex and who knows what else are occupational hazards. Thankfully, he has his health. Missionaries and volunteers usually fit into this category. Another high-risk group would be VFRs (Visiting Friends and Relatives), or those who have emigrated from lesser-developed countries who travel to visit their homeland.

A low-risk traveler might be the CEO of a Fortune 500 company, flying to Hong Kong for only three days and staying in the best hotel. A week in the Caribbean would also qualify. And then there are the majority of travelers, who fall somewhere in between Indiana Jones and your grandmother in Florida.

Each traveler is also involved in deciding which vaccines to receive. Some people are petrified of needles and will choose to forgo them. Often, when multiple doses of a vaccine are required (e.g., hepatitis B, rabies), there is not enough time to receive a full course of vaccination. Travelers who grew up in lesser-developed countries may have pre-existing immunity to certain infections, such as hepatitis A or B. Some parents will choose to worry only about their children. Many people feel that they can avoid infection through personal precautions alone.

Everyone seems to have their own perception of the risks involved in travel. Some of the vaccines are quite expensive, and this may play a role in choosing what to receive. Our hypothetical high-risk traveler might need to spend upward of $1,000 just to be fully protected from the vaccine-preventable risks.

It's up to the medical professional to advise the patient of the risks and to make recommendations, but it's up to you, the traveler, to decide which vaccines to receive. To make things a bit more confusing, I guarantee you that not every travel medicine professional will make the same recommendations for the same traveler.

Routine, Required, Recommended

There are lots of vaccines. To make things a little simpler, we divide the shots available into three categories. *Routine* are those with which all travelers should be up to date. *Required* are those which may be required to enter into certain countries or to cross international borders. *Recommended* are those that should be given according to your risk, as discussed above.

Routine	Recommended	
• tetanus, diphtheria, polio	• hepatitis A	• rabies
• measles, mumps, rubella	• hepatitis B	• influenza
• varicella	• typhoid fever	• pneumococcal pneumonia
	• meningococcal disease	• TB skin test / BCG
Required	• cholera	
• yellow fever	• Japanese encephalitis	
• meningococcal disease*	• tick-borne encephalitis	* for religious pilgrims to Saudi Arabia

Routine

TETANUS, DIPHTHERIA, POLIO. Although these infections have largely been eradicated in most industrialized countries, they continue to occur in the tropics and some eastern European countries. Polio, which had previously been declared eradicated from the Western hemisphere, made a brief reappearance in the Dominican Republic and Haiti in the year 2000. Global campaigns continue in an effort to eliminate it from the world. Unfortunately, wars hamper many of the efforts made. Diphtheria continues to thrive in lesser-developed countries and the states of the former USSR. Tetanus, also known as lockjaw, is a risk to the unprotected anywhere in the world. The vast majority of children are current with these vaccinations. Many adults, however, no longer have adequate immunity against these infections. That's because many of us do not visit the doctor regularly once we are adults, and doctors are probably less vigilant in keeping their adult patients up to date with their immunizations.

Boosters against tetanus and diphtheria should be given every 10 years, whether one is traveling or not. For those who are visiting countries where polio is still a risk, a booster dose of polio vaccine should be given to adults once in their lifetime. TdP is a combined vaccine against all three infections that provides continued protection for 10 years.

MEASLES. This viral infection is still quite prevalent in many lesser-developed countries. More than one million children die each year from measles. Measles vaccine is recommended for those born between 1957 and 1980 (Canada recommends it for those born between 1970 and 1980) who have not yet received a second dose of the vaccine. Children are immunized at the age of one, and again at five years of age. If you will be visiting a lesser-developed country with a baby where measles is a risk, the vaccine can also be administered between the ages of six and twelve months. Two doses will still be needed after the child's first birthday. Measles vaccine is usually supplied in combination with mumps and rubella vaccine (MMR).

Inoculations against varicella (chickenpox), meningococcal meningitis and pneumococcal disease are now given as routine childhood immunizations in North America. They should be up to date in all children, but are not specifically recommended for travel abroad.

Required

YELLOW FEVER. Yellow fever is a viral infection that occurs in both tropical Africa and South America. It is transmitted by the *Aedes aegypti* mosquito. These mosquitoes are also found in urban areas, and there is increasing concern that this infection could re-establish itself in major cities. Symptoms may range from a mild flu-like syndrome to severe hepatitis and hemorrhagic fever. There is no specific treatment for this infection, and it carries a mortality rate of at least 20 percent. While the disease is rare in travelers, perhaps because most people are immunized, it does occur. A luxury trip down the Amazon for only a few days warrants receiving the vaccine.

The regulations surrounding the need for yellow fever vaccine may be a bit confusing to some. Let me elucidate:

1. It's a requirement for entry into several countries in Africa, mainly in West Africa (see table at end of chapter). This is regardless of your point of departure (Canada, the United States or elsewhere).
2. It's required to enter certain countries in Africa and South America, and elsewhere, when one has recently traveled in another country which is reporting cases of yellow fever, or which lies in the traditional endemic zones for yellow fever (see Chapter 5, Region-by Region Guide).
3. Vaccination is highly recommended if one is entering rural and even some urban areas in the traditional endemic zones. The Centers for Disease Control and Prevention (CDC) regularly publish and distribute the "Blue Sheet," which lists countries currently reporting cases of yellow fever (and cholera and plague). It's also available on the Internet (see website at end of chapter). Even if one is traveling in a country in the endemic zone that is not reporting cases, it's prudent to be immunized. The disease may be under-reported, there is a time lag until reports actually get published, and the disease can spread very quickly when there is an outbreak.

Let me give you some examples. If you are visiting French Guiana (even if you are only getting off your cruise ship for the day) or Ghana, you will require a yellow fever shot for entry. If you are flying from Tanzania (which is in the endemic zone) to Egypt or South Africa or India (which are not), you will require a yellow fever shot. If you are traveling within Brazil or Kenya, it is recommended that you receive the vaccine. Should you be taking the bus across the border from Ecuador to Peru, you will require the vaccine—and it is in your best interest to receive it as well. Confused?

Yellow fever vaccine is administered only at centers that are specifically designated by the World Health Organization as yellow fever clinics. They understand the regulations. You should receive an International Certificate of Vaccination documenting your shot, which may have to be presented when crossing international borders. If you do not have this document, you may be "quarantined" at the border for 10 days, inoculated on the spot with the country's vaccine and needle, or asked to make a donation to the border guard's favorite charity. Get it done before you leave.

The vaccine, which is given as a single dose, is virtually 100 percent effective after 10 days and provides protection for 10 years. It is a live vaccine, and therefore is not recommended for pregnant women, anyone who is immunosuppressed (e.g., by HIV, steroids) or those with an egg allergy. A certificate of exemption should be issued instead. However, in some of these situations, one must weigh the risks against the benefits. It can be given to children as young as 6 months of age if they are at significant risk. Otherwise, it's best delayed until 9 to 12 months of age. The side effects are usually mild, and may not appear until 5 to 10 days after vaccination. It should be given at least 10 days prior to entering the "yellow fever" country, or your certificate may not be considered valid. Booster doses are effective immediately.

Recently, an increasing number of severe adverse reactions to the vaccine have been reported in elderly travelers. This does not suggest that the elderly should not receive the vaccine when there is a true risk of exposure, but it would be prudent to give it careful consideration if the vaccine is required only for "bureaucratic" reasons. A certificate of exemption may be preferred.

Contrary to some popular beliefs, no inoculations are required to get back into the United States, Canada or other Western countries.

Countries that require yellow fever vaccination for entry from North America

Benin	French Guiana	Mauritania
Burkina Faso	Gabon	Niger
Cameroon	Ghana	Rwanda
Central African Republic	Ivory Coast	São Tomé and Principe
Congo	Mali	Togo

Recommended

HEPATITIS A. Hepatitis A is a viral infection of the liver, which is transmitted through infected food and water or from person to person. A few weeks after becoming infected, you may become ill with fever, nausea, weakness and fatigue. This is followed by jaundice (a yellowing of the skin and eyes). There is no specific treatment for hepatitis A. Thankfully, it usually is a self-limited infection, but you can count on being under the weather and off work for at least a month. The disease is usually quite mild, or even undetectable in small children. In the elderly it is more serious, with the mortality rate approaching 3 percent.

Hepatitis A occurs primarily in lesser-developed countries. Yes, the risk of infection is greater for the backpacker or visiting relative than for the affluent or business traveler staying in five-star hotels. But, as I tell my patients, *You are only as safe as the last person who handled your dinner.*" Consider receiving this vaccine for most travel outside of North America, Western Europe, Australia, New Zealand and Japan.

Prior to 1994, we used gamma globulin or immune serum globulin to prevent this infection. This was an injection that was usually given in your buttock. It contains protective antibodies against hepatitis A that have been collected from your local blood donors. While no other diseases were ever transmitted through the use of this product, it no longer seemed like such a great idea with the perceived threat of HIV and hepatitis C. It still may be used by some doctors for those who need last-minute protection. This protection is only short-lived, lasting between three and six months, depending upon the amount injected into the aforementioned buttock. Fortunately, we now have three excellent inactivated vaccines, Havrix®, Vaqta® and Avaxim®. Even better is that these vaccines go in your arm, not your buttock.

The three vaccines are quite comparable, and in fact may be used interchangeably. The initial dose is followed by a booster from 6 to 18 months later. If you happen to wait longer for your booster, don't worry. It's still OK. The first dose provides protection for at least a year, and the booster for at least 10 years (probably much longer). Side effects are minimal. While it's preferable to get immunized at least two weeks prior to your departure, evidence suggests that even last-minute vaccinations are worthwhile. It is considered safe in pregnancy.

The vaccine is safe for all over the age of one, although many doctors do not immunize small children (under five years of age) because the disease is usually quite mild or undetectable at this age. There is the risk, however, that such a child may come back home infected, though not sick, and pass the infection on to other, non-immune children or adults.

If you grew up in a lesser-developed country where your food, water and hygiene were questionable, you may have contracted hepatitis A (also known as yellow jaundice) as a child. Even if you did not become ill, you would still have life-long immunity. A blood test can be done which will prove if you are protected. If you are immune but receive the vaccine anyway, no harm is done (except you might have spent the 60 bucks elsewhere).

TYPHOID FEVER. This is a serious infection caused by the bacterium *Salmonella typhi,* which is transmitted via contaminated food and water. It can affect the bloodstream, lungs, liver, spleen, intestine and brain. After an incubation period of from 7 to 21 days, you develop symptoms which may include a persistent fever, headache, nausea, loss of appetite, abdominal pain, cough, constipation and confusion. Intestinal bleeding or perforation may be serious complications of the disease. With proper antibiotic treatment, the mortality rate should be less than 1 percent. Quinolone antibiotics, such as ciprofloxacin, are the treatment of choice. Resistance has emerged to older antibiotics such as sulfa and ampicillin.

Paratyphoid fever is a similar, though less severe infection, which is transmitted and treated in the same way as typhoid. In the olden days, we used a vaccine known as TABT to protect against both infections. Those who claimed that the reaction to the vaccine was nearly as bad as the disease were almost correct.

There are now two types of vaccines available to help lessen the risk of typhoid fever. However, they are both less than 70 percent effective. Therefore, the most important measure is to take care with your food and water. Typhim Vi® and Typherix® are injectable vaccines which after one dose provide up to 70 percent protection. Remember, a club sandwich teeming with typhoid bacilli can still give you typhoid fever. In the United States, this protection is said to last only two years; in Canada, we say three. The side effects are usually minor, and include some soreness at the injection site. These are "killed" vaccines, and so are considered safe in pregnancy and for immunosuppressed individuals. They may be given to those two years of age and older.

Vivotif® is an oral vaccine which provides protection for up to five years. It consists of four capsules that must be taken on alternate days. It may cause an upset stomach. Being a live vaccine, it should not be given to pregnant women or anyone who is immunosuppressed. Due to the dosing schedule and the need to keep the capsules refrigerated, compliance with this vaccine is often less than perfect. You also need to avoid antibiotics and vomiting. It is, however, preferable for someone who dislikes injections, or who will need protection for a longer time. It may be used in those six years of age and older.

CHOLERA. Cholera is a bacterial infection (*Vibrio cholerae*) of the intestine which is contracted through infected food and water. Outbreaks of cholera continue to occur in more than 60 countries worldwide. While some people develop only a mild illness, others may suffer severe watery diarrhea and vomiting, which may quickly progress to dehydration and death. This infection is exceedingly rare in travelers (less than one in 500,000), particularly in those who stay on the beaten path and use even a small bit of common sense with their choice of water.

An oral vaccine is available against cholera, Mutacol/Orochol Berna®. It provides about 80 percent protection for at least six months, which makes it superior to the older, injectable vaccine. There are also very few side effects. It is a single dose which has to be mixed with water. The vaccine is a live vaccine and should not be used in pregnancy or for those who are immunosuppressed. Vaccination is not recommended under the age of two.

While this vaccine is a good one, it's probably rarely needed by

travelers, due to the rarity of the infection. Perhaps a health worker going to work in a refugee camp where cholera has broken out,
or someone returning to their village back home where there may
be no access to clean water, should have the vaccine. Most travelers do have access to clean food and water and should be instruct-
ed on ways to minimize their risk, namely, *"Boil it, bottle it, peel
it, cook it ... or forget it!"*

This vaccine is currently required for religious pilgrims traveling
to Mecca for the haj. As well, Zanzibar (off the coast of Tanzania)
and Madagascar may also require proof of inoculation. The World
Health Organization does not endorse these "requirements."
Many travel advisers will instead furnish the patient with a certificate of exemption.

MENINGOCOCCAL DISEASE. Meningococcal disease is caused by the
bacterium *Neisseria meningitidis,* which is transmitted from person to person via close contact such as coughing, sneezing or direct
contact (kissing, sharing coffee cups, etc.). It may involve the blood
(meningococcemia) or the brain and spinal cord (meningitis). The
symptoms may include fever, headache, vomiting, irritability,
changes in the level of consciousness and a stiff neck. While it
often begins like a mild illness, it may quickly progress to shock,
convulsions or coma. It's usually accompanied by a petechial
(small bruises) rash. Even with optimal therapy, the mortality rate
may range from 5 to 15 percent.

There are several strains of meningococcal disease. Serogroup A
is the most common cause of epidemics outside of North America,
but serogroups C and B may also be responsible. One of the currently available vaccines, Menomune®, provides protection against
four of the strains, A,C,Y and W-135. While this is an excellent
vaccine, it does not provide very good protection in children under
the age of four. In children over four and adults, immunity lasts
between three and five years. Children who are immunized under
the age of four should receive a booster dose after this age if they
continue to be exposed.

Meningococcal vaccine may be recommended for travelers who
are off to areas where meningococcal disease is prevalent, or where

there have been significant outbreaks in the recent past. This applies particularly to longer-term travelers who will have close contact with the local population. The "meningitis belt" in Africa stretches from Gambia in the west to Ethiopia in the east (see map at end of Chapter 5, Region-by-Region Guide). Outbreaks are common in the dry winter months between December and May. Young children are affected the most, although adults and older kids may also become infected.

In the past, outbreaks have occurred in other areas, such as northern India, Nepal, East Africa and Saudi Arabia. Considering that no new outbreaks have occurred among travelers in recent years, vaccination is no longer recommended for the first three. Saudi Arabia continues to require that religious pilgrims to Mecca, for both haj and umra, receive the vaccine within the preceding three years.

In North America, the number of cases of meningococcal disease in 15- to 24-year-olds has been climbing. Most but not all of these cases are due to serogroup C. The risk is greatest in college students living in dormitories. Vaccination with Menomune®, or a newer, "conjugated" vaccine which provides protection only against serogroup C (Menjugate®), is now recommended for these academic travelers.

HEPATITIS B. This viral infection of the liver is transmitted through blood, blood products and unprotected sex. It differs from hepatitis A in its mode of transmission, but more importantly in its ability to cause more severe acute or chronic liver disease. While most of those who are infected recover and develop immunity, about 5 percent go on to become carriers of the virus. This carrier state may lead to conditions such as chronic hepatitis, cirrhosis or cancer of the liver, as well as being a danger to sexual and other close contacts.

In North America, less than 3 percent of the general population are carriers of the hepatitis B virus. This figure may be as high as 15 percent in other parts of the world, particularly Africa and Asia. Therefore, the traveler to these destinations is at higher risk. It's not unreasonable to consider this vaccine for all travelers, as you never know when an accident or illness will necessitate less than sterile medical treatment. Unanticipated and unprotected sex has also been known to occur.

Vaccination is strongly recommended for longer-term travelers (more than six months) to areas of the world with a high prevalence of hepatitis B in the local population (the figure of six months is a bit arbitrary, and it would not be unreasonable to offer it to shorter-term travelers), or for anyone who will be at higher risk based upon occupational exposure or other dangerous behaviors (e.g., health care workers, those who plan to engage in sex, and especially those health care workers who plan to engage in sex). Tattooing, acupuncture, body piercing, IV drug use and close shaves are all to be avoided.

Two very safe and effective vaccines are available—Engerix B® and Recombivax®. The full schedule consists of three doses, traditionally given at 0-1-6 months. Accelerated but effective regimens for those lacking sufficient time are 0-1-2 months, 0-7-21 days or 0-14-28 days. With these latter schedules, a further booster dose is suggested after one year. The full course of hepatitis B vaccination provides lifetime protection. Very good, though not perfect, protection against hepatitis B exists after only two injections, so it's quite reasonable to at least offer this if that's all that time allows. The vaccine is safe at any age as well as in pregnancy. Side effects are minimal, and the two vaccines may be used interchangeably. It's not necessary to check your antibody levels after receiving hepatitis B vaccine. All children in North America are now routinely inoculated against hepatitis B in childhood.

For many, it will be convenient, and a little less expensive, to receive a combined hepatitis A and B vaccine, called Twinrex®. This vaccine is usually given at 0-1-6 months, but may also be accelerated when necessary. Both hepatitis A and B vaccines may go unrefrigerated for up to two weeks, so it's quite reasonable for the traveler to carry a dose along, to be administered after arrival if necessary. If carrying syringes, be sure to carry an explanatory note from your doctor.

There are other forms of viral hepatitis, including hepatitis C and E. Hepatitis C is transmitted in the same way as hepatitis B, and it may have similar consequences. Hepatitis E is passed through contaminated food and water, as is hepatitis A. It's found mainly in Mexico, Asia and Africa. This infection is especially serious in pregnant women, with a mortality rate of between 15 and 20 percent. Neither hepatitis C nor E is preventable through vaccination.

JAPANESE ENCEPHALITIS. JE is a viral infection of the brain which occurs in rural parts of Asia and Southeast Asia. It is transmitted by the *Culex* mosquito, which bites between dusk and dawn, particularly in areas with rice paddies and pig farming. The infection is somewhat seasonal, usually being more prevalent from May through October. In the more tropical regions, it may be a risk year round. JE is thankfully quite rare in travelers, with the vast majority of infections being asymptomatic. However, among those who are affected, 20 percent of cases may prove fatal and up to 50 percent may leave the victim with a disability. The young and the elderly are at greatest risk.

The vaccine is advisable for those who plan prolonged exposure (one month or more) in the endemic areas during the transmission season (see map at end of Chapter 5, Region-by-Region Guide). It consists of three doses, given at 0-7-28 days. This can be shortened to 0-7-14 days in the hurried traveler. Even two shots provide reasonable short-term protection. Side effects are a bit more common than with most of the other vaccines. In particular, serious allergic reactions sometimes occur, especially in those with other allergies. As these reactions are sometimes delayed by up to two weeks, you should not receive a dose of this vaccine less than 10 days prior to your departure. Considering the cost of the vaccine (about $100 per dose) and the relative rarity of the disease in travelers, you probably warrant this one only if you are at high risk. It's available overseas much more cheaply. Don't forget your insect repellents and mosquito nets.

RABIES. Rabies is a viral infection of the central nervous system which when contracted by humans is thought to be 100 percent fatal in the absence of proper pre- or post-exposure vaccination. It is transmitted by a bite, scratch or, rarely, lick from infected animals, most commonly dogs. Cats, bats and monkeys may also be infectious. Closer to home, foxes, skunks and raccoons are a threat. More than 50,000 cases, and deaths, occur worldwide each year. The majority of these happen in India. In many countries of the world, stray dogs, some having rabies, are a tremendous problem. They may be docile, and somewhat pathetic looking—just the kind of animal you'd love to pet. Don't!

The incubation period (time from the bite until symptoms appear) of rabies is usually between two weeks and six months. However, depending upon the severity of the bite and its proximity to the brain (the nearer the brain, the more urgent the situation), this may be as little as four days or as long as a year or more. The illness in humans begins with vague flu-like symptoms such as fatigue, fever or headache. There may be discomfort or tingling at the site of exposure (bite). This is followed within several days by spasm of the swallowing muscles and, hence, a fear of water (hydrophobia), confusion, agitation, convulsions, delirium, paralysis, coma and death.

Pre-exposure vaccination, which consists of three injections (on days 0-7-21 or -28), is recommended only for those at the highest risk. This may include those with occupational exposure, such as veterinarians and spelunkers (people who spend time in caves), or others who by the nature, location and duration of their travels may be at risk. I recall one patient who was off to work in a dog food factory in Thailand; indeed, a high-risk traveler. Children, in spite of repeated warnings from their parents, are more likely to play with animals and less likely to report a bite. Consider them higher-risk travelers. Rabies vaccine is quite expensive (at least $100 per dose), and this certainly puts a limit on the number of people who receive it.

There are three "brands" of rabies vaccine that are considered safe and effective. They are human diploid cell vaccine (HDCV), purified chick embryo cell vaccine (PCEC) and rabies vaccine adsorbed (RVA). They are considered interchangeable. Pre-exposure vaccination probably provides lifetime protection, though many authorities still recommend checking antibody levels every two years if exposure continues.

Rabies vaccine is usually given intramuscularly (in the deltoid muscle of the arm). In the case of HDCV, it's also effective if given intradermally (just under the skin, like a TB skin test). In this case, only one-tenth of the usual dose need be given. The main advantage of this route is that if you are going away with family or friends, you can share the vial of vaccine. One caveat is that this route may not be effective if you are already on an antimalarial such as chloroquine or mefloquine. If that's the case, you require the intramuscular route.

Pre-exposure vaccination does not preclude the need for further injections after a potentially rabid bite (all bites in lesser-developed countries must be considered potentially rabid). If you are bitten, it's imperative that the wound be thoroughly cleansed with soap and water. Let me say that again—wash the wound thoroughly with soap and water. If you have received pre-exposure vaccination, then there is still a need for two further injections of vaccine on days 0 and 3 after exposure. I repeat, there is still a need for two further injections of vaccine.

For the person who has not previously been vaccinated, it's also necessary to receive human rabies immune globulin (HRIG) as quickly as possible. This provides some immediate protection. HRIG should be injected into the site of the bite, not into a distant arm or buttock. As well, immunization with the rabies vaccine on days 0-3-7-14-28 should be started. HRIG must be given as soon after the bite as possible (measure in days, not hours or minutes). You should, therefore, always have time to get to good medical care. If rabies vaccine has been started more than seven days before the availability of HRIG, then HRIG should not be given, as it will interfere with your immune response to the vaccine.

Safe, effective rabies vaccines are not always available in some countries, and when they are, they may be exorbitantly expensive. Remember, if you are bitten, wash the wound thoroughly and seek good medical care as quickly as possible. If effective vaccines are not available, you should travel to somewhere where they are. This is a good time to call home or your travel clinic, just to make sure you are receiving the correct treatment. Rabies is 100 percent preventable if you receive the proper course of vaccination. It is 100 percent fatal if you don't.

TICK-BORNE ENCEPHALITIS. This viral infection of the brain is found in rural areas of both Eastern and Western Europe. The most common countries include Austria, Estonia, Latvia, the Czech Republic, Slovakia, Germany, Hungary, Poland, Switzerland, Russia, Ukraine, Belarus and northern parts of the former Yugoslavia. As the name implies, it is transmitted via ticks, which like to jump off the plants, grass and bushes onto unsuspecting and uncovered hikers. Ticks do their feeding from spring through fall, and only people who travel into rural areas for three weeks or more during this period are considered at significant risk. You can also become infected by drinking unpasteurized milk from goats, cows or sheep.

The infection, when it actually produces symptoms, begins with a flu-like illness, which is followed by more severe symptoms, such as neck stiffness, dizziness, tremors, drowsiness, delirium and coma. It is rarely fatal, but permanent neurological damage may occur.

The vaccine (FSME-Immun®) consists of two doses, given one to three months apart. Booster doses should be administered at twelve months, and then every three years if there is recurrent exposure. This vaccine is not currently available in the United States, and in Canada your doctor must order it through Health Canada's Special Access Program. Personal measures such as wearing long pants and socks, using insect repellents and inspecting your skin at the end of the day for embedded ticks are a great idea.

INFLUENZA. The flu, as it's better known, is a particular risk to the elderly (over 65) and to those with chronic, underlying medical problems. These include respiratory conditions such as asthma and emphysema, heart disease, immunodeficiency, diabetes and cancer. The flu season in the Southern Hemisphere occurs during our summer, as opposed to our season, which stretches from December through April. True influenza is not just a scratchy throat and a runny nose. It's *"My fever was 102°F, my throat was raw, my head was splitting, my chest ached from coughing and every part of my body including my eyeballs hurt!"* While most people recover within a week or two, high-risk individuals are more susceptible to complications such as pneumonia and even death. Influenza has been responsible for thousands of deaths in the past century.

The vaccine would be recommended for those at higher risk, as well as anyone wishing to reduce the risk of becoming ill with the flu. It should not be given to people with an egg allergy. As the influenza virus has a way of changing from year to year, vaccination is recommended annually.

PNEUMOCOCCAL PNEUMONIA. Like influenza, this common respiratory infection can be particularly lethal in the elderly and in those with underlying medical problems. Everyone over the age of 65, as well as anyone with chronic heart or lung disease, immunosuppression or diabetes, should receive the vaccine. People who have lost their spleen, either through trauma or because of sickle cell disease, should also be immunized.

TUBERCULOSIS. TB is a bacterial infection which primarily affects the lungs, though it may also affect other organs such as the kidney, bowel, bones and lymph nodes. Two million people die from TB each year. One-third of the world's population is infected, and 5 to 10 percent of these will become sick and infectious at some point in their lives. It is transmitted via respiratory droplets, that is, coughing and sneezing, just like the common cold. The disease is on the increase for a few reasons:

• HIV infection and TB are inextricably linked, and this has been the main reason for its resurgence.
• Strains of TB have developed resistance to all the commonly used medications.
• Treatment requires multiple drugs for a prolonged period and compliance is often poor, which tends to lead to further drug resistance.

- Public health systems are ineffective or nonexistent in many less developed countries.
- War, poverty and human migration all contribute to the increase in TB around the world. Refugees in Africa, prison inmates in Russia and the homeless in North America are only some of the victims.

Many people, especially in lesser-developed countries, have been exposed to TB in the past and have developed some immunity. However, this so-called immunity may break down, sometimes because of other medications or medical problems (e.g., HIV), and the infection may reactivate.

Infection with TB is a fairly small risk to most travelers, but it does occur. People who are at the greatest risk are those going off to highly endemic areas for longer periods of time and who will have lots of exposure to the local population. Long-term volunteers and missionaries fit this description.

There is a fair bit of controversy regarding immunization to prevent TB. Most of the world outside of North America routinely administers a vaccine known as BCG to children at birth. The North American view is that BCG does not work very well, and probably provides some protection only for the very young and only against certain forms of TB.

The North American approach is to do a two-step (two tests at least one week apart) TB skin test (Mantoux test) prior to travel. This test is usually normal (negative), unless there has been past exposure to tuberculosis or vaccination with BCG; the usual plan is to repeat the test about two months after your return. In this way, we detect those who have converted from negative to positive. Those who have converted are not ill with TB, nor are they contagious. But we know that they have been exposed and are at higher risk of developing active TB in the future. They are usually offered preventive medication, usually isoniazid (INH), for 6 to 12 months, which lowers the risk of developing an active infection. Other drug regimens (e.g., rifampin and pyrazinamide) may be used if a drug-resistant strain of TB is suspected.

Considering the spread of multi-drug-resistant TB and the difficulty in doing yearly skin tests, it may be worthwhile at least to consider the pros and cons of BCG, particularly for very young children who will be living in high-risk areas for prolonged periods.

SMALLPOX. This scourge of mankind killed millions of humans throughout history. In 1977 the last case of this viral infection was recorded in Somalia, and in 1980 the World Health Organization declared the disease eradicated. This was largely the result of vaccination and a tremendous amount of hard work. Today, the threat of smallpox as a biological weapon looms over the world, and smallpox vaccination may again become a necessity. For the time being, however, smallpox vaccination is not recommended or required for travel, nor is the vaccine available to the general public.

What Are the Side Effects of Vaccines?

For the most part, the side effects are mild, consisting of localized soreness and tenderness at the site of injection within the first 48 hours. Flu-like symptoms such as a fever and muscle aches occur, but are uncommon. Allergic reactions tend to be quite rare, but they can happen; so it is for this reason that you will be asked to remain in the office for at least 15 minutes after your injection.

What is not so rare is vasovagal syncope, or a simple fainting spell. The combination of anticipation and a bit of pain is sometimes enough to provoke this reaction. An empty stomach and three layers of clothing don't help either. If you are prone to such spells, let the doctor or nurse know in advance. They will have you lie down so that a little more blood remains in your head.

If you are acutely ill or feverish, you and your doctor should probably postpone your vaccinations. Runny noses, sprained ankles, tension headaches and tummy aches probably don't qualify as "sick," and it would be safe to proceed in such situations. There is no shortage of people out there extolling the dangers of vaccination. If you choose to believe everything that you hear, I suggest you do so at your own risk.

When Should I Get My Vaccines?

It would be nice to have all your vaccinations completed about two weeks before you leave. This may mean visiting your travel clinic six to eight weeks prior to your departure. All the vaccines will then be completely effective by the time you arrive at your destination. You won't have an achy arm on the plane, and there will be plenty of time to get everything else done. Remember that several of the vaccines which you may need, such as hepatitis B, Japanese encephalitis and rabies, require a series of shots. There are accelerated schedules in some cases, as described; but if you are leaving the next day, none of the schedules are that fast. Having said that, a last-minute TdP or hepatitis A shot on the way to the airport is still worthwhile. When you make your visit, take along your itinerary and a record of your past inoculations.

Several shots may be given at the same sitting (or "lying," if you happen to be a fainter). This may leave you with at least two sore arms, but the efficacy of the vaccines will not be affected. The only exception is as follows: Live vaccines (e.g., measles, oral typhoid, cholera, yellow fever) should be given at the same time or separated by at least four weeks, if possible. Unfortunately, we are not yet able to mix all the shots into one convenient cocktail.

Sometimes travelers have started a series of shots, but have not completed the whole series. At other times, they fail to come back at the recommended time for a booster. A booster dose can be given any time without the necessity of having to begin the original series all over again.

Key Points

- Immunize according to risk—not just the country visited.
- Vaccines may be divided into those that are Routine, Required and Recommended.
- The doctor/nurse advises, the traveler decides.

Summary of Pretravel Inoculations

Disease	Vaccine	Course	Duration
Hepatitis A	Avaxim® (AP)* Vaqta® (Merck) Havrix® (GSK)*	single dose good for 1 year; booster at 6-12 months	10 years or more after booster dose
Hepatitis B	Engerix B® (GSK)* Recombivax® (Merck)	0-1-6 months; accelerated: 0-1-2-12 months; 0-7-21, 0-14-28 days, booster at 12 months	life
Hepatitis A/B	Twinrix® (GSK)*	0-1-6 months; may also be accelerated as above if necessary	hep A: 10 years hep B: life
Typhoid fever	Typhim-Vi® (AP)* Typherix® (GSK)* Vivotif® (Berna)	single dose oral: 4 doses on alternate days	2 years (U.S.) 3 years (Canada) 5 years
Yellow fever	YF-Vax® (AP)*	single dose	10 years
Meningococcal disease	Menomune® (AP)* (A,C,Y,W-135)	single dose; children immunized before age 4 need a booster	3-5 years
Rabies	Imovax® (HDCV)(AP)* RabAvert® (PCEC) (Chiron)	pre-exposure: 0-7-21 (or 28) days post-exposure: 0-3 days if previously vaccinated; 0-3-7-14-28 if not, and must receive human rabies immune globulin (HRIG)	check immunity every 2 years if exposure continues
Japanese encephalitis	JE-Vax® (AP)*	0-7-30 days; accelerated: 0-7-14 days	2 years
Tick-borne encephalitis	FSME-Immun® (Baxter)	2 doses, 1-3 months apart	booster at 12 months, and then every 3 years
Cholera	Mutacol®/Orochol® (Berna)	single dose (oral)	at least 6 months

*GSK = Glaxo SmithKline
*AP = Aventis Pasteur
***Note**: Check dosages and instructions with doctor or pharmacist.*

Traveler's Diarrhea

CHAPTER 7

"Most travel is best of all in the anticipation or the
remembering; the reality has more to
do with losing your luggage."

REGINA NADELSON

"Travel expands the mind ... but loosens the bowels." At least it
does so in up to 40 percent of tropical travelers. Traveler's
Diarrhea is by far the commonest affliction of those going from
industrialized countries to tropical or lesser-developed countries.
For most, it is just an inconvenience, but for some it's severe
enough to keep you in the room close to the toilet, or may even
require hospitalization.

There are many definitions of this condition, with the scientific
one being "passing three unformed bowel movements within 24
hours." Perhaps a more practical one is when your stools become
so loose that they tend to take the shape of the container. This condition has received many nicknames, depending upon where you
become infected.

Affectionate Names for Traveler's Diarrhea

- Montezuma's Revenge
- Delhi Belly
- Seeping Slickness
- Aztec Two-Step

- Calcutta Craps
- _____
- _____

  (add your own here)

The risk of acquiring Traveler's Diarrhea depends upon a few factors. Destination plays an important role, with Africa, Latin America, the Middle East and southern Asia posing a 20–50 percent risk, and North America, Japan, Western Europe and Australia much lower, at less than 10 percent. The Caribbean, Russia, eastern and southern Europe and China fall in between, at 15–20 percent. But it's more than just your destination.

Younger travelers fall ill more often than the elderly. Either the latter have some additional gut immunity, or they are more careful. Your style of travel plays an important role. A cash-strapped backpacker shlepping through rural India for six months would be at much greater risk than a businessperson staying at the top hotel in New Delhi for just three days. Anyone lacking acid in their stomach, usually because they are taking medications which block the acid, may be more prone. So too would a traveler who is immunosuppressed, as with HIV/AIDS. Finally, being careful does make a difference, and we'll talk more about that in a moment. And, oh yes, luck. Some people barely think twice, and have no problem. Others are paranoid and picky—and they get sick.

What Are the Causes?

There are numerous infectious organisms responsible for Traveler's Diarrhea, with the majority of them being bacteria. Enterotoxigenic *E. coli* causes up to 70 percent of cases, and it generally causes mild, self-limited watery diarrhea, so it doesn't usually ruin your trip. It is said to follow the "rule of threes"—you become ill on the third day of the trip, you run to the bathroom three times a day and usually you are all better within three days. Having said that, many people have a way of falling ill just as they board their airplane for the long flight back home.

Other well-known bacteria, such as *Salmonella, Shigella* and *Campylobacter,* may not be so forgiving. They usually affect the large intestine, and are potentially more invasive, often leading to dysentery; that is, diarrhea accompanied by fever, or blood or pus in the stools. It's not always necessary to leave home to acquire these infections.

Viruses, such as rotavirus and Norwalk virus, account for up to about 20 percent of cases of diarrhea in travelers. Less common causes of infectious diarrhea include protozoan parasites, such as *Giardia lamblia* and various amebas, including *Entamoeba histolytica.* Infection with these parasites may range from being totally asymptomatic, to mild watery diarrhea or, in the case of amebiasis, full-blown dysentery, with blood and pus in the stools. Amebiasis (infection caused by amebas) may also spread to your liver, where it forms an abscess. This may in turn give you symptoms of fever, sweats, weight loss and pain over your liver (the upper-right-hand corner of your abdomen).

Giardiasis is particularly well known for causing gas, bloating, rumbling, nausea, fatigue and *"farts that curl your nose,"* according to one well-traveled and infected expert. Lactose intolerance, or an inability to digest the lactose in dairy products, may complicate giardiasis, or in fact almost any cause of diarrhea.

Some newer parasites such as *Cryptosporidium* and *Cyclospora* are emerging as more frequent causes of diarrhea in travelers. Cryptosporidiosis can cause fairly severe watery diarrhea that may persist for up to three weeks. In immunosuppressed patients such as those with HIV/AIDS, it may be particularly debilitating or even fatal. There is no specific treatment other than hydration. Infection with *Cyclospora* may begin acutely, with severe watery diarrhea and vomiting, and follow a chronic course characterized by loss of appetite and fatigue for up to 12 weeks if left untreated.

What about intestinal worms? Well, there certainly are a lot of them in the tropics, and several of them are transmitted through contaminated food. First, there are the roundworms (*Ascaris lumbricoides*) and the whipworms (*Trichuris trichiura*). Remember that human fertilizer or "night soil" may contaminate the local vegetable patch, and hence your food. Tapeworms (*Taenia solium, Taenia saginata, Diphyllobothrium latum*) are contracted by eating poorly cooked or raw pork, beef or fish. They can grow up to 30 feet in length. Hopefully, I have convinced you to order your meat well done. Hookworms (*Ancylostoma duodenale* and *Necator americanus*) and *Strongyloides stercoralis* are contracted by walking barefoot in areas contaminated by human feces. Don't walk there! Having mentioned all these lovely worms, I reassure you that in general, they are not usually a cause of diarrhea, nor are they common infections in travelers.

What you get, to a slight extent, may depend upon where you travel and when. Enterotoxigenic *E. coli* is particularly prevalent in Latin America, while *Cyclospora* tends to produce yearly outbreaks in Nepal between April and July. Giardiasis first attracted attention when Canadian hockey fans succumbed in Leningrad (now St. Petersburg) in 1972, and it is still a greater risk there, as well as in India and Nepal. *Campylobacter* is a significant threat in Thailand and Northern Africa.

Is it the food or the water that makes us sick? Well, both, but in fact the food is more often responsible. It may be washed in local water, inadequately cooked, contaminated by raw vegetables that share the same cutting board, left in the sun by the pool for hours or used as a landing strip by flies that are capable of transmitting disease. Food handlers are not always up to scratch either. I think it's easier for us to have control over our water than our food.

The above-mentioned infections are not only the property of tropical and lesser-developed countries. Almost all of them can be found right here in North America. Large outbreaks of cryptosporidiosis, involving thousands of people, have occurred in both Canada and the United States. Giardiasis is affectionately known as "beaver fever" throughout our parks and rivers. Food poisoning caused by *Campylobacter* and *Salmonella* is commonplace. *Cyclospora* has been responsible for several outbreaks in North America as a result of being imported along with Guatemalan raspberries. Therefore, the precautions we preach for travelers abroad should also be practiced at home.

Not everything that causes the runs, however, is infectious. Consider the traveler to the Caribbean suddenly exposed to too much sun, too much alcohol and too much fruit, or perhaps in other destinations where the spices or the grease play havoc with traditional bowel habits.

How Do We Prevent It?

The quick answer is *"Boil it, bottle it, peel it, cook it ... or forget it!"* But let me break this old Mexican proverb down into its different parts, and provide you with a little more detail.

Boiling water is the most reliable method of purifying your water. Unfortunately, for many travelers, it is not a practical option. The $64,000 question is, *"For how long do you have to boil your water?"* The correct answer is, *"Just bringing it to a rolling boil for a few minutes will suffice."* Persisting for 10 or 20 minutes will be a waste of fuel, water and time. Once you have boiled your water, be sure to store it in a clean, covered container. Portable heating coils may be more practical than stoves or raging campfires when it comes to sterilizing small amounts of water. Boiling water will not remove silt and other debris from your water.

Bottled water is available in almost every corner of the world. Most of it is probably safe to drink. But there is a fair bit of skepticism about disreputable people refilling bottles with contaminated local water and selling it back to you. So again, traveler beware. Inspect the seal to make sure it has not been tampered with. (I've heard that even the seals can be forged.)

Carbonated water offers the additional protection of being more difficult to forge, and the pH is lower, providing a less hospitable environment for bacteria. Other carbonated beverages, beer and wine are also safe to drink. Remember, ice is only frozen water, with the offending organisms well preserved. Avoid it, unless you are assured of its origin. Milk should be pasteurized, and if this option is not available, boil it.

Chemical disinfection (halogenation), using halogens such as iodine and chlorine, is very effective, but not always perfect. *Giardia,* and particularly *Cryptosporidium,* may be resistant. The dosage and contact time employed with these chemicals may depend upon the temperature of the water and its turbidity (can you see through it?). One drawback is the fact that iodine or chlorine may leave your water tasting a bit like your laundry. This can be rectified by adding some vitamin C, either as a tablet or via juice crystals. Iodine should be used cautiously, or not at all, by those with thyroid disease and by pregnant women. Long-term use is also not recommended. It is available as a liquid or tablet, or as a resin that is incorporated into some water filters. An excellent new product called Pristine® contains chlorine dioxide, which is effective against *Cryptosporidium* as well as all other water-borne infectious organisms. It does not alter the taste of your water.

Charcoal (activated charcoal) does not get rid of the organisms in water, but does remove organic wastes, chemicals and radioactive particles. This sounds like a good thing. If used after halogenation, it will remove the annoying taste left by iodine or chlorine. Charcoal is often a component of water purification systems.

Water purification systems are quite popular with many travelers. To describe every one on the market is beyond the scope of this book, but let me try to give you the basics. Choosing a water purifier is a bit like picking out a personal computer—it depends upon your needs. Take into consideration your itinerary, since that may determine which pathogens you are most concerned about. How much room do you have in your knapsack? How simple is it to use? How long does it have to last? Can you replace the parts as they age? How much water do you need to filter? How much money can you spend?

Most systems use a ceramic filter. These will remove the bigger items, like bacteria and parasites. But in spite of the fact that their pore sizes are as small as 0.2 microns, the filters cannot be counted on to remove viruses, such as hepatitis A and E, Norwalk and rotavirus. Therefore, many use an iodine resin to achieve this. Charcoal may also be a component, to remove the toxic wastes, along with the awful taste I mentioned. If your purifier does not both filter and halogenate, then these jobs may have to be done as separate processes.

Finally, we cannot survive on fluids alone. So what about the *food?* The bottom line is, it should be cooked—well cooked and recently cooked. Aside from causing diarrhea, contaminated foods may transmit several worms, which I have already described for you.

Vegetables must be washed in soapy water and soaked in a disinfectant such as iodine or chlorine. Lettuce is best avoided. Fruits must also be washed properly and peeled, preferably with a clean knife. Watermelons have the reputation of being injected with local water to make them heavier and thus increase the selling price. Juice stands are quite popular around the world. I remember vividly the market in Cuzco, Peru—nice ladies in bowlerlike hats with rows of infected blenders. Patronize them at your own risk.

Thankfully, bread and similar products are safe; but items that may act as a wonderful culture medium for bacteria, such as custards and salad dressings, are not.

A few other points need mentioning. First, wash your hands frequently. You are shaking hands constantly, and the local money may not be that hygienic either. Hand sanitizers containing ethyl alcohol, such as Purell®, are useful when there's no water nearby. Is it safe to shower using local water? I think so, though it may not be the best time to sing all your old Beatle songs. Can you brush your teeth in the local water? Probably, in that you are exposing yourself to only a small amount of water, and therefore very few infectious organisms. Preferably it should be as hot as you can stand. Personally, I brush with bottled water when away. My paranoia seems to increase with age.

So what do you really do about food and water when away? I think the answer is to do the best you can, realizing that a bit of diarrhea may be inevitable. Trying foods in the market is a bit risky, but fun. Getting invited into local homes for a meal is a great experience. But pulling out your $300 water purifier at the dinner table is probably in bad taste. Eating out with your business clients is a necessity. Many places where you eat do in fact follow good hygienic practices. You are entitled to ask a few questions before you eat. Tours of the kitchen are not recommended. As with everything in this book, a little bit of knowledge and a lot of common sense are what you really need.

What Do I Do When I Get Diarrhea?

The cornerstone of treatment of diarrhea is to replace your fluid losses. This is particularly important in children, who may become dehydrated more quickly. Rehydration can usually be achieved with oral fluids, such as purified water, soup with salt, canned fruit juice, tea with sugar or carbonated drinks. Breast-feeding should be continued in babies.

Oral rehydration salts (ORS), made to World Health Organization (WHO) and UNICEF standards, are readily available around the world. They contain the ideal amounts of sugar, potassium, sodium and bicarbonate, and can be added to clean water. Gastrolyte® is one brand that is available in North America. The formula for the ORS packet used by UNICEF and WHO contains 3.5 grams sodium chloride (common salt), 2.9 grams trisodium citrate dihydrate (or 2.5 grams sodium bicarbonate; i.e., baking soda), 1.5 grams potassium chloride and 20 grams glucose (anhydrous), all added to one liter of clean water.

You can make your own ORS if necessary by using the following formula: one level teaspoon of salt, eight level teaspoons of sugar and one quart or liter of clean drinking or boiled water (and then cooling the mixture).

For most cases of diarrhea, oral rehydration may be all that's required. Once you are getting better, solid foods may be added gradually. (One hint to help you decide how solid, is that the consistency of your food should resemble that of your stools.) Rice and bananas are good foods to start with. Dairy products are best avoided until you and your stools are back to normal. In a minority of cases involving both adults and children, diarrhea and/or vomiting may lead to severe dehydration and require medical attention and possibly intravenous fluids.

For those who need a bit of symptomatic relief, an antiperistaltic such as Imodium® (loperamide) will usually suffice. Contrary to popular belief, such medications do not plug you up or shut the trap door and throw away the key! Rather, they slow peristalsis (the propulsive movement of your intestine). It should be used in small amounts, lest you never go the bathroom again.

Some of you are probably saying, *"Isn't it better to let the infection get out of your system on its own?"* Those in favor of just letting nature take its course may change their minds on an eight-hour bus ride in the Andes, or when they see the local facilities. If it's your one day to see the Taj Mahal or the pyramids, you also might be looking for the quickest remedy. On the other hand, if you have plenty of time, a good book and plenty of toilet paper, medications are not always necessary, as most infections will resolve on their own. My advice to people is, *"If you are uncomfortable or inconvenienced, why not take something to make things better?"*

It's not advisable to use an antiperistaltic alone in the presence of fever, or blood and pus in the stools. Lomotil® (diphenoxylate) is a narcotic and may result in drowsiness. It is best avoided. Antiperistaltics should not be used by those under the age of two, or by pregnant women.

Pepto-Bismol® (bismuth subsalicylate), in a dose of two table-spoons or tablets every 30 minutes for up to eight doses, will also shorten the duration of your diarrhea. This medication should not be taken by anyone with an aspirin allergy or who is on anticoag-ulant medications. Pepto-Bismol® may turn both your stools and your tongue black.

What about antibiotics? Since bacteria cause most acute cases of Traveler's Diarrhea, the use of an appropriate antibiotic will usu-ally dramatically shorten the duration of your illness. A member of the quinolone family, such as Cipro®, Noroxin®, Floxin® or Levaquin®, given in a brief course of three days or less (e.g., 500 milligrams of Cipro® twice daily for three days), will usually do the trick. For those who want the quickest relief, a quinolone antibi-otic, in combination with a small amount of Imodium®, is your best bet. You'll likely be feeling better within 24 hours.

The quinolones are not recommended under the age of 16 (they affect the growing cartilage in rats), but they are likely not harm-ful if used in such a brief course should the situation demand it. *Campylobacter* has developed resistance to ciprofloxacin in Thailand, and a better choice there may be azithromycin (Zithromax®). Sulfa-containing antibiotics, such as Bactrim® and Septra®, are of little use any more due to drug resistance. An exception to this statement might be diarrhea caused by *Cyclospora,* where this medication is the drug of choice.

As mentioned, diarrhea caused by parasites is much less com-mon and usually much less acute than that caused by bacteria. If you are suspected of having giardiasis or amebiasis, the correct treatment would be metronidazole (Flagyl®) or tinidazole (Fasigen®).

To diagnose the cause of your diarrhea properly, it is necessary to perform both a stool culture (to grow the bacteria) and to look at a specimen under a microscope (to actually see the parasites). The reality in the tropics is that, much like with malaria, a proper diag-nosis is often not made. So you may initially be given an antibiot-ic. If you return no better in a few days, you will receive an antipar-asitic. In some countries, they are combined in the same pill.

If you are homeopathically inclined, there are numerous products which you might take to settle things down in your intestines, including yogurt, lactobacillus, acidophilus and grapefruit seed extract. If you are on that eight-hour Andean bus adventure and the next toilet is six hours away (I remember it well!), I personally would opt for the Imodium® and antibiotic.

I have seen long-term volunteers who seem to succumb to one episode of diarrhea after another. Every infection is eventually diagnosed as either bacterial or parasitic, or both. Every medication is taken—often more than once. They get quite rundown, lose weight and sometimes have to return home. This demonstrates that it really is worthwhile to take care with your food and water, and to try to get accurate diagnosis and proper treatment whenever possible.

Can I Take Something to Prevent Diarrhea?

The occasional person may need a bit of added help in avoiding turista. I would consider the use of a prophylactic antibiotic, again a quinolone such as Cipro® (500 milligrams daily), in someone who just can't afford to get sick, such as those with underlying medical conditions like diabetes, HIV/AIDS or inflammatory bowel disease. Also included in this group are the so-called VIPs, who because of the importance of their mission cannot afford the extra time needed to go to the bathroom if affected. Some unlucky people swear they get cramps as soon as they see a palm tree. This group may also benefit. Prophylactic antibiotics should be considered only in the short-term (less than three weeks) traveler. If you do take a preventive antibiotic, start it on the day of your arrival, and continue it until the day after you arrive back home.

Pepto-Bismol® has also been used successfully in preventing Traveler's Diarrhea. The recommended dosage is two tablespoons or two tablets four times daily. That's a helluva lot to carry, especially if you are using the liquid. Like a prophylactic antibiotic, this medication is suggested only for short-term travelers.

Some travelers will still have diarrhea and other joys such as gas, bloating and a tremendous amount of noise emanating from their abdomen after their return home. These symptoms may gradually disappear on their own, but it may be worth a trip to the doctor to see if you have returned home with some unexpected company, such as a parasite or two. (See Chapter 25, Hey Doc, I'm Home!) Remember, Traveler's Diarrhea is one of the more innocent consequences of consuming contaminated food and water. Typhoid fever, hepatitis A and E, intestinal worms and many other infections may be yours if you ignore the words, *"Boil it, bottle it, peel it, cook it ... or forget it!"* Having said that, never turn down the opportunity for a home-cooked meal.

Key Points

- Boil it, bottle it, peel it, cook it ... or forget it!
- Take along something for the treatment of diarrhea, such as Imodium® and Cipro®.
- Be sure to replace your fluids if you develop vomiting and/or diarrhea
- If you are at "high risk," consider taking a prophylactic antibiotic.

Malaria

CHAPTER 8

"The tourist who moves about to see and hear and open
himself to all the influences of the places which condense
centuries of human greatness is only a man
in search of excellence."

MAX LERNER

If you are off to the tropics and have time to read about only one topic, this would be a good choice. I apologize for it being a bit long, but I think that you need a good understanding of the disease, and the issues surrounding its prevention and treatment. Malaria is by far the most serious infectious threat faced by travelers to the tropics.

Every year, between 300 and 500 million cases of malaria occur worldwide. Some 90 percent of these take place in sub-Saharan Africa. About two million people die each year, the majority being children. The number of travelers returning to the United States and Canada with malaria has again been increasing in recent years, and more than a handful die each year.

Malaria should be a preventable and/or treatable disease. So why the problem? Perhaps it's the usual explanation that more of us are traveling to "off the beaten path" malarious areas. There certainly are many more North Americans of foreign descent returning to places like India and Africa to visit their families. Drug-resistant strains of malaria are spreading, and global warming might be allowing mosquitoes to transmit the infection in places where they haven't flown before.

But perhaps a major contributing factor is the deluge of misleading information, anecdotes and hearsay surrounding the topic of malaria and antimalarial medications. Many travelers that I encounter are dangerously influenced by some of the advice they receive once they are abroad, as well as at home. Personally, I think you should be armed with the "proper" advice before you leave. Your life may depend upon it. Hopefully, the following pages will give you the information you need to make intelligent choices about the subject.

What Is Malaria?

Malaria is a parasitic (protozoan, to be more specific) infection of the red blood cells transmitted by the bite of the female *Anopheles* mosquito. There are four human strains of this parasite, *Plasmodium vivax*, *Plasmodium ovale*, *Plasmodium malariae* and *Plasmodium falciparum*. It is this last strain, *P. falciparum*, that is resistant to many of our antimalarial drugs, and unfortunately it is this strain that may prove fatal. The first two strains, *P. vivax* and *P. ovale*, have the ability to lie dormant in the liver for longer periods of time, and hence may account for cases of malaria that occur months after exposure, or cases that relapse. But they do not cause death. *P. malariae* is the least commonly encountered strain.

Where Is There Malaria?

Before you get all hot and bothered, it's necessary to know whether or not you will be in a malarious area. The map at the end of Chapter 5, Region-by-Region Guide, gives an overview of where malaria occurs. However, such maps can be a bit misleading. In Southeast Asia and South and Central America, for example, urban areas and most tourist spots are free of malaria. A typical tour through Bangkok, Chiang Mai, the beaches of southern Thailand, Singapore, Kuala Lumpur and Bali presents almost no risk of malaria. Neither does a trip that includes Quito, the Galapagos, Lima, Cuzco and Machu Picchu. This may be because of the altitude (e.g., Cuzco, Quito), previous efforts to eliminate mosquitoes, or a lack of breeding sites for mosquitoes. The same cannot be said for India or sub-Saharan Africa, where malaria is also found in major cities such as Mumbai (Bombay), Lagos and Dar es Salaam, as well as in rural areas. In sub-Saharan Africa, the predominant species is *P. falciparum,* and transmission tends to be more intense than in most other parts of the world. Should you be off to the Caribbean, only the island of Hispaniola (Dominican Republic/Haiti) still has malaria, and most of it on the Haitian end of the island.

As far as the relative risk of contracting malaria goes, it's highest in sub-Saharan Africa and Oceania (Papua New Guinea, West Papua, Vanuatu, Solomon Islands), moderate in Asia and lowest in Southeast Asia, Central America and South America.

As you can see from the map, most of the tropical world has chloroquine-resistant *falciparum* malaria (CRFM). Only rural areas of the Middle East, the island of Hispaniola and parts of rural Mexico and Central America have solely chloroquine-sensitive malaria. Along the borders of Thailand with Myanmar (Burma) and Cambodia, *falciparum* malaria may be resistant to mefloquine as well. Strains of *P. vivax* which are resistant to both chloroquine and primaquine are found in Papua New Guinea.

Malaria was not always restricted to the tropics. Russia, Europe, the United States and Canada all played host to this infection in past centuries. Occasionally, a case of malaria occurs in someone who has not left North America, proving the point that the conditions for transmission still exist here.

In the future, the global malaria situation will continue to change, perhaps due to global warming, clever parasites, migration or failure of public health measures. It is therefore crucial that you get accurate, up-to-date information about your risk of malaria, from either a travel medicine professional or one of the sources provided in this book, such as the Centers for Disease Control and Prevention in Atlanta (CDC) (see website at end of chapter). Please refer to Chapter 5, Region-by-Region Guide, for greater detail regarding the risk of malaria at your destination.

A safe, effective, affordable vaccine would be of tremendous benefit to people living in malarious areas. Unfortunately, this may still take several years. Note that most diseases develop resistance to medications (e.g., TB, malaria, HIV), but not to vaccines.

How Do I Get Malaria?

Your risk of contracting malaria depends upon several factors, such as your destination, time spent at that destination, time of year and preventive measures taken.

As mentioned, malaria is transmitted via the bite of an infected female *Anopheles* mosquito. This mosquito prefers to breed in stagnant pools of fresh water. In fact, the name "malaria" came from the Italian for bad air, the *"mal´aria"* that emanated from the swampy breeding grounds of these mosquitoes. Its feeding hours

Life Cycle of Malaria

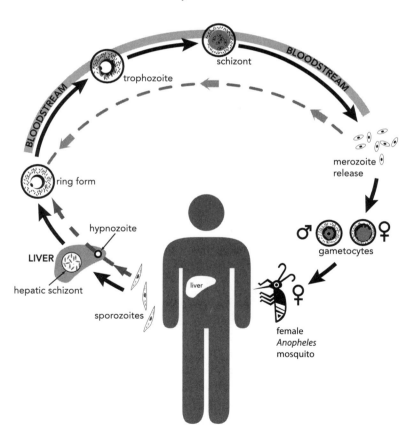

are between dusk and dawn. What the male mosquitoes do every evening while the women are out to dinner is beyond me. This feeding time is in contrast to another mosquito species, the *Aedes* mosquito, which transmits yellow fever and dengue. It prefers to bite during the day, and dwells in urban areas in small collections of water such as planters and empty tires found around human habitation.

Once you have been bitten, the young parasites (sporozoites) travel immediately to your liver (under your right ribcage). Here they spend at least six days dividing, though they may sometimes remain dormant there for many months (hypnozoites). At some point, usually within 30 to 60 days in the case of *P. falciparum*, the parasites exit the liver and invade your red blood cells (trophozoites).

In your red blood cells they then spend between 24 and 72 hours maturing (now schizonts) and dividing into as many as 8 to 24 new parasites called merozoites. The red blood cell eventually ruptures, releasing young parasites that will go on to reinvade other red cells. After a few or even several cycles of dividing, some parasites eventually develop into the sexual form of the parasite (gametocytes), and may be picked up by another feeding mosquito. The mosquito then requires human blood to allow these gametocytes to continue their development.

With each new cycle in the bloodstream, the number of red blood cells infected with malaria parasites becomes greater and greater, and the patient gets sicker and sicker. The infected red blood cells tend to become "sticky," thereby clogging the smallest arteries, especially in the brain. This leads to cerebral malaria, which is not a particular strain of malaria but rather a dreaded and often fatal complication of *falciparum* malaria. The kidneys and lungs may also be severely affected.

Malaria is not transmissible directly from person to person, with the exception of an infected pregnant mother to her fetus. Rare infections occur via blood transfusion, which is why blood services will decline your blood donation for at least three years after your possible exposure.

What Are the Symptoms?

"Malaria the mime" it is called, for it can mimic almost any other infectious illness. But to simplify things, it is most like "the flu," a really bad flu. An abrupt onset of fever, headache, chills, aches and pains—these symptoms and signs are the most common. Patients usually experience a feeling of extreme coldness, followed by the opposite, feeling hot. The "paroxysm" often ends with a drenching sweat and extreme fatigue. These episodes may assume a pattern (recurring every 48 to 72 hours), which occurs because the dividing parasites tend to become synchronized. However, this pattern is not always the case, and may be affected by the strain of malaria and recent antimalarial medications taken. Any other symptom known to medicine may occur with malaria. Suffice it to say that if you are in or have returned from a malarious area and have a fever, you may have malaria.

As I mentioned, the parasites spend at least six days dividing in your liver before reaching the bloodstream. So if you have a fever within your first week at your destination, it's highly unlikely that this is malaria. More likely it is something you picked up on the plane.

Untreated malaria, particularly with *P. falciparum*, may lead to complications. As more and more red blood cells are destroyed, you become anemic, and therefore quite weak. Should cerebral malaria occur, you may have a seizure or gradually become confused and lose consciousness. Both the lungs and the kidneys may also fail if these organs become obstructed by infected red blood cells. Gastrointestinal symptoms such as diarrhea may also occur, and may sometimes distract you or the doctor from the true diagnosis.

Malaria, whether it develops abroad or back home, is a medical emergency. From the onset of a fever until death may be as little as three days. There is not always time for delayed diagnosis or misdiagnosis, nor improper or inadequate treatment.

Other tropical infections, such as dengue fever, typhoid fever, meningitis, hepatitis, leptospirosis, Lassa fever and tick typhus, may all cause a similar illness. So may nontropical infections such as mononucleosis, pneumonia and the flu. But the first priority for both the patient and the doctor is to rule out malaria.

How Do You Prevent Malaria?

If you take some reasonable precautions and use the proper anti-malarial medication, properly, malaria should be a preventable illness. Unfortunately, a great many people ignore personal protective measures and shun antimalalarial medications because of perceived side effects. Let us first deal with the personal precautions that you can take to reduce your risk. Not all these measures are always desirable, practical, available or affordable.

Personal Protective Measures

1. Avoid outdoor exposure between dusk and dawn. This is not always practical, especially for those who want to be outside between dusk and dawn.

2. Use an insect repellent containg DEET (N,N-diethyl-metatoluamide). This compound is superior to citronella, Skin-So-Soft®, garlic, vitamin B1 and electric buzzers (the last three really don't work). Though it may be a bit irritating (don't spill it on your purse), and the smell isn't perfect, DEET has an amazingly safe track record. It's available as a spray, lotion, stick, gel or soap. It may damage plastics, synthetic fabrics or leather, but it's safe on cotton, wool and nylon ... and skin.

3. Wear long sleeves and long pants. This is a bit more practical. Be sure to take along lightweight clothing, as it may still be hot out in the evening. Clothing may be sprayed with DEET-containing repellents or permethrin.

4. Wear light-colored clothing. Darker colors tend to attract mosquitoes.

5. Avoid perfumes, aftershaves and the like, as these may attract mosquitoes. Having said that, it seems that everyone has something that attracts flying insects.

6. Sleep in a well-screened, air-conditioned room. This may be unavailable or unaffordable.

7. Sleep under a mosquito net, particularly one that's impregnated with permethrin. Tuck the edges of the net under the mattress. Insect nets are an extremely efficient way of reducing contact with mosquitoes (and who knows what else?) during biting hours. They have greatly lowered the incidence of malaria among many local populations.

DEET AND OTHER REPELLENTS. DEET is available in concentrations ranging from 2 to 100 percent. The higher the concentration, the longer the protection: 10 percent DEET provides about four hours of protection; 100 percent DEET provides up to eight.

Concentrations of 35 percent or less are probably adequate, as there is little additional protection gained from higher concentrations, and they offer less chance of toxicity. Small children should stick to no more than 10 percent. Under the age of two, the use of DEET is a bit controversial. There is no evidence that DEET is harmful to pregnant women or the fetus, but it's best to use a low concentration in combination with other measures.

A few of the better-known products include Muskol®, Sawyer®, Repel®, Cutter®, Deep Woods OFF®, Skintastic® and Skedaddle®. Each one is available in different forms and strengths. Ultrathon® and Sawyer Controlled Release Insect Repellent® are "controlled-release" products which employ a unique formulation of DEET that slows the absorption and evaporation of DEET from the skin surface. They therefore achieve prolonged protection (about 10 hours) while using a lower concentration. Either would be ideal for people with concerns about DEET toxicity, or for those who just don't want to keep lathering up with insect repellent every few hours. The availability of these products may vary from country to country.

DEET is toxic when ingested (it was not intended as a beverage), and is absorbed through the skin in small quantities. This is mainly a concern in small children. To minimize any risk, especially in children, adhere to the following guidelines:

• Apply it sparingly, and only to exposed skin.
• Avoid contact with the eyes, any open sores or cuts, or the hands, which usually end up in the mouth. (Let the adult apply the repellent.)
• Use lower concentrations (10 to 35 percent).
• Wash it off when you get indoors.

In my experience, DEET has an undeserved bad reputation, similar to Imodium® and mefloquine. Many people are frightened by the fact that it melted someone else's watchband or wallet. It was not meant to go on your fashion accessories. Keep it on your skin where it belongs. It's not carcinogenic. You will be fine.

DEET may be found in combination with sunscreens, which may seem like a handy idea. But in fact, DEET may reduce the effectiveness of your sunscreen, and the concentrations used of both products are often very low. If you are using both DEET and sunscreen, the latter should be applied first, with the repellent following about 30 minutes later.

A few words about the other repellents. Permethrin is a highly effective knock-down repellent which may be applied to clothing, insect nets and curtains. It's odorless and nonstaining, and will withstand several washings. It's available as a spray (Permanone®, Duranon®, Sawyer®), a liquid or coils. A properly impregnated insect net will remain effective for up to six months. It's readily available in the United States, but not in Canada. Perhaps the best way to avoid biting insects is to apply DEET to your skin and permethrin to your clothing and net.

Citronella is "natural" and therefore quite popular. Unfortunately it provides only short-term (one to two hours) protection. It's available as a lotion, coils and candles and is probably the best choice for those who choose not to use DEET.

Skin-So-Soft®, made by Avon, is another favorite. It's not clear how it prevents bites (certain preparations contain a small amount of citronella), though some think that it is by making your landing strip too slippery for the mosquito. Like citronella, it is effective only for a short time. Other natural oils which provide short-term protection include soybean oil, lemon, eucalyptus and lemongrass oil.

Finally, every time I give a talk about malaria, someone asks me about bananas as a repellent. Aside from slapping the little critters with the peel, I haven't heard that it's of much use.

Chemoprophylaxis

While personal measures are very important in reducing the risk of malaria, chemoprophylaxis is the mainstay of malaria prevention. However, it requires a well-informed traveler—in fact, a very well-informed traveler—to understand the risks and benefits of all the various antimalarial medications. The following points are critical to the understanding of this issue.

Malaria prophylaxis—some important points:

- Most antimalarial medications do not really *prevent* infection with the parasite; rather, they *suppress* the symptoms of the infection (e.g., fever, chills, death) by killing the parasites when they enter the liver or the bloodstream. There are many other medical conditions where we only suppress things rather than prevent or cure them, such as hypertension, diabetes and high cholesterol. This allows us to prevent more serious complications, like heart attacks, strokes and kidney failure.

- There is no perfect antimalarial; that is, one that's 100 percent effective and always without side effects.

- All antimalarials, in fact all medications, may have side effects; however, most side effects do not occur in most people most of the time. If one is aware of the potential side effects ahead of time, I think they may be more tolerable.

- When side effects do occur, they are often mild, tolerable (a bad dream once a week isn't the end of the world) and transient (the day after taking the pill), and they may diminish with time. Those who claim that the side effects are worse than the disease just haven't had the disease.

- Antimalarials are generally continued for four weeks after leaving the malarious area, in the hope that they will kill any parasites that may leave the liver during that time and, hence, prevent a case of malaria after returning home. But remember, malaria can still occur after these four weeks.

- If you believe that you have intolerable side effects from your antimalarial, get some good advice and make a switch to something different.

There was a time in the 1960s when all the strains of malaria could be prevented, or treated, with the drug chloroquine. However, as has happened with other infections, like TB and HIV, drug resistance started to occur—first in the Amazon and Southeast Asia, then, in the past decade, through sub-Saharan

Africa and the rest of Asia. Along the borders of Thailand with Myanmar (Burma) and Cambodia, *P. falciparum* is resistant to multiple drugs, including mefloquine. Sporadic cases of multi-drug-resistant malaria also occur in Africa.

Your choice of antimalarial may depend upon a few factors, including:

- your destination, and time spent there (one overnight stay might not necessarily warrant six weeks worth of antimalarial medication)
- other medical problems and medications
- age
- pregnancy
- sensitivity or previous side effects with certain medications in the past
- personal preference, availability and your budget

This summary of various antimalarials shows their indications, dosages, side effects, and some of the controversy surrounding them.

Chloroquine (Aralen®, Nivaquine®, Resochin®)

This drug, when used alone, continues to be the drug of choice for prevention and for treatment in chloroquine-sensitive areas such as rural parts of Mexico, Central America, the Middle East and the island of Hispaniola (Haiti/Dominican Republic). There was a time when it was adequate to prevent and treat all strains of malaria.

It is taken on a weekly basis, beginning the week before exposure, weekly while away and for four weeks after exposure. Aside from a bitter taste, its most common side effects include an upset stomach, headache, itchiness in black people (this is not a true allergy) and transient hair loss. It may also aggravate pre-existing psoriasis and seizure disorders and, hence, should be avoided in these situations. Psychosis may rarely occur. In long-term users (several years), there is a risk of damage to the retina of the eye, and therefore you should have a yearly eye exam if you are using it for a prolonged period. This is mainly a risk when it's used in much higher doses, as for rheumatoid arthritis.

Chloroquine is safe in pregnancy, but it is not protective in most parts of the world. Some parents will be anxious to give it to their children when they return home (to the tropics), because it is available overseas in a liquid form, but they must be cautioned that it provides inadequate protection in most countries. Chloroquine is quite toxic if taken in excess, so children must be kept away from the bottle.

Proguanil (Paludrine®)

In chloroquine-sensitive areas, proguanil is a reasonable alternative for those who cannot take chloroquine. It must be taken on a daily basis, beginning the day of exposure, daily while away and daily for four weeks after exposure. Its most common side effect is the occurrence of mouth ulcers. Proguanil is not available in the United States.

Before the advent of mefloquine and doxycycline, a combination of weekly chloroquine with daily proguanil was the regimen of choice in chloroquine-resistant areas. It is still used by many travelers, especially those from Europe. While it is a useful combination, it certainly lacks the efficacy of mefloquine, Malarone® or doxycycline. Side effects, while different in nature, occur as commonly with this regimen as they do with mefloquine. As well, the complicated regimen might make compliance difficult. This combination is best forgotten.

Mefloquine (Lariam®)

This drug has aroused more controversy than most. It was first introduced in the 1960s during the Vietnam War, because of the emergence of resistant strains of P. falciparum. Since then, as drug-resistant malaria has spread, it has become the antimalarial of choice for those visiting most malarious areas of the world. Most of the controversy stems from mefloquine's side effects. No one can deny that it may cause side effects, but I think it's fair to say they don't occur in the majority of people; and when they do occur, they are usually transient and tolerable. They tend to occur more frequently in young women, which is probably why it hasn't bothered me. There are other medications which may be useful, but like

Summary of Antimalarials

Medication	Adult dosage	How to take it	Pediatric dosage	Comments
chloroquine (Aralen®, Nivaquine®)	1 tablet = 150 mg base = 250 mg salt	Take 2 tablets *weekly* beginning 1 week prior to exposure, weekly while away and for 4 weeks after your return.	5 mg/kg base weekly to maximum 300 mg *or* 1–2 yrs: 75 mg base 3–4 yrs: 100 mg base 5–7 yrs: 125 mg base 8–10 yrs: 200 mg base 11–13 yrs: 250 mg base > 14 yrs: 300 mg base	• tastes bitter; may be crushed up and mixed with food • toxic if taken in overdose • available as a liquid overseas • safe in pregnancy
proguanil (Paludrine®)	100 mg tablets	Take 2 tablets *daily* while away, and for 4 weeks after your return.	< 2 yrs: 50 mg/day 2–6 yrs: 100 mg/day 7-10 yrs: 150 mg/day > 10 yrs: 200 mg/day	• not available in U.S. • may cause mouth ulcers • safe in pregnancy
mefloquine (Lariam®)	250 mg tablets	Take 1 tablet *weekly,* beginning 1 week prior to travel, weekly while away and for 4 weeks after your return.	< 15 kg: 5 mg/kg/wk 15–19 kg: ¼ tablet/wk 20–30 kg: ½ tablet/wk 31–45 kg: ¾ tablet/wk > 45 kg: 1 tablet/wk	• take with food and lots of water, not alcohol • contraindicated with epilepsy, psychiatric disorders, cardiac conduction disturbances
doxycycline (Vibramycin®)	100 mg tablets	Take 1 tablet *daily,* beginning the day before exposure, daily while away and for 4 weeks after your return.	>8 yrs: 2 mg/kg of body weight once/day, up to the adult dose of 100 mg	• contraindicated during pregnancy and breast-feeding, and under the age of 8. • take with food and lots of water during the day
atovaquone/ proguanil (Malarone®)	250 mg tablets/ 100 mg tablets	Take 1 tablet *daily,* beginning the day before exposure, daily while exposed and for 7 days after your return.	11–20 kg: 62.5/25 mg 21–30 kg: 125/50 mg 31–40 kg: 187.5/75 mg > 40 kg: 250/100 mg (1 tablet)	• contraindicated in pregnancy • commonest side effects are gastrointestinal
primaquine	15 mg tablets (base)	Take 2 tablets (30 mg) *daily,* beginning the day before exposure, daily while away and for 7 days after your return.	0.5 mg/kg base daily to maximum 30 mg/day	• must check G6PD level prior to taking it • contraindicated in pregnancy

Note : Check dosages and instructions with doctor or pharmacist.

mefloquine they may be less than perfect and also carry their own list of adverse effects.

Mefloquine is taken on a weekly basis (the same day each week), usually beginning the week prior to departure. Take it weekly while exposed and for four weeks after departing the malarious area. It must be taken with food and lots of water. Taking mefloquine with alcohol has been shown to exacerbate the side effects, and perhaps overindulgence in this and other substances contributes to side effects blamed solely on the mefloquine. I have had patients who found it beneficial to avoid caffeine as well while taking mefloquine. Some people find the side effects less bothersome if it's taken at bedtime.

Some travel advisers suggest that the medication be started a few weeks prior to departure, perhaps to ensure an adequate blood level, but mainly so that you will get used to it or discover any unwanted side effects before departure. It's thought that adverse effects usually occur when beginning the drug, and lessen with time. But this is not always the case, as I have seen many longer-term travelers who claim their side effects didn't happen until they had been on the medication for some time.

One final regime is that of a "loading dose"—one tablet daily for three days just prior to departure, and then one tablet per week. This may be appropriate for someone immediately entering an area with a high incidence of chloroquine-resistant malaria. This dosage may initially result in more side effects.

So what are these side effects? The most common, or minor ones, which may occur in about 15 percent of travelers, include:

- stomach upset
- dizziness
- sleep disturbances
- vivid (exotic, erotic, scary or all of the above) dreams
- mood changes (anxiety, depression)

These tend to happen more in the young adult traveler, especially females. They tend to be quite uncommon in children and the elderly. The most common description that I hear of is either a "free-floating tenseness," not attributable to external factors, or a sudden "jolt" of anxiety that makes you wake up from a sleep. Many people refer to their "hallucinations." But I maintain that hallucinations occur in the conscious, and most people are just describing a vivid dream while asleep. I also maintain that there is more paranoia *about* mefloquine than there is *from* it. To quote our peripatetic VSO volunteer in Rwanda, *"I don't know if this is a side effect or not, but I'm remembering my dreams more. Maybe it's just that my dreams are more interesting. What does it mean when you dream about lasagna, white crocodiles and bagels and cream cheese?"*

More serious "neuropsychiatric" side effects, such as seizures, extreme depression and psychosis, are quite rare, perhaps occurring in one in 10,000 travelers.

Mefloquine should not be prescribed for certain travelers, such as those with epilepsy; cardiac conduction disorders (irregular heart rhythms); a history of depression, anxiety or other psychiatric disorder; or a history of sensitivity or intolerable past side effects with the medication. These last two contraindications may take some judgment on the part of the medical professional and the patient. Mefloquine may, however, be used in children, with the dosage given according to weight. It comes as a scored tablet, so it can easily be broken into quarters. If necessary, it may be crushed and given with something tasty (and hopefully not infected), like pudding or ice cream.

It's also considered safe for pregnant women, beyond their first trimester, who must travel to a malarious area. For those in the first 12 weeks of pregnancy it is also used, but only after a thorough discussion of the risks and benefits. (See Chapter 21, Women and International Travel.) Remember, the first choice for a pregnant woman is, Don't go!

You will undoubtedly hear stories about the "long-term" effects of mefloquine, especially involving the liver (remember, under your right ribcage). As far as I know, there is no scientific evidence that this occurs, and studies done by the Peace Corps have shown that it can be well tolerated for more than a few years.

The cost of mefloquine (Lariam®) varies around the world. It is quite expensive in the United States ($8–$10 per pill), but less costly in Canada ($3.50 US per pill) and even cheaper in many other developed and lesser-developed countries. The presence of competition (i.e., another brand) seems to make a difference. (It's also available as Mephaquin®.)

Can I scuba dive and then climb Everest? These two questions come up frequently. Because of mefloquine's real and alleged side effects, it seems to be discouraged, or not allowed at times, in those going to both high and sub–sea level altitudes. If necessary, it is easy to find an effective alternative, such as doxycycline or Malarone®. But in my opinion, if you have not had a problem with the medication to date, there is no reason not to use it.

Enough said about mefloquine. Remember, there are other reasons to become anxious, sleepless and moody. As one patient put it, *"It could have been the mefloquine, but then again, maybe it was just India!"* Don't believe everything that you hear, or that everything that you hear will necessarily happen to you. Most people tolerate this drug quite well, it is easy to take and it provides excellent protection.

Doxycycline (Vibramycin®)

This antibiotic is an excellent antimalarial, and is a good alternative for those who cannot, or will not, take mefloquine. It may be used in all areas where chloroquine resistance occurs, including areas with mefloquine resistance, as is found along the borders of Thailand with Myanmar (Burma) and Cambodia.

It must be taken on a daily basis, beginning the day before entering a malarious area, daily while exposed to malaria, and for four more weeks after departure. It has side effects too, the most common being stomach upset and heartburn. If the pill is taken at night just before you lie down, it may severely irritate the esophagus, sometimes causing ulceration. So take it with lots of water, preferably during the day while upright. It may also cause photosensitivity, so sunscreens and sensible clothing are a must. Being an antibiotic, it may predispose women to a vaginal yeast infection, so carrying along a product such as Monistat® or Diflucan® for self-treatment is a good idea.

Doxycycline can cause a yellow staining of the developing teeth, so it must not be given to children under eight, pregnant women or nursing mothers. The final concern is that it may decrease the efficacy of oral contraceptives. Therefore, an additional form of protection against pregnancy should be used.

Atovaquone/Proguanil (Malarone®)

This combination of atovaquone and proguanil was introduced in the year 2000. It provides excellent protection against all strains of malaria. It differs from the previously mentioned antimalarials in that it is a "causal" prophylactic. That means it actually prevents development of the malaria parasite in the liver, whereas the others kill the parasites in the bloodstream. It is started one or two days prior to entering the malarious area, taken daily while exposed to malaria, and for seven days after departure. Its most common side effects include abdominal pain, nausea, vomiting and headache. It does not cause the so-called "neuropsychiatric" side effects attributed to mefloquine. Owing to insufficient data it is not yet recommended in pregnancy.

Malarone® is not cheap either, currently costing almost $5 US a pill (taken every day). Considering this, it is probably an excellent alternative for those who will be exposed to malaria for only a short time, travelers who cannot tolerate or don't want to try other antimalarials, and those with lots of money. In the United States it is available in pediatric dosages as well. Like Lariam®, it is much less expensive in other countries ($3 US in Canada).

Primaquine

This is another drug that has recently been shown to be effective in preventing malaria. Traditionally, it has been used to eradicate the persisting forms of malaria in the liver (*P. vivax* and *ovale*). It must be taken on a daily basis, beginning the day before entering a malarious area, daily while exposed and for only seven days after leaving the malarious area. Those taking primaquine must first be tested for an enzyme known as G6PD, since those with an inadequate level may have a severe reaction to the drug. It is not recommended in pregnancy. A longer-acting form of the drug, called tafenaquine, may be available in the future.

A word about some medications that should be avoided. Fansidar® (pyrimethamine/sulfadoxine) was briefly popular as an antimalarial in the 1980s, until it was observed that more people were dying from this drug than from malaria. This was due to severe skin reactions to the sulfa contained in the medication. It still has a place for short-term use in the treatment of malaria. Halofantrine (Halfan®) is another medication that is, in fact, quite effective, but has been associated with severe cardiac complications.

Finally, some people tell me they are going to use a homeopathic alternative. These remedies contain artemisinin, a Chinese herb also known as qinghaosu. While this and its derivatives have proven very useful for the treatment of malaria, they should not be trusted, or taken, for prevention.

A better approach to malaria prevention, not only for travelers but also for the millions inhabiting malarious areas, would be a vaccine. At the present time, there are several candidates being used in clinical trials, but it is doubtful that we will have an effective vaccine available for several years. I realize that once you are overseas, you will be exposed to many different viewpoints about malaria and antimalarials. My suggestion is that you learn about the various medications for prevention and treatment before you leave.

What If I Think I Have Malaria?

Fever in a returning traveler, or one residing in a malarious area, is malaria until proven otherwise. If you and your doctor stick to this adage, you should both be able to stay out of trouble. The reality of long-term travel is that many people do not end up taking their antimalarials, or perhaps they end up taking something less than adequate. People do develop malaria while away or after they have returned home.

If you are back home and you develop a fever, with or without the headache, chills, etc., I would suggest that you seek immediate medical attention from a knowledgeable family doctor (one who knows something about tropical diseases) or a tropical disease clinic, or in the emergency department. You should request, or demand if necessary, a blood smear for malaria. If this is positive, you should then make absolutely sure that your doctor knows how to treat malaria properly. If not, insist that you be referred to someone who does.

If your blood smear is negative, this does not necessarily mean that you do not have malaria. Rather, it means that they didn't find any parasites in your smear this time. If your fever persists or recurs, you should return in 12 to 24 hours to have the smear repeated. It may be positive the next time, or the next. People have died because they were incorrectly assured that they couldn't have malaria—*"it must be the flu"*—based on one negative blood smear. As well, North American doctors are not usually on the lookout for malaria and may not be well acquainted with its seriousness, how to make a diagnosis and the proper treatment. Patient beware, and be knowledgeable.

If you get your fever and headache in the tropics, it may be a different story. Again, seek medical attention if possible. In places such as Africa malaria may be over-diagnosed, but that's understandable since it's a very common disease over there. As well, the diagnosis is often if not usually made on clinical grounds (as opposed to a blood smear). And if a blood smear is done, it may or may not be accurate. But over-diagnosis and treatment, as long as it is the proper treatment, beats a missed diagnosis or inadequate treatment, which is often the case back home.

A common scenario may have you going to see the local doctor because of a fever. It's assumed you have malaria, and you're treated accordingly. Two days later, when you are no better, the doctor tells you that you have typhoid, and treats you accordingly. One of my feverish patients in Burkina Faso went to the clinic with a high fever. The doctor told him, *"You may have any one of five infections, and I am going to treat you for all five!"* Thankfully he recovered, but from what we aren't certain.

One other point. Local people, who have some immunity to

malaria owing to their constant exposure, may recover from their malaria with simpler treatment than you may require. So beware that you don't just receive a bunch of chloroquine tablets for what is likely chloroquine-resistant *falciparum* malaria.

Can I Treat Myself?

What if you are nowhere near medical care? Well, there is a place for standby emergency treatment (SBET). People who may find themselves in remote areas more than 24 hours away from medical care should be aware of the options. There are several medications that should successfully treat chloroquine-resistant *falciparum* malaria. Perhaps the gold standard would be a five- to seven-day course of quinine (600 milligrams three times daily) plus doxycycline (100 milligrams twice daily) for seven days. The quinine will make your ears ring, but it should work. An alternative to doxycycline for children would be clindamycin. Fansidar® (pyrimethamine/sulfadoxine) may also be used along with quinine, though it is relatively ineffective in Southeast Asia. This drug must not be used in anyone allergic to sulfa.

A newer and excellent option is Malarone®, taken as four tablets daily for three days. Medications that are not available in North America, such as artemesinin and its derivatives (e.g., Artenam®, Cotexcin®, Arsumax®) are also very effective, but should probably be taken along with another antimalarial, such as Fansidar®. Mefloquine has been used in larger doses for treatment, but it's not advised because of an increased risk of side effects. Halofantrine (Halfan®), as mentioned, may be available, but should be avoided on account of its potential cardiac toxicity. Self-treatment should be only a stop-gap measure, and it's still best to seek medical care.

If you know you are in a chloroquine-sensitive area (e.g., Central America), the treatment would be with chloroquine—four tablets right away, two more in six hours and two tablets per day for two more days (a total of 10 tablets). If you have an infection with *P. vivax*, it should be followed by a course of primaquine to prevent a relapse.

Several kits for self-diagnosis of malaria are now available (MalaQuick®, Parasite-F®, OptiMAL®, ICT Malaria Pf®). In fact, that's how many doctors and labs now make a diagnosis of malaria in lesser-developed countries. While the kits are quite reliable when used under laboratory conditions, they lose quite a bit of their accuracy when performed by a shivering soul with a temperature of 104°F (40°C).

There are more myths and misconceptions surrounding malaria than almost any other disease I know. Unfortunately, many travelers (and some doctors) believe them, thus putting themselves and others at risk.

Common Misconceptions

1. *Taking antimalarials only masks the disease.* Well, sort of true, but by doing that it sort of masks or suppresses the symptoms and complications of the disease as well, including death. We feel that this is a good thing.

2. *If I take antimalarials, there will be nothing left to treat me with if I get sick.* While extra caution may be needed when using certain drugs together, this certainly does not preclude effective treatment.

3. *If I am taking antimalarials, it will make it more difficult for the doctors to diagnose it if I get infected.* Not correct. First, you probably won't get malaria. Second, if there are malaria parasites there, they should be visible under the microscope. This may take a good lab technician and more than one blood smear, but if the parasites are truly there, they should be seen.

4. *The drugs are worse than the disease.* Again, any of the aforementioned side effects of any of the medications do not compare with the discomfort and possible fatal outcome of a case of malaria.

5. *I am immune to malaria.* Those who grew up in malarious areas such as Africa may indeed have developed some relative immunity to this infection. However, this protection tends to wane with time, and cannot be counted on for that next trip back home.

6. *Once you have malaria ... you have it for life.* Not true. While I have seen numerous patients who are convinced that they have suffered relapses on a yearly basis since World War II, this is rarely the case. As I mentioned, there are two strains, *P. vivax* and *P. ovale,* which may persist for months and even years in your liver, but they can easily be eradicated with the drug primaquine.

I sympathize with travelers who are exposed to numerous different opinions while abroad as to what is best for preventing and treating malaria. On the other hand, at least you're away on a vacation. My suggestion is that you try to educate yourself about these issues before you leave, or others will do it for you—sometimes with disastrous results. In addition to the websites of CDC and Health Canada, I would recommend the Malaria Foundation International (see below).

Key Points

- Malaria is a potentially fatal illness. However, it should be preventable and, when necessary, treatable.
- Don't believe everything you hear about malaria and antimalarials (only what you read in this book!).
- Fever while you are away or after your return is malaria until proven otherwise.

Related Websites

Centers for Disease Control and Prevention (CDC): http://www.cdc.gov/travel/regionalmalaria/index.htm

Health Canada: http://www.hc-sc.gc.ca

Malaria Foundation International: http://www.malaria.org

Other Insect-borne Diseases

CHAPTER 9

"Not all who wander are lost."

While malaria is certainly the most important insect-borne infection to which travelers may be exposed, it's far from the only one. Throughout history, these little creatures and the diseases they transmit have been responsible for more deaths than all of history's wars combined. And the situation is not improving.

Let's take a look at some of these insects and the diseases that they transmit. Keep in mind that most of these infections are quite uncommon in travelers, but I thought you'd want to know about them anyway.

Mosquitoes

There are more than 3,000 species of mosquitoes around the world, but only a few species are responsible for disease transmission to humans. To be more specific, it is the female mosquito that is responsible, as she requires blood for the development of her eggs. Mosquitoes may vary in appearance (you need to get up pretty close to see these differences), but more importantly, they differ as to their breeding habits, feeding habits and which infectious organism they are capable of transmitting. Let me acquaint you with the more important mosquito-borne infections.

DENGUE FEVER. Dengue (rhymes with "Schmenge") fever is a viral infection transmitted by the *Aedes aegypti* mosquito. In recent years it has been making a worldwide resurgence, likely due to increased urban migration (of people), continued poverty and global warming. Cases have been transmitted in Texas as well, and many southern U.S. states harbor the appropriate vectors.

Unlike the *Anopheles* mosquito, *Aedes aegypti* breeds in small collections of water in close proximity to humans—empty tires, cans, planters, vases and so on. Therefore, it is a particular risk to those who visit urban and tourist areas. The infection may be somewhat seasonal, with the worst time of year being during or after the rainy season. You don't need to travel across the globe to catch this one—the Caribbean or Central America will do just fine.

You wouldn't wish dengue on your worst enemy. It begins abruptly with a high fever, a severe headache located behind the eyes, and tremendous pains in the bones. Hence its nickname: "breakbone" or "bonecrusher" fever. A rash may appear on the fourth or fifth day. Dengue usually gets better on its own in a week or so, although the victim may remain fatigued, achy and even depressed for some time afterward. Treatment consists of rest, fluids and analgesics such as acetaminophen. Aspirin-containing medications must be avoided.

In his book *The Testament,* John Grisham probably did the most to raise awareness about dengue. In it, Nate, a recovering alcoholic lawyer, contracts the infection in the Amazon while hunting down a missionary who is destined to inherit $11 billion. To quote his description, *"His head ached and throbbed like no hangover he'd ever experienced. His muscles and joints hurt too much to move. And he was growing colder. The chills were starting."* It was the appearance of a rash that enabled the local storeowner to diagnose his illness as dengue rather than malaria.

Dengue, when not diagnosed clinically, is diagnosed by means of blood tests that measure antibodies to the virus. The illness must be differentiated from other infections such as malaria, typhoid and measles.

A more severe form of dengue exists, known as dengue hemorrhagic fever (DHF). In this syndrome, bleeding abnormalities develop —possibly leading to shock (dengue shock syndrome) and death. There are four strains of the dengue virus, and DHF is felt to occur when someone who has previously been exposed to one strain encounters another. This happens mainly in children living in endemic areas, rather than tourists passing through.

The prevention of dengue fever rests mainly with the use of DEET-containing repellents, especially during daytime hours. If you are living in an endemic area, it is worth your while to make sure the area surrounding your home is free of potential breeding spots for the *Aedes* mosquito.

YELLOW FEVER. This viral infection is limited to sub-Saharan Africa and parts of South America. It is also transmitted by *Aedes aegypti*. As this mosquito continues to thrive in urban areas, and as people move from the countryside into the cities, it is becoming a greater risk.

Yellow fever causes an acute illness with fever, headache, chills, muscle pains, nausea and vomiting. When complications such as jaundice or bleeding problems occur, the mortality rate may range from 20 to 50 percent. Not a nice disease.

It is completely preventable by receiving the yellow fever vaccine. Cases in travelers are quite rare, but do happen in the occasional unimmunized traveler.

FILARIASIS. Filariasis is transmitted by mosquitoes throughout most of the tropics. These worms find their way into your lymph nodes and vessels, usually in the groin. The initial symptoms, which don't occur until at least three months after infection, include fever and inflammation of the lymph nodes. With chronic and repeated infections, the lymph tracts become obstructed. The obstruction in turn may cause chronic swelling of the leg or foot, as well as fairly grotesque changes to the skin. This condition is better known as elephantiasis, as it is an elephant's foot which it most resembles. The infection is quite rare in travelers.

WEST NILE FEVER. This viral infection has been making more headlines recently on this side of the ocean than on the banks of the Nile in Uganda, where it was first reported in 1937. It may cause an acute illness similar to dengue fever, although most infected people have only mild flu-like symptoms or none at all. Severe illness causing encephalitis (inflammation of the brain) is more likely to happen in the very young, the elderly and the immunosuppressed. It may prove fatal in 3–15 percent of cases.

Mosquitoes become infected by feeding on infected birds, and then transmit the virus to us. This infection is a fine example of the vector and/or the virus coming here, rather than us going there. West Nile fever first surfaced on this continent in New York in 1999, when there were 62 confirmed cases and 7 deaths. In the year 2000 there were cases in New York, Georgia and Florida. This infection will probably remain with us in North America for years to come. Anti-mosquito measures—wear long sleeves, stay indoors between dusk and dawn and use insect repellent—are the only means of prevention.

JAPANESE ENCEPHALITIS. This one is also caused by a virus, and occurs in Asia, from India in the west to Korea, Japan and Indonesia in the east. The *Culex* mosquito responsible for transmission is found mainly in rural, agricultural areas, where it prefers to feed on animals such as birds and pigs. Its larvae develop in rice paddies and marshes.

JE is extremely rare in travelers. Most of those who become *infected* do not become *affected,* that is, they do not become ill. Both the very young and the elderly are more susceptible to serious infections. Prevention consists of the usual anti-mosquito measures, particularly between dusk and dawn. Immunization is recommended for those who will be spending at least three or four weeks in rural, agricultural regions, particularly during the main transmission season between May and October. Considering the rarity of the infection in travelers, and the high cost of the vaccine, I recommend the vaccine mainly to the higher-risk traveler.

OTHER VIRUSES. There are a few other mosquito-borne viral infections. I don't think you'll get them, but here they are. Rift Valley fever occurs in East Africa, and it may also be transmitted through close contact with animals such as sheep and goats. Chikungunya virus is transmitted by the *Aedes* mosquito, and causes an illness quite similar to dengue fever. It may be found in Africa or Asia. And finally, Ross River virus is a threat to travelers to Australia, Papua New Guinea and the Solomon Islands. This infection causes a flu-like illness, along with pains in the muscles and joints that may persist for some time.

Lice

There are three types of lice *(Pediculus)*, each making themselves comfortable on a different part of the human anatomy. Head lice are common in school children and basically cause an itchy scalp. Pubic lice are much more common in consenting adults, and tend to cause an itchy pubic area. Body lice *(Pediculus humanus corporis)* are able to transmit infections, the most important of which is epidemic louse-borne typhus.

LOUSE-BORNE TYPHUS. Body lice live in clothing and multiply rapidly under poor hygienic conditions, as are found with war or natural disasters and in refugee camps. In recent years, Burundi, Ethiopia and Rwanda have been sites of major outbreaks.

The infection is caused by the organism *Rickettsia prowazekii.* Like several other infections, it may present with fever, headaches, chills, muscle pains and weakness, and a rash which may appear after five or six days. Treatment is with doxycycline in adults, or erythromycin in children.

LOUSE-BORNE RELAPSING FEVER. This one is caused by a spirochete, as are syphilis and Lyme disease. Symptoms include fever, headache and muscle pain that lasts four to ten days and subsides. An afebrile (feverless) period lasting five or six days follows, and then there is a recurrence of acute symptoms.

Fleas

Fleas are wingless little insects that we usually associate with our itchy dog or cat. But in the 14th century, they were the cause of 200 million deaths during the Black Death, an outbreak of bubonic plague.

PLAGUE. Plague is a bacterial infection *(Yersinia pestis)* which is spread to humans by rat fleas. At times when all the rats are dying off, these fleas are only too happy to jump to nearby humans. We can also acquire the infection by handling the infected animals. Rats are a pretty good index of poverty, and unfortunately this infection is still found in many countries in the world, including parts of the western United States.

Bubonic plague is the most common form of the disease, producing enlarged, tender lymph nodes in the groin, fever, chills and prostration. It may spread through the bloodstream and cause meningitis, bleeding and shock. The most dreaded complication is pneumonic plague, which leads to a cough and difficulty in breathing, and if left untreated is usually fatal. This form of plague is directly transmissible from person to person by respiratory droplets.

Plague is rare, very rare in travelers, and is treatable with antibiotics such as tetracycline. A vaccine is available, but is only recommended for those at the highest risk. Prophylactic tetracycline or doxycycline is also a good option if exposure is likely.

In 1994, an outbreak of pneumonic plague occurred in Surat, a city in western India. Aside from the loss of 56 lives, the economic loss to India was incalculable. The outbreak caused widespread panic in India, but also on this side of the Atlantic, where baggage handlers refused to touch bags arriving from India.

TUNGIASIS. A less serious, but more common flea-borne infection is tungiasis, or jiggers, passed by the flea *Tunga penetrans.* The female of this species burrows and embeds itself in the skin of the host (that's you), usually under the toenails or between the toes. Here it lays its eggs. Once established, the flea must be surgically removed. Secondary infection may occur, and cases of tetanus have been recorded. Sounds like a good enough reason to keep your shoes on.

Flies

This group of insects is responsible for a wide variety of diseases. Mosquitoes actually fall into this family, though I decided to give them a section of their own. Most of us are well acquainted with the housefly, better known as *Musca domestica*. While being mainly a nuisance to us as we flail away with our flyswatter, it is capable of transmitting several important infections in the tropics. These include amebiasis, shigellosis, typhoid fever, cholera and other infections contracted through the food and water. Flies are associated with poverty, and I don't know how many undernourished children with runny noses and hovering flies I have seen around the world.

AFRICAN TRYPANOSOMIASIS (SLEEPING SICKNESS). Our parents joked that we had this one in high school. Fortunately not! It is a protozoal infection caused by *Trypanosoma gambiense* and *Trypanosoma rhodesiense*. The clinical symptoms of these two infections differ somewhat, with the latter following a more acute course. Initially, the symptoms may include a painful sore at the site of the bite, followed by fever, swollen glands, headache and insomnia. In the later stages, six to nine months later, irritability, restlessness, drowsiness by day and insomnia by night may occur. Mental functions decline, and death eventually occurs from malnutrition or other infections.

It is transmitted by the tsetse fly, which has one of the more painful bites to be had. As you can see from the names of the organisms, this infection is found only in sub-Saharan Africa. It's extremely rare in travelers, but if you are on safari, insect repellents are highly advisable.

AMERICAN TRYPANOSOMIASIS (CHAGAS' DISEASE). This infection is endemic from Mexico to Central and South America. The organism, *Trypanosoma cruzi*, is transmitted by the reduviid bug (not really a fly), also known as the "assassin" or "kissing" bug. This delightful creature (it's big!) lives in thatched roofs or the crevices in mud or stone walls. Again, this is a disease of extreme poverty. At night, the bug drops down onto your face while you are asleep, and while biting also defecates on you. You promptly rub the excrement into your eye. The acute symptoms begin after 7 to 14 days, and may consist of fever, fatigue, swollen glands and swelling of the liver and spleen.

In the late stages, many years later, the heart and/or the intestines become tremendously enlarged or dilated, and death may result. This infection is also rare in travelers, but has caused a problem in that it can be transmitted through blood donations.

Onchocerciasis (river blindness). This is a helminthic or worm infection caused by *Onchocerca volvulus,* a member of the filarial family. It is found in parts of Central and South America, but mainly in West Africa. The black fly *(Simulium damnosum),* which most Canadians know and hate, is the vector. It is found along fast-moving rivers and streams.

The adult worms may be found in nodules under the skin, but the real damage is done by the larvae, or microfilaria. These may cause intense itching of the skin and chronic skin changes. More importantly, in heavily exposed populations the larvae may spread to the eye and cause blindness. I've seen a few itchy returning travelers with this infection, but the serious complications usually occur in local people exposed to the worm for prolonged periods.

Loa loa. Yet another filarial worm, this infection is found mainly in the tropical forests of West Africa. It is passed by the fly *Chrysops.* The adult worm may be more than 1.2 inches (3 centimeters) in length, and crawls under the tissues of the skin, where it creates a moving swelling. This is known as a Calabar swelling, named after a port city in Nigeria. Much more exciting is when the worm wanders across the surface of the eye.

Leishmaniasis. Various female sandflies *(Phlebotomus)* are responsible for transmitting this important protozoan infection. The disease may present in three forms. Cutaneous leishmaniasis is found in parts of Asia, the Middle East, Africa and South America. It can produce large numbers of skin ulcers—as many as 200 in some cases—on the exposed parts of the body, such as the face, arms and legs, causing serious disability and leaving the patient permanently scarred. Mucocutaneous leishmaniasis occurs predominantly in Brazil, Peru and Bolivia. In this infection, the parasite may spread or metastasize to the cartilage and mucous membranes of the nose and mouth, producing extensive destruction and disfigurement. Visceral leishmaniasis, also known as kala-azar, is the most severe form of the disease, which, if untreated, has a mortality rate of almost 100 percent. It is characterized by irregular bouts of fever, substantial weight loss, swelling of the spleen and liver, and anemia. In patients who are also infected with HIV, the infection is especially deadly. More than 90 percent of the world's cases of visceral leishmaniasis occur in Bangladesh, Brazil, India, Nepal and Sudan.

MYIASIS. This one is a bit disgusting. Myiasis is an infection of the skin caused by the larvae of certain flies that are present in the tropics. The two main species are *Dermatobia hominis* (the human botfly) in South and Central America, and *Cordylobia anthropophaga* in Africa. Both of these can also infect animals such as cattle, dogs and cats. Most of the infections I've seen have been in travelers visiting the rainforests of Costa Rica and Belize.

The eggs of the fly manage to get attached to the underside of a female mosquito and penetrate the unbroken skin when the mosquito feeds. It may also be possible for these eggs to be deposited on clothing or towels left out to dry, and then rubbed into the skin. At the site of penetration, a boil-like lesion develops fairly rapidly. It will be red and tender. People often complain of transient, shooting pains in the lesion, as if there is something moving inside. There is! A tiny opening is usually visible at the top, through which the little maggot gets his, or her, air.

Getting rid of these things is the most fun. While it is always tempting to make a small incision and cut it out, this is not usually the wisest decision. There are better ways to entice the little critter out, and most of these ways involve suffocation. Try occluding the little air hole with Vaseline® overnight, and you might see him or her wriggling at the opening in the morning. It can then be grasped with tweezers and gently extricated. Peanut butter, toothpaste or chewing tobacco may also work.

The most popular and successful method in my experience is to cover the opening with raw bacon, and wait. It might not be immediately successful. As well, if your botfly is located in a conspicuous spot like your face or scalp, it would be best to try this method at night, as going to work with raw bacon strapped to your head might provoke some odd looks. When all else fails, just good old squeezing it out will usually work, though it may be a little uncomfortable.

Don't spend your time worrying about this one. But use your insect repellents, shake out your towels and iron your clothing. And if you do end up with one of these things, take it out and send it to me. I have a little museum.

Ticks

For many years, ticks were the Rodney Dangerfield of the insect world ... they didn't get any respect. But since the discovery of Lyme disease in Connecticut in the mid 1970s, they have finally received the attention they deserve. Though they are not responsible for as much morbidity or mortality as mosquito-borne infections such as malaria, ticks transmit a greater variety of organisms than any other group of arthropods.

Tick-borne diseases are ubiquitous. They are of concern to the New England backpacker (Lyme disease, babesiosis), the couple on safari in South Africa (African tick typhus), the student spending the summer in the forests of Eastern Europe (tick-borne encephalitis, Crimean-Congo hemorrhagic fever), the hiker in most of the United States and western Canada (Rocky Mountain spotted fever) and even the golfer in South Carolina (ehrlichiosis). More than 25 different infections are passed worldwide by these innocent-looking insects.

Ticks come in two varieties—hard and soft. They differ from each other mainly in appearance and their feeding habits. In temperate climates, ticks do their feeding from spring through fall, so the incidence of many of these diseases is seasonal.

When it comes to lunch, ticks can usually be found feeding on their animal hosts, such as dogs, deer, birds and rodents. It's when we veer off the beaten path in pursuit of mountain streams, big game or lost golf balls that we tend to end up as a tick's aperitif.

The skin is often the first site of a tick-borne infection. In Lyme disease, a bull's eye–shaped lesion usually appears at the bite site. In African tick typhus, a black eschar, or lesion, is often found. Fever and other flu-like symptoms are common to most tick-borne infections.

Lyme disease is caused by *Borreleia burgdorferi*. Weeks or months after the initial illness, symptoms involving the nervous system, the heart and the joints may occur. The diagnostic blood tests for Lyme disease are less than perfect. Treatment consists of antibiotics, such as amoxicillin, tetracycline or doxycycline.

Skin rashes, encephalitis, kidney failure, bleeding disorders and chronic arthritis are other potential and occasionally fatal complications of some tick-borne infections. In travelers, these infections may mimic other tropical illnesses such as malaria, typhoid, dengue and meningococcemia. South African tick typhus is the most commonly acquired tick-borne infection among my traveling patients.

Ticks and the gifts they bear can be avoided. If you must walk through wooded areas where ticks live, cover up. Wear long pants and tuck them into your socks. Light-colored clothing is recommended. Insect repellents containing DEET should be applied to the skin, and permethrin-containing repellents (e.g., Permanone®, Duranon®) may be sprayed on clothing. This chemical does not smell or stain, and will remain in your clothing and provide protection for a few weeks. This product may not be readily available in Canada. At the end of your day in the woods or the game park, examine yourself, or your friends, from bottom to top for embedded ticks. Don't forget the scalp.

Should you discover a tick having dinner by your ear, don't panic. It usually takes a couple of days of attachment before any infection is transmitted. Try to grab the tick with a pair of tweezers right at skin level, and apply gentle traction to extricate the insect from your skin. Be careful not to squish it in your bare fingers. Blowtorches or Vaseline® and other smothering substances are not recommended, as the panicking tick might decide to regurgitate under your skin.

A vaccine (FSME-Immun®) is available for the prevention of tick-borne encephalitis, a viral infection prevalent in Eastern

Europe during the spring and summer months. As well, there is a vaccine (Lymerix®) that is effective against strains of Lyme disease found in North America, but not those in Europe.

Mites

These minute arthropods are close relatives of ticks, and are a great source of irritation to human beings and domesticated animals. This is mainly due to the creatures' biting and burrowing habits.

SCRUB TYPHUS. This rickettsial infection is found in Japan, India and Southeast Asia, parts of Australia and some of the Indian and Pacific Ocean islands. Once transmitted to the host by a mite bite, *R. tsut-sugamushi* incubates for about 10 to 12 days. After that, victims may experience headaches, fever, loss of appetite and general apathy. The site of infection is marked by a lesion—the chigger bite or

eschar, which gradually enlarges and turns black. A rash may appear after 5 to 8 days. This infection is similar to louse-borne typhus, and is treated with the same antibiotics—doxycycline or erythromycin.

CHIGGERS. Chiggers are the larvae of the harvest mite, *Trombicula alfreddugesi.* Just sitting down in the grass is the best way to become infected, or infested. On its host, the chigger usually moves about until it reaches a place where it is somewhat confined, such as around ankles, under socks or behind knees. When people sit on chigger-infested ground, frequently they may get severe chigger bites around the waistline or in the crotch area, especially under belts and elastic bands of underwear.

Chigger bites will usually result in intense itching at the bite site. The saliva from the initial bite can trigger an allergic response, and a rash may appear on surrounding areas of skin. This may persist for several weeks. If you do enough scratching, these spots may become infected. While chiggers do not transmit any infection, they are irritating enough on their own.

SCABIES. One last irritating mite, *Sarcoptes scabiei,* is found world-wide. It is passed from person to person through close contact, which often involves sharing the same bed. This mite burrows under the skin, especially around the wrists, between the fingers and on the feet, waist, armpits, breasts and male genitalia. It does not usually affect the neck and head, although it may in infants. Symptoms appear between two and six weeks after exposure.

The itching is due to an allergic reaction to the tiny mites, and is associated with a rash of red, raised spots. The itch is worse at night, and may often affect more than one family member. Treatment is with topical creams, such as Kwellada® (lindane), Eurax® (crotamiton) and Nix® (permethrin, 1 percent). Antihistamines will help to control the severe itching. Again, no infection is transmitted by this infestation, only misery.

Aside from all these interesting infections that you probably won't get, insect bites are responsible for lots and lots of itching and scratching. Cool compresses or baths, calamine lotion, cortisone creams, After Bite® (contains ammonia and mink oil), antihistamines and various natural creams all might help to take away the sting and itching.

Finally, if reading this chapter isn't enough to make you cover up and put on your insect repellent, I don't know what will. Insects can be a pain in the neck, or the butt, or wherever else they choose to bite. But the diseases they transmit can be much worse.

Key Points

- Sensible clothing, insect nets and DEET- and permethrin-containing repellents will help prevent insect-borne infections.
- Insect-borne diseases are present around the world.
- Most of them are uncommon in travelers.

Sexually Transmitted Diseases

CHAPTER 10

"Stop worrying about the potholes in the road
and celebrate the journey!"

FITZHUGH MLLAN

There is no shortage of statistics in the press regarding the prevalence of HIV in lesser-developed countries. And there is no shortage of sexually transmitted diseases (STDs) above and beyond HIV, some of which are resistant to many antibiotics. Therefore, all travelers, especially the longer-term traveler, need to be very aware of the risks involved and the measures necessary to reduce these risks. Travelers do return infected with HIV and much more. The risk is real.

At the end of the year 2000, the World Health Organization (WHO) estimated that more than 36 million people were living with HIV or AIDS. Some 95 percent live in the developing world. About 22 million have died since the first reported case in 1981, and most of these fatalities have been in sub-Saharan Africa. This is also where the great majority of infected children live. While great progress in fighting AIDS has been made in countries such as Uganda and Thailand, the incidence is increasing in Eastern Europe, Asia, southern Africa and Latin America. Life expectancy is barely more than 40 years in some African countries.

Why Is the Situation Different over There?

There are several reasons why the prevalence of STDs is greater in lesser-developed countries:

- HIV is transmitted primarily through heterosexual sex, putting many more people at risk.

- Blood, blood products and medical instruments such as syringes are much more likely to be contaminated.

- Infections causing genital ulcers are much more common, and these make the transmission of the HIV virus much more efficient.

- Promiscuity and contact with prostitutes is extremely common. Migratory prostitution—or the movement of commercial sex workers from country to country—is increasing.

- Drugs that can reduce the transmission of HIV from pregnant mother to child are not readily available or affordable in lesser-developed countries.

- Intravenous drug abuse is widespread in some countries.

- Educational and public health measures have been unable to stem the epidemic in many places.

What About Travelers?

While they may be well informed, travelers are certainly not always well behaved. The rate of casual sex is much higher than expected, and the use of condoms much lower. For some, sex is the sole purpose of their trip abroad, just as climbing Mount Kilimanjaro is for others. The commercial sexual exploitation of children is rampant around the world. While not all casual sex abroad could be described as "sexual tourism," exposure does occur among all groups, both male and female, young and old, backpackers and businesspersons, and medical professionals and missionaries.

The risk of acquiring HIV or other STDs varies from geographic region to region. While I could provide you with endless statistics comparing the rates of HIV positivity around the world, I would prefer that you treat all sexual contacts as potentially infectious. Certainly commercial sex workers are more likely to be infected than other members of society. The type of sexual exposure will also affect the likelihood of acquiring HIV, with anal intercourse being a riskier proposition than vaginal intercourse.

It is fair to say that inhibitions are lessened in many while abroad, perhaps because of the anonymity of travel. Isolation, the availability of sexual partners, alcohol and a desire to experience "something new" are other factors. To be fair, when I recently cautioned a patient about the risks of unprotected sex, he replied, *"Hell, I won't even touch the water!"*

HIV (and hepatitis B and C) is transmitted in the following ways:

- unprotected sexual intercourse (vaginal, anal and oral)
- infected blood, blood products, needles and syringes
- from an infected mother to her unborn child

Also worth knowing is how it is not transmitted:

- casual contact such as kissing, hugging, shaking hands
- toilet seats and doorknobs
- insects
- food and water
- eating utensils

What Are the Symptoms of STDs?

The answer to this one will vary from person to person, and infection to infection. First, the incubation period, that is, the time from exposure until the appearance of symptoms, varies greatly among these infections. Gonorrhea or *Chlamydia* may produce symptoms in as few as three days, while infection with HIV or hepatitis B may not be detectable for two months or more. Women infected with gonorrhea or chlamydia often have no symptoms.

The following are symptoms which you should be aware of, and for which you must seek medical attention if they occur:

- discharge from the vagina or penis (*Chlamydia*, gonorrhea, *Trichomonas*, yeast infections)
- painful urination (*Chlamydia*, gonorrhea)
- sores, ulcers or growths around the genitals or anus (syphilis, chancroid, granuloma inguinale, lymphogranuloma venereum, genital herpes, venereal warts)
- a rash (scabies, pubic lice)
- swollen glands in the groin (genital herpes, chancroid, lymphogranuloma venereum, granuloma inguinale)

A SLEW OF STDs		
Viruses	**Bacteria**	**Protozoal**
• HIV	• gonorrhea	• yeast (*Candida*)
• hepatitis B	• *Chlamydia*	• *Trichomonas*
• hepatitis C	• syphilis	
• hepatitis A	• chancroid	**Other**
(oral-anal contact)	• granuloma inguinale	• scabies
• genital herpes (type 2)	• lymphogranuloma	• pubic lice
• human papilloma virus	venereum	
(genital warts)		

These are only the early or initial symptoms. Gonorrhea and chlamydia may cause pelvic inflammatory disease and infertility in women, and urethral strictures in males. Genital warts increase the risk of cervical cancer. The later stages of syphilis can produce an entire textbook of symptoms. Chronic liver disease and liver cancer may be the consequences of hepatitis B and C. HIV may progress to AIDS and all the opportunistic infections that accompany this disease.

In addition to the infections listed in the box above, intestinal infections with *Entamoeba histolytica*, *Giardia lamblia*, *Salmonella* and *Shigella* may all be passed through high-risk anal-oral contact.

While many sexually transmitted diseases are treatable and curable, some, such as HIV, genital herpes, genital warts and hepatitis B and C, will be with you for life. They may pose a risk to future sexual partners and unborn children. Let's hope I have at least got your attention, and now, please read on.

Reducing the Risk

With this information in mind, let us look at the various measures that can be taken to reduce the risk of infection with HIV and other STDs.

Reducing the risk of STDs:

- Remain celibate—this may not be for everyone, but it's the only method that is 100 percent effective.
- Be monogamous, with someone whose HIV status you know.
- Avoid high-risk sexual partners (strangers, commercial sex workers).
- Always use a latex condom (more information to follow).
- Beware of local doctors, dentists, acupuncturists and their medical instruments. Find out where you can get safe medical care before you need it.
- Avoid blood transfusions unless absolutely necessary.
- Carry your own first aid kit with sterile syringes and suture equipment.
- Know your blood type.
- Be sure that you are vaccinated against hepatitis B.
- IV drugs, tattoos, acupuncture and body piercing should be avoided.
- So should higher-risk behaviors, which may help expose you to blood, blood products and unsafe sex, such as motorcycle driving, nighttime travel and excessive alcohol consumption.
- Carry adequate medical insurance, so that if you need to return home for safe medical treatment you can afford it.
- If you are at greater risk by virtue of your occupation, wear latex gloves (not for sex), and be very careful.

About Those Condoms

While condoms are not perfect (they sometimes leak or break), they are your best protection if you plan to be sexually active while away. They must be used every time. Restrict yourself to the use of latex condoms. If you have a latex allergy, use polyurethane. For females, don't count on your male partner to provide the condom. Carry your own. Female condoms are available as well, but they are not quite as effective as the male condom in preventing pregnancy or STDs.

Condoms should be stored away from heat and light, so leaving the same condom in your glove compartment for a few months is not a good idea. Try your fridge instead. One final note: Up to one-third of condoms manufactured overseas may not measure up to North America's rigid standards, so consider taking along your own.

Lubricants and spermicides will further reduce the risk of HIV transmission. However, be sure these are water-based (e.g., K-Y® Jelly), as oil-based lubricants such as Vaseline® and baby oils may weaken latex condoms.

What If You Think You Have Been Exposed to HIV?

If you're working abroad as a health care worker and have accidentally sustained a needle-stick injury or some other form of exposure, it would be reasonable to immediately seek Post-Exposure Prophylaxis, better known as PEP. This treatment, which is probably only of benefit within the first 72 hours after exposure, has been shown to greatly reduce the risk of developing HIV infection as a result. Obviously, every health center in the developing world will not have this sort of treatment available, but if you're at high risk by nature of your occupation, you should find out what to do before anything happens.

Assuming it's available, the type of treatment offered will depend upon factors such as the type of exposure, the severity of the exposure and the likelihood that the source of exposure was HIV positive. So a drop of blood on your intact skin from someone who is known to be HIV negative would not warrant treatment. A deep puncture wound from a needle previously used on an

HIV-positive individual would necessitate four weeks of treatment with multiple medications. Some very high-risk travelers (e.g., a doctor delivering babies in Zimbabwe) may, in fact, choose to carry their own PEP, or at least the first few days' supply.

If you have been exposed through unsafe sex, you should be screened for STDs either while you are away or upon your return home. If the testing is to be done locally, be sure of the safety of any medical equipment used. Should you decide to wait until your return, you should receive pretest counseling as well as the appropriate blood tests and swabs. The latent period, that is, the time it may take until an HIV test may turn positive, may be up to 12 weeks or more. Remember that if you do become infected, early treatment lessens the likelihood of damage to the immune system in the future.

Should you develop symptoms of an STD such as a discharge, an ulcer or sore, or swollen glands, you should seek immediate medical attention. A diagnosis may be made clinically, and hopefully confirmed with laboratory testing if this is available. Remember that STDs often travel in pairs, or even in small crowds, so testing for other infections, including HIV, must also be performed.

The joy of sex and the joy of travel do not have to be mutually exclusive. But before you go, make sure you're fully aware of the risks involved, and how you can minimize them.

Key Points

- Use a condom all the time (if you are having sex).
- There's a greater variety and a greater risk of STDs in lesser-developed countries.
- Avoid high-risk activities such as tattooing, acupuncture, piercing and drunk driving.

A Few Other Concerns
CHAPTER 11

"The traveler sees what he sees, the tourist sees
what he has come to see."
GILBERT K. CHESTERTON

It may sometimes seem as though we travel health professionals spend all of our time telling you what *not* to do. But it's really a matter of making you aware of the various risks. Then you can choose to do what you want. So having cleared the air, do have a great time. And now here are a few more things that you should not do, or at least you should know about.

There are a few health concerns which don't fit neatly into some of the other chapters, so I have given them a chapter all of their own.

Swimmers Beware

SCHISTOSOMIASIS. This one may not roll off the tip of your tongue, but it's an infection that affects more than 200 million people throughout the tropics. It also goes by the name of bilharzia, in honor of its discoverer, Theodor Bilharz. It is caused by a tiny worm whose eggs are passed by humans in their urine or feces, depending upon the species. Assuming our human has no access to toilets or latrines, then the local fresh-water river or lake is the next best spot. These eggs will then inhabit certain types of snails; after a month there, they are released into the water.

Local people and tourists who play or work in fresh water become infected when these immature worms, known as cercariae, penetrate their unbroken skin. After a complicated migration in the human body through the lungs and the heart, they develop into adult worms and go about producing more eggs. The eggs can cause damage to various organs, including the liver, bowel or bladder. Prolonged and repeated exposure results in more serious infections. A true disease of poverty! If we could somehow provide the developing world with proper hygiene, sanitation and education, this disease would disappear. Travelers most often are just looking for a place to cool off.

The symptoms of schistosomiasis will depend upon which stage of the infection you are at. When the cercariae first penetrate your skin, you may notice an itchy rash, known as "swimmer's itch." This goes away on its own. Three to six weeks later, as the developing eggs are laid down in the veins of your bladder or bowel, you may develop something more interesting called "Katayama syndrome." This may consist of a fever, sweating, muscle aches, coughing and diarrhea. It takes a clever doctor to suspect this one.

Eventually, if enough worms have penetrated your skin, you may develop the painless passage of blood in the urine (in the case of *Schistosoma haematobium*) or various gastrointestinal symptoms (in the cases of *Schistosoma mansoni* or *japonicum*). Most travelers have limited exposure, and since worms do not divide in humans, most infections remain mild or asymptomatic. The majority of cases in travelers are diagnosed first by suspecting the infection, and by performing appropriate blood, urine or stool exams. Most infections are treatable and curable with the drug Praziquantel®.

And that's why we suggest to people that they avoid swimming in fresh water, particularly in tropical Africa, the Amazon and rural areas of Southeast Asia. If you have no choice (Lake Malawi looked too inviting), then try to swim in the deeper water, where there are no snails. Fast-moving streams, which are where whitewater rafters get exposed, are probably less of a risk. Having said that, they sometimes get infected. If you do think you have been exposed, rubbing your skin down vigorously with a towel will lessen the risk of larval penetration. Taking a shower or bath, with or without your mouth open, probably does not constitute a significant risk, and should be encouraged if the hot water is running.

LEPTOSPIROSIS. This infection is caused by a type of bacteria known as a spirochete, as is syphilis. But sex has nothing to do with it. Rather, it's contracted by swallowing water that has been contaminated with the urine of domesticated or wild animals, such as cattle, pigs, horses, dogs and rodents. Direct contact with broken skin may also lead to infection. Leptospirosis is found worldwide, but is most common in warmer climates.

Initially the illness may resemble malaria and other febrile illnesses. Anywhere between 2 and 21 days after exposure, you may experience fever, headache, chills, muscle aches, red eyes, vomiting and diarrhea. More serious complications include meningitis, kidney failure and jaundice (yellowing of the skin due to liver inflammation). The diagnosis is made by testing the blood or the urine, but this is another scenario where *"if you or the doctor don't think of it, you won't diagnose it."* Treatment with penicillin or doxycycline is helpful if it is begun within the first few days of the illness. The latter antibiotic can be used preventively for someone who has likely been exposed.

Leptospirosis can usually be avoided by refraining from swimming or wading in swamps or ponds that may be infected with animal urine. In September 2000, a large outbreak occurred among participants in the Eco-Challenge Sabah 2000 Expedition Race, who had no choice but to disregard this advice.

THE CANDIRU FISH. And now for something completely different ... the candiru fish (*Vandellia cirrhosa*). This delightful parasitic catfish is found in the waters of the Amazon and Orinoco rivers of South America. It's a bit of a vampire, and its main target is the gills of other fish, where it anchors itself and feeds on their blood.

If you are swimming in the buff and happen to heed nature's call to empty your bladder, this little guy (about an inch long) will be attracted to you. After having found the source of the urine, he will then swim upstream into your urethra (or anus or vagina), lodge itself with its spines and gorge itself on your blood. This is, in fact, a big mistake for the fish, since once he is engorged and stuck, there is no way out. It's also bad news for you, because the pain, I am told, is something else.

There are many treatments, the most definitive of which may be amputation or some lesser form of surgery. It has been reported that the folk remedy of inserting the juice of either the xaqua plant or the buitach apple into the urethra will both kill the fish and actually dissolve it. Alternatively, native Amazon residents report that drinking tea made from the green fruit of the jagua tree can also dissolve the fish.

So what have we learned? Don't swim in the Amazon. If you do, keep your bathing suit on. If you can't do that, at least pee before you swim. And now that you have learned about all these exotic infections and infestations, keep in mind that the greatest risk to swimmers is drowning, often under the influence of alcohol.

Barefoot Walking

There's nothing like kicking off your shoes and going for a walk on the beach. Why else did you fly down to the Caribbean? Just keep in the back of your mind that there are sometimes microscopic worms, fleas, men-of-war and discarded syringes waiting to puncture your skin.

Cutaneous larva migrans, or "creeping eruption," is an interesting infection caused by dog and cat hookworms. These larvae, which may have been left on the beach by the local pet, can penetrate your unbroken skin. This usually occurs on your foot, though it can happen anywhere, depending upon how you choose to sunbathe. It will cause an itchy, blistered, winding rash which seems to advance up to an inch a day. It does not creep anywhere else, such as to your brain, liver or spouse.

It can usually be recognized by a doctor who has seen it before, though it may not be by one who has not. It is treatable with a drug called albendazole or ivermectin. Try to avoid doctors who are anxious to freeze the worm or, worse still, cauterize it. I would not go so far as telling people not to walk barefoot, but do try to avoid places where the local dogs, cats and sometimes people have left their droppings or used syringes and other dangerous objects. Staying close to the water's edge is a bit safer, because the tide can wash away anything harmful.

In addition to animal hookworms, there are also human hookworms that may be lurking in the soil where proper sanitary facilities are lacking. These can also penetrate your bare feet and, after
a lengthy migration through your body, end up "hooked" onto the
lining of your small intestine, where they happily feed on your
blood. Hookworm is a major cause of iron deficiency anemia in
those who are constantly exposed to such conditions. Since most
travelers can afford very nice shoes and wear them most of the
time, your risk of developing anemia due to a hookworm infection
is remote.

Finally, these infections may sound trivial when compared to a
snakebite. If you are out at night in the grass, wear your shoes and
read Chapter 18, Snakes, Scorpions and Other Scary Creatures.

More About Your Feet

Your feet are among your most important possessions. Look after
them so that you can avoid *"the agony of da feet!"* (admittedly not
original). Make sure you have comfortable footwear. Fungal infections are extremely common on the feet. Fungi prefer moist, dark
locales, like in-between your toes. Use some powder between your
toes, wear socks that help to absorb the moisture, and take along
an antifungal cream such as Canesten® or Lamisil®. Cuts, blisters
and calluses should be attended to promptly, lest they interrupt
your hike or climb.

Here are some tips to make sure your feet last as long as your
vacation:

• Don't try out your new boots on the slopes of Kilimanjaro. Buy
them well in advance, and take the time to work them in.
Consider buying them later in the day, when your feet have done
all the swelling they plan to do till tomorrow.

• Boots should feel snug, but comfortable. Make sure you can still
wiggle your toes. Try walking up, down and sideways to make
sure your feet do not slide around excessively. Movement means
friction, and friction means blisters. Look for a salesperson who

seems to know something about hiking boots.

- Buy what feels the most comfortable, not what looks the best. You probably get what you pay for. Try on the boots with the socks you plan to wear.
- Be sure your socks fit well and do not bunch up. Synthetic materials such as polyester will help to keep your feet dry.
- Lace your boots up properly. Once again they should be snug, not tight.
- Pay attention to tender spots, or "hot spots," as soon as they appear, before they result in disabling blisters. Place some moleskin, duct tape or Vaseline® on the sore spot to reduce the pressure and friction.
- Take a cab, mule or rickshaw once in a while.

Breathing the Air

Well, this one will probably be unavoidable, but it's not always without hazard. Many cities around the world are tremendously polluted. Mumbai (Bombay), Bogotá, Manila, Jakarta and Beijing are just a few that come to mind. Children in Mexico City choose the color gray, rather than blue, when painting the sky. If you suffer from respiratory problems such as asthma or emphysema, make sure you go prepared with an adequate supply of your inhalers and other routine medications. In addition, it may be prudent to carry along an antibiotic in case you feel like you have developed a respiratory infection that may worsen your condition.

Flu vaccine is a reasonable measure for those who are at higher risk of becoming quite ill should they contract influenza. For that matter, it is not unreasonable for others as well. Remember, the flu season in the Southern Hemisphere is at the opposite time to ours. Recently, a large outbreak of influenza occurred on a ship cruising up to Alaska. So respiratory infections are not at all tropical. Rather, they tend to spread when lots of people get together. People over 65, as well as those with certain underlying medical problems, should also be vaccinated against pneumococcal pneumonia.

Ciguatera Poisoning

Sometimes you think you've done everything right and followed all the rules … and you still get sick. Ciguatera poisoning might be one of those instances. It has been described since the 18th century, with Captain Cook and his crew being among the first chronicled sufferers. Remember, it's not always necessary to travel to get a "travel disease," and outbreaks have occurred in North America from imported fish.

This condition was named after a Caribbean snail known as "cigua," which was thought to be the cause of the illness. The actual cause is a toxin produced by a tiny organism or dinoflagellate called *Gambierdiscus toxicus,* which is found along the coral reefs in the Caribbean and South Pacific between the latitudes 35° south to 35° north. This little organism is consumed by the local coral reef fish, which in turn may be consumed by larger and larger fish. The most commonly affected fish include barracuda, red snapper, grouper, kingfish, sea bass, Spanish mackerel and surgeon fish. The toxin does not harm the fish in any way, has no odor, color or flavor, and it's not destroyed by cooking, freezing, smoking, marinating or whatever else you may choose to do with your fish.

The initial symptoms of ciguatera poisoning are related to your gastrointestinal tract. Abdominal pain and cramps, nausea and vomiting usually begin within 12 hours of eating the guilty fish, and may persist for one to two days. More interesting are the neurological symptoms that develop. These include numbness and tingling around the mouth and the extremities, severe itching, weakness and what is known as temperature reversal. That is, what should feel hot feels cold, and vice versa. These symptoms usually last for two to three weeks, but sometimes they may continue for months or years. Alcohol and exertion may make your problems worse.

This condition is usually diagnosed clinically. In medical school, we are told that you can't diagnose something that you don't know about, so it will probably require a doctor with some "tropical" experience, or the local doctor, to make the diagnosis. Specific tests may be available for the fish, but not for you.

The initial treatment of ciguatera poisoning is mainly supportive, though the drug mannitol, a diuretic given intravenously, can help reduce the neurological symptoms if used early. More chronic symptoms, such as the numbness, may be treated with amitriptyline (Elavil®).

So how do you avoid this one? Well, the obvious answer is to avoid eating coral reef fish on your vacation. If you are not willing to make that sacrifice, these suggestions are usually adequate:

- Avoid eating larger fish weighing more than five pounds.
- Avoid the head, roe or viscera (organs) of the fish, since the toxin is more heavily concentrated in these areas.
- Listen to the locals if they tell you not to eat the fish.
- Avoid eating fish after large reef disturbances.

Viral Hemorrhagic Fevers

There are several interesting infections around the world that you will undoubtedly read about in the newspapers or see in the movies. That's likely as close as you'll get to them. But in the interest of full disclosure, let me provide you with some information about viral hemorrhagic fevers. Their names and distribution are as follows:

- Lassa fever: West Africa (Guinea, Liberia, Nigeria and Sierra Leone)
- Ebola hemorrhagic fever: Africa (Congo, Gabon, Ivory Coast, Sudan and Uganda)
- Marburg hemorrhagic fever: Africa (Kenya, Uganda and Zimbabwe)
- hantavirus pulmonary syndrome: United States; Canada; Central and South America (Argentina, Bolivia, Brazil, Chile, Panama, Paraguay and Uruguay)
- Argentine, Venezuelan and Bolivian hemorrhagic fevers: South America
- hemorrhagic fever with renal syndrome : Europe and Asia
- Crimean-Congo hemorrhagic fever: Africa; Europe (most recently, Kosovo); Asia (Iran, Pakistan)

These infections share several characteristics. First, as is evident from their name, they are all caused by somewhat similar viruses belonging to four separate families: the arenaviruses, filoviruses, bunyaviruses and flaviviruses. Unlike some other infections such as dengue fever or influenza, humans are not the natural host for these viruses. So how and why do we get infected? There are several possibilities.

The most common route is through direct contact with the host animals and/or their urine, feces or saliva. Rodents such as the multimammate rat (Lassa fever), the cotton rat, the deer mouse (hantavirus) and the house mouse are the usual hosts. Each particular host dwells only in a few restricted areas, so these infections are thankfully not widespread. Vectors such as ticks or mosquitoes are also capable of transmitting certain infections from the natural hosts to humans, as well as to other animals such as cattle, sheep and goats (Crimean-Congo hemorrhagic fever). People who handle these animals may also become infected.

Once a human becomes infected, the infection can be passed on in two ways—either by direct contact with another person (including sexual contact), or via contaminated syringes and needles that have been used to care for the sick patient. This latter route, in fact, is how many of these small outbreaks become "amplified." Health care workers are at great risk during an outbreak. This is why Dustin Hoffman wore that fancy suit in the movie *Outbreak*. Considering that an infected but asymptomatic person or monkey could fly from the jungles of Africa to New York City within a day or two, it's understandable that these infections create a bit of hysteria from time to time.

The symptoms of the various infections are quite similar and initially include fever, muscle aches, headache, weakness, sore throat, vomiting and diarrhea—not unlike several other illnesses that you have read about in this book. In more serious cases there may be bleeding under the skin, from internal organs or from body orifices. Kidney, liver or lung failure may also occur.

The treatment of these infections is mainly supportive—that is, with intravenous fluids and excellent nursing care. The drug ribavirin has proven useful in the treatment of Lassa fever. The mortality rates are quite high, ranging from about 15 percent in the case of Lassa fever to more than 50 percent with Ebola.

If you develop a fever with or without other symptoms during or after your trip, seek medical attention. Please do not try to convince your doctor that you have Lassa fever or Marburg hemorrhagic fever. I can almost promise you that you don't. Tell them that you have malaria. You will be better for it.

Anthrax

Diseases come and go on the world stage. After the tragic events of September 11, 2001, anthrax certainly had its 15 minutes of fame. It's an acute infection caused by the bacterium *Bacillus anthracis*. It's usually of concern mainly to hoofed animals, such as cattle, sheep, goats, camels, antelopes and other herbivores, which acquire the infectious spores from the soil. Humans become accidentally infected if they are exposed to these infected animals or their tissues. History has now taught us that biological terrorism is another potential route of infection.

There are three distinct forms of anthrax—cutaneous (skin), gastrointestinal (stomach or intestine) and inhalational (lungs), depending upon how the infection is contracted. Skin infections start as a red bump, which goes on to develop into a painless ulcer with a black base. Nearby lymph nodes may be swollen. In the intestinal form, there is fever, nausea, vomiting, abdominal pain and severe diarrhea. Finally, the respiratory form begins innocently like the common cold, but quickly progresses to breathing difficulty, shock and usually death. The infection is not contagious from person to person. The incubation period of the disease is usually less than a week, but may be as long as two months.

Anthrax is found around the world, particularly in lesser-developed countries where the host animals are raised, such as in South and Central America, Southern and Eastern Europe, Asia, Africa and the Middle East. Humans are rarely infected. When anthrax does occur, it is usually through some type of occupational exposure.

Treatment is with commonly available antibiotics, such as penicillin, tetracycline or ciprofloxacin. Cutaneous anthrax is rarely fatal when properly treated. Intestinal anthrax is fatal in about 50 percent of cases, and treatment of inhalational anthrax is unfortunately unsuccessful most of the time.

Yes, there is a vaccine. No, it's not for you! Rather, it is reserved for the following groups:

- laboratory workers who work directly with the organism

- those who are exposed to animal hides and furs in areas where standards are low

- persons who handle potentially infected animal products in high-incidence areas

- military personnel deployed to areas with high risk for exposure to the organism (as would be the case with biological terrorism)

So this is another disease that you should know about, and probably already do. But you really don't need to worry about it when you travel. I know I didn't while I was riding my camel in the deserts of Rajasthan.

Key Points

- There are lots of interesting infectons out there.
- You probably won't get any of them.
- Perhaps you should know about them just in case.

PART THREE
The World Around Us

Hello FROM CHINA!
Just a quick note to
say Thanks for all
your help. I'm healthy &
happy here in the land
of walls & rice & waterfalls.
take care

George & Michelle

Dr. Mark Wise
2300 John Street
Thornhill, Ontario
L3T 667
CANADA 加拿大

空野于大殿 皇野子の大殿 好全 내전
The Hall of Imperial Vault of Heaven
Salle de la Voûte céleste impériale
(Huangqiongyu)
Die Halle des Himmelsgewölby
La Sala Huangqiongyu

The Joys of Flight

CHAPTER 12

*"For my part, I travel not to go anywhere, but to go.
I travel for travel's sake. The great affair is to move."*
ROBERT LOUIS STEVENSON

Wilbur and Orville Wright first started out in the printing business. From there, they moved on to the bicycle business. Finally, at the turn of the 20th century, they settled on the airplane industry. On December 17, 1903, Wilbur made the first flight, which lasted 12 seconds and spanned 120 feet. Not a lot of frequent flyer points to be had there. On May 21, 1927, Charles Lindbergh landed in Paris after a solo flight from New York in his *Spirit of St. Louis*. Five years later, on May 20, 1932, Amelia Earhart became the first woman to successfully fly alone across the Atlantic. She preferred smelling salts and soup to coffee and tea. Likely none of these pioneers of flight gave much thought to jet lag, economy class syndrome, popping ears, pregnant passengers, terrorism or air rage. But we have progressed since then ... or have we? There is a tendency to blame the airline industry for everything that goes wrong when we are aloft. However, if flyers were more willing to modify their behavior, they just might find themselves more comfortable.

Man and woman were not made to travel at 35,000 feet scrunched up in a seat, to quickly cross 12 time zones, to eat and drink every three hours whether they were hungry or not, or to watch second-rate movies on a six-inch screen. And when we finally arrive, it gets worse. We succumb to jet lag.

Understanding the Problems

To understand a few of the problems, it is necessary to be acquainted with Boyle's law. I will understand if this does not leap out from your memory, so let me review it for you. Pressure times volume equals a constant (P x V = C). That is, as we fly higher and the ambient pressure in our pressurized aircraft becomes lower, the volume of any trapped gases increases.

As we eat and drink, and eat and drink, and sit bent at a right angle, and don't feel comfortable breaking wind, the gas that is trapped in our intestinal system may expand. This makes us feel bloated and uncomfortable. While that's not the end of the world, I thought you should at least know about it. Going easy on the baked beans and Brussels sprouts, and in general not overeating, is probably the best solution. Loose-fitting clothing and a belt with a few extra notches may also help.

We may also have air trapped in our Eustachian tubes. These are the passageways leading to the eardrums from the nose, mouth and sinuses. This does not usually create a problem during flight. As we descend, however, this trapped air contracts, creating a "sucking" effect on the eardrum, which may be quite painful and can even lead to bleeding behind the eardrum. This effect may be particularly bothersome if you're already congested due to an allergy or cold, in which case it may be best to postpone your flight. To attempt to equalize the pressures, the following measures may help:

- Drink or chew gum, or at least swallow frequently, as you descend.
- Breast-feed, if you are a baby.
- Use an oral or topical decongestant before and/or during the flight if you are already congested.
- Perform the Toynbee maneuver (pinch your nose, shut your mouth and blow). This will help re-expand your Eustachian tubes.
- Politely ask the pilot to make a very gradual descent (this may not be an option!).

There are a few other medical conditions where trapped air may be a problem. If you have recently had abdominal surgery, such as a laparoscopy or a tubal ligation, air may have been introduced into your abdominal cavity. You should probably not fly for a few weeks after such procedures. I had one young patient develop a spontaneous pneumomediastinum in Ecuador. What's that? It's the spontaneous (for no obvious reason unless you've been stabbed) leakage of some air from the lungs, which gets trapped around the heart. I must add that his medical care in Quito was superb. A pneumothorax is a similar condition, where air leaks from the lung and may compress the rest of the lung. Don't fly for three weeks if possible. Finally, if you have just broken your wrist and plan to fly home, it may not be a great idea. The air bubbles in your fresh cast may expand during your flight and compress the circulation to your hand. The problem can usually be managed by "splitting" the cast to allow for some extra breathing room during flight.

Oh, yes. I have read of someone's breast implant, which contained some air, exploding while in flight. I am sure that the person who suffered this fate was quite uncomfortable and distressed, but I assure you it is not a common occurrence.

Economy Class Syndrome

Economy class syndrome has been with us for many years. It received media attention in October 2000, when a 28-year-old British woman collapsed and died following 20 hours of flight from England to Australia. The cause was a deep vein thrombosis (DVT) or blood clot, which had traveled from the deep veins of her leg to her lung (pulmonary embolus). Since then, many more cases have been reported, and lawsuits against the airlines have been launched.

While there probably is a link between DVT and air travel, the risk remains quite low. DVT also occurs among people who have not flown long distances, or even short distances. Most cases in travelers occur in those with one of the following risk factors:

- pregnancy or recent pregnancy
- over 60 years of age
- obesity
- smoking habit
- use of estrogen medication (hormone replacement or the birth control pill)
- varicose veins
- previous DVT or pulmonary embolus
- recent surgery or injury
- chronic disease such as heart disease or cancer

The majority of reported cases of economy class syndrome have occurred in people with at least one of these risk factors. As well, sitting in economy class rather than business or first class does not seem to make much of a difference. Therefore, the term "traveler's thrombosis" may be more appropriate. I have yet to hear of this condition occurring in NBA basketball players, who might be a bit more cramped. But on the other hand, they are rarely obese, pregnant or on oral contraceptives. There's no reason to think that the same condition does not occur in those taking prolonged motor or train trips.

The symptoms of DVT include pain and swelling in the leg, usually in the calf. Should a piece of the blood clot break off and travel to the pulmonary artery in your lung, you may experience a cough, shortness of breath, hemoptysis (coughing up blood) and pleuritic (it hurts when you breathe) chest pain. The prognosis for someone with a DVT depends upon the size and location of the blood clot and the availability and quality of medical care. Certainly this is a potentially life-threatening condition. The symptoms of DVT or a pulmonary embolus may not become evident for one or two weeks following travel.

Whether or not you're at higher risk of developing this condition, there are several steps that would decrease your risk, such as:

- Drink lots of water, and minimize your alcohol and coffee intake, in an effort to prevent dehydration.

- Ask for an aisle or bulkhead seat, where there is more legroom; or even beg for first class.
- Exercise while you're aloft—wiggle your toes and stretch your legs, and hopefully all that water will send you walking down to the lavatory on a regular basis.
- Wear elastic compression stockings during flight—this has been shown to be of great benefit.
- Wear loose-fitting clothing.
- Consider walking to your destination.
- An aspirin taken four hours before flight is recommended for those at a higher risk of venous thrombosis (commonly called traveler's thrombosis). If you do choose to take an aspirin, be sure to take it with food.

There is currently no shortage of controversy regarding economy class syndrome or traveler's thrombosis. Certainly more research will take place in the coming years. For the time being, if the flight attendant offers you some water, take it.

Fainting

Fainting, or vasovagal syncope, is one of the most frequent "emergencies" aboard aircraft. It's more likely to occur in people who have been sitting for so long a time that the blood pools in their legs. They drink and eat too much and have on too much clothing, so some of the blood is diverted to their intestines and skin. Their bladder fills, and then they get up quickly to go to the lavatory, where they have to stand in line. By this time, most of their blood is in places other than their brain. They are usually pale, sweaty and somewhat "fuzzy" before they hit the floor. Treatment consists of lying them down and elevating their legs.

The Air

How about the air onboard a 747, or any other aircraft? Well, when you put 350 people in an enclosed space with the windows shut for eight hours, it's inevitable that some respiratory infections may be transmitted. The same thing occurs daily on our buses, in our classrooms and in our doctors' offices. Supporters of the airline industry claim that air quality has improved in recent years and is in fact quite good. Opponents say that it stinks, in order to save the airlines money. Personally, I don't think that I have caught anything aloft.

Having said that, the infections transmitted may include viruses, such as those causing the common cold or influenza, bacterial infections and even tuberculosis (TB). Considering the ease with which people can travel from one part of the world to another, TB raises some concern. The risk of contracting TB during flight is exceedingly low and probably not any greater than from being in close contact in other confined quarters. However, it may occur, with the risk being greatest among passengers or flight crew in prolonged, close contact with an infectious person—that is, someone actually coughing up the tuberculosis bacillus. People who are exposed to TB do not immediately become ill. Rather, a recent infection is detected by a "conversion" of one's TB test from negative to positive. Treatment to reduce the risk of developing active TB is available. If you don't hear from your public health department soon after your flight, you probably don't need to worry about this one. People with active TB should fly on private aircraft, or be adequately treated prior to travel.

Not for Everyone

Air travel may not be for everyone, and some prospective passengers should discuss the risks with their physician, or the airline doctor, before flying. Aircraft are pressurized with compressed atmospheric air, but it's economically unfeasible to maintain "sea level" pressures at cruising altitudes of 30,000 feet. So, in fact, the cruising altitude mimics an altitude of about 8,000 feet above sea level. This results in a drop in the partial pressure of oxygen (PO_2) in our blood. Most of us have no difficulty with this, considering we are mainly sitting there like couch potatoes during the flight. But for some it may present a problem.

If you or your loved ones suffer from heart disease or anemia, it's worth speaking to your doctor or the airline's doctor.

Supplemental oxygen may be indicated, but it needs to be arranged in advance. You will not be allowed to carry your own oxygen tank onboard. Pregnant women and scuba divers also have special considerations.

HEART AND LUNG DISEASE. People with severe heart disease, such as unstable angina, congestive heart failure or a recent heart attack or stroke, should preferably not fly. The same goes for those with significant respiratory disease, such as emphysema, acute asthma or infection. Thankfully, we are rarely exposed to cigarette smoke any more when we fly. Patients with pacemakers are not at higher risk, and these are not affected by security devices.

ANEMIA. Anemia, or a low red blood cell count, may also adversely affect your well-being while aloft. The usual adult hemoglobin level is between 12 and 15 grams per 100 milliliters; anyone whose hemoglobin is less than 8.5 (85 in Canada) should probably not fly. Sickle cell anemia, an inherited disorder in blacks, may also be a risk factor.

PREGNANCY. Aircraft double as movie theatres, restaurants and meeting rooms, but they were not designed to act as delivery suites. For that reason, pregnant women are not permitted on international flights after 36 weeks of gestation. A note documenting your due date may be required. Other than the risk of having your baby over the Rocky Mountains (there's probably a doctor onboard who never did any obstetrics), there is no increased risk to the mother or fetus.

SCUBA DIVERS. Scuba divers are at risk of decompression illness if they fly in a low-pressure environment too soon after diving. The accepted safe interval between one's last dive and the flight home is 24 hours, though some feel that a shorter interval may be sufficient.

Other Concerns
Flying, in my opinion, can be stressful ... very stressful. Getting to

the airport on time, kissing your baggage and your loved ones goodbye, pulling out your boarding pass umpteen times, being searched, squeezing your handbag into the overhead compartment, standing in line at the lavatory, trying to figure out where to plug in the earphones, wondering if you will make that connecting flight … it all adds up. I imagine that experienced flyers have it down to a science, or an art. For the rest of us, take a deep breath, count to 10 and try to relax.

I suppose one of the unexpected risks of flight is the other passengers. "Air rage," or particularly obnoxious, belligerent, rude and sometimes dangerous behavior, is on the increase. Reasons, or excuses, for such behavior include excessive alcohol consumption, smoking bans, flight delays, bad movies, crowding, long flights, psychological feelings of a loss of control, or problems with authority figures. Flight attendants are not trained as bouncers or security guards, and such trained personnel may in fact become standard on flights in the future.

Finally, many travelers suffer from an intense fear of flying. This is known as *aviophobia*. Such anxiety can result from not feeling in control, flying over water, turbulence, weather, small spaces, bad food, crowds, lost baggage, fear of terrorists, fear of heights, or all of the above. Many people with this problem will request a mild sedative, such as lorazepam, to take just before or during the flight. Nicotine chewing gums or patches may help hard-core smokers. Some instruction in meditation or relaxation may be appropriate. Courses are available, however, which will help you deal more definitively with such a problem, and apparently their success rate is quite high. There's a website that will provide you with lots of good advice in addition to information on the safest airlines, planes, countries, etc. (see end of chapter).

Before we leave this subject and move on to jet lag, let me reiterate something I will say over and over—most people are fine most of the time, but you should at least be aware of some of the things that can go wrong.

JET LAG

"Getting there is half the fun," or so goes the popular cliché. While this may hold true for a lazy driving trip through New England, or a flight to Florida, it generally does not apply to a 20-hour flight to Bangkok or the long return home from Capetown. It can be tough enough to survive the rigors of economy class flight.

What Is Jet Lag?

Whether you feel it or not, your body has rhythm. In fact it has many different "circadian" rhythms, which fluctuate during the course of the day and night. These control functions such as your blood pressure, heart rate, digestion, thinking and wakefulness. Ideally all these individual clocks work in harmony. We take it for granted that we generally get hungry at the same times every day, we are full of energy at certain times of the day and we are ready to put our head on the pillow at 10 o'clock each night. The time of night may vary from person to person and does not necessarily mean that your clock is broken.

Jet lag occurs when our internal body clock, which happens to have 25 hours, becomes out of sync with that of our new destination. This can occur after crossing as few as three time zones. For example, you may be rushing off to see the pyramids in Egypt just when your brain was expecting to crawl under the covers for some badly needed sleep. Or, conversely, it may be time for lights out, and you're occupied counting sheep because you can't get to sleep. Fortunately, traveling north–south is not a problem, though a 12-hour flight to Chile may still leave you a bit under the weather.

There are 24 time zones, each one hour apart. Greenwich, England, which is just a stone's throw from London, is the anchor point for this system. There, they operate according to Greenwich Mean Time (GMT). It's estimated that you may suffer from jet lag one day for every time zone you cross, so for that trip to the Orient you may be looking at more than 10 days out of whack. For someone with six months to recover, this is not the end of the world. But for business travelers flying a long way for a short time, the impact may be great.

The symptoms of jet lag are numerous. They may include difficulty falling asleep or staying asleep at bedtime, and fatigue during the day. You may be irritable, have difficulty concentrating or remembering things, or even be somewhat confused. Sounds like middle age. Perhaps you know a few people who seem that way even without traveling. Finally, you may lose your appetite and suffer with heartburn, and your magical bowel clock may be thrown off. All in all, not a great way to begin that vacation.

The severity may depend upon the direction of your travel (west to east is said to be worse than east to west), the number of time zones crossed and your personal susceptibility. Older people tend to adjust less well than younger people, perhaps because their sleeping habits may not be that great to start with. Personally, I recall an unquenchable desire to sleep for a week after my return from India a few years ago (east to west), and have generally found that returning home is the worst, regardless of the direction of travel. On the other hand, the excitement and anticipation of starting an amazing trip may overcome the deleterious effects of jet lag. My appetite seems to survive no matter where I go.

Somewhere at the bottom of the jet lag riddle is the ubiquitous hormone melatonin. It's produced by a small gland in our brain called the pineal gland. It's also produced by private manufacturers, but more on that in a moment.

What Can Be Done About It?

There are a few remedies for jet lag. Unfortunately, some of them are either ineffective or impractical, or both. Let's take a look at them. First, there is the Argonne Anti-Jet-Lag Diet®. This diet allegedly helps travelers adjust their body clock to the new time zone. It involves manipulating your food intake, caffeine intake and proportions of protein and carbohydrates, and is a bit complicated, to say the least. It's begun four days prior to departure, with alternating days of relative "feasting" and "fasting." Caffeinated beverages may be imbibed between 3 and 5 p.m., except on day four, when they may be taken in the morning if you are traveling west, or between 6 and 11 p.m. if traveling east. No alcohol is allowed on the plane. Bet I lost most of you right there.

This diet may be the best thing since sliced bread (which is allowed), but I really think that most of us have a hundred and one other things to worry about in the days before we travel. Impractical, in fact almost impossible, in my opinion. Whether it works is also open to question.

Another potential method is to vary the amount and timing of exposure to light before you travel, and upon your arrival at your destination. Recall that light exposure has an effect upon the production of melatonin in the brain. Natural light is usually available and quite inexpensive, but it may not always fit into our crowded schedule. Your boss may in fact get a bit perturbed to find you in the parking lot taking in those rays (with sunscreen, of course). Apparently, eastward travel requires exposure to bright light early in the day after arrival, and westward travel requires it at the end of the day. Artificial sources of light are also available, with Northern Light Technologies being one manufacturer. Some hotels actually cater to the jet lagged by providing rooms with either a source of bright light or total darkness.

Want to try something else? How about acupressure? This

involves balancing our meridian system by massaging specific pressure points regularly while we travel and upon our arrival. The Jet Lag Eliminator® will help you discover these points.

No-Jet-Lag® is a homeopathic remedy containing arnica, bellis perennis, chamomilla, ipecacuanha and lycopodium. The tablets need to be taken at take-off, every two hours in flight and then after each landing (including at intermediate stops). Many people swear by it and studies have suggested that it's effective, so consider giving it a try. I took this on my way to and from Nepal, and found the tablets tasted quite good. Maybe it helped minimize my jet lag. Check the website (see end of chapter).

Finally, there is melatonin. Levels of melatonin are lowest during the day, when we are awake and exposed to lots of light, and highest at night—helping us sleep, we think. There are many studies supporting the use of melatonin for jet lag as well as other sleep disturbances. It supposedly works by causing a "chemical darkness."

For eastward flight, it may be taken in the early evening for two or three days prior to departure. Upon arrival, take it a bit later at the local bedtime for as many nights as it takes you to get properly adjusted to the local time. If you are going west, then melatonin may be used at bedtime at your destination.

The recommended dosage is between 3 and 5 milligrams. I am sure you will find other dosages and schedules if you look hard enough. Melatonin may cause some drowsiness and should not be used in the young and the pregnant. Those on anticoagulants and with epilepsy should also avoid it. Its long-term effects are not known. It's available in the United States, but not in Canada, where Canadians went a little bit overboard thinking that it may cure everything from baldness, to cellulite, to sexual dysfunction. (It doesn't!)

Travelers often request a short-acting sleeping pill for use on the plane, as well as for a short time at their destination and/or when they return home. This does nothing to readjust the body's clock, but it may get you a decent night's sleep. Sleeping pills may also cause drowsiness (that seems rather obvious), and some people may have difficulty with their short-term memory. In the elderly, these should be used cautiously, or not at all. The risk of addiction to such pills is remote when used for only such a short time.

For those who are traveling across several time zones but only for a few days, most of these methods are probably not of benefit, and in fact it may be better just to leave your watch at home time. If you're looking for something interesting to read during that long flight, try *SLAM Jet Lag,* by Michael Klompas and Colin Shapiro (see references at end of book).

So there you have it—several choices to help minimize your jet lag. Now that I have given you those, let me offer some more advice which may help to improve your mood upon your arrival:

- Drink lots of fluids while in flight, preferably water. Avoid, or minimize, the coffee and alcohol. They cause dehydration and upset your sleep patterns, and alcohol can contribute to air rage.

- Don't eat everything that comes your way. Gases expand in the air up there. Your belt will need an extra notch or two by the time you arrive.

- Take a stretch or stroll every hour to make sure your blood is still flowing, especially after spending a few hours curled up like a pretzel.

- If you fly at night, try to get some sleep on the plane. Use the complimentary earplugs and blindfold. Invest in an inflatable pillow.

- Switch to the local time schedule upon your arrival. A cold shower or a quick swim may invigorate you for the day ahead. Try to avoid napping during the day, and hit the sack at night, local time, when you're totally bushed. Caffeine is allowed during the day if necessary.

- Schedule a one-night (or longer) stopover on your way if possible. If two nights in London on the way to New Delhi doesn't fit into your budget, I understand.

- Don't plan to perform brain surgery (particularly if you are not a brain surgeon) or high-level negotiations as soon as you arrive.

Jet lag is one of the joys of travel, right up there with motion sickness and lost baggage. Thankfully, many of its unwanted effects can be minimized with some careful planning and sensible behavior. For many of us, traveling is a reward for working too hard for several months or years. A glass of white wine and a nap may be a nice treat. Remember that your flight is also part of your vacation. Enjoy it.

Related Websites

Air Safety: http://www.airsafe.com

No-Jet-Lag: http://www.nojetlag.com

Key Points

- Dress, eat and drink in a way that you will be most comfortable during your flight.
- If you have medical problems, make sure that you're fit to fly.
- Jet lag may occur after crossing as few as three time zones. There are several medical and nonmedical ways to minimize it.
- Be happy that you are going somewhere far away!

Motion Sickness

CHAPTER 13

"Traveling is like flirting with life. It's like saying, 'I would stay and love you, but I have to go; this is my station.'"

LISA ST. AUBIN DE TERAN

To travel means to move, and for many to be on the move means motion sickness. This is one of the more humbling experiences of travel. Here's how it goes. You may feel stomach discomfort, nausea, drowsiness, lightheadedness and the need to gasp for air or to sigh. People around you notice that you are pale and sweaty. Eventually, these feelings may culminate in an uncontrollable desire to throw up.

Why Me?

Motion sickness has been with us for centuries, in fact, ever since men and women started moving faster than our maker intended. Julius Caesar was nauseated in his chariot, and Tom Hanks and other astronauts upchucked in *Apollo 13*.

This unpleasant condition is just another example of information overload—too many conflicting signals reaching the brain from the inner ear, the eyes and other body receptors all at the same time. As with other travel favorites such as altitude sickness and jet lag, some individuals may be more susceptible than others.

It rarely occurs in children under the age of two or in the elderly (let's call that over sixty). Young children aged two to twelve are affected the most. Women tend to become ill three times more commonly than men. While the likelihood of becoming ill may depend upon the size of your ship or dinghy or the amount of turbulence in the air, for some just to be on the move is enough. Having said that, traveling by boat gives you the best chance of becoming ill, followed by plane, car and train.

For most people, motion sickness will be only a slight nuisance, but for others it may take a few days to adapt. Up to 5 percent of travelers will not get better unless they change their surroundings. Some unlucky souls actually experience the same problem when they get back onto dry land, as they readjust to their new reality. This is termed *"mal d'embarquement* syndrome."

Can I Avoid It?

There are several measures which travelers can take to minimize their risk of becoming ill. First, choose the best available seat. This would be in the middle of the boat, over the wing of the plane or in the front seat of the car, where unwanted movement may be the least. Driving the car is preferable. Try to stay relatively still, in a semi-reclining position if possible. Focus on distant objects, such as the horizon or whatever is on the TV screen. This helps to keep your inner ear, which is responsible for your balance, relatively stable.

Stay away from big meals, alcohol and cigarette smoke. If fresh air is available, take advantage. Avoid reading. With young children, try to keep them occupied and distracted by playing games; that is, unless you're suffering from motion sickness.

As usual, there are several medications and remedies available to help prevent your misery. Ideally these should be taken prior to your moving experience, since they may have to be administered by suppository or injection if you wait too long.

- Dimenhydrinate (Gravol®), meclizine (Bonamine®) and promethazine (Phenergan®) are the most commonly used oral remedies. Their main side effect is drowsiness. Dosages may need to be repeated every four to six hours. Needless to say these should not be taken by pilots, captains or drivers if they intend to remain in charge. Nor should they be taken by pregnant women or young babies.
- Transderm-Scop® (in the United States) or Transderm-V® (in Canada), the scopolamine patch, is stuck just behind your ear and has the advantage of providing up to three days of relief. However, it may make the wearer drowsy and a bit dizzy and could cause some blurred vision. If, in fact, the waters are quite calm, the effects of the patch may be worse than the disease. This drug must be avoided by the young, the pregnant and anyone with glaucoma or an enlarged prostate (usually slightly older men). I sometimes offer the suggestion that would-be travelers try the patch at home before hitting the high seas.
- Ginger root *(Zingiber officinale),* which may be taken as capsules or in the dry root form, is available for the naturally inclined.
- Travel Ease® is a homeopathic concoction (made by the makers of No-Jet-Lag®) containing borax, cocculus indicus, gelsemium, kreosotum, rhus toxicodendron and tabacum.
- Acupressure, applied by a small device worn around the wrist known as the Sea-Band®, has not been shown to be effective but does make some people happy.

So if your dreams include sailing the high seas, flying eight-seater aircraft in the Himalayas or just driving the kids to Myrtle Beach, pick your seat well, take along some medication and, oh yes, perhaps pack a plastic bag or two.

Key Points

- Motion sickness results from sensory overload to the brain.
- Choose your seat strategically.
- Pills, patches or pressure may alleviate your misery.

Culture Shock

CHAPTER 14

"I dislike feeling at home when I am abroad."
GEORGE BERNARD SHAW

Imagine being dropped in a foreign place where the language was incomprehensible, the people dressed differently, the food burned your stomach, the temperature was 95°F in the shade, the local currency looked funny, you had no friends and the water was always cold. Now imagine staying there for a year. Sounds a bit disconcerting? Well, many of you who are reading this book will be doing just that. So why don't we talk about culture shock, so that it doesn't get the better of you?

What Is Culture Shock?

Many people believe that getting off the plane on a Caribbean island and driving to their hotel is an example of culture shock. I agree that the hot, humid air, the barefoot children begging and the donkeys walking along the road may be shocking. But this is not culture shock. Culture shock is a syndrome brought on by the stress that results from the loss of all the familiar signs, symbols and surroundings that we take for granted and the plunge into a totally unfamiliar environment. We go from air conditioning, nearby friends and family, a familiar language, civilized drivers, microwaves, endless electricity and 20 varieties of bagels and coffee—to something totally different. We are like a fish out of water. Well, perhaps that fish out of water has a bit more to worry about than we do.

This syndrome may be experienced by all travelers, though it's probably most significant for those who spend a longer time away

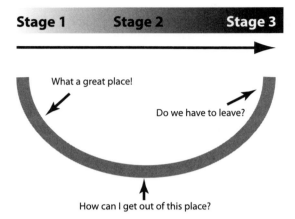

from home. As well, it's a bit like jet lag or motion sickness in that not everyone suffers to the same extent or in the same way. Although you may not be able to avoid all the stresses of adapting to a new country and culture, with some understanding of culture shock you should be able to make the transition that much easier.

Arriving in a foreign country, we usually experience a "honey-moon phase" (Stage 1) for several weeks or even a few months. (This is especially true if you're on your honeymoon.) Everything is new and exciting. The local people are polite and gracious and anxious to help out. The new sights, sounds, tastes and smells make us feel even more alive and excited. We look forward with great antic-ipation to getting on with the new job or adventure. It's not unlike the first few days at summer camp, college or even that new job.

This may be followed by Stage 2, the *"What am I doing here?"* stage. Stage 2 may be characterized by a hostile and aggressive atti-tude toward the host country and its people. This hostility grows out of the genuine difficulty that you may experience in the process of adjustment. In spite of your good intentions, feelings of frustration, irritability and anxiety may occur. There's a tendency to personalize everything negative that happens. Changes in mood, sleep patterns, energy level, sex drive and appetite may also be noticeable. Your sense of humor, one of your most valuable assets, may disappear.

You may feel guilty about these negative feelings. But there are problems with the phones, there's no fresh fruit available, cobras are on your porch, you have diarrhea, you got robbed, you can't get the hang of the language … and the local people seem indifferent to these problems. Indifference becomes interpreted as being insensitive and unsympathetic, so you decide, *"I just don't like them."* Expatriates often tend to congregate in their own little "cocoon." While this refuge may provide a sense of security and a convenient forum for complaining, it doesn't help much with integration into the local way of life. Let me balance that by saying that there is no reason not to get together with friends and fellow countrymen and -women: It doesn't hurt to let out your frustrations once in a while, you were not meant to give up your former identity, and it's probably lots of fun.

Keep in mind that the symptoms of anxiety and depression are not restricted to people visiting foreign countries. My office and the waiting rooms of most doctors are busy with people suffering from these same problems for a multitude of reasons, including stresses resulting from family, work, money (or lack thereof), illness and, sometimes, all of the above. Traveling, working and living abroad are not always easy. In fact, they can be downright impossible at times. We leave many of our stresses behind at home, but we acquire new ones, whether it's the difficulty in getting things done, a lack of privacy, local corruption, lack of resources for our work, or whatever.

Finally comes Stage 3, typically after about six months, when the visitor accepts the customs and other quirks of the host country as just another way of living. You become willing to see local values and behaviors as *different* from yours, rather than worse or wrong. At this point, you not only understand and accept all the cues of social intercourse—the food, drink, habits and customs— you actually enjoy them and make them part of your daily life. Your sense of humor resurfaces. Getting the hang of your new job may help, too. While you may never be totally Ethiopian, Mongolian, Peruvian or Nepalese, you certainly are a lot closer than when you began. Unfortunately, for many travelers it's during this final stage that they end up returning home.

In someone taking a much briefer trip, the same stages probably occur, but much more quickly and superficially. Imagine a one-week holiday to Mexico. The first day or two are filled with anticipation and new experiences. Midweek may be plagued with water shortages, a bit of diarrhea and other frustrations. And by the time you're ready to board your plane back home, you finally feel at home and wish you could stay for another week.

When I'm feeling a bit overwhelmed by it all, I let myself wallow in home comforts. I look at photos from home, read magazines, listen to music from home (on occasion I will play my Christmas CDs nowhere near December, because I find them comforting and they make me happy), and eat food that is as close to "home" as possible. Before leaving, we printed about 90 envelopes with our overseas address and handed them out at our going-away party. We arrived at our placement with two letters in our pigeonhole! Receiving news from home makes being away much easier for me. I've asked for photos from everyone and have set up a wall collage with pictures of all my friends and family. Hanging out with other Westerners provides a good opportunity to discuss our experiences, but I try to limit the negative talk. Yes, I think it's important to get things off your chest, but if you make a habit of talking about all the bad stuff all the time, you tend to forget that there is good stuff! I highly recommend journalizing to clear your head space.

—VSO volunteer

What Can We Do About It?

It's important to recognize that culture shock is a natural and common experience. Here are several ways in which you can make your adjustment to life overseas a bit easier:

• Realize that culture shock may occur.

- Take time to acclimatize to the jet lag, the food, the living conditions, the weather. You may have plans to change the world; just don't try to do everything in the first week.
- Learn as much as you can in advance about the country you're visiting.
- Commit yourself to learning the local language.
- Develop a social life—hopefully one that involves local people as well as other expatriates.
- Keep in touch with family and friends, and with events back home.
- Don't lose sight of your personal goals.
- Make the most of your work. Set small, realistic goals and try to tolerate what you cannot change. (This suggestion may be extremely difficult if it involves ignoring things we wouldn't tolerate at home, like corruption, corporal punishment, poor treatment of women and other behaviors.)
- Make use of and offer peer support.
- Deal with stress as it arises.
- If you happen to be a nonworking spouse, use the time to get in shape, volunteer, develop a new skill, travel and discover the culture.
- If you've brought children along, take advantage of the time together.
- Be proactive about your physical health. Pay attention to your diet and hygiene, and get regular rest, exercise and relaxation.
- Take along some special things from home—your favorite photos, packaged teas, snacks, music, magazines—which you can enjoy when you're feeling lonely or blue.
- Ask for help if you need it.

E-mail has made communication with family and friends back home quite easy. I've seen travelers spend most of their days glued to a computer at the local Internet café. There's the danger, however, that staying too connected may limit your incentive to get involved with local events and, hence, prolong your culture shock. So take advantage of e-mail, but use it in moderation.

Aside from staying in touch with distant family and friends, keep in touch with yourself. Meditate. Take a walk. Record your feelings and experiences in a journal. For some great advice on that journal, take a look at the book by Dr. Mel Borins entitled *Go Away—Just for the Health of It* (see references at end of book). Privacy is one thing that many people cherish, and it's sometimes difficult to find when you're the village novelty.

It's important to learn as much as you can about the country and its culture before you leave home. They say that 10 percent of your job success depends upon your particular skill, and the other 90 percent upon how well you communicate with others. It's difficult to communicate with those whose customs, traditions and ways of operating you do not understand. Many volunteer agencies invest a great deal of time and usually money in preparing volunteers and employees for their experience abroad. Considering the time, energy, financial cost and distress involved in repatriating someone and/or their family, it's time well spent. For an exhaustive list of written material on the subject of cross-cultural training and adaptation, visit the Intercultural and Community Development Resources (ICDR) website (see end of chapter).

What If I Have Problems?

Depression is a common occurrence, no matter on which side of the ocean you find yourself. It's one of the most frequent reasons for expatriates returning home early. The symptoms of depression may include mood swings, crying spells, irritability, fatigue, lack of appetite, loss of motivation or get-up-and-go, feelings of worthlessness or guilt and thoughts of death or suicide. If you feel yourself falling into this pattern, it's essential that you get help. If you recognize it in somebody else, lend a helping hand.

Substance abuse, particularly alcohol, is sometimes a problem for those working abroad. Whether it's the hot weather, the cheap beer, the local custom or peer pressure, it may end up affecting your job and relationships while abroad. As well, substance abuse will undoubtedly lower your inhibitions, which in turn may lead to the dangers of unsafe sex and unsafe driving. Once again, if this appears to be becoming a problem, ask for help.

If you have had emotional or substance abuse problems in the past, be sure that you find out what support services, if any, are available at your destination.

When we arrived at our placements, acceptance in the local community appeared to be dependent on our conforming to a set of cultural norms that was fundamentally different from anything we had experienced before. We felt that the ideal volunteer was one who threw herself wholeheartedly into local life, who spoke the language fluently, whose smile never cracked, who never needed escape—be it physically or mentally. As time went on we realized how important it was for us to keep a sense of self. A small example of this recognition was that we all wore Western clothes more and more as time went on. There is no ideal degree of integration, and you must not feel that there is. Preservation of a healthy sense of self is as important as anything else: It is a sign of success, not of failure.

—VSO volunteer

What Qualities Will I Need When I Travel Abroad?

Undoubtedly you'll need many qualities if you're going to manage successfully. These may apply whether you travel for pleasure or work, and whether you're gone for a week or a year. Which one is most important? That probably depends upon the person and the situation, but one volunteer I met was adamant that a sense of humor is paramount. *"If you can't laugh about some of the things that go on, you will have to cry."* Here are some of the qualities you will need: open-mindedness, sense of humor, ability to cope with failure, communicativeness, flexibility and adaptability, curiosity, positive and realistic expectations, tolerance for differences and ambiguities, positive regard for others, and a strong sense of self.

How About Returning Home?

For some, the adjustment upon returning home may be even more difficult than the move abroad. In fact, you may go through the same stages you experienced when you arrived in Borneo. You have just left a place that you had grown to love, along with its people. The new values that you acquired abroad now seem a bit out of place. People would love to hear your stories and see your slides, but they don't have time. (An estimate from one returnee is that, aside from family, most acquaintances will listen to your stories for up to five minutes and then begin to talk about themselves.) You're not sure what the future holds. And finally, you have to get used to your mother's cooking again. (In the case of my mother, this would be a pleasure!)

So what can you do? In fact, it's much the same as when you arrived at your destination. Be aware that re-entry shock can occur. Re-establish your social life. Get involved with work. Keep in touch with your friends overseas. Offer to give a talk or slide show about your experiences. Look after your mental and physical health. You may encounter difficulties, such as re-entering the job market, returning to school or re-establishing old relationships. Given time, things usually work out.

Just as jet lag can be made milder with a stopover, so can culture shock. One VSO volunteer from Cameroon told me that she spent two weeks relaxing in Europe, adjusting to the weather, the food and the traffic before returning home. A nice option if you can swing it.

But don't worry about that for now. Remember, culture shock is as natural as that first bout of diarrhea. Anticipate it. Understand it. And things will get better.

Related Website

International and Community Development Resources (ICDR): www.icdr.com

---

Key Points

- Realize that culture shock may occur.
- Understand why it may occur.
- Try to take measures to minimize its negative impact.

Your Personal Safety

CHAPTER 15

"The world is a book, and those who do
not travel, read only a page."

SAINT AUGUSTINE

While we spend a lot of time talking about exotic and not-so-exotic tropical diseases, in fact they account for only a small fraction of the serious morbidity (illness) and mortality (death) in travelers. Personal injuries, on the other hand, play a significant role. When my children and people who remind me of my children travel, I really don't worry so much about tropical infections, which are usually either preventable or manageable. Rather, I lie awake at night thinking of them riding in those buses, walking those streets and being exposed to unexpected events abroad.

In March 2000, I was looking at a newspaper headline and gruesome photo from Nairobi: *"A speeding bus swerved to avoid a pothole and collided head on with another bus yesterday, killing at least 101 people in Western Kenya, police said."* It was only when I visited Kenya in the summer of that year that I learned a British volunteer had died in that accident. I also met a volunteer who had decided not to get on that bus because it was dark and raining, and the bus was horribly overcrowded. To quote another volunteer, who was asked about the greatest threat to her health abroad, *"I suffered with water-related illness, but I think that the greatest threats are road accidents and public transport."*

Several studies have focused on the causes of death in travelers. Medical illnesses usually account for about 66 percent of these deaths. This is not unlike the situation back home, where heart attacks and strokes are the major causes of mortality. (Older travelers are at greatest risk.) For this reason, it would be reasonable to see your doctor before you travel, just to make sure that everything is as good as can be with your health. Of course, there's no guarantee of perfect health while you are away.

Infectious diseases, such as malaria, typhoid fever, rabies and hepatitis, typically account for less than 3 percent of deaths abroad. Talking about these infectious risks, however, probably takes up about 90 percent of the time you spend with the doctor before you leave.

Trauma, whether it's through motor vehicle accidents or other forms of personal injury, consistently accounts for at least 25 percent of the deaths abroad. This more often involves young travelers, and more often males than females. The latter finding may be because males are more prone to taking risks, or that they are just not as intelligent as females. Probably a bit of both. The nature of these deaths tends to vary from country to country.

Of this 25 percent, the greatest cause of death is motor vehicle accidents. Motorcycles and the backs of open trucks do not fare well when it comes to ranking the methods of safe travel. In fact, the Peace Corps found that between 1962 and 1983, 33 percent of their deaths on the road were due to motorcycle accidents. Other gruesome causes of death in travelers included drowning, airplane crashes, homicide, suicide, poisoning, electrocution and avalanches. Some of us tend to pursue much riskier activities when we travel than we do at home. We mountain climb, bungee jump, hitchhike, scuba dive, parasail and so on. Unfortunately, accidents happen.

It's not surprising that motor vehicle accidents are particularly high on the list of causes of death among travelers. Cars and buses in lesser-developed countries are often poorly maintained and teeming with masses of people and chickens. I won't forget the sight of a giant crab strutting down the aisle of my Peruvian bus.

Roads are usually poorly lit and lack a white line down the center. Potholes the size of swimming pools abound. Seatbelts are rarely seen. You may be sharing the road with bicycles, rickshaws, cows, elephants and baboons. Perhaps the drivers are not as careful as we are here. Their remuneration may depend upon how quickly they reach their destination, and how many passengers they deliver. Hopefully they have a driver's license. I realize that I may be libeling an entire group in society, but I am just trying to make you aware.

I vividly remember several harrowing bus rides through the Andes back in the 1970s. Every few hundred yards there was another cross on the roadside commemorating where a bus had tumbled over the edge. On a bus in Guatemala, as my daughter Carrie closed her eyes, I couldn't help but notice the Spanish messages over the driver imploring El Dio to bless this bus. I understand why. My cab driver in Dar es Salaam had a great smile, but no dashboard.

For better or for worse, you can't always avoid the local form of transportation. Often there is no other practical choice. And what better way to see the country and its people than by staying on the ground.

Rules of the Road

- Avoid driving at night in rural areas.
- If traveling by bus, try to find the best one you can afford.
- Stay off motorbikes if at all possible; get some proper training if you will be riding one regularly.
- Don't drink and drive, and don't drive with someone who has been drinking.
- At least *look* for a seatbelt.
- If you are taking along young children, make sure you arrange for a proper car seat.
- Use a local driver when possible. This decision may depend on the amount of confidence you have in the local driver versus yourself.
- Sitting in the back seat is statistically safer than in the front seat.
- Choose your taxi with care. Anecdotes abound of unsuspecting travelers being driven to remote spots, robbed and left on the roadside.
- Avoid driving at night in rural areas. (Yes, I'm mentioning it again. It's important!)

When I look back on my travels, I realize that I've broken most of these rules. But as I get older and wiser and have children of my own, I see their importance.

I should also mention that just crossing the road as a pedestrian has its hazards. In many popular destinations where the English flag once flew or still does, such as England, Kenya, Tanzania and Nepal, they tend to drive on the wrong side (the left) of the street. Looking over your left shoulder before you cross the street rather than your right may be a disastrous mistake. It almost cost me my life in Nairobi. In some places, just crossing the street—no matter which way you look—can be a challenge.

Now that I've frightened you out of getting into a moving vehicle while you're away, let's talk about other ways of maintaining your safety. That is, how can you avoid getting mugged, robbed and worse? Remember, my intention is not to make you paranoid and distrustful, but rather to make you aware of what may be going on around you.

Personal injury due to violence is, unfortunately, common, particularly in certain countries. As the Canadian government stated in one of its travel advisories back in 1995 after an American military base had been blown up in Saudi Arabia, *"There remains the risk of being in the wrong place at the wrong time. Exercise vigilance and caution."* Unfortunately, that risk remains, and will always be with us.

Here are some tips to avoid unwanted trouble. Many apply particularly to women. The list is long, but it's based on the anecdotes of many unfortunate travelers over the years. Pick the pointers that apply to you:

- Leave your nice jewelry at home. Don't even bring your costume jewelry.
- Leave any valuables in the hotel safe, if there is one.
- Make copies of your passport and other important documents. Keep one copy with you and leave one at home.
- Carry a few extra passport photos. They might come in handy.
- Do not carry a purse. If you must, keep it close to your body, not dangling by a long strap.
- Change your travelers' checks and money only at "licensed" establishments. Count your money inside, not as you walk out the front door. Be vigilant at ATMs.
- Do not carry large amounts of money.
- If you are wearing a money belt, it's best to have it concealed under your clothing around your waist. Don't keep one around your ankle or neck.
- Sew zipper pockets into your jacket.
- Consider dividing your money and valuables among different pockets. (Some of those new pants with 30 pockets make it tough for even me to remember where my money is.)
- If you value your possessions, do not let them out of your sight. What gets stored on the top of the bus may not be there at the end of your 12-hour ride. When on a train, or anywhere else, do not leave your bags unattended.
- Be aware of your surroundings at all times. Be especially vigilant around markets, airports and train and bus stations. If all of a

sudden there are eight people surrounding you, something may be going on. Get yourself out of there as quickly as possible.

- Be sensitive to the local culture. Dress appropriately, and perhaps somewhat conservatively. You already look like a wealthy tourist without making it more obvious.
- Don't try to photograph any sensitive buildings. They can usually be identified by the armed guards out front.
- Be tactful when it comes to taking pictures of local people. Some cultures consider it *"stealing their soul."* Others just don't like it. Be sure you have "implied consent" before snapping away.
- Be alert to scams (*"Oh, I'm sorry. I seem to have dropped my baby on his head. Would you mind picking him up while my accomplice checks out your back pocket?"* Or *"Pardon me for pouring that ketchup on your lovely sweater. Let me look in your purse for a hankie!"*) Scams can in fact be quite elaborate. In Nairobi, people allegedly throw themselves in front of your car, feigning injury. You, being a good person and feeling a bit guilty, get out to see if they are OK. Next thing you know, your car has been stolen. If someone seems too accommodating or friendly, think about it for a second.
- Consider taking along your own padlock for your hotel room door.
- Do not open your room door unless you are absolutely sure who is on the other side.
- Learn the location of hotel exits and stairways in case you need to make a quick departure.
- Take along a flashlight and extra batteries.
- Don't walk alone in dark, isolated areas, or even, in some of them, if you have company. Romantic strolls on the beach are not always a good idea. Think twice in some well-lit areas as well.
- If you will be in a country for some time, or if there is significant unrest in that country, register with your local embassy or consulate. Make sure that someone you trust knows of your whereabouts at all times.
- Walk with some purpose in your step. That is, at least *try* to look like you know where you are going. As Yogi Berra once said, *"If you come to a fork in the road, take it."*

- Don't abuse alcohol. It may lead you into unsafe vehicles, unsafe sex and unsafe back alleys. An intoxicated tourist makes a much better target. The potency of local Russian vodka and Peruvian chicha may be greater than you think.
- Don't accept a drink from someone you don't know unless you saw it being poured.
- Avoid riots and political demonstrations, and generally stay away from unruly crowds.
- Do not carry "mystery" packages across borders for people you do not know, and even for some you do.

I haven't had any problems with thievery, but this may be due to a technique I have developed when I am in a crowded environment. As soon as I am feeling closed in, I make sure to push a space between myself and the throng. The volunteers I know who have been mugged usually don't realize it because it occurs among a crowd. I feel a bit like an aggressive foreigner, but it keeps a fair distance between myself and groping hands.

—VSO volunteer

Remember that while you are away, you are subject to the laws of the land—not the land of your origin, but the country where you are traveling. If you are caught using or trafficking illegal drugs, or are suspected of any other crime, you may languish for years behind bars in some foreign land. Inhabiting foreign jails may in turn be hazardous to your health. Neither your high-priced lawyer back home nor your local government officials will wield much influence in such situations. Some offenses may be punishable by death.

Finally, in some countries, kidnapping for ransom is almost a daily occurrence. Colombia comes to mind. Money is usually the motivation for such acts. If you are living and working abroad, give some thought to the following:

- Select the location of your residence carefully.
- Consider the need for additional security—alarms, security lighting, special locks, gates, security guards.
- Choose your security guards and domestic employees with care. Do not entrust them with important information, such as where you have left your valuables, or the fact that you won't be home until next week.
- Always look in the back seat of your car before getting in. Change your route to work regularly. Keep your vehicle well maintained. Keep your doors and windows locked. Drive along well-lit and well-traveled streets. Most abductions take place on the way to and from work.
- Be well acquainted with at least one local neighbor, as well as the location of the nearest hospital, police station and government buildings—their government and yours.
- Be cautious about giving information over the telephone.
- Discourage the delivery of packages to your private residence.

Well! If this chapter hasn't made you paranoid (no, it's not the mefloquine!), then I don't know what will. But really, most of it is pure common sense, or should be. Sometimes we just need to see things in writing. Most of the people you meet when you travel will be friendly, sincere and honest. Do not put your guard up too high.

With the exception of losing my Swiss Army® knife from my pack on the top of an Ecuadorian bus in the 1970s, I've been quite fortunate over the years. I have survived Peruvian cliffs, downtown Nairobi, the traffic in Kathmandu and much more. I feel a bit lucky to have fared so well.

Two indispensable resources to check before you leave, or even before you book your flight, are the websites of the U.S Department of State and the Canadian Department of Foreign Affairs and International Trade (DFAIT) (see end of chapter). These sites will tell you the places to which you should not even dream of going, and how to stay safe in the ones where you do go.

Related Websites

U.S. Department of State:
http://travel.state.gov/travel_warnings.html

Canadian Department of Foreign Affairs and International Trade:
http://www.voyage.gc.ca/consular_home-e.htm

Key Points

- Be aware of your surroundings.
- Avoid driving in rural areas after dark.
- You look wealthy in most tropical countries, even though you may not feel it.

The Sun Did It

CHAPTER 16

"The man who goes out alone can start today; but he who travels with another must wait till that other is ready."

HENRY DAVID THOREAU

"The sun did it!" This cheery advertising slogan used to refer to that bronze tan and subtle blond bleaching of the hair so popular back in the Beach Boys era. Now when we give credit to the sun, it's more likely to be because of premature aging of the skin, photosensitivity reactions and skin cancer. A tan is no longer considered a sign of good health. Rather, it represents skin injury. The main beneficiaries are the cosmetic surgeons. Sounds depressing. I, along with many other people, happen to like a bit of a suntan.

The ABCs

Let's look at the ABCs of the sun's rays, that is, the different types of ultraviolet radiation to which we are exposed:

- *UVA.* This is long-wave radiation (320–400 nanometers). It is responsible for most photosensitivity reactions, and also contributes to chronic skin damage and sunburn. It penetrates deeper into our skin than UVB radiation. Its level is relatively constant during daylight hours.
- *UVB.* The midrange of ultraviolet radiation (290–320 nanometers) is the major cause of sunburn and chronic skin injury, including aging and skin cancer. It is most intense between 11 a.m. and 4 p.m. It can penetrate through one meter of water, and is reflected 17 percent by water, 50 percent by sand and up to 80

percent by snow. When we trek at high altitudes, the atmosphere is thinner, and these rays become much more intense. This is also true as you get closer to the equator.

- *UVC.* This wavelength of radiation (less than 280 nanometers) does not reach the earth's surface, as it is blocked by the ozone layer. However, it is found in artificial light sources such as tanning beds. It may cause redness or sunburn.

Certain people may be more susceptible to the effects of the sun. This includes redheads; those with fair skin, freckles or numerous moles; people who tend to burn easily or tan minimally; and anyone with a family history of skin cancer. Many of the medications that we use may cause photosensitivity. Doxycycline, which is

often used for malaria prophylaxis, is one of them. Diuretics and sulfa-containing medications are others. Some people develop allergic reactions to the sun. These reactions may show up after only a short time in the sun. Bumps, hives, blisters or red blotches are the most common symptoms of a sun allergy. Women who are pregnant or on the birth control pill may develop increased pigmentation on their face as a result of sun exposure.

There are three types of skin cancer—basal cell carcinomas, squamous cell carcinomas and malignant melanomas. Melanomas are the least common, but by far the most serious. They may arise out of a pre-existing freckle or mole, or out of nowhere. All forms of skin cancer are on the increase. Most of our sun exposure occurs by the time we are 20 years old, so protection is particularly important in children.

How Do We Avoid It?

Sun damage can be avoided by

- minimizing exposure to the sun, especially between the hours of 11 a.m. and 4 p.m. (If your shadow is shorter than you are, it's time to get out of the sun.)
- wearing protective clothing, especially a hat
- using sunscreens or sunblocks

Regarding the first point, don't be lulled into a false sense of security just because it's cloudy, there's a cool breeze or you're spending your day in the water. If you walk along the streets in most tropical climates, the local people can usually be seen sitting in the shade with a wide-brimmed hat.

All protective clothing is not created equal. The degree of protection depends upon the style, weave and chemical enhancement. Not to be outdone by sunscreens, clothing may be ranked according to its UPF (ultraviolet protection factor). So a shirt with a UPF of 50 allows only $\frac{1}{50}$th, or 2 percent, of the rays to hit your skin. Lighter colors may feel cooler because they reflect the sun, but in fact darker fabrics absorb UV rays better and provide superior protection.

Sunscreens and Sunblocks

Sunscreens work by "absorbing" the sun's rays so that they do not hit the skin. Their relative effectiveness is measured by the SPF (sun protection factor). The higher the SPF, the longer the protection you receive. Theoretically, an SPF of 15 will allow you to remain in the sun 15 times longer without burning than if you didn't apply it. These numbers may be an overestimate. In addition, many sun worshippers do not apply their sunscreen properly or adequately.

The various components of your sunscreen may include PABA, padimate, benzophenones, cinnamates and salicylates. Parsol should be a component of any sunscreen, as it's the only chemical that blocks UVA.

True *sunblocks,* which may be less cosmetically pleasing (or perhaps more), include titanium dioxide and zinc oxide. They are particularly useful on the more exposed body parts such as the ears and nose. They are available in many pleasing colors, and more recently can also be found in less ostentatious preparations as well.

When choosing a sunscreen, consider your own sensitivity to the sun. Everyone should use a sunscreen with an SPF of at least 15. Those who are more susceptible should use something stronger. If you're going to be spending time in the water, or sweating, choose a sunscreen that is water resistant or, even better, waterproof. If not, reapply it when you get out of the water. Sunscreen should be applied to the skin at least 20 minutes before exposure to the sun. Remember again that at higher altitudes the sun's rays are even more dangerous on account of the thinner air.

For people exposed to the sun and disease-transmitting mosquitoes at the same time, it's best to apply sunscreen first, followed by an insect repellent. There are preparations available that combine both a sunscreen and a repellent, but they are often low in strength and, therefore, the protection is not long-lasting. There's evidence that DEET lessens the efficacy of sunscreens, so it may be wise to reapply your sunscreen a little more frequently.

Many people feel that sunscreens give us a false sense of security, and they may be right. While your intentions may be good, sunscreens may in fact be less than adequate for the following reasons:

- not enough sunscreen is used (it can be quite expensive)
- it may wash off in the water or because of your sweat
- vital spots, such as the nose, ears, lips, feet and bald spots, may be missed
- whoops ... I fell asleep!

Sunglasses

Finally, don't forget your eyes. UV exposure may be responsible for cataracts, macular degeneration and the growth of pterygium (a yellowish tissue) across your eye. Therefore, sunglasses, ideally of the wraparound variety, should be worn when you are out in the bright sun. This goes for kids as well. Like clothing, not all lenses are created equal. Read the small print.

How Do I Treat My Sunburn?

Simple measures include aspirin or ibuprofen for pain, and perhaps an antihistamine such as diphenhydramine (Benadryl®). A cool bath or compresses will be soothing, as will topical preparations such as menthol or cortisone cream. Topical anesthetics such as Lanacaine® should be avoided.

And stay out of the sun!

Related Websites

American Academy of Dermatology: http://www.aad.org

Canadian Dermatology Association: http://www.dermatology.ca

Key Points

- Use your sunscreen, and use it properly.
- Wear a hat and other protective clothing.
- Minimize your sun exposure between 11 a.m. and 4 p.m.

Into Thin Air— Altitude Sickness

CHAPTER 17

"When you travel, remember that a foreign country is not designed to make you comfortable. It is designed to make its own people comfortable."

CLIFTON FADIMAN

Whether or not you have mastered marathons and triathlons, you may be thinking of making your next physical challenge a vertical one—climbing a mountain. If you do decide to head up into thinner air, however, you'd better be aware of the risks of altitude sickness. While it's not absolutely necessary to understand all of the physiology behind it, a good grasp of the basics is worth your while.

Most travelers are not headed for the peak of Everest (29,036 feet above sea level), but there are many other destinations that pose a risk of altitude sickness, including the rest of the Himalayas and the Andes, which are above 10,000 feet, and the peak of Mount Kilimanjaro, at 19,340 feet. Each year there are fatalities among climbers and trekkers to all these spots, in spite of the fact that altitude sickness should be a preventable condition and, when necessary, a treatable one.

In fact, altitude sickness may occur at any altitude greater than 7,000 feet above sea level. For practical purposes, we classify high altitudes as:

• high: 8,000–12,000 feet above sea level

• very high: 12,000–18,000 feet above sea level
• extremely high: over 18,000 feet above sea level

While the risks are greatest at extremely high altitudes, more people seem to become sick and die between 12,000 and 18,000 feet. Part of this may be explained by the "Mexico effect"; that is, more people get traveler's diarrhea in Mexico, because more people go to Mexico. Most people don't ascend higher than 20,000 feet, and the risks are much lower below 12,000 feet. But there are lots of visitors to very high altitudes, where the risk is significant; hence, this finding.

Some Common High-Altitude Destinations

• Mexico City: 7,572 feet	• Mount Kinabalu, Malaysia: 13,455 feet
• Aspen, Colorado: 7,773 feet	• Mount Kilimanjaro, Tanzania: 19,340 feet
• Bogotá, Colombia: 8,678 feet	• Mount Logan, Yukon: 19,850 feet
• Quito, Ecuador: 9,446 feet	• Mount McKinley (Denali), Alaska: 20,320 feet
• Cuzco, Peru: 10,581 feet	• Mount Aconcagua, Argentina: 22,831 feet
• La Paz, Bolivia: 12,001 feet	• Mount Everest, Nepal: 29,036 feet
• Lhasa, Tibet: 12,090 feet	

What Is It?

As we ascend, the partial pressure of oxygen in the air decreases, so we have less oxygen for our red blood cells to deliver to vital organs such as our brain and lungs. This relative lack of oxygen is called "hypoxia." The body immediately attempts to acclimatize to this situation by increasing the heart rate and the respiratory rate, which in turn increases the amount of oxygen our tissues receive. Our bone marrow also starts to produce more red blood cells, but this does not have much of a beneficial effect for several weeks.

In March 2001 I hiked in the Annapurna region of Nepal with my son Benjamin. I vividly recall all of that acclimatizing—my rapid breathing and pounding heart, and the need to stop and rest every few minutes. Benjamin, on the other hand, easily kept up with our Nepalese guide. I suppose that differences in age and fitness level had a role to play.

Aside from the beneficial changes in our heart and respiratory rates, other, deleterious changes occur which may lead to altitude sickness. In the lungs, our pulmonary arteries constrict, or narrow, and the pressure in the arteries increases. This increase in pressure may lead to unequal blood flow to different parts of the lung. The blood vessels soon become more permeable, or leaky, and fluid accumulates in the lung. We tend to retain fluid anyway at high altitudes because of changes in certain hormone levels. This only aggravates the situation. All these changes lead to high altitude pulmonary edema (HAPE).

In the brain, similar events take place. Blood flow increases (which ordinarily is a good thing), but the vessels become leaky, and high altitude cerebral edema (HACE), or swelling, occurs.

The risk of developing altitude sickness will depend upon several factors, most of which should be within your control. These factors are

• the altitude reached
• the time taken to acclimatize at each altitude before ascending further
• the rate of ascent
• the duration of time spent at high altitude
• your personal susceptibility
• common sense (level of exertion, keeping warm and well hydrated)

Let me expand upon a few of these points. First, the amount of oxygen available to our red blood cells decreases as the altitude increases. Furthermore, it is the "sleeping altitude" that is most important. In other words, we may be able to wander up higher during the day but we should come back down to sleep, so that we have not exceeded the safe increase in altitude for a given day. Hence, the dictum *"Climb high ... sleep low."*

When we rest for a few days in Cuzco at 10,581 feet above sea level, it gives us the time to acclimatize. But this does not prepare us for any altitude. It's necessary to rest, and re-acclimatize, every

3,000 feet or so. We cannot safely acclimatize to huge changes in altitude in short periods. The accepted guideline is that your sleeping altitude should not increase by more than 1,500 feet per day.

What determines our personal susceptibility? It's probably something called our hypoxic ventilatory response (HVR). That is, in the face of hypoxia, or not enough oxygen, how quickly do you tend to breathe? The control for this response is located in the carotid body, which sits in the carotid artery on the way to your brain. The rapid breathers probably fare better than the under-breathers. A good rule of thumb is that if you have had troubles at high altitude in the past, you may be at greater risk in the future.

The last point is particularly important. It's likely a lack of common sense that results in many of the tragedies that occur at high altitude. It's not just the altitude that's important, but the other variables, including our level of exertion and how well we keep ourselves hydrated and insulated from the cold.

It should be well noted that being in great physical shape does not offer any protection against altitude sickness. On the contrary; it may increase the risk. Such fit individuals may go faster than common sense dictates. People who climb or trek in groups are also at higher risk. Their desire to keep up with the group may put them in grave danger. Having said that, it sure doesn't hurt to be in shape.

The symptoms of altitude sickness will vary, and may depend upon the altitude reached, the time taken to reach that altitude, and individual susceptibility. Individuals with a past history of altitude sickness, as well as those who tend to retain fluids and hypoventilate, are at greater risk. And finally, perhaps those on a budget need to be extra careful. I am told that guides on Mount Kilimanjaro cost $100 per day, so there may be a necessity for budget climbers to get up and hopefully down more quickly.

There are different forms of altitude sickness, some of which I have already mentioned.

ACUTE MOUNTAIN SICKNESS. Acute mountain sickness (AMS) is the mildest and most common of the altitude-related syndromes. To compare it to something to which most of us can relate, it resembles a hangover. You know, a throbbing headache, nausea, vomiting, fatigue, dizziness and insomnia. It will usually begin within 24 hours of arrival at a high altitude (more than about 7,000 feet). Most people will successfully acclimatize, and the symptoms should dissipate. However, AMS may progress on to the more serious forms of altitude sickness if you continue to ascend. So don't.

HIGH ALTITUDE CEREBRAL EDEMA. The most lethal form of altitude sickness is high altitude cerebral edema (HACE). In addition to the symptoms of AMS, unsteadiness, confusion and/or irrational behavior are characteristic. Someone who seemed quite pleasant yesterday may seem unsociable or downright bitchy. The inability to walk a straight line is a very specific sign of HACE.

Perhaps this is one of the reasons that unfortunate Everest climbers find themselves falling into crevasses. If immediate measures are not taken, coma and death may result. Sometimes, the climber may seem relatively well at night and be unrousable in the morning. It typically takes a few days from the onset of AMS until HACE sets in.

HIGH ALTITUDE PULMONARY EDEMA. High altitude pulmonary edema (HAPE) is characterized by fatigue, a dry cough and shortness of breath. Almost all of us will be short of breath as we climb. I sure was, and that's OK. But it's not OK to remain short of breath at rest. If you notice that your buddy is falling behind and can't catch his breath at rest, be concerned. Because more fluid returns to our chest when we lie down, HAPE will usually worsen at night. It may become difficult to breathe while lying down flat, and the sick person may cough up pink or blood-tinged frothy sputum. Once again, if this condition goes unrecognized and untreated, coma and death may be the end result. HACE and HAPE may coexist, and each one may contribute to the development of the other.

HAPE and HACE are not always totally predictable or preventable. In the vast majority of cases, however, serious cases of altitude sickness are preceded by more subtle signs. Denial is a serious disease at high altitudes. The crucial thing is to recognize the early symptoms in yourself or your fellow climbers before the situation deteriorates and treatment becomes more difficult.

HIGH ALTITUDE RETINOPATHY. Small hemorrhages may occur at the back of the eye (the retina) at altitudes above 15,000 feet. These usually cause no symptoms unless they are located over the macula, the part of the retina with the most acute vision. One need not descend. The small hemorrhages will generally resolve themselves in 10–14 days.

HIGH ALTITUDE FLATUS EXPULSION. Let's include this one for completeness. Boyle's law, which you probably remember from physics class and other chapters in this book, states that pressure times volume = a constant (P x V = C). Therefore, at higher altitudes, where the barometric pressure is lower, trapped gases, such as might be found in your intestine, expand. This may lead to some bloating and, eventually, excessive farting. This may in fact be a beneficial aspect of high altitude, since it will help keep your tent a little warmer at night.

A few other things go on at high altitudes. As the altitude increases, the temperature drops and the sun's rays penetrate the thin air more effectively. Warm clothing, sunscreens and sunglasses are a must. One Canadian making an attempt on Everest in 2000 developed HAPE, probably because his jacket zipper broke and he was overexposed to the cold overnight.

Many climbers will develop a troublesome dry cough or bronchitis on the mountain. On the way to Everest, it's known as the "Khumbu cough." It may be due to the dry air, the leftover smog in Kathmandu or perhaps the fact that there are 12 people sleeping in a small tent passing their germs back and forth. This condition may be confused with high altitude pulmonary edema, though it should not make you so short of breath.

Fluid retention, or edema, is a common problem, especially in women. This will cause some facial puffiness and swelling of the hands and feet. As long as no other symptoms of altitude sickness are present, you may continue to climb.

And finally, periodic breathing occurs to some extent in almost everybody at high altitudes. Periods of hyperventilation, or overbreathing, are followed by periods of apnea (little or no breathing), which may last from 3 to 15 seconds. While not life-threatening or a harbinger of more serious things to come, it may be a little disconcerting to wake up thinking that you can't breathe or may have HAPE. Whether or not you suffer from periodic breathing, many people suffer from insomnia at high altitude.

Am I Fit to Climb?

High altitudes are not for everyone. Children and adults are equally susceptible to altitude sickness. The issue here is that very young kids may not be able to verbalize that they have a headache or feel rotten. They may feel compelled to keep up with Dad, rather than disappoint him. One record-breaking teenager who managed to get to the top of Mount Kilimanjaro described the experience as dreadful. So if you do plan to take, or drag, your children to high altitudes, make sure you follow all the rules, know how to recognize the early signs of altitude sickness, and will be willing to descend without reaching the summit.

Pregnant women, along with the fetus, are probably fine to ascend to altitudes of up to 12,000 feet or so, but it may be better not to remain there for a prolonged time. If you have had or have a complicated pregnancy, stay home. Keep in mind that obstetrical care is not readily available in the Andes or Himalayas.

Heart attacks are no more common at high altitudes than at sea level. Therefore, high altitude need not be a barrier to those with known heart disease. If you have frequent angina or congestive heart failure, it may be prudent to stay down below. Hypertension, which affects up to 15 percent of the adult population, is not affected by the altitude.

Those with chronic obstructive lung disease or emphysema may find themselves more short of breath. So hiking the entire Inca Trail is probably out of the question, but getting a relaxed view may be possible. Supplemental oxygen should be available just in case. Asthma is not necessarily exacerbated at high altitudes. For some the cold air may trigger problems, but for others the clear and somewhat thinner air may make things easier. Be sure you carry your medications with you.

Severe anemia may cause problems above 7,000 feet out of doors, just as it does on aircraft. People with sickle cell anemia should not travel to high altitudes.

Two other questions often seem to pop up. First, *"Should I remain on my birth control pill when I trek to Everest Base Camp?"* This one is pertinent because of the increased risk of phlebitis, or blood clots in the leg, associated with the pill. At high altitudes, dehydration and the tendency to sit in a cramped tent for hours on end may make the situation even worse. I don't think there's a consensus on this one, though there is agreement that sex goes on above the treeline.

Second, *"Is it safe to take mefloquine (Lariam®) at high altitudes (e.g., Mount Kilimanjaro), since the side effects may mimic the symptoms of altitude sickness?"* My opinion is that as long as you have not previously suffered serious adverse effects while on mefloquine, it should not be a problem. The main symptom of altitude sickness is headache, which is really not that common with mefloquine. If in doubt, doxycycline or Malarone® are good options. A useful guideline is that any illness at high altitude should be considered altitude sickness until proven otherwise.

Altitude Sickness—How to Prevent It

If you're intent on reaching a higher altitude, you need the proper attitude and some advice:

- Avoid rapid ascent when possible (e.g., flying directly from sea level to a high altitude). Considering this is not always possible, take a few days to acclimatize at the higher altitude. In other words, take it easy. So, for example, before you set out on the Inca Trail, spend a few days wandering in and around Cuzco. Or better still, start from Bolivia. Most people fly directly into Lhasa, Tibet, at 12,090 feet. Lie down and take a rest upon arrival.
- Climb slowly. Overexertion will not get you to the top any faster, but it will exacerbate altitude sickness. As they say in Swahili, *"pole, pole, pole"* ("go slow, go slow, go slow").
- Climb high, sleep low. It's the sleeping altitude that's particularly important. This should not increase by more than 1,000–1,500 feet per day. Every three days, take a day of rest. Here, your destination may play a big role. Taking the example of Mount Kilimanjaro, it usually involves an ascent from the base at about 6,500 feet to the peak at 19,340 feet. Most travelers will do the ascent in four or five days. Simple math shows that this means more than 1,500 feet per day. In the Andes and the Himalayas, on the other hand, the rates of ascent are much more gradual, and most people have more time at their disposal.
- Avoid the use of sedatives and tranquilizers. They may depress your respiration.

- Dress warmly. Hypothermia will exacerbate the symptoms of altitude sickness.
- Avoid alcohol. Its effects may seem a little more profound at high altitudes.
- Stay well hydrated. Drink enough to keep your urine clear. This point is strongly stressed by most successful climbers.
- A diet high in carbohydrates and low in salt may be beneficial.
- *Do not ascend with symptoms of altitude sickness.* Those climbing with a group may be at higher risk because peer pressure or fear of "failure" may inhibit some from admitting a problem. Leave your ego at home!
- Recognize the early signs and symptoms of altitude sickness in yourself and your fellow climbers.

WHAT ABOUT DIAMOX®? Diamox® (acetazolamide) is a medication that may help you acclimatize if necessary, as well as being useful to treat mild forms of altitude sickness. It's a diuretic (it makes you pee), which acts by making the kidneys excrete bicarbonate into the urine, hence making your blood become more acidic. This in turn tells your system to hyperventilate in order to blow off carbon dioxide. Hyperventilation is the body's chief method of increasing the amount of oxygen delivered to the tissues.

If you must ascend rapidly, or have a past history of altitude sickness, consider the use of Diamox®. The dosage is 125 milligrams twice daily (it comes as a 250 milligram tablet, so cut it in half). It should be started the day before ascent, and only needs to be taken the first two or three days at high altitude. This drug contains sulfa, and therefore must be avoided by anyone with a sulfa allergy. It may cause some tingling around the mouth and extremities, similar to what happens during a panic attack, where we also tend to hyperventilate. The taste of beer and carbonated drinks may be altered, because the enzyme that Diamox® inhibits, carbonic anhydrase, is present in the tongue.

In my humble opinion, Diamox® is underused and over-maligned. It does not work by "masking" the symptoms of altitude sickness; rather, it actually prevents it by speeding up acclimatization. In situations such as the aforementioned flight to Lhasa or the ascent of Kilimanjaro, I generally recommend or offer it to my patients. These trips are usually once-in-a-lifetime opportunities, and a little bit of help is often appreciated. In other geographic locations such as the Himalayas and the Andes, the preventive use of Diamox® is usually not recommended so long as you follow the other common sense guidelines. For those who do take Diamox® preventively, it should not be construed as a license to rush up the mountain.

For the rare person with a sulfa allergy who must make an abrupt ascent to a very high or higher altitude, dexamethasone (Decadron®) could be used (4 milligrams every 12 hours). This should be started the day before ascent and continued for two days at the new altitude.

If you have suffered from HAPE on a previous climb, studies have shown that using Adalat® (20 milligrams [slow release] every eight hours) may reduce the chances of a repeat performance.

Studies using gingko biloba appear promising in reducing the incidence and severity of AMS. One well-conducted study used 120 milligrams orally twice a day, starting five days prior to the ascent and continuing at altitude. This may also be helpful if you have trouble remembering where you are. Viagra® (sildenafil citrate) has recently been mentioned as beneficial in preventing high altitude pulmonary edema. I'll leave the jokes to you.

Other popular folk remedies which you may find the locals using are coca leaf tea or garlic. While they may not have any proven beneficial effect, when in Peru or Nepal do as the Peruvians or Nepalese do. I have!

How Do We Treat Altitude Sickness?

It seems that we often don't prevent some of the preventable things in life, so let me say a few words about treatment. Mild symptoms of AMS can usually be treated with rest, simple analgesics such as acetaminophen or aspirin, and perhaps Diamox®. Symptoms will usually resolve within a day or two. If they do not, then it's probably best to descend until you feel better, at which time it would be safe to re-ascend cautiously.

Treatment of Altitude Sickness

• stop, rest, acclimatize
• ASA, acetaminophen
• acetazolamide (Diamox®)
• *descend*

• oxygen
• nifedipene (Adalat®)
• dexamethasone (Decadron®)
• hyperbaric therapy

HAPE and HACE are medical emergencies. If they're not recognized promptly and treated properly, disaster may follow. The definitive treatment of both these conditions is *descent!* Denial is a common "condition" of climbers, and suggestions such as *"It's just a migraine,"* or *"I think it's the flu"* should be vehemently disregarded. How far should you descend? Usually 2,000–3,000 feet, or at least down to the altitude at which the ill person last spent a normal, restful night. If in doubt about that altitude, keep going lower. Improvement with HAPE may occur with descent of as little as 500 feet.

In reality, it's not always practical or desirable to descend immediately. Other measures should be instituted as well. These include

• oxygen, if it's available
• minimized exertion, warmth
• nifedipine (Adalat®): 20 milligrams by mouth and 20 milligrams every six hours, for the treatment of HAPE
• dexamethasone (Decadron®): 8 milligrams intramuscularly or by mouth and 4 milligrams every six hours, for the treatment of HACE. Dexamethasone works by reducing swelling, rather than aiding acclimatization. Rebound symptoms may occur after it's discontinued. Before climbing again, wait until you have been well for a day while off medication.
• hyperbaric oxygen (Gamov Bag®). The Gamov Bag® is a $2,000 device that may not always be available. When it is, however, it works very well. It consists of an airtight sleeping bag, which may be pressurized by means of a simple foot pump. The increased pressure in the bag simulates descent and improves the available oxygen in the bloodstream of the inhabitant. It may

treat AMS in as little as one or two hours, HAPE in two to four hours, and HACE in four to six hours. It will not be of use for someone who is comatose or severely claustrophobic, though I am sure the latter could be convinced to stay inside. This form of treatment is not a substitute for descent, but it may buy some time until the sun rises, the weather clears or that helicopter arrives.

Remember, descent is the definitive treatment for serious forms of altitude sickness, namely HAPE and HACE. It's much easier to descend with someone who is rational and conscious as opposed to comatose and coughing up blood-laced froth. Once a climber has recovered from altitude sickness, it's acceptable to re-ascend, as long as it's done cautiously and, perhaps, with the aid of Diamox® or Adalat®.

Serious altitude sickness is usually avoidable by following the above preventive guidelines and learning to recognize and treat the early symptoms of altitude sickness. Unfortunately, ambition and egos sometimes get in the way. So, try a bottle of champagne, vodka or red wine (or all of the above) if you want to find out what altitude sickness feels like in its mildest form. And if you still want to get to high altitudes, use your common sense.

Related Websites

CIWEC Clinic, Kathmandu:
http://www.ciwec-clinic.com/altitude/alti2.html

High Altitude Medical Guide:
http://www.high-altitude-medicine.com

Key Points

- Climb high … sleep low.
- Do not ascend with symptoms of altitude sickness.
- Go slowly. Drink lots of water.

Snakes, Scorpions and Other Scary Creatures

CHAPTER 18

*"If you look like your passport picture,
you're too ill to travel."*

AUTHOR UNKNOWN

I really don't know anyone who is fond of snakes or scorpions (but I know there are some), and I would venture the guess that the vast majority of people are somewhat petrified of them. Fortunately, some of the things we fear the most are the least likely to happen. Other species, however, such as cars and buses, should be approached with great caution.

Snakes

Snakes are certainly something I fear, but I, and you, should take comfort in the following:

- The risk to most travelers of snakebite is very low.
- Snakes are not very aggressive creatures—they bite only when provoked.
- Only a small minority of snakes are dangerously venomous to humans.
- Not all bites from poisonous snakes result in significant envenomation.

An estimated 30,000 to 40,000 deaths occur worldwide each year from snakebites. Most of these are in Africa and Asia. About

8,000 people a year receive venomous bites in the United States; between 9 and 15 victims die.

About 700 of the world's 3,200 snake species are venomous, and their venoms are extremely complex substances, being made up of 20 or more components. Snakes cannot hear sounds as we hear them. Instead, they rely on vibrations through the ground, which are sensed through a delicate organ at the base of a snake's jaw. Snake charmers may play charming music, but that snake is actually swaying to the movement and the tapping foot of the charmer.

There are five main families of poisonous snakes. Their names and most prominent family members are as follows:

- *Viperidae:* viper, adder, asp
- *Elapidae:* cobra, krait, mamba, coral snake, Australian poisonous snakes, sea snake
- *Colubridae:* boomslang, bird snake
- *Hydrophiidae:* sea snake, sea krait
- *Crotalinae* (pit vipers): rattlesnake, American and Asian lancehead, copperhead, cottonmouth, fer-de-lance, bushmaster

All snakebites, regardless of their type, may cause immediate fright, which is understandable. The victim may quickly appear as if in shock; that is, semiconscious, with cold, clammy skin, a feeble pulse and rapid, shallow breathing. This occurs much more quickly than the effects of any venom. Further symptoms depend upon the type of venom and the severity of the bite, and may be divided into local and systemic effects.

LOCAL EFFECTS. At the site of a poisonous bite, one may see two small holes left there by the fangs of the snake. If you have had a nonpoisonous bite, the local reaction will be no worse than any other bite. If venom has been injected, there will be immediate swelling, pain and discoloration of the surrounding skin. This is most typical of cobra and pit viper bites. These effects may proceed on to necrosis, or death of the superficial tissues.

SYSTEMIC EFFECTS. *Elapidae* produce primarily a neurotoxin. Reactions include pain and muscular weakness; the ability to swallow, speak, keep one's eyes open or breathe may be affected.

Viperidae secrete a hemorrhagic toxin, which may be manifested by minor bleeding from the gums, or more serious bleeding into the internal organs (e.g., the gut or brain). Shock may result from massive bleeding. Some cobras are able to project their venom several feet into the victim's eye, causing intense pain and swelling.

Sea snakes may cause breakdown of the muscles (myotoxicity), neurotoxicity and kidney failure.

Although death may occur as early as 15 minutes after an elapid bite, this is the exception and not the rule. There is usually time to get to qualified medical care. A snake does not use up all its venom with each bite. It has a "replacement fang" behind its active fang, and it can in fact bite up to 10 times. Most poisonous snakebites probably don't leave evidence of envenomation. This may be due to a lack of coordination or synchronization between the bite and the release of venom.

How Can I Avoid Snakebites?

Here are some tips for avoiding snakebites:

- Never walk in unknown areas without footwear and protective clothing. Stay on the hiking path. Be especially careful at night. Outhouses and latrines are favorite resting places for snakes.
- Carry a flashlight and a walking stick at night.
- If you encounter a snake, stay still (snakes only attack moving targets), and it will eventually slink away on its own.
- Don't put your hands into holes in the ground, under rocks or into woodpiles.
- Cut the grass around your house regularly and keep the area clean (if you live in an area with snakes; otherwise, it's optional).
- Don't swim in swamps or rivers matted with vegetation.
- Check your footwear, your clothing and the corners of your rooms.
- Keep a safe distance from snake charmers.

I Got Bitten—What Now?

Do:

- Try to remain calm. Help others remain calm. Get the victim away from the snake to avoid a second bite.
- Immobilize the limb with a splint, and keep it at or below the level of the heart.
- Immediately call for transport to the nearest hospital.
- Gently cleanse the wound to remove any excess venom.
- Remove rings, bracelets and other potentially constricting devices.
- Mark any reddened area or swelling with a pen to assist in monitoring any changes.
- Apply a crepe bandage to the whole limb. The idea of this bandage is to slow venous and lymphatic flow. It should not block the arterial blood flow. Make sure you can feel a pulse distal to the bandage (toward the extremities). Do not remove this bandage until you reach medical care and, if it's necessary, antivenom is at hand.

- If the snake is dead, take it to the hospital (on a stick). Otherwise, do your best to identify the snake.

Do not:

- attempt to catch and kill the snake. Even a severed head can bite.
- cut into the wound or attempt to "suck out" the venom
- apply ice, heat or electric shock to the wound
- apply a tourniquet
- administer aspirin
- panic!

When you have reached medical care, you will be monitored for signs of envenomation, such as bleeding, swelling or paralysis. If these appear, you should be treated with the appropriate antivenom (antivenin). This is usually administered intravenously and very slowly. Allergic reactions to antivenom sometimes occur, so medical personnel must be prepared for that complication. Other treatments may include supportive care and antibiotics.

Remember, snakebites are rare among travelers, and using some common sense will make them rarer. Now let's move on to something more pleasant—like scorpions.

Scorpions

There are about 650 species of scorpions worldwide, and I recall vividly when our local host in Burkina Faso brought one to the breakfast table to show us. These arachnids are equipped with a pair of pincers, used to hold on to prey, and a stinger. They tend to be nocturnal, and are more active in hot, humid weather. Now that I recall, Burkina Faso (in western Africa) is very hot and humid. Scorpions have their own outdoor hiding places, such as under rocks, wood and leaves, as well as indoor spots—in corners, inside shoes and under clothing. If my son Benjamin lived in the tropics, his floor would be a major meeting place for scorpions. Shake out your shoes, sleeping bag or tent before getting too comfortable.

As with snakes, not all scorpion stings produce severe reactions. But when they do, children, by virtue of their size, are at greatest risk. Intense pain may occur at the site of the sting, and this feeling may be associated with severe thirst, vomiting and diarrhea. The scorpion's venom has a neurotoxic effect and may cause respiratory paralysis or convulsions. Cardiovascular effects and hemorrhage may also occur. An acute anaphylactic (allergic) reaction may happen as well, requiring immediate treatment.

Anaphylaxis is, hopefully, treated with the EpiPen® that you brought along; that is, with injectable adrenaline plus an antihistamine. Local pain can be controlled with topical cool compresses and potent painkillers. Antivenoms may be available, but their usage is a bit controversial. Once again, try to seek qualified medical care as quickly as possible.

Spiders

The most famous and dangerous spiders include the brown recluse spider, the black widow spider, the funnel web spider of Australia and tarantulas. I remember sharing a Haitian shower with one the size of a hockey puck. Most of these spiders are not aggressive (thankfully), so the trick is to keep your distance. They hang out in all the same places as scorpions.

Spider bites may cause severe local pain, tissue damage and muscle spasm, progressing to nerve dysfunction and respiratory difficulty. Treatment consists of immobilization of the affected extremity, compression with a bandage, and ice. Analgesics and antivenom should be given if necessary.

Let's see. Centipedes, fire ants, beetles, bees, wasps, ticks and many more creepy crawlers are out there, but in general, you are not part of their usual diet. So try to keep out of their way, and they might keep out of yours.

Jellyfish

A pleasant stroll down the beach and frolic in the surf may sometimes prove to be more memorable than you had anticipated. Jellyfish, and a few of their relatives, belong to the family known as coelentrates. These transmit their toxins to us by means of an ingenious mechanism called nematocysts. There are millions of these on the tentacles of the jellyfish. Upon contact with living tissue (you or me), small tubes in the nematocyst puncture your skin and inject their poison directly into your small blood vessels.

The species responsible for the most deaths worldwide are the chirodropids, commonly called box jellyfish. Box jellyfish are most commonly found off the shores of North Queensland, Australia. Their sting can cause death from cardiac arrest within 60 seconds. They get washed onto shore by the currents, wind and tides, and are usually not easy to see. Thus, the symptoms are usually a bit unexpected.

The initial symptoms of a jellyfish sting are intense pain, stinging and burning at the site of the "bite." A fairly rapid death from severe envenomation can also be one of the initial symptoms. The skin may be red, discolored or blistered, and the linear pattern of the tentacles can usually be seen. The injury may look as if you were branded. Women and children are more susceptible to severe stings, perhaps because of their relatively hairless legs. Most stings occur on the lower legs, until you start to pick at the tentacles, at which point they also occur on the hands and arms. Other symptoms of envenomation may include nausea and vomiting, pains in the joints, wheezing and difficulty breathing, and paralysis.

The Portuguese man-of-war (Physalia physalis) is found along both the Atlantic and Pacific coasts. This creature can also cause extremely painful stings, although death is uncommon. Tentacles that have washed up on the beach and may look "dead" are still capable of envenomation.

Fire coral, which actually looks like true coral, attaches itself to rocks and coral. Divers who lean against or handle coral are often in for a painful surprise.

To treat jellyfish stings:

- Prevent drowning; remove the victim from the scene.
- Wash off any remaining tentacles with sea water. Fresh water or hot water will cause the remaining nematocysts to fire.
- Pour on 5 percent acetic acid, better known as vinegar. This will inactivate the nematocyst toxins. Rubbing alcohol and urine may be immediately available and are also effective.
- Gently remove remaining nematocysts with shaving cream and a razor, not with vigorous rubbing.

- As necessary, provide pain relief, topical ice packs and other supportive measures (e.g., oxygen, intravenous fluids).
- Help control the pain and prevent further absorption of venom by using compression bandages and immobilization.
- Make sure the victim is given tetanus toxoid if necessary (i.e., if due for it). In Australia, antivenom is available for severe evenomation from box jellyfish.

As you can see, before you head for the beach you will need icepacks, shaving cream and a razor, vinegar and a full bladder.

Other Sea Creatures

There are a few other sea creatures, fascinating or irritating, depending upon your point of view. Echinodermata include sea urchins, starfish and sea cucumbers. I suppose sea urchins are a bit like aquatic porcupines. When we accidentally step on them or handle them, their spines, which may be either venom-bearing or non-venom-bearing, penetrate our skin, usually in the foot. The initial symptom is severe, burning pain along with local swelling, redness and muscle aches. Generalized symptoms such as nausea and vomiting, muscle weakness and low blood pressure may occur with multiple puncture wounds.

This time, hot water for about an hour (not urine or sea water) is the best treatment. Spines which may have broken off in the skin should be removed if possible, as they may go on to cause chronic problems if left in place. These wounds often become infected, so preventive antibiotics are a good idea.

Starfish are also covered with spines that may be venomous. Fortunately there is only one important poisonous starfish, which is located in the Pacific. *Acanthaster planci,* commonly known as the crown of thorns starfish, causes immediate pain, redness and swelling when touched. Other symptoms may include numbness, nausea and vomiting, and muscle weakness. If possible, broken spines should be removed. Hot water is the treatment of choice. Other measures, such as pain relief and antibiotics, may be required.

Sea cucumbers are bottom feeders that also possess nematocysts. Contact with the tentacles usually causes only a mild skin irritation. However, if one touches your eye, severe inflammation may occur. Treatment would be topical anesthetics and irrigation, and a visit to an eye doctor would probably be a good idea.

Coral, which tends to attract divers like a magnet, is actually a living creature. Some species may have nematocysts. The main complication of cuts from coral is secondary bacterial infection; treatment consists of thorough cleansing with soap and water or other antiseptics, as well as topical and oral antibiotics. If stinging is present, vinegar or urine will deactivate the firing nematocysts. If you happen to stroll by a large group of people in bathing suits urinating on each other, you may safely ignore them, since it's likely just another coral outbreak.

Of course, the best method of treatment is always prevention. That's why they build hotel swimming pools.

Key Points

- The risk of snakebites, especially poisonous snakebites, is extremely low for travelers.
- Learn what to do if you encounter a poisonous snake.
- Keep your eyes open as you stroll along the beach.

PART FOUR
Specific Concerns

The Business Traveler

CHAPTER 19

"In the business world, everyone is paid in two coins:
cash and experience. Take the experience first;
the cash will come later."

HAROLD GENEEN

"Traveling on business, are you? That sure sounds great.
First-class flights. Five-star hotels. Expense account. Foreign
lands. A break from the kids. Frequent flyer points. A chance
to get out of the office."

"Not quite. Dash out to the airport in rush hour traffic as
I try to make the last of my phone calls. Stand in line to check
in at the airport. Flight delays. Work like a dog while I'm
there. Miss my daughter's karate tournament. The work is
piled three-feet high when I get back. Miss my wife. Picked
up a cold on the plane. Oh yeah, real great."

Well, maybe business travel isn't all it's cracked up to be. But that
may depend upon the type of business, where you travel and how
often you travel. Certainly all so-called business travelers are not
alike. The "typical" ones wear suits and ties, carry attaché cases
and travel only to big cities for a short time—every other week.
But others, such as United Nations peacekeepers, maintain the
peace in unstable places like Kosovo and East Timor. Geophysical
engineers fly over the jungles of Peru and Indonesia. Filmmakers
make documentaries in Rwanda. Software developers develop in
southern India. All in the name of work.

Let us look at the medical risks involved before we examine the
psychological ones.

Starting with pretravel inoculation, business travelers are no different from anyone else. Where are you going? When are you going? For how long? What will you be doing? Do you have any medical problems? Might you be pregnant? Many will be low-risk travelers, some will be high-risk. At a minimum, be sure you're up to date with your tetanus-diphtheria-polio vaccination.

Hepatitis A, which is contracted through infected food and water, is the most common vaccine-preventable disease. Your hotel may have five stars, but your food and water are only as good as the last person who handled them. Furthermore, when you do business with local people in a far-off land, it may be politically correct to eat where they eat, eat how they eat and eat what they eat. Hepatitis B is transmitted through contaminated medical instruments, blood, blood products and sex. While you might not anticipate the need for any of these things while you're away, appendicitis, bleeding ulcers, kidney stones, motor vehicle accidents and unprotected sex have been known to occur. If you're traveling on business to the tropics or lesser-developed countries, consider inoculation against hepatitis A and B. The combined vaccine, Twinrix®, will give you long-lasting protection against both.

If I may interject a little bit more about sex. Hepatitis B vaccination is a good start toward preventing sexually transmitted diseases. Abstinence is even better, as is using a latex condom every time. The reality is that not everyone abstains, and not everyone uses condoms. Loneliness, alcohol, lowered inhibitions and anonymity all may increase the likelihood of casual sex while away. If you don't follow the rules, you, your friends and your family back home may all be at risk of contracting an STD.

I think I got sidetracked. The need for other vaccines really depends upon your risk factors. Remember that yellow fever vaccination may be a requirement for entry to certain countries. Your employer is obligated to provide you with as safe a workplace as possible. This applies whether that workplace is in Colorado or Colombia. Be sure to check out the recommended vaccinations for your destination.

Although the likelihood of contracting something unpleasant from the food and water is lower for most business travelers, it is not zero. As well, the impact of that bout of diarrhea may be much greater on you, with only 10 minutes to spare, than on a backpacker who has another six months to recover. Be careful with your food and water, and take along your Imodium® and Cipro®. Consider prophylactic Cipro®, if you *"just can't afford to get sick"* and you're visiting a high-risk destination for a short time.

Mosquitoes have a hard time distinguishing business travelers from backpackers. Sure, some of them stay in air-conditioned hotels and stay for only a week (business travelers, not mosquitoes). Their risk of developing malaria is low. Others work in the mines of Africa. I vividly recall one young man who returned home to Canada from Zambia with a fever. He was seen in the local emergency department and was told he had the flu, since his malaria smear was negative. He didn't, and it wasn't. He died at home the next day of *falciparum* malaria.

Find out if you will in fact be in a malarious area. Use personal precautions such as DEET-containing repellents and mosquito nets if you will not be spending your nights in well-screened, air-conditioned digs. There are a few effective antimalarials to choose from now. Malarone® may be ideal for the short-term business traveler, since it is relatively free of side effects and need only be taken for seven days after leaving the malarious area. Never forget, if you develop a fever while you're away, or after you return, you may have malaria. Seek good medical care. Dengue should also be kept in mind, since it occurs in urban areas, where typical business travelers tend to congregate.

Carry a small, or large, first aid kit, so that you won't have to commandeer a cab into town every time you need an antacid, some Imodium® or a Band-Aid®. Be sure your company provides you with contacts in the event of a medical or other emergency.

All North Americans appear wealthy when they travel to lesser-developed countries. You may not all feel that way, but that's how you're perceived. The truth of the matter is that some are wealthier than others, or have employers with deeper pockets. Please read or reread Chapter 15, Your Personal Safety.

Business travelers share the infectious risks of travel along with everyone else, though it is probably true that in most cases they are relatively low-risk travelers. But from the point of view of stress, they are at the top of the heap. While many other travelers are off schmoozing in youth hostels, reminiscing with family or lying on the beach (sounds nice, doesn't it?), you have a job to do, and you have to do it well. All the while you're suffering from jet lag, separated from family and the conveniences of home. To make things a bit easier on yourself, and on your family as well, consider some of the following suggestions:

- Try to arrange a lighter workload for a few days before you leave, and for a few days after your return. Easier said than done.
- Schedule your flights strategically—take nonstop flights to avoid layovers and delayed or canceled connections; give yourself some extra time to get to your destination; travel at nonpeak times if possible.
- If jet lag is a problem, try to give yourself a day to adjust before undertaking important tasks. Try out any of the methods to reduce jet lag. (See the section on jet lag in Chapter 12, The Joys of Flight.)
- Keep in touch with your family—by phone, e-mail, letters, pictures. Make a separate call to your kids so they get adequate airtime of their own.
- Leave "secret" messages for your spouse and your children to open while you're away.
- Go over your trip with your kids. Give them a map, and let them keep track of where you are each day.
- Plan your travel so that you will be home for the weekend.
- Carry a small album of your favorite family photos.
- Plan some time for yourself while you're away—get some exercise, visit friends, read a book, visit a museum, go to a baseball game.
- Practice meditation or deep breathing to help you through those stressful moments.

- Make use of your down time. Catch up on your journals or correspondence. Write some letters. Doodle! Dream! Sleep!
- Maintain a positive attitude. Consider how lucky you are to visit the Taj Mahal on your day off.
- Look after yourself on the plane. Avoid too much coffee and alcohol; drink lots of water.
- If you're relocating to another country with or without your family, learn about culture shock and what can be done to minimize it. See if your company can provide you with cross-cultural training and other forms of assistance to make the transition easier for you and your family. To learn more about such services, check out the website of Family Guidance International (FGI) at http://www.fgiworld.com.

And finally, remember the well-known saying, *"Grant me the serenity to accept the things I cannot change, the courage to change the things I can and the wisdom to know the difference."*

Key Points

- Arrange your travel plans to minimize your stress, if at all possible.
- Keep in touch with your family as much as possible.
- Look after yourself—both your mental and your physical health.

Women and International Travel

CHAPTER 20

Just about everything in this book applies equally to both males and females. But there are still a few issues which pertain only to the latter. (Pregnancy is the most notable example.) So at the risk of upsetting some men out there who didn't get their own chapter, and even some women who probably feel offended that they "need" a chapter, here is some health information geared toward the female traveler. If you are a guy, there is a good chance that you will be traveling with a woman, so it may be of interest to you as well.

TRAVELING FOR TWO—THE PREGNANT TRAVELER

There's a time and place for everything, and when it comes to travel, women must sometimes decide whether pregnancy is the time, and Botswana the place. Certainly, pregnancy should not be a bar to traveling, but it's necessary to consider some of the additional risks involved and to take measures that can reduce these risks.

Almost every medical aspect of travel, including pretravel inoculation, malaria prophylaxis, safe medications, problems associated with flight, and availability of medical care must be considered.
Sometimes it's best to postpone your trip until after delivery, but I
must admit that most pregnant women I see have already made up
their minds to travel. My job is to make it as safe as possible.

If you do plan to travel, perhaps the first step should be to ensure
that you're in as good health as possible. If you're suffering from
morning sickness or extreme fatigue, or are anemic, it may be best to
delay your travel until these conditions go away or are corrected.
Miscarriage, when it occurs, usually happens during the first
trimester, and this may be a prudent time to avoid extensive travel.
Delivery is usually scheduled during the ninth month. It's generally
felt that the fourth to sixth month of pregnancy is the ideal time to
take that trip—you should be feeling the best, you can still walk
down the aisle of the plane and complications are less likely to occur.

When picking your destination, in addition to checking out the
hotels and sights make sure there is adequate medical care available—not just for cuts and scrapes, but for unexpected emergencies such as eclampsia, bleeding and Caesarean sections. Is the
local blood screened for HIV, hepatitis B and C, and syphilis? Is
high-quality pediatric care available if your baby decides to enter
the world prematurely? If you're planning on having your baby
abroad, the answers to these questions are even more important.
Do your research well in advance.

In general, trips to urban centers are probably quite reasonable.
Trekking to the middle of nowhere would not be. Also, examine
your medical insurance very carefully to be certain that you, and
your baby if necessary, are covered for any medical treatment that
may be required abroad.

Are the Inoculations Safe?

Travel to the tropics requires a few more considerations than a trip
to California demands. Certain inoculations may be required or
advisable, depending upon your destination and other risk factors.
The risks and benefits of the various vaccines must be carefully

weighed against the risks of the infections they are meant to prevent. Mixed into that decision is the mother's concern about receiving anything "foreign" during her pregnancy.

As you have already read, we immunize according to risk, not just the country visited. Hopefully, most women will be able to minimize their risks by choosing destinations and "styles" of travel where the risk of disease is lower. Having said that, let us take a look at the vaccines that may need to be considered.

Vaccines can be divided into those that are "killed" or "inactivated," and those that are "live." The first group, the inactivated ones, are felt to be safe in pregnancy if indicated. It would still be prudent to defer vaccination until at least the second trimester of pregnancy whenever possible. This group of vaccines includes tetanus-diphtheria-polio (the injectable form of polio vaccine), hepatitis A and B, meningococcal meningitis, rabies, influenza, pneumococcal pneumonia and typhoid (the injectable form—Typhim Vi® or Typherix®). There is no experience with Japanese encephalitis vaccine in pregnancy, so it should probably be used only if the risk of exposure is high.

Live vaccines, including measles, mumps and rubella; oral typhoid (Vivotif®); and oral cholera (which is rarely indicated anyway), should not be administered during pregnancy.

Yellow fever vaccine is a live vaccine, but the situation here gets a bit more complicated, as evidence of vaccination may be required to enter certain countries. As well, the disease has about a 30 percent mortality rate. The first suggestion may be, Don't go. If the destination is a low-risk one, that is, a country included in the traditional endemic zones (see maps on page 63) but not currently reporting cases of yellow fever, a "certificate of exemption" may be in order. Finally, if there is truly a significant risk, the vaccine should probably be given, considering that there have never been any reports of fetal abnormalities in children of women who have received the vaccine. Again, it's best to defer this vaccine until at least the second trimester, if possible.

Remember, the risk of many diseases can be greatly reduced through the use of personal protective measures, a.k.a. common sense.

What About Malaria?

Malaria may be a threat to anyone off to the tropics, but it presents an even greater risk to a pregnant mom and her fetus. My first piece of advice to a pregnant woman heading off to West Africa is usually, Don't go! This may in fact be the best advice. Having said that, it's often not heeded.

Personal precautions against mosquitoes, such as staying indoors in the evening and wearing long sleeves, pants and socks, are extremely important. Insect repellents containing DEET may be used, but a concentration of 35 percent or less, used sparingly, is advisable. Other repellents such as citronella and Avon's Skin-So-Soft® may also be used, but they may provide shorter protection than DEET. If possible, sleep in a well-sealed, air-conditioned room or under a permethrin-impregnated net.

The decision to use antimalarials, and which one to use, will depend upon your destination. For women traveling to chloroquine-sensitive areas such as rural Central America, chloroquine is both adequate and safe.

Most of the malarious world, however, harbors chloroquine-resistant *falciparum* malaria. If you must travel to these areas, the prophylaxis of choice would be mefloquine (Lariam®). It's "officially" OK during the second and third trimesters. As well, considering that no adverse affects have been observed when used in the first trimester, it would be the best choice then as well.

Doxycycline is an effective antimalarial, but causes a yellow staining of the baby's teeth and, hence, must not be used during pregnancy or while breast-feeding. There is currently no information regarding the safety of atovaquone/proguanil (Malarone®) during pregnancy, so it should therefore be avoided if possible.

And If I Get the Runs?

Montezuma's Revenge and dehydration are no treat for anyone. Strict attention must be paid to food and water when traveling. Boiling the water or choosing reliable bottled water are the best choices. While beer, carbonated beverages and hot tea or coffee are usually safe, many women prefer to avoid alcohol and caffeine during their pregnancy anyway. Iodine, whether as a pill or part of a water purifier, should not be used for more than a few weeks. Meat must be well cooked and dairy products pasteurized. Uncooked veggies and peeled fruits are best avoided. If it's the Four Seasons Hotel in New York where you're eating, it's probably OK to disregard this advice (well, not all of it). Other potentially dangerous infections in pregnancy, which may be acquired from contaminated food and water, are hepatitis E, toxoplasmosis and listeriosis.

Oral rehydration is the cornerstone of treatment for diarrhea. This may be accomplished with clear fluids such as soup with salt, tea with sugar, or safe bottled drinks. Oral rehydration salts (e.g., Gastrolyte®) are usually available worldwide, or can be taken along with you.

Imodium® (loperamide) is almost everyone's choice for the treatment of diarrhea, but it should be avoided if possible in pregnancy. So should Pepto-Bismol® (bismuth subsalicylate). Antibiotics should also be used only if necessary. In this case, the best choice may be erythromycin or a cephalosporin. Quinolones, such as ciprofloxacin (Cipro®), are advised against.

Not everyone gets the runs. Pregnant women in particular sometimes have problems with constipation. Do your best to maintain a high fluid and fiber intake. As for medications during pregnancy, it's best to avoid most of them if you can. Acetaminophen, amoxicillin and erythromycin are three useful ones that would be considered safe.

Is It Safe to Fly?

What about the flight itself? The actual oxygen content of the air in most pressurized commercial aircraft is equivalent to what we would find at an altitude of between 5,000 and 8,000 feet. This does not pose a problem for Mom or the fetus, as long as there are no complicating factors such as anemia. If your hemoglobin is less than 8.5 gm/dl (85 gm/L in Canada), it would be best not to fly. Supplemental oxygen should be used if travel is unavoidable.

I'm sure you remember Boyle's law (gases expand at higher altitudes as the pressure decreases). Keep that in mind before digging into the beans, as they will compound the bloating or distension that you already may feel.

Pregnant women are at greater risk of developing a blood clot in the veins of their legs during flight. This is because of an increase in clotting factors during pregnancy and a tendency for the legs to swell. Remember to drink plenty of water, stretch your legs and walk frequently. Sitting at the bulkhead, on the aisle or, best of all, in first class will provide a bit more leg room. Elastic stockings are a good idea. If you have previously had phlebitis, it may be best to stay put at home.

Airplanes double as meeting rooms, movie theaters and restaurants (some of them, anyway). But they were not meant to be maternity wards. Hence, most airlines will not accept passengers who are more than 36 weeks pregnant. A letter from your doctor may be required to prove your actual due date. If you have had, or are having, a complicated pregnancy, consult your doctor if you plan to fly earlier than 36 weeks.

Jet lag is probably the same for the pregnant as for the non-pregnant traveler. One would assume it would affect the fetus as well, but, understandably, no studies have been done to prove this. Melatonin and sleeping pills should not be taken, so this may be an instance where light exposure or acupressure is worth trying.

Can I Skydive, Mountain Climb or Scuba Dive?

Now that you have finally arrived, can you have any fun? Well, that depends upon your definition of fun. Skydiving, parasailing, whitewater rafting and waterskiing are not allowed, but you probably weren't planning on those activities anyway. I'm sure there are other sports I haven't heard of. Let's assume they're not such good ideas either.

Walking and hiking are fine, depending upon the altitude. A consensus is that pregnant women should not climb higher than about 12,000 feet. Women with complicated pregnancies should probably avoid travel to high altitudes. Aside from concerns about effects on the fetus, there is also the issue of availability of medical care, should the need arise. Scuba diving is another activity to avoid during pregnancy. There is enough evidence to suggest that decompression sickness, should it occur, can affect the baby as well as the mom. Use a snorkel instead. It should be kept in mind that up to 5 percent of babies will be born with some sort of congenital abnormality. Most women will give up their coffee, alcohol and cigarettes for

this reason. It seems reasonable to forgo some of these higher-risk activities as well (said the male doctor!).

Finally, motor vehicle accidents are the greatest cause of death in travelers. Remember the rules of the road (Chapter 15, Your Personal Safety). Pick your vehicle carefully, don't travel at night in rural areas, avoid motorbikes and, above all, use your seatbelt and lap belt. They are safe and may be life-saving.

When it comes to traveling with children, it may seem convenient to carry your baby tucked in your uterus. But give your plans some thought before you fly. Your health care provider should be able to provide you with the information you need, but, in the end, the decisions will be yours.

Key Points

- The second trimester of pregnancy may be the best time to travel.
- You are at higher risk for venous thrombosis when you fly.
- Get expert advice regarding pretravel inoculations and malaria prophylaxis.

OTHER GYNECOLOGICAL ISSUES

Now let's look at some other gynecological issues.

IRREGULAR MENSTRUATION. A woman's menstrual cycle, which usually runs like clockwork, I am told, may in fact become quite irregular with travel. Drastic changes in diet may play havoc with your cycle, but stress is probably the main reason for making periods disappear altogether. This does not mean that you will be uptight with a tension headache for four months, but rather that travel and all it implies is much different for your body than is your regular routine. Always to be kept in mind when you miss a period is the possibility of pregnancy. For women who experience irregular or more frequent menstrual bleeding when they travel, going on a birth control pill may help regulate the problem.

FEMININE HYGIENE PRODUCTS. Along with menstrual bleeding comes the need for feminine hygiene products. You may take their availability for granted in North America, but my consultants tell me that things are not always so rosy in other parts of the world. Tampons may be unavailable, or perhaps may only be found in tourist areas. When they can be located, they may be considered a luxury item and be quite expensive to purchase.

According to one VSO volunteer, *"The North American standard type are awfully costly in Rwanda, and the Rwandan type do not look particularly convenient. I would encourage anyone coming here to bring a full complement for the duration of their stay."* I realize that Rwanda is not representative of the entire world, but if your travels are taking you off the beaten path, plan ahead. Disposing of the aforesaid tampons may also present a problem, as you may find the local dog carrying them down the road the next day. They are best burned. One solution recommended to me by a worldly female traveler is "The Keeper®," a small, bell-shaped natural gum rubber menstrual cap that is worn internally. It is a comfortable, hygienic, sanitary, safe alternative to tampons and pads. It's very easy to use, and one cap will last for many years, according to the manufacturer. For more information, go to www.keeper.com. One final point—swimming during your menstrual period does not put you at any greater risk of shark attacks!

BIRTH CONTROL. Birth control is also high on the list of female concerns, whether you are traveling or not. If you're taking an oral contraceptive, it's probably best to carry more than enough for your entire trip abroad. You may have difficulty finding your particular brand when you travel. When you're crossing several time zones, the timing of your pill can get a bit tricky. Try to keep a watch at your home time, and take your pill every 24 hours until you're settled at your destination. You can then gradually move your pill up to a more convenient time. Err on the side of taking the pill at less than a 24-hour interval.

Doxycycline, a commonly used antimalarial, may decrease the efficacy of your birth control pill. A barrier method of birth control (e.g., condom) should be used as well. A bad bout of vomiting may mean that your pill didn't get absorbed. Should this happen to you within three hours of taking your last pill, take another pill. If this one comes up as well, continue with barrier methods of birth control for the remainder of your cycle. Forgetting to take your pill can also be a problem. If you remember within 12 hours, take that forgotten pill and you will be OK. If more than 12 hours have elapsed, take that forgotten pill but also use a barrier method until your package is finished. Remember that birth control pills are for birth control. Only condoms will protect you against sexually transmitted diseases.

The issue of taking the birth control pill at high altitudes is controversial. It may increase your risk of developing a blood clot, as will the dehydration. I would suggest that you stay well hydrated, and perhaps continue the pill if you are sexually active.

For various reasons, some women would like to do away with their period for a month. This can be safely done by taking two packages of the pill back to back, without a seven-day break between cycles.

Regarding condoms ... if you plan to be sexually active abroad, and probably even if you don't, it would be wise to carry at least a few of your own latex condoms. Preferably these should be from back home, where the quality of said condoms is reliable. Men, whether they are from the host country or from anywhere else, cannot be counted on to carry or use condoms. Language or cultural barriers may make such encounters even more difficult.

Female condoms boast a high degree of efficacy when it comes to preventing pregnancy and sexually transmitted diseases—that is, if used properly and every time. The female condom, which is made from polyurethane, can be inserted into the vagina up to eight hours before intercourse. It may be used with both water-based and oil-based lubricants. There's no need for the male to use a condom at the same time. While you may be able to find female condoms at home, I would not count on their being available in most tropical or lesser-developed countries.

Depo-Provera® is an injectable form of birth control which must be given every 12 weeks. It's more than 99 percent effective in preventing pregnancy, and it's available worldwide. This sounds ideal, but side effects are not uncommon. These may include irregular bleeding, increased appetite, headaches, depression, abdominal pain and increased or decreased sex drive. These unwanted effects are not reversed until the medication wears off (up to 12 weeks).

Other forms of birth control, such as IUDs, caps, sponges and diaphragms, are probably not as convenient or effective as the pill and condoms when it comes to preventing pregnancy and STDs.

Emergency contraception, also known as "the morning after pill," may be necessary for some women when the unexpected occurs—a broken or forgotten condom, or rape. In this situation, there's concern not only about unwanted pregnancy, but also STDs. The oldest method (well, probably not the oldest) of emergency contraception is known as the Yuzpe method. This consists of taking two tablets initially, each containing 50 micrograms of ethinylestradiol and 250 micrograms of levonorgestrel, and then again in 12 hours. This combination is contained in the birth control pill Ovral®. The first dose must be taken within 72 hours of intercourse, and perhaps with some Gravol®, because it may cause nausea. While very effective, this method is not perfect, and pregnancy may still occur.

Another effective option is known as Plan B®, a pill which contains 0.75 milligrams of levonorgestrel. This pill must also be taken twice: the first one within 72 hours of intercourse, and the second 12 hours later. It's as effective as the Yuzpe method and may cause less nausea. When deciding upon the need for emergency contraception, it's probably best to ignore where you are in your menstrual cycle; the exact timing of ovulation can be tricky, especially when you're traveling.

These two methods work by either delaying ovulation or preventing implantation of a fertilized egg in the uterus. Hence, they prevent pregnancy; they do not induce abortion. They will not be effective if you are already pregnant. Remember, it may be advisable to seek medical care to deal with the possible risk of exposure to STDs. Considering that medical care and/or the latest medications are not always available in Timbuktu, you may choose to carry emergency contraception with you.

Not every woman is interested in birth control. Maybe it's part of your plan to become pregnant while you're away. The getting pregnant part may be easy, but assuming you're staying abroad for a long time, the question becomes whether it's safe to have your baby overseas. In most "westernized" countries, the answer will probably be yes. But what about lesser-developed countries?

Consider the following:
• What is the quality of the medical facilities?
• Is good pre- and post-natal care available?
• Can the local medical staff handle unexpected emergencies or complications should they happen to Mom or the baby?
• Is blood screened for HIV, malaria, syphilis and hepatitis B and C?
• Will you be the first expatriate woman to have a baby there?
• Is it wise to remain in a highly malarious area during pregnancy?

VAGINAL INFECTIONS. These may happen at the best of times, and traveling, especially in warm climates, may make the problem worse. Antibiotics, including the antimalarial doxycycline, may also contribute to this problem. Take along a vaginal cream such as Monistat® or a single-dose tablet like Diflucan® in case you develop a yeast infection.

LOCAL CULTURE AND PERSONAL SAFETY

Adapting to a culture that differs from your own can present its challenges. Not all foreign cultures are as "liberated" as ours. This is not a huge issue if you are just leaving your cruise ship for a day to tour Zanzibar. But if you're planning to live there, it is. First, what should you wear?

This is up to you, but remember that how you dress may have the effect of offending local women, making you more of a target for harassment by local men or, on a more positive note, making it easier for you to integrate into the local community. The best way to find out about the proper dress code is to do some research before you leave or, better still, spend a day or two just observing the local women—how they dress, how they walk, how they interact with each other and with men. As Yogi Berra, the great Yankee catcher, once said, *"You can observe a lot by watching."* I don't think he was talking about Zanzibar.

Whether or not you decide to go native and adopt the local dress, perhaps the best guideline is to be conservative. If tradition suggests that your bare shoulders or legs be covered, then cover up. This need not necessarily be in local clothing, but anything light, cool and loose-fitting would be fine. To quote our helpful VSO volunteer, *"A sarong is the most important thing. I used mine as clothes, curtains, towel, beach bag, blanket, temple dress, pillow, etc. I would never leave home without it!"* Dressing like the local people does not imply that you should give up your blue jeans, Old Navy T-shirts and Birkenstocks. You need to maintain your own culture and identity as well.

BE CAREFUL ... BE AWARE. Personal safety is important to both genders, but female travelers have some additional concerns. There are very few instances where local women whistle at and harass foreign men. Unfortunately, the opposite is often true (that is, local men harassing foreign women). Assuming you don't want to be harassed and whistled at, or even worse, remember the following suggestions:

- Whenever possible, do not walk or travel alone. In many cultures, women walk arm in arm or holding hands. They talk nonstop and laugh incessantly. This is not just a show of affection. They may be having a good time, but they are also avoiding the local men. If you can find a male companion you like and trust, that's great. Groups of friends are even better.
- Dress with common sense and respect for the local culture. Act in the same way.
- Walk with a sense of purpose, even if you're a little bit disoriented. It's easier to ignore somebody while you're moving and not looking at them.
- Wear a cheap wedding band, and have some stories ready to tell about your "husband and children."
- If there are "women only" buses or train cars, take them. They are probably there for a reason.
- Make sure that your hotel room is locked. Don't open the door unless you know who is on the other side.
- Follow your gut reactions. If a situation doesn't feel comfortable, you should remove yourself from that situation as quickly as possible.
- Don't accept a drink unless you have seen it poured.
- Make certain your living accommodations are secure.

Women, don't forget everything else as well, of course: boil it, bottle it … use your insect repellent … climb high, sleep low … get your vaccinations … carry adequate travel insurance … use your common sense … and have a great time. Amelia Earhart once said, "Adventure is worthwhile in itself." Good luck on your adventure.

Key Points

- Carry adequate supplies of your feminine hygiene products.
- You are ultimately responsible for your own birth control and prevention of STDs.
- Staying safe requires common sense and an awareness of your surroundings.

Let's Take the Kids— The Young Traveler

CHAPTER 21

*"The world is a book, and those who do
not travel read only a page."*

SAINT AUGUSTINE

Traveling with children certainly presents its challenges, but many parents refuse to go anywhere without their young ones. Of course, those challenges will vary, depending upon your destination, the duration of your trip, the mode of transport, the number of children, the age of those children and the nature of those children. The rewards usually outweigh the trials and tribulations, and you, the parents, will require patience, flexibility, some hard work and a sense of humor. Even on our long driving trips to the Baseball Hall of Fame when we were kids, my parents exercised all these characteristics.

Perhaps the first thing to keep in mind is that children are not just little adults; they are usually little children. Their endurance, desires and culinary preferences will be different from yours. To keep them happy and, hence, yourself happy, a few general tips are in order:

- Get the children involved in planning the trip. Help them learn about their destination before they arrive.
- Check out in advance which supplies, such as diapers, car seats or baby foods, you will be able to get abroad, and which ones you should bring from home.

- Take along plenty of their favorite books, toys, stuffed animals and blankets—and lots of batteries.
- Plan outings specifically for the kids. If I am correct, most children do not like museums.
- Remember that children need some unstructured time, some down time, so don't be afraid to leave an afternoon for rest, relaxation or just horsing around.
- Keep in mind that kids get tired and hungry. When they get that way they get crabby, sort of like we do. While it might be your goal to walk from one end of the Great Wall of China to the other, kids will usually benefit from a short cab ride, a trip in a rickshaw or some time on the back of an elephant.
- Have them keep in touch with friends, relatives and events back home. Suggest that they keep their own journal. Let them take their own pictures.

I had the pleasure of taking my 18-year-old son Benjamin (not really a child) to Nepal in March 2000. His endurance was far superior to mine. I got tired ... he got hungry. We both benefited from that ride in the rickshaw. He got hungry. It was wonderful for him to experience how others in the world live, and great for me to watch him gain confidence as a traveler. He still got hungry.

Before You Go

Before you take your kids abroad, make sure that their identification papers are in order. If you are traveling as a single parent with your child, a legal document signed by the nontraveling parent should be obtained. Ensure that your travel and medical insurance policies apply to your children as well as to yourself. If you are going to be very far from good medical care, take the time to learn how to recognize and treat common medical conditions that may arise with your children, and carry adequate medications and supplies.

How Old?

It has been traditionally thought that infants under the age of two weeks or so should not be flying because their lungs are not mature. This is no longer thought to be the case. So go ahead. Drive to the airport as soon as you have given birth. Why you might want to do this is beyond me and, I'll bet, most of the readers. But it is considered safe, as long as your baby is healthy. He or she will, however, have to be accompanied by an adult. Certainly you'll save on the fare for the extra seat. I'm just glad I'm not sitting beside you. (I have three kids of my own, thank you!)

Kids may have the same problems with popping ears as adults. This usually occurs during descent, at which time it may be worthwhile to offer your child some chewing gum, a drink or a breast if appropriate. While it may seem like a good idea to sedate that rambunctious son of yours for the 24-hour flight to Hong Kong, this is not always the best course of action. The effects of sedating medications such as diphenhydramine (Gravol®) or antihistamines may be unpredictable. A familiar blanket and stuffed animal may just do the trick.

Motion sickness tends to occur more among children between the ages of 2 and 12. Medications such as Gravol® are best given before they are actually necessary. If your child is prone to motion sickness, choose a seat over the wing of the plane or in the front seat of the car. On a boat, have kids lie relatively still and stare off at the horizon. Keep them occupied if you can, though reading should be avoided. Carry a plastic bag just in case.

Inoculations and Antimalarials

Travel to lesser-developed countries requires more advance planning. Pretravel inoculations for diseases such as yellow fever, typhoid, hepatitis A and B, Japanese encephalitis and meningitis may be required or recommended, depending upon the destination. There are lower age limits for most of the vaccines (see table on the next page). Certain components of the meningococcal meningitis vaccine may not be as effective in children under the age of four. If you have very young children, discuss this with your travel doctor. Routine inoculations such as diphtheria, tetanus, polio, measles, mumps and rubella, varicella and *Hemophilus* influenza should be up to date before you leave.

Travel Vaccines: Age Limits	
Vaccine	**Lowest Age**
yellow fever	9 months
cholera (oral)	2 years
hepatitis A	1 year
typhoid fever	
Typhim Vi®/ Typherix®	2 years
Vivotif®	6 years
hepatitis B	birth
meningococcus (A,C,Y, W-135)	2 years
rabies	1 year
Japanese encephalitis	1 year

Measles continues to be a major cause of mortality among children in poorer countries, mainly owing to a lack of immunization. In North America, children receive the first of two measles shots (along with mumps and rubella—MMR) at the age of one. If you happen to be taking a child who is under one year of age to a less-developed country, a measles shot should be given as close to departure as possible. This should then be repeated after the baby's first birthday.

If a vaccine is appropriate for Mom or Dad, it's generally appropriate for the children. Vaccination against rabies is one situation where we may be even more anxious to inoculate the kids. Children, in spite of numerous warnings, may still want to pat that drooling dog or tease that cute monkey. If they do sustain a bite, they may be less likely to report it to you. Rabies vaccine is not recommended for every child traveling off to the tropics, but those who will be living abroad for an extended time, in India, for example, may be best receiving this vaccine.

As I mentioned in Chapter 6, Pretravel Inoculation, vaccination with BCG to prevent tuberculosis may be appropriate in some very high-risk young children who will be living in TB-endemic areas for a prolonged time. The usual approach, however, would be yearly TB skin testing.

Kids tend to tolerate the vaccines fairly well, but some Tylenol® may be helpful following or even before vaccination. Bribery is also quite useful.

Malaria is the most important infectious risk to travelers to the tropics, regardless of age, and it can be even more serious in children. Mefloquine (Lariam®), the drug of choice in most malarious areas of the world, is safe and well tolerated in children. The pill is scored, so it's easy to break it up into quarters, or even smaller pieces. If necessary, it may be crushed up and mixed with something more appetizing. Febrile seizures are not uncommon in children under the age of four. A history of this condition should not be considered an impediment to the use of mefloquine.

Malarone® (atovaquone/proguanil), a newer antimalarial, is available in pediatric dosages in the United States, though not in Canada. Its main side effect is stomach upset, so it should be taken with food. Doxycycline, an alternative to mefloquine, is contraindicated in children under eight and in breast-feeding moms. Chloroquine would still be an appropriate antimalarial in rural areas of Central America, the Middle East or Haiti. It's available as a liquid, but neither the liquid nor the pills are very pleasant to swallow. Mix it with some chocolate. Remember that antimalarial medications, and most medications for that matter, can be very dangerous when ingested accidentally. Keep them far away from your children and in safe containers.

An excellent website containing information on inoculations and antimalarials in children has been written by Mary Wilson, M.D., and Caroline Zeind, Pharm.D., of Mount Auburn Hospital in Cambridge, Massachusetts (see end of chapter).

Other Dos and Don'ts

MOSQUITOES. Personal protective measures such as staying indoors between dusk and dawn, wearing protective clothing and

sleeping under a permethrin-impregnated mosquito net are vital to children who will be exposed to malaria and other insect-borne diseases. DEET-containing insect repellents are safe, but should be used only in concentrations of less than 35 percent. In small children this should be reduced to 10 percent. Slow-release DEET products are available that reduce the absorption (Ultrathon®, Sawyer Controlled Release Insect Repellent®). Remember to avoid putting it around the lips, the eyes or open cuts. You, the adult, should apply the lotion, so that it ends up on your hands, not theirs. It should be washed off with soap and water after your child returns to his or her mosquito-proof home for the night.

TRAVELER'S DIARRHEA. Montezuma's Revenge knows no age limits, and it has been shown that little children not only get sicker, but also stay that way longer and more often require hospitalization for dehydration. Be extremely careful when it comes to what goes into your child's mouth. Oral rehydration salts (ORS) such as

Gastrolyte® are ideal for rehydrating a small child with vomiting and/or diarrhea. They are readily available around the world. Breast-feeding should be continued in the presence of vomiting and diarrhea in infants.

If you are traveling to the tropics with small children, you should probably be aware of the symptoms and signs of dehydration. These would include:

• thirst
• warm, dry skin
• reduced urine output
• weakness and lethargy
• sunken, dry eyes
• dry mouth and tongue
• loss of skin elasticity
• rapid, weak pulse

Traveler's Diarrhea is usually caused by a bacterium, such as enterotoxigenic *E. coli, Salmonella, Shigella* or *Campylobacter.* Most of these have become resistant to trimethoprim/sulfamethoxazole (Bactrim®), which used to be the drug of choice in children. A better choice these days would be azithromycin. Ciprofloxacin, which probably has a broader spectrum of action, is not recommended under the age of 16. Most experts agree, however, that the benefit of a brief course of this antibiotic likely outweighs the risk.

High altitudes. If travel to high altitudes is in your plans, give it some extra thought before you go. Adults don't seem to mind getting up at three in the morning in the freezing cold with a pounding headache so they can reach the top of Kilimanjaro. Kids might not find this their cup of tea, or hot chocolate. Depending upon their age and temperament, they may be less inclined to verbalize that they are feeling unwell, thus putting themselves at greater risk. This does not mean that you can't take your kids to Nepal. But do be aware of the measures to reduce the risks of altitude sickness (see Chapter 17, Into Thin Air), and be prepared to stop and descend should problems arise. Diamox® (acetazolamide), which can help to treat or prevent altitude sickness, may also be used in children, but slow ascent and plenty of fluids are the keys to prevention.

Of course there are other dos and don'ts that you need to bear in mind when you take the kids, but most of them are common sense things and apply to adults as well. Don't play with dogs. Cover up and use plenty of sunscreen. Be on guard for their personal safety, especially when around water. Even sexually transmitted diseases may need to be considered, depending upon the age of your children. Take a night light for small children, and outlet covers to use in hotel rooms. The list goes on, but so will your fun.

Not only will you enjoy your children more when you are away from the everyday stresses of home, but they will help enrich your trip by breaking down some of the barriers that may keep you apart from the local people. Life is a collection of experiences, and the ones away with your kids will be the best.

Related Website

Inoculations and antimalarials in children (Mary Wilson, M.D.; Caroline Zeind, Pharm. D.):
http://www.istm.org/pharmacycharts

Key Points

- Children tend to get sicker, and sicker faster, than adults.
- Involve your children in planning their adventure.
- Set a pace that is appropriate for the kids.
- You are responsible for keeping your kids out of all kinds of trouble.

The Traveler with Medical Conditions

CHAPTER 22

"A journey is like a marriage. The certain way to be wrong is to think that you control it."

JOHN STEINBECK

Not all travelers are created equal. Some are small. Some are old. Some are adventurous. And some have underlying medical problems. Regardless of who you are and where you go, the travel medicine specialist and the traveler must take these factors into consideration when considering the inoculations, antimalarials and other precautions which you should take. Over the years I have seen travelers with almost every imaginable medical condition set off on a trip. My job is rarely to tell people not to travel; rather, it is to advise them how to make it as safe and enjoyable as possible.

Let me say a word about the "elderly" traveler. Being old, or older, is not a disability. Nor are disabilities and chronic diseases solely the domain of the elderly. Unfortunately, the elderly may be more likely to suffer from medical problems such as diabetes, heart disease, arthritis and deafness. They are also blessed with common sense and somehow know whether they should be traveling to Bhutan or Boca Raton.

The following are just a few of the conditions that make travel, especially to the tropics, a little bit more challenging.

INFLAMMATORY BOWEL DISEASE

There are many medical conditions which make us think twice before traveling. Inflammatory bowel disease (Crohn's disease and ulcerative colitis) is one of them. Just the thought of Montezuma's Revenge may be enough to change your destination from Burkina Faso to Boston, or even decide to stay home. We are usually concerned that a routine bout of Traveler's Diarrhea will lead to a flare-up of your underlying IBD. In addition, should you develop diarrhea while you are away, there may be some confusion about whether this is an infection or your underlying disease. The treatments are not the same.

By sticking to the following suggestions and by ensuring that your disease is well controlled before you leave, that trip of your dreams or living abroad may be a lot closer to reality.

- Take along a few rolls of toilet paper. This may not apply if you are staying at the Hilton, but if you are hiking the Inca Trail it's a good idea.
- Carry an address book with the name and phone number of your doctor, as well as those of a doctor abroad to contact in an emergency.
- Take more medication and other supplies than you really need. Keep your medications in their original labeled containers. Pack them with your carry-on baggage, or you might never see them again.
- Purchase medical insurance. Don't skimp on this item.
- Always know the location of the next toilet, and know how to ask for it in several languages.
- *"Boil it, bottle it, peel it, cook it ... or forget it!"* I don't expect any traveler to achieve absolute perfection when it comes to choice of food and beverage. Much of what we eat is beyond our direct control. However, I am suggesting that someone with IBD be a little, make that a lot, more discriminating when it comes to dietary choices.
- Ice cubes are a no-no. Also, watch what you eat in the days preceding your trip.
- Take along medications such as Imodium®, as well as an antibiotic

such as Cipro®, for the prompt treatment of traveler's diarrhea. Consider using a "preventive" Imodium® before a long flight, drive or camel ride.

- As well, it may be reasonable, if you are traveling to a higher-risk destination (Egypt, for example) for less than three weeks, to consider the use of a daily prophylactic antibiotic, such as Cipro®. This will lower your risk of developing Montezuma's Revenge by about 80 percent.
- Be prepared to recognize the danger signals which may suggest a flare-up of your Crohn's disease or ulcerative colitis.
- Discuss with your doctor, prior to departure, what you should do if you think you are having a flare-up of your IBD. This may involve medications such as cortisone (prednisone).
- Eat lightly and sensibly, especially on the airplane. Gases expand as the plane ascends. So will your intestines.
- Plan your visits to the airplane bathroom to avoid peak times (after meals, after the movie, before landing).
- Don't forget the other health risks of traveling, such as bugs, the sun and exotic infections.
- Travel only with understanding, patient people.
- Have a great time! And, oh yes, don't forget the toilet paper! This statement may seem a bit facetious, but it comes from the mouths of several people who have traveled extensively with IBD.
- Visit the websites of the Crohn's and Colitis Foundation of America (http://www.ccfa.org) and of Canada (http://www.ccfc.ca).

HIV/AIDS

Although several health issues are unique to someone who is infected with HIV, others may also apply to anyone who is immunosuppressed (e.g., with leukemia; on chemotherapy or corticosteroids). Food- and water-borne diseases, insect-borne infections and the inoculations themselves may pose important risks to this group of travelers. Aside from the medical concerns, the logistics of crossing borders or carrying medications may also pose a formidable task.

Pretravel Inoculations

From the point of view of pretravel inoculation, the risk factors such as destination, duration and style of travel should be considered as with any other traveler. However, there are a few points to keep in mind if you are HIV positive. First, live vaccines should be avoided, especially in anyone who is immunosuppressed, as evidenced by a CD_4 count of less than 200. This would preclude yellow fever, oral typhoid (Vivotif®), oral polio and measles vaccines. Measles vaccine may be given to someone infected with HIV if they do not have severe immunosuppression. Typhim Vi®, an inactivated vaccine, is a safe alternative for typhoid, as is IPV (injected polio vaccine).

Those who must venture to an area of high risk for yellow fever may still consider receiving this vaccine; although the risk is theoretical, it has been given in the past without adverse effects. Where the risk is likely low, a certificate of exemption may be given. Another choice, if possible, is to select a different destination. Other vaccines, such as those against hepatitis A and B, are quite safe and highly recommended.

Tuberculosis is usually of little threat to travelers, but not if you're HIV positive. Therefore, TB skin testing should be performed prior to and after any extended travel where exposure is likely. BCG, a live vaccine with questionable efficacy against TB, is not recommended.

Another concern is whether the immunosuppressed person will respond adequately to any particular vaccine. In the case of hepatitis B, a double dose of vaccine has been advocated. Because of this possible limitation, personal measures to avoid disease, be it care with your food or the use of condoms, are critical.

Food and Water Precautions

For most travelers a bout of diarrhea is just an inconvenience, but it may be debilitating and life-threatening to someone with AIDS. People with AIDS often have a decrease in stomach acid, which reduces the defenses against gastrointestinal infections. It takes a much smaller inoculum, or a smaller mistake, to become ill.

Bacterial infections such as *Salmonella, Shigella* and *Campylobacter* are often much more severe and prolonged in those who are HIV positive, sometimes leading to a chronic-carrier state. They may spread to the bloodstream as well. A group of spore-forming parasites, including *Cryptosporidia, Microsporidia, Isospora* and *Cyclospora,* may also lead to severe, dehydrating and sometimes fatal diarrhea. The severity of the infection is proportional to the immune status of the individual. Effective treatment for these particular infections is unfortunately lacking.

Therefore, the need to adhere to food and water precautions is critical. Bottled water, if sealed, should be safe. Water filters and chemicals such as iodine do not eradicate *Cryptosporidia,* and therefore boiling is the best alternative. Beer and carbonated drinks are usually trustworthy. Ice cubes are not.

Prophylactic antibiotics such as Cipro® are an excellent idea in the short-term (i.e., not more than three weeks) traveler who is off to a location where the food and water may be contaminated. Sulfa (Bactrim®, Septra®), in addition to predisposing you to photosensitivity or a drug rash, is less likely to be effective, and hence is a poor choice. Fortunately, enterotoxigenic *E. coli,* the commonest cause of traveler's diarrhea, is no more severe among HIV-positive travelers.

Some Other Concerns

Malaria is also not an increased risk, but a risk just the same. Use DEET-containing repellents and mosquito nets, and take other personal precautions. Two other insect-borne infections, Chagas' disease and visceral leishmaniasis, may be associated with more severe illness in HIV-infected individuals. Luckily, they are quite rare in travelers.

Sexually transmitted diseases such as syphilis, gonorrhea and chancroid are much more common in the tropics. Abstinence or safe sex must be the rule for all travelers.

There are several "bureaucratic" issues that need to be dealt with if you are HIV positive and plan to travel. At least 50 countries, particularly in Eastern Europe and the Middle East, prohibit the entry of HIV-infected individuals. Proof of HIV testing may be required, depending upon the purpose and length of stay in the host country. This applies mainly to longer-term travelers and those on work permits. Most countries will accept the result of a recent test done in North America. Others insist upon doing it when you arrive at their border. You can find these specific guidelines at http://travel.state.gov/HIVtestingreqs.html.

Anticipation is paramount. Carry adequate supplies of all current medications and those which you anticipate you may need. These should be accompanied by a letter from your physician. As well, hopefully you will have the name of a doctor or clinic you can contact abroad should you require medical care. Make sure you have adequate medical insurance and, once again, read the small print.

Many people infected with HIV will be on antiretroviral treatment (ARV), which may involve a combination of up to three medications. This may in itself pose some problems. First, will your lifestyle while you are away allow you to be compliant with a complicated regimen of medications? Will you have access to additional medications, or alternative medications, should you require them? You will need to be monitored—your blood count, liver and kidney function tests, CD_4 count, viral load. Will these tests be available at your destination?

Realistically, traveling with medical problems such as HIV infection may present limitations. But hopefully, with proper pretravel counseling, thorough planning and careful attention to personal behavior, you can safely travel the world. AEGIS (AIDS Education Global Information System) provides plenty of helpful information at their website (http://www.aegis.com).

DIABETES

Cruising the Nile ... trekking in Nepal ... elephant rides in Thailand ... the Taj Mahal. The places to go are endless, as are the reasons for going. But regardless of where and why you go, travel should be relaxing, stimulating and fulfilling. Diabetes should not be a barrier to traveling. However, the diabetic traveler's planning needs to go well beyond the usual itinerary and clothing list. If you use Murphy's law (whatever can go wrong will go wrong) as your guide, you will realize what I mean.

Imagine the following scenario. Your early morning flight to Greece sits on the runway for three hours in a snowstorm. The lovely breakfast you anticipate never materializes. You forgot to pack the "just in case" granola bars. The flight attendant seems to ignore your requests for orange juice. What about the time zones? When should you take your next dose of insulin? How much? Where is your insulin? (Great! It's in my suitcase in the hold. It'll freeze.) Finally, you land in Athens. Your baggage lands in Tokyo. The lovely customs agent takes away your syringes. What do you mean there's no Diet Coke in Greece? A lovely cruise through the Greek islands. Motion sickness! I wonder what my blood sugar is now? Get the picture?

Close control of blood glucose is always desirable in the management of diabetes. While traveling, however, particularly during long flights, the goal should be to avoid any extremes that may result in symptomatic hypo- or hyperglycemia. Once you arrive at your destination, you may then get back to a pattern of tighter control. The trick is to plan ahead.

Diabetic Supplies

Skimp on your underwear and socks, but not on your supplies. You never know when something may get damaged, lost or stolen. It's probably prudent to carry double the supplies that you will actually require. That goes for your insulin, syringes, batteries for your blood glucose monitor, testing strips and alcohol swabs. It may not always be possible to purchase the same supplies abroad. For example, the U-100 strength insulin you use here may not be available in certain countries. The same goes for your syringes or the insulin cartridges for your pen. It may be worthwhile to check with the manufacturer of your insulin about its availability at your destination. Premixed combinations of insulin are available and may be appropriate for someone with stable insulin requirements.

Insulin pens are perhaps ideal for travel. There is less risk of damage or theft. Many people with diabetes find them easy to use, which can be particularly important for the traveler who requires more frequent injections and adjustments than usual.

Carry your supplies in your hand baggage. Insulin that travels in the baggage compartment may freeze and lose its potency—or it may end up in Tokyo. Consider giving a bottle of insulin to your traveling companion, just in case you become separated from your hand luggage.

It is important to carry some identification such as a MedicAlert® bracelet or a wallet card, along with a letter from your doctor explaining that you have diabetes. A written prescription for your insulin, needles and other supplies will smooth your passage through customs, as well as help you out should you require more supplies abroad. Lancets, which are used for finger-pricking when checking blood glucose levels, may be carried on board the plane, as long as they are capped and accompanied by a reputable glucose meter (e.g., Accu-Chek®, One Touch®).

Remember that mealtime while traveling may be anytime. Flight delays, flat tires, power failures, long-winded tour guides and *coups d'état* are only a few of the factors that will conspire against you and your ideal schedule. So always be prepared. Pack some cheese, granola bars, crackers or dried fruit at all times, as well as some hard candy should you require a fast-acting source of sugar. A glucagon kit, for treatment of severe hypoglycemia, may be a good idea for someone with "brittle" diabetes, or for someone going a bit farther off the beaten path. Check this one out with your doctor. If you do take a kit along, be sure to instruct a traveling companion on its use.

Pay particular attention to your feet and footwear. If you are planning to hike, or even to walk more than usual, make sure your shoes or boots are broken in before you begin. Inspect your feet daily for cuts, infections or blisters. Seek prompt medical attention for any infection that develops anywhere, or carry appropriate antibiotics that you can use on your own.

Insulin Storage

The insulin you are using does not need to be refrigerated. However, it must be protected from temperature extremes and direct sunlight, or it may lose its potency. Crossing the Sahara in a Land Rover while your insulin swelters in the glove compartment is not ideal. And remember, unpressurized airline baggage compartments may lead to your insulin freezing. Unopened bottles of insulin should be refrigerated as soon as possible.

Insulin may be protected from temperature extremes by carrying it in a Thermos or other insulated container. Cool down the container, put the bottle in a plastic bag, and line the container with a wet washcloth for protection. Specially designed kits for carrying diabetic supplies and for protecting insulin may simplify your life while traveling.

Travel Tips for People with Diabetes

- Take along double the supplies and medications that you anticipate you will need.
- Carry these things with your hand baggage.
- Take along some identification, such as a MedicAlert® bracelet.
- Always have a snack handy in case you need a quick source of sugar.
- Aim for reasonably good, not perfect, control while you are on your way to your destination.
- Carry a note explaining why you are carrying syringes.

Blood Sugar Control

Before you leave, contact your airline and request diabetic meals. Then, while you're in flight, keep your watch at the local time of your departure city.

In addition to the time changes, the nature and timing of your meals are often a bit unpredictable, and your level of physical activity dwindles to nothing as you recline in your crowded airline seat for what seems like an eternity. Obviously, adjustments need to be made to your customary insulin schedule. The keys to avoiding significant hypo- or hyperglycemia during travel are frequent self-monitoring of blood glucose, and flexibility.

A newer form of insulin, insulin lispro (Humalog®), has the advantage of a very quick onset of action, so it can be given just before eating your meal. This is preferable to regular insulin, which needs to be injected 30 to 60 minutes before eating. Considering the uncertainty of mealtimes when we travel, this can help avoid unwanted bouts of hypoglycemia, or low blood sugar.

There are several ways to calculate insulin requirements, and it's best that you discuss them with your doctor or the staff of a diabetes education unit. What you choose to do will depend upon the duration and direction of your flight, your time of departure and your usual regime (single vs. multiple daily injections, and the type[s] of insulin you use).

Eastward travel results in a shorter day and, hence, lower insulin requirements. You may choose to give yourself a smaller dose of your intermediate-acting insulin in the morning, and then supplement it later in the day with short-acting insulin, according to your glucose readings. For westward travel, with a longer day, your requirement will increase, depending upon how many time zones you're crossing. Good control may be achieved simply by the addition of some short-acting insulin late in your day to cover the extra hours. Some people switch to a split dosage (i.e., twice daily) before their departure, if they are not already on such a regime. Remember, never take your insulin unless your next meal is in sight, and don't forget to carry your own sources of carbohydrate and sugar (crackers, dried fruit, nuts). For those who will be traveling across five time zones or fewer, it's probably unnecessary to adjust insulin dosages. However, close monitoring is still essential.

If you're among those now using insulin pumps to regulate blood glucose, make sure to take along extra batteries and supplies. In case of equipment failure, it's also a good idea to bring along a supply of syringes and insulin. Frequent blood glucose monitoring is still required. In general, insulin pumps do not set off airport metal detectors and are safe to use while in flight.

People on oral medications for diabetes do not usually have to make any adjustments in their dosage, though they should be aware of all the potential problems that can arise.

Once you're on the ground again, whether for seven days or two years, keep in mind that your activities may differ from what they were at home. If you're staying in a hot climate, you may find that your insulin gets absorbed more quickly, resulting in hypoglycemia. If you're trekking, don't forget the need for lots of fluids and the fact that your insulin requirements may be less because of your level of exertion. Glucose monitors may give incorrect readings at high altitudes, so you should take the time to calibrate your machine.

There are countless ways of managing your blood sugar during a prolonged flight and while away. But there is no one right way. It's probably best to sit down with your diabetes educator or doctor and work out what would be best for you. With a little bit of advice, lots of planning, frequent blood sugar testing and flexibility, the traveler with diabetes should be able to choose where, when and how to travel. *The Diabetic Traveler* is a quarterly newsletter which is dedicated to helping people with diabetes travel safely and with peace of mind. (*The Diabetic Traveler,* PO Box 8223 RW, Stamford, CT 06905; (203) 327-5832)

HEART AND LUNG DISEASE

Cardiovascular and respiratory conditions are extremely common in the general population. If you suffer with angina, congestive heart failure, asthma, emphysema or other problems, it's probably best to visit your doctor before your trip. Certain precautions may be in order, most of which involve common sense.

First, is it safe to fly? The cruising altitude of most commercial aircraft is about 30,000 feet. In a pressurized aircraft, the cabin pressure is equivalent to that found at between 5,000 and 8,000 feet above sea level, about the same as Aspen, Colorado. The resultant decrease in the oxygen level is not a problem for most passengers. For others, however, it can be.

Certain cardiac patients should not be traveling by plane, if at all. These would include the following situations:
- uncomplicated heart attack in the past three weeks
- complicated heart attack (heart failure, abnormal heart rhythms) in the past six weeks

- unstable angina (i.e., angina that is not well controlled with medications) or angina at rest
- symptomatic congestive heart failure
- recent coronary bypass graft (safe to travel one to two weeks later)
- serious cardiac arrhythmias (irregular heart rhythms), such as recurrent ventricular fibrillation

These guidelines may be flexible and depend upon factors such as whether you plan to fly unaccompanied on a commercial airline as opposed to an air ambulance with full medical supervision.

A cardiac pacemaker should not present a problem even as you go through airport security devices. Should you happen to have an implanted defibrillator, I would suggest that you visit your cardiologist well before takeoff.

When you arrive at your destination, you should be able to do everything you do at home. If this is usually limited to clicking the remote to keep up with 16 NFL games on Sunday afternoon, you should probably seek some medical advice if mountain climbing or other such activities are now on your agenda.

In the case of lung disease, as with heart problems, it's probably the severity of your condition that will dictate what precautions you should take and what limitations you may have. If you have low oxygen levels when you are on the ground, it may be best to have supplemental oxygen available for your flight. This will involve contacting your airline well in advance. Most airlines will not permit you to use your own oxygen equipment while in flight. Special organizations exist which specifically plan trips for travelers who are on oxygen.

If you plan on visiting a high-altitude destination such as Nepal or Peru, speak to your doctor before you go. People with stable angina are not adversely affected by the altitude itself, although the increased exertion of an activity like trekking may be a problem. For those with chronic lung disease, if you have a low oxygen level at home, anticipate the need for supplemental oxygen at your high-altitude destination, just as you would on an airplane. It's not just the destination that's important, but also what you plan to do up there that's critical. Common sense helps. Asthma is often better at high altitudes, since the air is thinner. On the other hand, for some people cold air and exertion act as triggers.

We take for granted the relatively clean air we breathe in most parts of North America. But asthma, chronic bronchitis and emphysema all may be adversely affected by the air quality in cities such as Mumbai (Bombay), Beijing, Kathmandu and Manila. In Mexico City, the local traffic cops often wear a mask. This may not be a bad idea for you, too. It may also be wise to carry a course of antibiotics to be used if you develop a respiratory infection.

Whether it is your heart or lungs, or both, keep in mind the following tips:
- Visit the doctor well before departure to be sure that your condition is as well controlled as possible.
- Carry more medication than you expect to need, and keep it in your hand luggage.
- Keep a separate list of your medications and dosages.
- Take a list of your personal physicians, specialists, etc., with their contact phone numbers.
- Keep a copy of your most recent electrocardiogram and other pertinent reports.
- Contact the airline well in advance if you will need supplemental oxygen, boarding assistance, a special diet or anything else.
- Get the recommended inoculations before you travel, with particular attention to pneumococcal and flu vaccines.
- Try to minimize the stress involved in travel. Arrive at the airport early. Plan a sensible itinerary.
- Carry adequate medical and travel insurance.

OTHER DISABILITIES

In May 2001, Eric Weihenmayer, a blind American climber, stood on top of the world's highest peak, Mount Everest. One of my blind patients, Euclid Herie, recently stepped down as the head of the Canadian National Institute for the Blind and the World Blind Union. For the past 10 years I have been trying to keep up with his world-

wide adventures, which ranged from paddling the Nahanni River to going on safari in Botswana to delivering speeches in India.

Most people, with or without disabilities, are not as adventurous as these two individuals. But travel should be available and accessible to those who are

• hard of hearing/deaf
• sight impaired
• on dialysis
• wheelchair dependent
• arthritic
• oxygen dependent

This is, of course, only a partial list.

There may be limitations when it comes to certain disabilities, certain destinations and certain activities. But these should not keep many people from experiencing an enjoyable, adventurous and fulfilling time abroad. Dialysis can be arranged at numerous centers around the world. Oxygen can be transported or made available at your destination. Wheelchair access is improving, though not perfect.

The key to a successful trip is advance planning, and those plans should be realistic. As I said at the beginning of the chapter, not all travelers are created equal. Neither are all travel agents. Find a good one who can help you with the details. If you are flying, hopefully you can get a nonstop flight and avoid transfers. The trip from one terminal to another at Chicago's O'Hare International Airport is almost as long as the Inca Trail. Moving ramps are available at the airport. So are neat little motorized carts, which you may request. Schedule plenty of time between flights if you must change planes. Contact your airline in advance if you will need advance boarding, special seating, oxygen, wheelchair access or a special diet.

When it comes to hotel accommodations, someone should be asking about the following:
- ramp to entrance
- location of elevators
- distance from the lobby to your room
- handicapped parking
- low-pile carpet
- raised toilet seat
- fire exits for people with disabilities, or first-floor rooms in case of fire
- accessibility and availability of heated pools for exercise and relaxation

Try to pace yourself so that you do not become overtired. Set aside times for rest and relaxation and time on your own, when perhaps your traveling companions can go out to do something more strenuous. Don't plan to do everything on the first day. And remember all that other advice you read in the beginning of the book, namely:
- Take along plenty of your medications in their original containers.

- Carry copies of any important medical records.
- Have the name and phone number of a doctor abroad, as well as your doctors back home.
- Get sufficient medical and travel insurance—don't leave home without them!

The Society for Accessible Travel and Hospitality (SATH) (http://www.sath.org) provides excellent information and innumerable useful links for those traveling with a disability. Its address is: SATH, 347 Fifth Ave., Suite 610, New York, NY 10016; (212) 447-7284/Fax 725-8253; e-mail: sathtravel@aol.com. As well, there are many other organizations and travel companies devoted to making your travel dreams a reality.

Key Points

- Traveling with any sort of medical condition takes advance planning ... lots of it!
- Look for a travel agent or organization with experience in helping travelers with medical conditions.
- Realize your limitations and plan accordingly.

Traveling to Adopt

CHAPTER 23

"Travelers never think that they are the foreigners."
HERMAN MELVILLE

There are countless reasons why people travel, and I've heard them all: to lounge by the ocean, climb a mountain, pray at holy shrines, visit friends and family, conduct business or volunteer time and skills. But perhaps the most exciting, for both me and the traveler, is to adopt a child from a completely different country and culture. The commonest destinations for adoptive parents tend to be Eastern Europe (Romania, Ukraine), Asia (China, Korea, Vietnam, India) and Latin America (Guatemala, Peru).

Several factors have led to the upsurge in international adoption, not the least of which are the extremely long waiting times to adopt a child locally. But perhaps the most important is the desire to be able to provide a loving home and endless opportunity for a child who would never get to experience these in their native country.

Adoptive parents share some of the same health-related anxieties that all travelers do: *"Do I need any shots?"* *"Can I drink the water?"* *"What about malaria?"* and *"What do I do if I get sick?"* The answer to many of these questions can be found by reading this book. But a visit to your local travel clinic is still a good idea. The shots you may receive will depend upon your particular destination, how long you plan to be there and whether you will be visiting rural areas. At a minimum, you will need to be up to date with your routine inoculations, such as tetanus-diphtheria-polio and measles. Protection against hepatitis A and typhoid fever may also be recommended, assuming you're traveling to a lesser-developed country where the safety of the food and water may be suspect. And don't forget your Imodium®.

Hepatitis B is a very important issue. The first concern is the fact that you may become ill and require medical care that is less than sterile in the middle of China. Added to this is the worry that the baby you adopt may be a carrier of the hepatitis B virus, and hence be infectious to you. As you recall, hepatitis B is transmitted via bodily fluids—and such contact is usually an occupational hazard of parenting. These children may have become infected directly from their mother during pregnancy, or from contaminated needles or blood. The bottom line here is that you should be immunized against hepatitis B. Also consider vaccinating siblings and grandparents eagerly waiting at home.

Whether you will need any other vaccines or malaria prophylaxis will depend mainly upon your destination. You should also be aware of the noninfectious risks where you are going, whether it be the buses in Guatemala or the pollution in Beijing. Many excellent organizations now exist to help adoptive parents through every step of their incredible journey.

Having looked after yourself, your concerns should then focus on the soon-to-be-your baby. New questions should enter your minds, such as:
• How will I know if the baby is healthy?
• What tests should he or she have done when we return home?
• Could the baby be carrying any diseases that may be a risk to friends and family back home?

Ideally, there will be a complete written record of your baby's and the birth mother's medical history. Hopefully, this can answer some of the following questions:
• Is there a family history of any medical problems?
• Were there any problems during pregnancy or surrounding the delivery?
• Did the mother smoke, take any drugs or drink alcohol during pregnancy?
• What inoculations, if any, has the baby received to date?
• What were the results of testing for hepatitis B and HIV, stools for parasites, etc.?
• Has the baby had any medical problems or required hospitalization to date?
• Has the baby grown well and passed the usual milestones, such as smiling or sitting at the appropriate times?
• Under what sort of conditions has the baby been brought up so far (living with birth family, foster care or an orphanage, quality of caring)?

That was ideally. It's quite conceivable that any records will be few and far between, and what is available could even be fraudulent. Certain infections, such as hepatitis B and HIV, have a long incubation period, so a negative test when you meet your baby could subsequently become positive in the months ahead. There's no guarantee that the vaccines your baby "received" were actually given; and if they were, the vaccines may not have met our standards. As well, a malnourished child may not respond adequately to immunization. What this usually means is that you will repeat the appropriate tests when you return home, and consider repeating some or all of the vaccinations.

Upon return, your baby should obviously have a medical examination. This need not be on the way home from the airport, but preferably within two weeks of arriving home. Should there be any acute illness, however, it should be attended to immediately. Remember that a child adopted from a malarious country may develop malaria days, weeks or even months after arrival. Respiratory infections, diarrhea and skin problems such as scabies and impetigo are common conditions in these children.

Aside from performing a thorough general examination, the doctor should be on the lookout for any sign of growth disturbance (height, weight, head circumference), malnutrition and hearing and visual problems. A developmental assessment is crucial to detect signs of past emotional deprivation or abuse. This may require a referral to a specialized facility.

Routine investigations may vary according to the age and origin of the child, but should probably include most of the following:

- CBC (complete blood count to detect anemia, sickle cell disease and other inherited conditions)
- urinalysis
- chest x-ray
- TB skin test (if negative, repeat in six months)
- stool for culture and sensitivity (to test for bacterial infections such as *Salmonella* and *Shigella*)
- stool for ova and parasites (to detect protozoal infections such as giardiasis and amebiasis, and helminthic [worm] infections)
- VDRL (for syphilis)
- HIV (should be repeated in six months if negative)
- hepatitis B screen (for antigen and antibodies—should be repeated in six months if negative)

Any further testing or treatment will depend upon the results of the above assessment.

If it's felt that your child needs to be reimmunized, the exact schedule for those vaccines may depend upon the child's age and past records. The routine vaccines that will be necessary are DPTP (diphtheria, polio, tetanus, pertussis), MMR (measles, mumps, rubella) and Hib (*Hemophilus* influenza). If there's no evidence of past exposure to hepatitis B, this vaccine should also be given. Newer vaccines against varicella, meningitis and pneumoccocal infections may also be worthwhile.

Just as there are organizations specializing in international adoption, there are also medical clinics across North America that have expertise in assessing your new bundle of joy. He or she may not appreciate all the probing, prodding and needling, but you will rest easier after it has all been done. Go to the COMEUNITY website (see end of chapter) to find a clinic near you.

I suppose there are certain health risks involved in adopting a child from a lesser-developed country. But if you and your family are properly immunized and take sensible precautions such as washing your hands after changing a diaper, these are really quite negligible. Some babies may be harboring intestinal worms. These are generally not contagious to others in North America, since the life cycle of most worms requires some time spent outside the body in a different home (e.g., in the soil) before they become infectious to others. This is quite unlikely in countries with indoor plumbing.

Traveling is stressful, and I would assume that traveling to a foreign country to adopt a child must be very stressful. Your new child may not bond with you as automatically as you had hoped. This may be distressing, but imagine how it must be for the child. Giant, strange-looking humans stare and make silly faces and noises at you, and then whisk you to a foreign country by airplane, where you receive a multitude of needles. But I am sure that for all parties involved, things get better and better. Good luck!

Related Websites

Children's Bridge: http://www.childrensbridge.com

COMEUNITY: http://www.comeunity.com

International Adoption for Canadians (information for Americans too): http://www.interlog.com/~ladybug/home.htm

Open Arms to International Adoption: http://www.open-arms.com

U.S. State Department: http://travel.state.gov/adopt.html

Key Points

- Take the appropriate medical precautions for yourself before and during your trip.
- Assume that your child will need to be retested and reimmunized when you arrive back home.

PART FIVE
Now That You're Home

TROPICAL BIRDS

COSTA RICA

COSTA RICA CORREOS

Dear Mark,

Our kids have stayed fairly healthy — some are fatter, some are thinner — they all now speak Spanish and are very happy.

This place is a fascinating mix of cowboys, volcanoes, pumas and BEER!

Cheers, Brad

Dr. Mark Wise
2300 John Street
Thornhill, ON
CANADA L3T 6G7

1. Edita: Publicaciones Ibera S.A.T

Foto Patricia Aguilar

Hey Doc, I'm Home!

CHAPTER 25

*"A man travels the world over in search of what he needs,
and returns home to find it."*

GEORGE MOORE

Welcome home! Now that your bags are unpacked and your laundry is done, the question comes up, *"Do I need to see a doctor?"* That depends. There are two kinds of returning travelers—those who feel great when they get home, and those who don't. Those who don't should see their doctor, sometimes right away. Those who do should see a doctor if they have been abroad for more than a few months, if they have had a significant illness while away or if they have likely been exposed to contaminated food and water, unsafe sex, tuberculosis, schistosomiasis and so on. Let's look at the "sick" group first.

Fever—The Most Important Problem

There are a few common problems among returning travelers, the most important of which by far is a fever. *Fever in a returning traveler is malaria until proven otherwise.* If both you and the doctor looking after you can remember this, then everything should be OK. There are several other "tropical" illnesses that may also present with a fever, including typhoid, dengue, hepatitis, tick typhus, leptospirosis and brucellosis, among many others. As well, many nontropical infections may also occur after your arrival home, such as pneumonia, influenza, strep throat, infectious mononucleosis and the flu. But the priority is always to rule out malaria.

If you develop a fever soon after your return (within the first few months, particularly the first 60 days), see a doctor. Your family doctor should suffice, assuming he or she knows something about malaria, although you may be safer in an emergency department or with an expert in tropical diseases. Temperatures are best measured with thermometers. We see many people who feel warm but do not have an elevated temperature. A blood smear for malaria is the most important test that should be done, and it must be done promptly and interpreted promptly. You can die of *falciparum* malaria in as little as three days from the onset of the fever.

Not all laboratories have extensive experience in performing and interpreting malaria smears. There are two types of smears, a "thick" smear and a "thin" smear. The thick smear concentrates the red blood cells and washes away many of the other cells seen on a regular blood smear. This makes it easier to pick out the malaria parasites, especially when the infection is very light. A thin smear is like a regular blood smear. It allows the technician to determine the species of malaria, which is very important, and in the case of *falciparum* malaria the percentage of red blood cells containing parasites. This gives an indication of the severity and urgency of the infection. More than likely you will have a thin smear done.

If your test is negative, it does not mean that you do not have malaria, in spite of what the doctor has told you. It means that malaria parasites were not found on this initial smear. You should return within 24 hours for another test if your fever persists or returns. It sometimes takes a few tries before the parasites can be found and a diagnosis is made. People have died because the doctor has told them they have the flu, sending them home with useless antibiotics. You must be your own advocate in this situation.

Should your malaria smear be positive, your next task is to make sure that you receive the proper treatment. North American doctors in general are not eagerly waiting for cases of malaria to appear on their doorstep, nor are they experienced in its treatment. Help (for the doctor), however, is never more than a phone call away. Depending upon the strain of malaria you have and the severity of the infection, you may require hospitalization for treatment and observation.

Malaria caused by *P. vivax* or *P. ovale* (this one is quite uncommon) is initially treated with chloroquine (these strains are sensitive to chloroquine), followed by a 14-day course of the drug primaquine, which eradicates any parasites that may be persisting in the liver. If this latter treatment is not given, then these strains of malaria can relapse. Strains of *P. vivax* that are found in Papua New Guinea and West Papua (formerly Irian Jaya) have managed to develop some resistance to primaquine. In this case, a higher dose of the medication needs to be used. Primaquine must not be taken until your doctor has checked something called your G6PD level. If the level of this enzyme is low, there's a risk that you will have a serious side effect to the medication.

Falciparum malaria is a medical emergency, and the proper treatment probably requires a specialist in tropical or infectious diseases. In someone who is well enough to take oral medications, the treatment may consist of

- Malarone® (atovaquone/proguanil)—four tablets daily for three days (adult dose), or
- quinine sulfate—600 milligrams three times daily for seven days *plus* either doxycycline—100 milligrams daily for seven days; *or* Fansidar®—three tablets in a single dose

This strain of malaria, if not promptly treated, may lead to cerebral malaria, respiratory failure and kidney failure. In complicated cases, intravenous quinine, as well as expert supportive care, is required.

Malaria is a treatable disease, but much like a heart attack it must be treated promptly and properly. Returning travelers occasionally die from malaria due to:
- incorrect or delayed diagnosis
- incorrect or inadequate treatment

The fault for these errors may lie with the physician or the patient, or both. To be sure you are not partially responsible for your own demise, you should be well acquainted with the symptoms, diagnosis and treatment of malaria.

If it's not malaria you have, then you and your doctor must keep

looking for other causes of fever, such as typhoid fever, meningococcal disease, dengue fever, hepatitis, leptospirosis, tick typhus,
brucellosis and exotic viral infections such as Ebola and Lassa
fever. The entire list is as long as your arm.

Common Causes of Tropical Fevers in Returning Travelers	
• malaria	• dengue fever
• typhoid fever	• tick typhus
• hepatitis A	• leptospirosis
• *Salmonella, Shigella, Campylobacter*	• malaria (just a reminder!)

Aside from malaria smears, testing may include blood, urine and
stool cultures, serological (antibody) tests, chest x-ray and ultra-
sound. Remember, many people with a fever upon their return do
not have a tropical disease. In fact, the cause of the fever goes
undiscovered in about 30 percent of cases.

In September 2000, a sudden surge in reported cases of leptospirosis (an infection transmitted via the urine of rodents and
other animals) was noted around the world. With a little detective
work and cooperation, tropical disease experts were able to determine that all the infected patients had recently participated in the
Eco-Challenge-Sabah (Borneo) 2000. We usually follow the guideline in medicine that "common things are common." In Borneo,
that is not always the case.

My Stomach Hurts!

Gastrointestinal problems are the commonest ailment in returning
travelers. There is a host of things that might have hitched a free
ride home to North America by way of your intestines. If you
developed an acute diarrheal infection just as you flew back home,
it may be caused by a bacterium (*E. coli, Salmonella, Shigella,
Campylobacter*). Perhaps you had an undercooked meat patty as
you were leaving the Ethiopian airport. In this case, it may be

advisable to see your doctor, who may in turn request that you provide a fresh stool sample in a container no bigger than a shot glass. (The stool should also not be bigger than a shot glass.) This is used to culture, or grow, the potentially infecting bacterium.

If you are very sick, it may be prudent to resort to the previously described and prescribed treatment of acute diarrhea, by taking a small dose of Imodium® along with a brief course of an antibiotic such as Cipro®. The stool culture may take up to 48 hours before you get the final result, so waiting for the result is not always the most desirable course of action. Don't forget to drink lots of clear fluids, such as soup, juice, tea or water mixed with oral rehydration salts.

If your intestinal problems are a little more chronic in nature, then you may need to fill a few more bottles for examination. These should be checked for parasites, such as *Giardia, Cryptosporidium, Cyclospora* and *Entamoeba histolytica*. Many parasites, in spite of what you may read, often live in perfect harmony with you and your bowels. *Blastocystis hominis, Entamoeba coli, Dientamoeba fragilis, Entamoeba hartmanni* and *Endolimax nana* are a few of the ones that need not arouse fear, and may be left untreated if you have little in the way of symptoms.

If nothing of note is found in your stools, then a little more investigation is in order. Lactose intolerance (an inability to digest the lactose in dairy products) may cause diarrhea, gas, bloating and abdominal pains. It may follow any severe form of diarrhea that you might have had while away. Lactose intolerance can be proven by means of blood or breath tests, but a trial period off lactose products will often help make a diagnosis. This problem is not always an "all or none" situation. That is, you may be able to tolerate some milk in your tea or a cup of yogurt, but not an extra large chocolate milkshake or a tall half-decaf latté. Products such as Lactaid® or Lacteeze® are available if this turns out to be your problem. In fact, the condition often improves and resolves on its own with time.

Other conditions which I have seen in returning travelers that may initially resemble an infection include inflammatory bowel disease (ulcerative colitis, Crohn's disease), hyperthyroidism, tropical sprue and bowel cancer. Therefore, your doctor should be careful to consider "nontropical" conditions as well.

Perhaps the commonest diagnosis we are left with after a full investigation is a post-infectious irritable bowel syndrome. This means: *"I spent two years in* _____ *[insert the name of your country here]. I got sick (several times). I got better. But I'm still not the way I was before."* You may suffer with gas, bloating, rumbling and abdominal discomfort. Your stools may be loose, ribbony, pellet-like (rabbit turds) or all of the above. You may be sensitive to certain foods or drinks that didn't bother you before. You shouldn't be losing weight or noticing any blood in your stools. This condition usually improves with time (measured in months), a careful diet, some additional fiber and reassurance. Other gastrointestinal infections and conditions must be ruled out before arriving at this diagnosis. An occasional few unfortunate travelers never return to the way it was before.

Honey, I Passed a Worm!

This is undoubtedly one of the most exciting things that can happen to you after you get home. If you had the good fortune while abroad to ingest some food that had been contaminated with human feces, or perhaps you didn't cook your beef, pork or fish adequately, then you might have been playing host to a worm for some time. While a bit alarming, this is not life-threatening.

Roundworms *(Ascaris lumbricoides)* are round, whitish and up to six inches long. They often crawl out into the world because they are having trouble finding a sexual partner inside. Little do they know that they won't find one outside. The likelihood of acquiring this parasite seems to be inversely proportional to one's budget while away. The whipworm *(Trichuris trichiura)* is much smaller than the roundworm and is rarely found in the stools. Rest assured that these worms cannot be passed on to your family or dearest friends. They are treatable with the drug mebendazole (Vermox®).

Tapeworms *Taenia saginata* (beef), *Taenia solium* (pork) and *Diphyllobothrium latum* (fish) are the ones that can grow up to 30 feet in length, but usually only short segments are passed at one time. They are white and ribbony in appearance. Contrary to popular belief, tapeworms are probably not responsible for your weight loss. If you would like to adopt one of these worms, have your meat rare, or even raw. If not, stick to well done. The treatment of choice for tapeworms is the drug Praziquantel®.

Pinworms *(Enterobius vermicularis)* can also be seen wandering around your rear end, usually late at night. This is when the female pinworm comes out of the bowel to lay her eggs. (It's also the best time to catch reruns of *Leave It to Beaver.*) The worms are white, and only about half an inch long. The eggs they lay on the skin are quite irritating, typically prompting the infectee (usually a child) to scratch, get the eggs on a couple of fingers, put those fingers in the mouth (or on a little brother) and keep the whole cycle alive. This is not really a tropical or traveler's infection. Rather, it affects close-knit families in temperate climates.

Most travelers are not heavily infected with worms, as presumably their exposure has been minimal. As well, these worms do not divide inside of us, preferring instead the great outdoors or the inside of a snail for their development. The pork tapeworm, however, has the ability to form a cyst and spread elsewhere in the body, including the brain, the muscles or the skin. Most helminthic, or worm, infections are easily treated, though they too may require the expertise of a tropical disease specialist.

What's That Spot on My Skin?

BITES. There are many interesting skin conditions that people discover on their return home. But perhaps the most common are nonspecific (we're not really sure what bit you) bites. Mites, bedbugs, fleas, mosquitoes and many other insects may be responsible. Most of these result in a rash that can be quite itchy. The problem may persist for some time after your return, even though the bugs have been left far behind. This may be due to an allergy or hypersensitivity to the bite itself. Other bites, such as those from the deerfly, tsetse fly or black fly are usually quite uncomfortable.

BOILS. Sometimes quite large and painful, boils may be a common problem in travelers. A moist climate, an abundance of bacteria such as *Staphylococcus* and *Streptococcus* and perhaps a relative lack of hygiene may all be responsible. Boils tend to be recurrent and show up over different parts of the body. This is because it is very easy to "inoculate" oneself, simply by touching the infection and then scratching somewhere else. In addition, some people become nasal carriers of the bacteria, and let's face it, most of us get our fingers near our nose on a regular basis. The treatment of an acute boil may be warm saltwater compresses and antibiotics, but an incision to release the pus inside is often required. A longer course of oral antibiotics such as cloxacillin, erythromycin or cephalexin, combined with a topical antibiotic in the nose, may be needed to prevent recurrences.

OTHER CONDITIONS. Boils may sometimes be confused with myiasis (see Chapter 9, Other Insect-borne Diseases), which is caused by the larva of the botfly, either *Dermatobia hominis* or *Cordylobia anthropophaga*. These flies manage to get their eggs under your skin, either via the bite of a mosquito or by laying them on your clothing, from which they can penetrate your unbroken skin. Most of the travelers I have seen with this condition have just returned from the rain forests of Central America. People with a botfly have the sensation, often a painful one, that there is something alive and moving under their skin, and indeed there is.

The developing larva requires air to survive, and the best way to entice him or her out is to cut off the air supply. This can be accomplished in a few ways (see Chapter 9). Minor surgery is not usually the way to go. If you are living in the tropics, you may find your pet dog, cat or cattle complaining of the same thing.

For the traveler who has just returned from the beaches of Jamaica and has a creeping, itchy linear rash on the foot, this is undoubtedly cutaneous larva migrans, or a "creeping eruption." (It is present in other countries as well.) The eruption may appear anywhere else on the body, depending upon which part of the anatomy was lying in the sand. It is caused by the larvae of a dog or cat hookworm (*Ancylostoma braziliense* or *Ancylostoma caninum*), which have been left in the sand by the local dog or cat. These larvae can penetrate your unbroken skin, and once having done so they wander aimlessly, in a very serpiginous (winding) pattern under the skin. The red line is intensely itchy, it may blister, and it advances up to an inch per day. It will not enter any vital organs, nor is it transmissible from person to person. While this rash will usually be evident before the end of your vacation, I have seen it appear many months after a return from the tropics. In days gone by, we would treat the rash by either burning it or freezing it, or using a medication called thiabendazole. Today, being much more humane and having better drugs, we use oral medications such as albendazole or ivermectin.

Cutaneous leishmaniasis is a parasitic disease transmitted by sandflies in many parts of the tropics, particularly Asia and South America. If you have a skin ulcer that just won't heal, this could be what you have.

An eschar is an easily recognizable skin lesion (by someone who can easily recognize it) left by the bite of a mite or tick. It begins as a small red bump, but gradually turns into a black, crusted ulcer. It is associated with infections such as African tick typhus and scrub typhus. If you have just returned from the game parks in southern Africa with a fever and an odd-looking ulcer on your skin, suggest this diagnosis to your doctor.

Leprosy still exists in many parts of the world. It is caused by *Mycobacterium leprae,* which is most likely transmitted from person to person via nasal secretions. It's not spread by simply touching an infected person. The skin lesions of leprosy do not look particularly ominous. However, they are usually "numb," or anesthetic, because the underlying nerve is also affected. Leprosy also affects much larger nerves, such as those to the hand and foot, and it is the involvement of these nerves which ultimately leads to the horrible deformities that are often seen with untreated cases. I mention this disease mainly to make you aware that it still exists around the world, but it is not, I repeat not, a risk to travelers.

An interesting though harmless condition called phytophotodermatitis occurs in people who have chosen to lighten their hair with lime juice. The juice drips onto the shoulders or face, or it may be rubbed onto other parts of the body after a squeeze of lime into a gin and tonic. The lime reacts with the sunlight, and the result is a streaky, pigmented rash, almost like a mild burn. Fortunately, it fades with time.

And last but not least, I have recently seen a few people who have received henna—or alleged henna—tattoos around their ankles and arms. Rather then fading over a few weeks as promised, the tattoo causes an allergic reaction and takes on a three-dimensional appearance. This one tends not to fade with time.

There are many other causes of skin problems. I have discussed the most common ones. And as I've said repeatedly, it may take the experienced tropical disease doctor to recognize some of these interesting rashes. So if it isn't going away, look for the right help.

I Feel Great. Do I Need a Checkup?

It wouldn't hurt to have a checkup, particularly if you have been away for some time and exposed to many infections. Hopefully, the doctor will ask you some pertinent questions:

- Where have you been?
- For how long?
- When did you return?
- What were you doing over there?
- Did you have any illnesses while away?
- Were you swimming in fresh water?
- Were you walking barefoot?
- Did you have any unsafe sexual exposure or medical care?
- How are you feeling now?

Then, after a thorough physical exam, some routine tests may be advisable, depending upon your answers to the above. These tests would include:

- CBC (complete blood count)
- stools for O & P (ova and parasites)
- serology (blood tests looking for antibodies to certain infections; e.g., schistosomiasis)
- a TB (tuberculosis) skin test, about two months after your return. If your TB test has converted from negative (before you left) to positive (on your return), this means you have been infected with TB while away. It does not mean that you are sick with TB or infectious to others. Your lifetime risk of developing active TB will be between 5 and 15 percent, assuming you are otherwise healthy. The risk is greatest in the first two years after infection. To minimize this risk, the doctor may recommend a course of the drug INH for 6 to 12 months. Other drug regimens may also be considered because of the increasing incidence of drug-resistant TB.
- HIV, VDRL, cervical or urethral cultures (if you have been exposed to STDs)

Most people who return well, are well; but don't forget the possibility that malaria might surface weeks and months after your return. Fatigue is another common problem in returning travelers. Possible causes may include jet lag, reverse culture shock and depression, various infections or perhaps some post-travel variant of chronic fatigue syndrome.

This chapter does not mention every "tropical" disease known to man and woman, but it does cover the most common problems that occur in returning travelers. Hopefully, you have returned with none of the above. But even if you have, don't let that discourage you from planning your next adventure. Worms go away, but memories last forever.

Key Points

- Fever in a returning traveler is malaria until proven otherwise.
- If your malaria smear is negative, it does not mean you don't have malaria. Have it repeated in 12–24 hours if your fever persists or recurs.
- If you are feeling well when you get home, you probably are!

Sources of Information

There is no shortage of information available on travel and health. The more you know about your destination(s) and the problems you may encounter, the more likely you will be to avoid these problems. Below are some resources from the Internet and elsewhere that you will find helpful, current and mostly free. Remember, the information you will find out there is for everybody. It's my job, and yours, to figure out how it applies to you.

SOME WEBSITES

International Organizations and Medical Sites

Centers for Disease Control and Prevention (CDC): http://www.cdc.gov/travel

CIA—World Factbook: http://www.odci.gov/cia/publications/factbook

CIWEC Clinic, Kathmandu, Nepal: http://ciwec-clinic.com

Department of Foreign Affairs and Trade (Canada): http://www.dfait-maeci.gc.ca

Department of State (United States), Travel Warnings: http://travel.state.gov/travel_warnings.html

Drugs and Vaccines for Pediatric Travelers: An Integrated Table: http://www.istm.org/pharmacycharts

Health Canada: http://www.hc-sc.gc.ca/main/lcdc/web/osh/pub_e.html

High Altitude Medical Guide: http://www.high-altitude-medicine.com

HIV and Travel: http://www.cdc.gov/travel/hivtrav.htm

IAMAT: http://www.sentex.net/~iamat

International Adoption, U.S. Department of State:
http://travel.state.gov/adopt.html

International Society of Travel Medicine (ISTM):
http://www.istm.org

Malaria Foundation International: http://www.malaria.org

The Travel Clinic™: http://www.drwisetravel.com

Travel Clinics (worldwide list): http://www.istm.org

World Health Organization (WHO): http://www.who.int

Helpful Travel Sites

Airsafe.com (useful information for the airline passenger):
http://www.airsafe.com

Disability Travel and Recreation Resources:
http://www.makoa.org/travel.htm

Intercultural and Community Development Resources Inc.
(ICDR): www.icdr.com

Izon's Backpacker Journal: http://www.izon.com

Journeywoman: http://www.journeywoman.com

Lonely Planet: http://www.lonelyplanet.com

National Geographic: http://www.nationalgeographic.com

Perry-Castañeda Library Map Collection:
http://www.lib.utexas.edu/maps/index.html

Society for Accessible Travel and Hospitality (SATH):
http://www.sath.org

Universal Currency Converter: http://www.xe.net/ucc

WeatherHub (international weather): http://www.weatherhub.com

References and Suggested Reading

Auerbach, P.S. (editor). *Wilderness Medicine, Management of Wilderness and Environmental Emergencies*. St. Louis: Mosby, 1995.

Borins, Mel. *Go Away: Just for the Health of It*. Dallas: Holistic Press, 2000.

Centers for Disease Control and Prevention—*Health Information for International Travel 2001–2002*. Atlanta: Centers for Disease Control and Prevention, U.S. Department of Health and Human Services, 2001.

Dupont, Herbert L., and Robert Steffen. *Textbook of Travel Medicine and Health*. Hamilton, Ontario: B.C. Decker, 1997.

Gallmann, Kuki. *I Dreamed of Africa*. New York: Penguin, 1992.

Garrett, Laurie. *The Coming Plague*. New York: Penguin, 1995.

Hargarten, Stephen W. "Overseas Fatalities of United States Citizen Travelers: An Analysis of Deaths Related to International Travel." *Annals of Emergency Medicine* 20:6 (June 1991).

Herzog, Maurice. *Annapurna*. New York: Dutton, 1953.

Isaac, Jeffrey. *The Outward Bound Wilderness First-Aid Handbook*. New York: Lyons Press, 1998.

Journal of Travel Medicine (various issues). Hamilton, Ontario: B.C. Decker.

Keystone, Jay (editor). *Don't Drink the Water* (5th edition). Ottawa: Canadian Public Health Association, 2000.

Klompas, M., and C.M. Shapiro. *SLAM Jet Lag*. Thornhill, Ontario: Joli Joco Publications, 2000.

Krakauer, Jon. *Into Thin Air*. New York: Doubleday, 1997.

Lessell, Colin B., and Lyn Greenwood. *The World Travellers' Manual of Homeopathy* (revised). Essex, U.K.: C.W. Daniel Co., 1999.

Moss, Maggie, and Gemma Moss. *Handbook for Women Travellers*. London: Piatkus, 1995.

Piet-Pelon, Nancy J., and Barbara Hornby. *Women's Guide to Living Overseas* (2nd ed.) Yarmouth, Maine: Intercultural Press, 1992.

Preston, Richard M. *The Hot Zone*. New York: Doubleday, 1994.

Rose, Stuart. *2001 International Travel Health Guide*. Northampton, Massachusetts: Travel Medicine Inc., 2001.

Schlagenhauf-Lawlor, Patricia. *Traveler's Malaria*. Hamilton, Ontario: B.C. Decker, 2001.

Werner, David. *Where There Is No Doctor*. Berkeley: Hesperian Foundation, 1998.

World Health Organization: *International Travel and Health—Vaccination Requirements and Health Advice*. Geneva: World Health Organization (annual).

Index

Acknowledgments

I am grateful to many people for helping to make this book a reality. Lionel Koffler and Michael Worek of Firefly Books gave me the chance to write the book I have been dreaming about. My editor, Dan Liebman, continually complimented me on my writing, and I have the same opinion of his editing. Max Licht, who is responsible for the cartoons, was a pleasure to work with. I am certain you have enjoyed his illustrations.

Many friends and colleagues were kind enough to read my writing, or listen to me talk about it. Their suggestions are all part of this book. They include Diana Charlebois, Michelle Rot, Ken Hundert, Paula Gutfreund, Heather Hubley, Estelle Wolf, Steve Emmins, Martha Bailkowski, Zoe Jackson, Sue-In Pak, Angie Dornai, Joanne Veldman, Barb Hogan, Glenna Ottenbreit-Born, Evelyn Hannon, Harvey Medland, Jason Lewis, Lisa Sawyer, Christy Afuwape and Barry Borden.

Doctors constantly learn from their patients, and in my case I have many thousands to thank for allowing me to share in their travels.

My mother and father, Mimi and Sydney Wise, have supported me and encouraged me all the way through my life, and I thank them for everything. I'm sure they were nervous when I took that first trip to South America. My dad is a proofreader without equal, and I thank him especially for his hard work.

And finally my family—my wife Gayle, and lovely and talented children Carrie, Benjamin and Michael. They have allowed me to travel, they have traveled with me, they have seen all of my slides and read all of my writing. Over the years, they have valiantly put up with the "old man." I thank them all. I love them all.

Notes

Notes

Notes

Notes

Notes

Notes

Notes